Training Effectiveness Handbook

A High-Results System for Design, Delivery, and Evaluation

Lester T. Shapiro, CFP

McGraw-Hill, Inc.

New York San Francisco Washington, D.C. Auckland Bogotá
Caracas Lisbon London Madrid Mexico City Milan
Montreal New Delhi San Juan Singapore
Sydney Tokyo Toronto

Library of Congress Cataloging-in-Publication Data

Shapiro, Lester T.
  Training effectiveness handbook : a high-results system for
design, delivery, and evaluation / Lester T. Shapiro.
    p.   cm.
  Includes bibliographical references and index.
  ISBN 0-07-057109-0 (alk. paper)
    1. Occupational training—Handbooks, manuals, etc.
  2. Occupational training—Evaluation—Handbooks, manuals, etc.
  I. Title.
  HD5715.S53   1995
  658.3'124—dc20   94-42613
                                                       CIP

To Herman Bass, my mentor,
who challenged me to defend my ideas
and supported me when
most of my attempts to teach *Guided Discovery* failed.

For Lesley J. Shapiro, my daughter,
so that someday, if you choose to,
you can help people learn new skills
that will help them achieve their objectives.

1 2 3 4 5 6 7 8 9 0   DOH/DOH   9 0 0 9 8 7 6 5

ISBN 0-07-057109-0

*The sponsoring editor for this book was James H. Bessent, Jr., the editing
supervisor was Fred Dahl, and the production supervisor was Pamela A. Pelton.
It was set in Palatino by Inkwell Publishing Services.*

Printed and bound by R. R. Donnelley & Sons Company.

 This book is printed on recycled, acid-free paper
containing a minimum of 50% recycled de-inked
fiber.

Contents

**Part 3.
Program Development:
A System for Designing and
Delivering Effective Training**

Acknowledgments

I would like to thank Diana, my wife and special editor, for her encouragement, support, research assistance, time, patience and extensive editorial advice.

I would also like to thank Arthur N. Caso, Ph.D., professor of English and corporate consultant, James M. Wendt, Marketing Analyst, Aon Auto Capital Corporation, Harry A. Morrison, Ph.D., Dean of Science, Purdue University and Stephen C. Taylor, Vice President Profession Development, Aon Corporation, who examined the manuscript and provided ideas, insight and encouragement.

Special thanks to David N. Roberts, Ph.D. Sales and Training Consultant, Key Royal Automotive Company and Douglas B. Smith, Manager Credit Claims, Ryan Insurance Group, Inc. who not only examined the manual but who also provided extensive editorial advice.

Thanks also to Jim Bessent, editor, McGraw-Hill, who championed the publication of this book and to Fred Dahl of Inkwell Publishing Services for his efforts in making this a quality product.

I also owe tremendous gratitude to Patrick G. Ryan, Chairman and Chief Executive Officer of Aon Corporation, who has actively supported my work and provided the research laboratory through the assignments he gave me.

I would like to thank my *Guided Discovery* students in the USA and United Kingdom. Each of whom have directly contributed to the process of perfecting my concepts and therefore were instrumental in helping me write this book.

Finally, to all my friends, family and colleagues. I wish to express my appreciation for the support and encouragement that each of you have provided me.

Lester T. Shapiro

Permissions

Grateful acknowledgment is made to the following for permission to use material appearing on the pages listed below:

Page 1, 8, 155: "Training Evaluation: What's the Current Status?" by Dale C. Brandenburg. Reprinted with permission from *Training and Development Journal*, August 1982, © 1982, the American Society for Training and Development. All rights reserved.

Page 14: Table 1 (p. 48) and Table 2 (p. 51) from "Instructional Designer's Decisions and Priorities: A Survey of Design Practice" by John Wedman and Martin Tessmer. Reprinted with permission from *Performance Improvement Quarterly*, Volume 6, Number 2, pp. 43–57, © 1993, Learning Systems Institute, Florida State University.

Page 16, 155: From *The Adult Learner, A Neglected Species*, by Malcolm Knowles, © 1973 by Gulf Publishing Company, Houston, TX. Used with permission. All rights reserved.

Page 20, 21, 24, 28, 30, 31, 37, 38, 531, 533: Reprinted with permission from *Preparing Instructional Objectives*. California by Robert F. Mager, © 1984, Lake Publishing Company.

Page 30, 448: Excerpt from *The Conditions of Learning* by Robert M. Gagne, copyright © 1965 by Holt, Rinehart and Winston, Inc. and renewed 1993 by Robert M. Gagne, reprinted by permission of the publisher.

Page 30: "Learning A Process of Change" by E. A. Haggard and "Basic Principles in a Good Teaching-Learning Situation" by W. H. Burton. Reprinted with permission from *Readings in Human Learning*, edited by L. D. and Alice Crow, © 1963, McKay.

Page 81, 523, 530: Reprinted with permission from *How to Write Learning Objectives* by Sarah A. Lutterodt and Deborah J. Grafinger, © 1985, GP Courseware.

Page 84, 85, 86, 90, 155, 156: Reprinted with permission from the *Taxonomy of Educational Objectives, Book 1: Cognitive Domain* by Benjamin S. Bloom, © 1984, Longman Publishers USA.

Page 84, 85, 86, 156: Reprinted with permission from the *Taxonomy of Educational Objectives, Book 2: Affective Domain* by Benjamin S. Bloom, David R. Krathwohl and Bertram B. Masia, © 1964, Longman Publishers USA.

Page 135, 136, 138, 184: Reprinted with permission from *The Human Side of Enterprise* by Douglas McGregor, © 1960, McGraw-Hill, Inc.

Page 135–137: "Teach 'Win-Win' Selling with 'Win-Win' Training" by Thomas Kramlinger. Reprinted with permission from *Successful Meetings*, July 1975, © 1975 Bill Communications. All rights reserved.

Page 146: Reprinted with permission from *Training for Performance* by John E. Morrison, ed., © 1991, John Wiley & Sons, Ltd., Sussex, United Kingdom.

Page 156, 157: "What's Ahead in Human Resources" by Mary F. Cook. Reprinted with permission from *Management Review*, April 1988, © 1988, American Management Association, New York. All rights reserved.

Page 176, 177, 264: Reprinted with permission from *The Handbook of Selling* by Gary M. Grikscheit, Harold C. Cash and W. J. E. Crissy, © 1991, John Wiley and Sons, Inc.

Page 257, 258, 349: Reprinted with permission from *The Psychology of Selling* by Harold C. Cash and W. J. E. Crissy, © 1966, John Wiley and Sons, Inc.

Page 260, 263, 448: Reprinted with permission from *The Encyclopedia of Human Behavior: Psychology, Psychiatry, and Mental Health* by Robert M. Goldenson, Ph.D., © 1970, Doubleday & Company, Inc.

Page 270: Excerpt from *Language in Thought and Action*, Fourth Edition by S. I. Hayakawa, Arthur A. Berger and Arthur Chandler, copyright © 1978 by Harcourt Brace & Company, reprinted by permission of the publisher.

Page 353-510: Appendixes A through H are reprinted with permission of Aon Corporation, Chicago, Illinois, © 1991. All rights reserved.

Introduction

A. Training and Quality

Quality is on the mind of almost every business leader in America. Managers are trying to find new ways to respond to their customers and increase effectiveness in all parts of their organizations. The emphasis on quality, whether it focuses on Total Quality Management or continuous improvement or quality assurance, is related to the need to compete within the context of a global economy.

Training plays a key role in conveying the "quality" message. However, and this is an important distinction, the quality movement has not been associated with the quality of training. In a 1982 survey on the status of training evaluation, Brandenburg stated, "When I first conceived the idea for this study, I thought I would use the term 'Quality Assurance of Training' rather than Training Evaluation." He goes on to say that his colleagues in the business community discouraged him from using the *Quality Assurance* term because it could be considered jargon not generally accepted. (Brandenburg, 1982)

Brandenburg found that no universally accepted model of training evaluation existed. Quality is about judgment, measurement and accountability. Without adequate evaluation tools, quality and training cannot be linked.

There is also an assumption that a quality initiative will permeate every part of the organization, including training. However, because of the difficulty associated with measurement, training has been immune from application of the processes used to achieve total quality elsewhere.

With today's worldwide competition, an organization must leverage every available resource to survive and prosper. The need for quality has never been greater. This includes the quality of the training the organization provides for itself or its customers.

The measure of a training program's quality is its effectiveness. Training is effective to the degree that it produces the desired behavior in the population being trained. In concise terms, total quality occurs when each participant is able to use the knowledge and skills taught in the program to bring about a desired result on the job.

1

B. Total Customer Satisfaction

The quality movement is driven by total customer satisfaction. In a training transaction there are a number of customer relationships, each requiring satisfaction. These involve both internal and external customers. The following illustrations show these relationships.

CEO   Manager   Trainer   Performer   End User

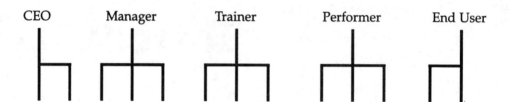

Chairs facing back to back symbolize that an individual plays different roles in related transactions. For example, if the performer is a salesperson, he or she is accountable to the manager for selling the product and satisfying the customer (end user). In the transaction with the customer, the salesperson is responsible for bringing about a buying decision.

| | Manager | Performer | End User |

| Managing Performance |

The end user is the manager's customer. The need for training is motivated by the need to satisfy the end user. In some cases, the performer may perceive the need for training and request it from the manager.

| Contracting for Training |

Trainer   Manager

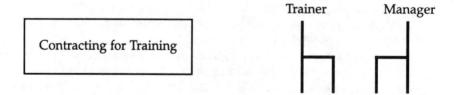

The manager is the trainer's customer. The manager contracts with the trainer to correct a discrepancy in one or more performer's knowledge and skill. While conducting the training, the trainer acts on behalf of the manager. Satisfaction occurs when the investment made in training brings about organizational results and the conduct of the training supports the desired culture. Compensation for the trainer occurs in the form of a fee or a salary and in recognition for solving a problem.

The performer (student) is also the trainer's customer. Performers must feel that the training provided solutions to real-world problems that justified their time and effort. Total satisfaction is realized when they are effective in their transaction with the end user.

Total quality has been achieved when the training enables all performers to bring about the desired results on the job. When this occurs the investment made in training is justified and everybody wins: the end user, performer, manager, trainer and the organization.

C. Is Training Really an Investment?

Organizations in America spend in excess of 40 billion dollars a year on training. Are they getting the quality they deserve? Are they getting the maximum return on their investment?

An investment is an outlay of money usually for income or profit. We invest in stocks, bonds and real estate for the purpose of realizing a gain. We measure our success, as investors, by the amount of our gain. Investments which go down in value are considered a loss.

Training is effective to the degree that it enables each performer to produce results on the job using the knowledge and skills taught. When this occurs, the organization gets a return on its investment. If the performer continues to use the skills we can say that the investment has grown in value.

However, if the skills acquired in the training proves to be ineffective or the performer does not use them, the organization must look at the time and money spent as a loss. If the product of the training is only a certificate on a wall or a book gathering dust on a shelf, then the purchaser of training has lost on that particular investment.

Loss, in this instance, does not mean a total loss. For example, a share of stock purchased for $40 that drops to $20 still has value. Likewise, all training will have some value; at worst, it may convince the performer that there must be a better way to approach the issue under discussion.

If you, as a decision maker, approve an expenditure for training but cannot demonstrate the impact of the training on your organization's results, then you have made a questionable investment.

D. Have You Invested in Poor Quality Training?

Here is an informal survey. Answer each question by inserting the appropriate number from this rating scale:

3	Frequently
2	Occasionally
1	Seldom
0	Never

How often have you attended training where you:

____ Felt your time was wasted by attending the program.

____ Had a good time, were entertained, but can't remember what was taught.

____ Knew more than the person conducting the training.

____ Disagreed with what was being taught.

____ Felt the instructor's explanation of the subject was inadequate.

____ Were exposed to a large quantity of knowledge-based material but did not receive an adequate explanation or demonstration of how to put it into practice.

____ Did not have adequate opportunities to practice the skill taught and receive feedback.

____ Were not challenged.

____ Were unable to challenge and explore the relevance and efficacy of the skills being taught.

____ Learned about a skill for which you had no practical application.

____ **Learned a skill that seemed to work in the classroom but did not work on the job.**

____ **Attended a course, which appeared to meet your need, only to discover that it did not deliver the knowledge or skills needed for you to achieve your goals.**

____ **Were unable to use the skills taught with confidence or competence.**

____ Total Score.

A total score over 25 or a rating of 2 or 3 on the last two items suggests that you or your organization have invested in poor quality training.

E. What About the Quality of the Training You Deliver?

Let's look at the effectiveness of training from the developer's or instructor's viewpoint. Answer each question by inserting the appropriate number from this rating scale:

3	**Frequently**
2	**Occasionally**
1	**Seldom**
0	**Never**

How often have you experienced the following problems with the training you designed or conducted:

____ Students were reluctant to be trained.

____ Students felt their time could be better spent doing their job.

____ You had difficulty getting people to participate in class discussions.

____ You had difficulty controlling a discussion and reaching a focused conclusion.

____ Students were reluctant to engage in role play activities.

____ You ran out of time for role play and performance evaluation exercises.

____ Students were reluctant to change their behavior.

____ You frequently hear students say that their situations are different.

____ Managers were reluctant to send their people to training.

____ Skills being taught were not reinforced by the manager.

____ Top management did not support the training effort.

____ You were unable to determine the student's needs prior to training or during the early stages of the training.

____ You had difficulty writing learning objectives.

____ You had difficulty planning and organizing a training manual.

____ You had difficulty replicating instructor performance. Instructors who facilitated the program depart from the training manual.

____ **You were unable to measure the effectiveness of the training.**

____ **You were unable to link the training conducted to the results produced on the job.**

____ **Students did not use the skills taught in the program on the job.**

____ Total Score

A total score over 25 or a rating of 2 or 3 on the last three items suggests that you are less than satisfied with the quality of the training you developed or conducted.

F. Questions for the Chief Executive Officer

Is your organization getting the maximum return from its investment in training?

If your answer is yes, and you have convincing evidence, then disregard this section. If you are not certain, then see if you, or anyone in your organization, can answer the following questions:

1. What are your organization's training standards?

2. How does your organization measure the effectiveness of existing training, new projects or programs purchases from outside vendors?

3. What process is used by decision makers to purchase sales and management training from an outside vendor?

4. What are training personnel in your organization held accountable for?

5. Can you demonstrate the impact of training on your organization's results?

If you cannot answer these questions, your organization may be wasting valuable time and money on ineffective or inappropriate training programs.

G. Mistakes Can Be Expensive

Every person who invests time and money for training is a consumer of training. This includes company executives, managers, developers, facilitators and students. Depending on your level of authority within an organization, that investment can be considerable. For example:

A CEO purchases a 5-day training program to train 500 managers to be more effective in their transactions with employees. Assuming a cost of $500 per manager, $250,000 will be paid to the vendor. 2500 worker days will be spent in the classroom, which, at an average salary of $800 per week, represents a $400,000 opportunity cost. Assuming no travel and expenses, the training investment is $650,000.

If the training fails to bring about the desired skills, $650,000 is essentially lost. Also, if the organization does not measure the change or link the skills to its production or sales results, then the prudence of the investment must be questioned.

H. What Types of Training Are Subject to Quality Problems?

Training related to skills that can be quantitatively measured are less subject to quality problems. A typing course is a good example. If 80 percent of the students can type 60 words per minute with 90 percent accuracy, you can rate the training a success. By contrast, skills that involve qualitative factors, like communication and decision making are more difficult to measure.

There are many vendors offering programs on sales, management, communication, decision making and the development of training. How can you determine which programs will be effective? Will the skills you learn in any of these programs enable you to negotiate agreements with people that result in the achievement of your goals?

I. Can You Recover Damages for Poor Quality?

When you spend $795 for a product, such as a freezer, you have something to show for your expenditure. However, let's say that the freezer fails to perform as promised. It cannot hold a constant temperature, breaks down frequently and causes $500 worth of food to spoil. You would probably take legal action against the seller and you may recover both your $795 and the spoilage loss.

What about the training that you purchase? What is your basis for measuring whether you or your organization got its money's worth? Just as important, how do you recover the loss if the training is not effective? Most professionals have to carry malpractice insurance as they are held accountable for their performance. Unfortunately, there is no equivalent of malpractice insurance in the training field.

J. How Can You Ensure That You Invest in Quality Training?

Getting the most from your training investment means being an informed consumer. If you were buying an automobile, an appliance, an insurance policy, a common stock, a mutual fund or a roll of paper towels, you would have access to a wealth of consumer information. Companies like Consumer Union, the publisher of *Consumer Reports*, evaluate products and services against established criteria. Their ratings enable you to choose the product that gives you the best value for your money. There are no equivalent services available to the training consumer.

K. The Problem

"No universally accepted model for evaluation of training exists, nor are there generally accepted modes of operation or behavior." (Brandenburg, 1982)

As Table i.1 illustrates, Brandenburg found that the "most used evaluative techniques, regardless of criticisms heaped upon them, are the 'smile' indices, i.e.,

Table i.1. Brandenburg's 1982 Study of 33 Training Units[1,2]
Data Collection Techniques

In conducting evaluation of training, whether before, during, or after the activities, how frequently are the following data collection techniques used by you or your operational unit? (Scale: 4 = Very Often, 3 = Fairly Often, 2 = Once in a While, 1 = Never)

| | Group | | | |
| | Sales | | SIG | |
Technique	Mean	Rank	Mean	Rank
1. Objective questionnaire or survey	3.6	2	3.0	2
2. Open-ended comments or reactions	3.9	1	3.4	1
3. Multiple-choice (or similar) achievement measures	3.0	4	2.5	3
4. Essay (open-ended) achievement measures	1.9	12	1.9	10.5
5. Participant self assessment	2.9	5	2.3	6.5
6. Task performance measures (e.g., simulation, role playing)	3.1	3	2.5	4.4
7. Observation or anecdotal record	2.7	6	2.5	4.5
8. Use of video tape	2.5	7.5	1.7	12
9. Structured interviews	2.4	9	2.3	6.6
10. Later on the job performance appraisal	2.5	7.5	2.1	8
11. Indirect follow-up studies	2.2	10	2.0	9
12. Collection of cost analysis information	2.0	11	1.9	10.5

[1]The Sales group consisted of 14 training units who were members of the Chicago Sales Training Group (ASTD). The SIG group consisted of 19 organizations in the Training in Business and Industry Group of the American Educational Research Association.

[2]From "Training Evaluation: What's the Current Status" by Dale C. Brandenburg, *Training and Development Journal*, August 1982 pp. 15–19. Copyright 1982 American Society for Training and Development. Used by permission. All rights reserved.

questionnaires and comments. Cognitive and performance based outcome measures are used less often, while the least used techniques are those that require longitudinal follow-up of participants."

Six years later, Brandenburg surveyed 45 Fortune 500 companies and found that only 30 percent used measures of learning and only 15 percent used measures of behavior. However, 100 percent of the companies used some type of participant reaction form that measured the participant's perceived satisfaction with the training. (Brandenburg & Schultz, 1988) Basically, little had changed and few organizations seemed concerned with the measurement of training effectiveness.

Evaluation of training effectiveness and total quality are integral. The ability to evaluate training enables an organization to make cost effective decisions that ensure the greatest return on its training investment.

L. The Solution

This book provides a system for evaluating any training program regardless of instructional style, method or format. This enables you to predict the likelihood that the training and the behavior contained within the training will be effective. As a result, you will be able to:

- Make decisions about the purchase or development of training that significantly increase the return on the training investment.
- Plan, organize, conduct, evaluate and modify training that brings about measurable results.
- Use training to bring about change in an organization.
- Identify programs that are ineffective or inappropriate to your needs or the culture of your organization.
- Negotiate the time and resources needed to produce training that impacts results.
- Enable people to acquire skills that will help them achieve their goals.
- Manage the overall training function including internal program development and assessment of new training projects.
- Evaluate instructor performance using objective measurements.
- Achieve training effectiveness in an organization of any size.

M. The Method

The Training Effectiveness Handbook is organized into three parts.

Part 1: **Learning Objectives:** The Foundation.

Part 2: **Training Effectiveness Evaluation:** The key to maximizing the return on your training investment.

Part 3: **Program Development:** A system for designing and delivering effective training.

In Part 1, **Learning Objectives**, you will participate in a training program on writing learning objectives. There are five benefits. You will:

1. Discover that learning objectives are the foundation of instructional design and delivery.
2. Gain considerable skill in writing and evaluating learning objectives.
3. Experience an effective training program. This will give us a common frame of reference to discuss training.

4. Gain considerable skill in using an evaluation system that will enable you to measure the quality of any training program.

5. Be able to design a reliable Performance Evaluation System for measuring student competence with complex interactive sales, management and teaching behaviors.

Part 2, **Training Effectiveness Evaluation,** explains a system that can be used to bring about training effectiveness in an organization. The system consists of (1) the *Total Quality Training Standards,** (2) *Guidelines for Meeting the Standards* and (3) *Expert Criteria to Measure the Standards.*

In Part 2 the need for standards and the guidelines for meeting each will be discussed. Then you will use the Standards to evaluate the training you experienced in Part 1. You will also evaluate a module which teaches an interactive training behavior. These will enable you to practice using the systems to evaluate training. Finally, we will look at the process and systems required to implement the Standards in an organization and the use of the Standards for evaluating training to be purchased from a vendor.

Part 3, **Program Development,** explains a system that will enable you to design and deliver effective training. In this section I will discuss the development process, the structure of an instructor guide that links program content directly to a set of learning objectives and the control of time.

Part 3 introduces *Guided Discovery*, an interactive training style that enables you to conduct discussions that reveal student understanding and acceptance of program content. *Guided Discovery* addresses the difficulties associated with getting active participation and guiding discussions to a focused conclusion within pre-set time frames.

Also provided is a reference manual, *Expert Criteria for Measuring the Standards.* It contains criteria to measure 37 components of training design, organization and delivery. These criteria along with the knowledge in Parts 1, 2 and 3 enable you to measure any program against the *Total Quality Training Standards* and to plan, organize, conduct, evaluate and modify an effective training program.

---

*Total Quality Training Standards are also referred to as the Standards

PART 1

Learning Objectives

The Foundation

1
Foundation or Formality?

Are learning objectives the <u>foundation</u> of instructional design and delivery or are they only a <u>formality</u>, a ritual that each developer of training performs because it's expected?

Before you answer, consider the definition of the word foundation: a basis (as a tenet, principle or axiom) upon which something stands or is supported.

To answer the question of whether or not objectives are a foundation or a formality, I examined programs from the annual conventions of the National Society for Performance and Instruction (NSPI) and the American Society for Training and Development (ASTD), the nation's largest and most prestigious training organizations. I reasoned that they would:

1. Establish standards for the workshops which would, at a minimum, include standards for objectives, and

2. Provide workshops on the writing of learning objectives at their annual conventions.

A. Available Training

A review of recent convention programs revealed no specific workshops on the writing of learning objectives from either the NSPI or ASTD. A two day course offered by a training consultant for a fee of $600 contained a list of 16 objectives of which only one dealt with the writing of objectives.

My first conclusion: The area of useful objectives is not perceived as a problem.

This conclusion was supported by a survey conducted by John Wedman of the University of Missouri in 1991. Wedman surveyed 73 practicing instructional designers in two states to determine the degree to which they used various activities of the instructional development process.

Approximately 40 percent of the subjects were from the same training and development group within a large organization. The other subjects were from a wide variety of contexts (e.g., business, government, etc.). Their training experience ranged from a few months to over 25 years.

The subjects were asked to rank the frequency which they completed each of eleven design activities listed in the chart below. Notice that 82 percent of the subjects stated that they <u>always</u> "write learning objectives." The combination of the <u>always</u> and <u>usually</u> responses indicate that learning objectives are used in 94 percent of the projects executed by these designers.

Instructional design activity	Frequency of Completion*			
	Always	Usually	Occassionally	Never
Conduct a needs assessment	29	34	23	8
Determine if need can be solved by training	36	34	21	8
Write learning objectives	**82**	**12**	**4**	**1**
Conduct task analysis	30	36	23	8
Identify the types of learning outcomes	36	38	16	10
Assess trainee's entry skills and characteristics	27	27	34	10
Develop test items	59	23	11	4
Select instructional strategies for training	50	35	10	3
Select media formats for the training	52	34	8	3
Pilot test instruction before completion	33	16	33	18
Do a follow-up evaluation of the training	38	34	22	5

Wedman then asked the subjects to identify reasons why an activity was excluded from some projects. The chart below shows that learning objectives are rarely excluded. In fact, only two respondents cited a lack of expertise as a reason for not using objectives. (Wedman and Tessmer)

Instructional design activity	Reason for Exclusion*						
	Lack expertise	Client won't support	Decision already made	Considered unnecessary	Not enough time	Not enough money	Total (across)
Conduct a needs assessment	0	6	31	15	13	3	68
Determine if need can be solved by training	3	2	29	5	6	1	46
Write learning objectives	**2**	**0**	**2**	**5**	**5**	**3**	**17**
Conduct task analysis	5	5	12	17	14	3	56
Identify types of learning outcomes	7	7	13	12	9	2	50
Assess trainee's entry skills and characteristics	0	6	11	16	8	4	45
Develop test items	0	2	3	12	7	3	27
Select instructional strategies	3	1	12	1	9	4	30
Select media formats	0	2	11	2	9	9	33
Pilot test instruction	1	9	4	15	32	14	75
Do a follow-up evaluation	1	8	2	9	9	7	36
Total (across activities)	22	48	130	109	121	53	

*Used by permission from the *Performance Improvement Quarterly*.

B. Consistency and Uniformity

Approximately 95 percent of the workshops in the NSPI and ASTD Convention Programs contained learning objectives. However, there was no consistency among them. Nor is there any consistency in the objectives contained within the numerous advertising brochures I receive from training vendors. Consider the following examples:

- "Accelerated Learning": Participants learn how to use the key elements of accelerated learning.
- "Accelerated Training": The objective of the workshop is to acquaint people with the concepts, philosophies and methods of accelerated learning as applied primarily to corporate training, seed people's imagination in terms of the infinite possibilities for enhancing human learning and enable people to exercise more of their innate creativity in designing and delivering more effective training.
- "The Course Developer Workshop": You will learn how to write high level objectives in three domains: cognitive, psychomotor and affective.
- "Designing Seminars that Work": You will learn how to select the right training activity to meet your objective.
- "Influencing the Performance of Others": You will learn how to identify important problems worth solving, find the most likely cause of each problem; select practical solutions that will eliminate the causes; effectively implement your solutions; and prevent potential problems.
- "Increasing Effort and Job Performance Through Intrinsic Motivation": Describe the effects of perceived challenge and competence on job performance. Identify methods which increase levels of self efficacy, self determination and ultimate intrinsic motivation.
- "Equipment Analysis Framework": Given an equipment analysis job aid, task selection criteria and examples, participants will select an appropriate method of training for each task identified in an equipment analysis.
- "Instructional Skills for New Trainers": As a result of participating, you understand how to design and present an effective training session—the kind that gets results for your organization.

The above objectives are all flawed when measured against the criteria in this book. Several are not even learning objectives, despite what their authors may claim.

The NSPI uses three criteria to judge the usefulness of the objectives for training sessions at their annual convention. First, objectives may "contain no more than 25 words." This limit is imposed, undoubtedly, to control the size of the program booklet. However, there is no basis in the literature for limiting the number of words in an objective.

The second states that objectives must be "clear and specific." Since "clear" and "specific" are abstract words, this criterion is anything but clear and specific.

The third criterion requires the objectives to be "performance based." The term "performance based" is too general, and therefore it is not useful as a criterion.

My second conclusion: There is no agreement between people in the training field with regard to the structure and content of objectives.

C. The Raging Controversy

Malcolm Knowles in <u>The Adult Learner: A Neglected Species</u> (1973), presents a range of positions with regard to the relevance and need for objectives held by learning theorists. They range from the behaviorists, who "insist that objectives are meaningless unless they describe terminal behaviors in very precise, measurable and observable terms" to the "theorists who see learning as a process of inquiry expressly (and sometimes vehemently) reject the idea that there should be preset or prescribed objectives at all." (Knowles, 1973, pp. 126–129) Knowles attempts to reconcile these positions "by assigning the terminal-behavior-oriented procedures to training and the more inquiry-process-oriented procedures to education." (Knowles, 1973, p. 130)

My third conclusion: There is no agreement among learning theorists as to the need for learning objectives.

D. "Because You Say It Is, Does Not Make It So"

Some time ago an associate asked me to look at a set of objectives he had written. After studying them, I told him that they were useless and not objectives. My associate was rather upset by my assertion that his objectives had no value. He persisted in claiming these were objectives and suggested I did not know what I was talking about.

To help him understand the problem, I pointed to the dictionary on my desk and declared that it was a telephone. My friend, who by now was very angry, told me I was crazy. I maintained stubbornly that the dictionary was a telephone and he persisted that I had lost my mind. Finally, I said "how do you know that I'm crazy?" To which he replied; "I know what a telephone is and a dictionary is not one, unless the dictionary is a disguise and there is one hidden inside." "How do you know?" I asked. Indignantly, he replied that "there are certain criteria that distinguish a telephone from a dictionary or for that matter anything else. A telephone has a device for dialing, a speaker, a transmitter and produces a dial tone that indicates its connection to the telephone system when actuated."

"You are absolutely right, I said, my dictionary is not a telephone. It does not meet the basic criteria you just defined. In fact, that's the beauty of criteria. They enable reasonable people to agree that something falls within a particular category and in doing so permits them to communicate with each other and accomplish their goals."

Objectives present us with a special problem. They are written statements that use abstract symbols (words) to stand for human behavior. They are not tangible items that are easily subject to classification. However, objectives can be classified and measured if we can agree on a set of criteria.

E. Where Do You Stand?

This section will help you measure your level of comfort with learning objectives. It does so by measuring your use of objectives, technical knowledge and your actual skill in developing a set of objectives.

Task 1—Developing Learning Objectives

You are to teach a course on writing learning objectives to a group of new instructional developers. **Write a set of objectives for this program.** Use a separate sheet of paper for this task.

Task 2—Use of Learning Objectives

The following statements describe a particular use of learning objectives. **Rate your ability to use each with this scale:**

10	**Can document my use of objectives for this purpose**
5	**Questionable or not documented**
0	**Never used objectives in this way**

____ Describe, with precision, the knowledge and skills that the training will bring about.

____ Plan the structure of a training program in terms of time and modules.

____ Negotiate with management (or a client) the time, money and personnel required to conduct the program.

____ Measure the learner's need for training.

____ Make decisions with regard to content, resources and training methodology for each module of the program.

____ Organize the students' efforts and activities toward accomplishing the desired behavior.

____ Measure the learner's acquisition of the desired behavior (and, therefore, the program's effectiveness).

____ Measure the learner's perception of the value and effectiveness of the training.

____ Construct instructor guides (manuals) that enable certified instructors to conduct the training program in a predefined manner.

____ Determine the effectiveness and relevance of a vendor's training program.

____ Total. This is your **Utilization Score** (maximum score is 100).

Task 3—Technical Knowledge—Self Test

Use the following questions to **test your actual knowledge** with regard to the definition, use, structure and measurement of objectives.

1. Write a definition of a learning objective.

2. List five components of a useful objective.

3. List four types of objectives that are relevant to <u>structuring</u> a training program and write a precise definition for each.

4. List six criteria (standards) that you would use to measure the usefulness of a Core, Terminal, Program or Module Objective.

The solutions to this self test are found on pages 511-512. Compare your answers to mine and determine your **Knowledge Percentage** (percentage of correct answers). Insert these below.

Important: A model set of learning objectives for a course on objectives is located on page 19. These are my answers to Task 1 and the learning objectives for Part 1. You will evaluate the objectives you wrote later in the book.

F. How Did You Do?

Insert your **Utilization Score** and **Knowledge Percentage** in the spaces below. Then calculate your **Objective Utilization Rating**:

> **Utilization Score**   _____
> **Knowledge Percentage**   _____%
> **Objective Utilization Rating** _____

Determine your **Objective Utilization Rating** by multiplying your **Utilization Score** by your **Knowledge Percentage**. For example: Your **Utilization Score** was 60 and your **Knowledge Percentage** was 90 percent. Your **Objective Utilization Rating** is 54 (e.g., 60 x .90 = 54).

Here is an interpretation of your **Objective Utilization Rating**:

Rating	*Explanation of Rating*
71 to 100	You have specific knowledge of the nature and structure of objectives. *Objectives are the foundation of your training programs* as they are used at every juncture of the program development process. Your programs are totally objective driven.
35 to 70	Your use of objectives in your training is very limited or your technical knowledge of objectives limits their use. Utilization of objectives could result in a substantial improvement in training effectiveness.
Below 34	You have limited technical knowledge of objectives or do not use objectives in your training. *They are not the foundation of your training programs.*

If your **Utilization Score** is high and your **Knowledge Percentage** is low you may want to reread the ten utilization questions. Remember, to score 10 you must be able to <u>document</u> each use.

If your **Knowledge Percentage** is high and your **Utilization Score** is low you are missing the benefits of using objectives. Knowledge without application is of very limited value.

Whatever your score, I invite you on a journey. At the end of the journey you will have the ability to achieve an **Objective Utilization Rating** of <u>100</u> and use learning objectives as the *foundation of your training programs.*

G. Objectives of Part 1

Objectives are powerful tools in the design and delivery of training. The explanation that follows will help you measure the objectives you are currently using and make corrections to them that will increase the effectiveness of your training. The following are the learning objectives for Part 1 and my answer to Task 1:

Module Objective

Write a Learning Objective: Given a performance discrepancy that is caused by a lack of skill or knowledge on a subject that the instructional developer has mastered, the developer (reader) will be able to write a learning objective that contains performance, criteria, conditions and time components within 12 minutes which achieves an Effectiveness Rating of 10 (on a 10 scale) against prescribed criteria.

Unit Objectives

To accomplish the Module Objective, the Instructional Developer will be able to:

1. Write a definition of a learning objective.

2. List six components of a useful objective.

3. List six criteria (standards) that would measure the usefulness of a Core, Terminal, Program or Module Objective.

4. Given six criteria, a Rating Scale and a learning objective, calculate the Effectiveness Rating of the learning objective with an accuracy of +/− 1.0 against the author's solution.

5. Differentiate between Core, Module and Unit Objectives. (List and specifically differentiate four types of objectives that are relevant to <u>structuring</u> a training program.)

6. Calculate an Effectiveness Rating for a set of learning objectives.

A Note to the Reader: With the exception of the words learning objective and desired behavior, all terms with special meanings are capitalized in the text and defined in the glossary.

2
The Learning
Objective Principle

In <u>Preparing Instructional Objectives,</u> Robert F. Mager stated: **"An objective is a description of a performance you want learners to be able to exhibit before you consider them competent."** He further stated that: "An objective describes an intended result of instruction, rather than the process of instruction itself." (Mager, 1984, p. 5) Could Mager's definition represent the principle of a learning objective?

A Definition or a Principle?

A principle is a fundamental truth, law or doctrine serving as the basis to support existence or to determine the structure or function of something. The word principle comes from the Latin word *principium* meaning beginning or basis. Notice the similarity of principle to the definition of the word foundation on page 13. A principle is a foundation upon which something stands. Here are two examples:

Bernoulli's Principle
> An increase in the speed of a fluid produces a decrease in pressure and a decrease in speed produces an increase in pressure.

The Theory of Relativity
> $E = MC^2$

The first example explains lift in an airfoil, the ability of a sail to make forward motion up wind and the process of drawing fuel into the flow stream of an engine's carburetor. It was postulated by Daniel Bernoulli (1700–1782). The second example was postulated by the world renowned physicist, Albert Einstein. It brought about the atomic age.

I suggest that Mager's definition is, in fact, the comprehensive principle for the form and structure of a Learning Objective and therefore the foundation of instructional design and delivery.

Mager's Learning Objective Principle
"A description of a performance you want learners to be able to exhibit before you consider them competent."

On the following pages we will derive the structural components of an objective from Mager's Principle and the criteria for measuring the usefulness of each. This will enable us to agree on a measurement system that will, in turn, enable you to write objectives and predetermine the effectiveness of a training event.

A. The Performance Component

"A description of a <u>performance</u> you want learners to be able to <u>exhibit</u> before you consider them competent."

The word performance in this sense is synonymous with the word behavior. An objective must describe the desired behavior you wish to observe. Webster defines behavior as follows: To act, function or react in a particular way. Anything that an organism does involving action and response to stimulation. For our purposes, behavior is:

Behavior: An action or response to a situation.

Behavior involves action. The English language uses verbs to denote actions. For example: plan, write, conduct and evaluate are verbs which describe human action. To describe performance we must also know the object of the verb. In other words, what is being acted upon. For example, *give a sales talk, conduct a sales discussion, evaluate a learning objective, plan a vacation or write a poem.*
Bob Mager refers to the combination of the verb and the object of the verb as a performance statement. I will refer to it throughout this book as the Performance Component.

Measuring the Performance Component

Listed below is the criterion for measuring the usefulness of the Performance Component of a learning objective:

Contains **the performance** to be exhibited. (Active verb[s] and the object of the verb describe <u>the desired behavior</u>.)

The Performance Component is the core or central component of the learning objective. Stated another way, if there is not a performance to be exhibited there is no objective. To test for a performance using the above criterion, the statement must:

- Contain an active (action) verb and the object of the verb.
- Describe the behavior of the student, not the instructor.
- Be observable during the training event.

For example, the Performance Component *"give a sales talk"* meets each of the above criteria.

Here is a quick test for any Performance Component: Can you observe the student performing the desired behavior in the classroom?

Test Your Skill

Consider the following four statements: Only one meets the criterion for a Performance Component. For reference purposes, I have repeated the criterion for the Performance Component and the sub criteria (tests) to aid you in your analysis. My answers and explanation follow.

1. To provide participants with a systematic approach to the design, development and delivery of training.
2. Be able to improve ability to conduct training.
3. Be able to plan a module of training.
4. Be able to sell an automobile.

For Reference

Performance Component Criterion

Contains **the performance** to be exhibited. (Active verb[s] and the object of the verb describe <u>the desired behavior</u>.)

To test for a performance using the above criterion, the statement must:

- Contain an active (action) verb and the object of the verb.
- Describe the behavior of the student, not the instructor.
- Be observable during the training event.

Quick Test: Can I observe the student performing the desired behavior in the classroom?

Statement 1

To provide participants with a systematic approach to the design, development and delivery of training.

This statement does not contain a performance to be exhibited. The word **"to"** at the beginning of any objective is a "red flag." Objectives starting with **"to"** are usually written from the instructor's viewpoint. The words that are not usually shown are: "The purpose of this course is to ..." The completed statement reads:

<u>The purpose of this course is to</u> provide participants with a systematic approach to the design, development and delivery of training.

This is the instructor's purpose. Not a student's performance. Ask yourself: What will the <u>student</u> be doing to demonstrate skill with the "systematic approach to design, development and delivery of training?" It is not apparent from the statement.

Statement 2

Be able to improve ability to conduct training.

This appears to be a benefit of participating in the training, not a performance. In order to observe improvement, we would need to have the student perform, but this is not evident from the statement. Therefore, it is not an objective.

Statement 3

Be able to plan a module of training.

<u>This is a performance.</u> It contains an active verb, **plan** and the object of the verb, **a module of training.** It describes the behavior of the student and is observable during a training event.

Statement 4

Be able to sell an automobile.

This one is a bit tricky. While it contains an active verb, **sell** and the object of the verb, **an automobile,** the behavior is generally <u>not observable during a training event</u> unless you bring in living, breathing, customers. Most training professionals agree that simulating reality in the classroom is desirable. However, bringing in actual customers tends to be a logistical nightmare. I would judge this to be a <u>questionable</u> performance.

Did you experience difficulty with this exercise? If you did, you are not alone. As the book continues, you will have many opportunities to practice identifying the Performance Component of an objective. For now let's return to Mager's definition and identify the five other components of a useful objective.

B. The Conditions Component

"A description of a performance **you want learners to be able to exhibit** before you consider them competent."

The key word is "to exhibit." To measure the behavior we must see the behavior. Again, we must return to our description of behavior and specifically the words <u>response to a situation.</u> Bob Mager uses the word <u>Conditions</u> to describe this element of an objective. I define <u>Conditions</u> as **the situation under which the performance occurs, limitations imposed on the performer or non-implicit resources available to the performer.** Which of the following statements is a <u>Condition</u>?

1. Given a narrative describing customer history, a product description booklet, a price list and 15 minutes to prepare.

2. Given 4 hours of training by an experienced instructor.

The first statement describes the situation and resources the person will have to work with along with a limitation (15 minutes to prepare) that you plan to impose. This is a <u>Condition</u>.

The second statement describes <u>the training</u> and is <u>not a Condition</u>. It describes **the process of instruction** from the trainer's point of view. The reference to the length of the training program, 4 hours, is a limitation on the trainer. It is not a limitation on the performance we desire the student to exhibit.

Notice the word **"given"** in each of the previous statements. The word **given** is often found, but not always, as the prefacing word of the objective's Condition Component. However, to qualify as a Condition Component of a learning objective, the statement must meet the following criterion:

It must describe the situation under which the performance occurs, limitations imposed on the performer or non-implicit resources available to the performer.

The Condition: <u>"Given a narrative describing customer history, a product description booklet, a price list and 15 minutes to prepare"</u> could also be worded as follows:

Condition: The salesperson will read a narrative describing the company's history with a customer in preparation for the performance. Only the product description booklet and the price list can be used during the performance. Fifteen minutes will be allowed for preparation.

C. Criteria and Performance Time

"A description of a performance you want learners to be able to exhibit **before you consider them competent**."

Before you consider them competent. In order to measure competence we must establish criteria to measure the behavior. For example, consider our performance "give a sales talk." To know that the person has performed competently we impose measurable standards. For example, the talk should be given word for word (no errors) and be completed in 6 minutes.

An important note to the reader. The performance, **give a sales talk** *word for word* <u>within 6 minutes</u>, is an example of a canned sales presentation (or stimulus response behavior). While you may not agree that this is a desirable behavior for a salesperson, this is not the issue. It is used to illustrate two components of a learning objective, *Criteria (shown in italics)* and <u>Performance Time</u> (underlined) that permit measurement of the behavior in the classroom or for that matter on the job in a live sales interview. These are defined here:

- <u>Criteria</u>: **The standard or standards by which you will measure the desired behavior.**

- <u>Performance Time</u>: **The time for the performance expressed in hours, minutes or seconds** (not the length of the training program or module).

D. The Criteria Component

Criteria refer to one or more criterion. A criterion is defined as a standard upon which a judgment or decision can be based. It is through criteria that we can judge whether or not the student acquired the desired behavior. Hence, a useful objective contains **criteria** to measure the desired behavior <u>at program's end</u>. For example, here is an objective for an exercise on identifying criteria. The <u>Condition is underlined</u>, the **Performance is bolded,** and the *criteria are shown in italics*: The Performance Time is shown in plain text.

> <u>Given three learning objectives containing one or all of the components (performance, condition or criteria)</u>, the reader will be able to **identify (by underlining)** *correctly* **the words** *that are used as criteria in each* within 2 minutes.

Here are the three objectives referred to in the above model objective. Go ahead and do the exercise (underline the criteria). The answers follow.

1. Give a sales talk word for word within 6 minutes.

2. Given a narrative describing an employee's performance and stage of development, the manager will be able to choose a course of action that is appropriate to the problem and the employee's stage of development.

3. Given an unprogrammed VCR, the purchaser will be able to program five events without reference to the manual.

I have shown the *Criteria in italics*. I have also **bolded the Performance** and underlined the Condition (where applicable) to make the structure clear. Performance Time is shown in plain text. How did you do?

1. **Give a sales talk** *word for word* within 6 minutes.

2. Given a narrative describing an employee's performance and stage of development, the manager will be able to **choose a course of action** *that is appropriate to the problem and the employee's stage of development.*

3. Given an unprogrammed VCR, the purchaser will be able to **program** *five* **events** *without reference to the manual.*

When examining an objective for Criteria look for the following words: **that, which, in relation to or based on**. These often precede the criteria. In example 4 and 5, the **prefacing word is underlined**, *the Criteria are in italics* **and the Performance is bolded.**

4. **Construct an algorithm for claim decisions** based on *the provisions of the policy.*

5. **Conduct a disciplinary discussion with an employee** which *contains two transactions that maintain the employee's self esteem.*

Only the principal Criteria need to be shown in the objective. For example, in our training course for managers on disciplinary interviews (objective 5), we may want to measure the structure of the behavior (a four step procedure for conducting the discussion). Subordinate criteria, such as each of the four steps, can be shown on the performance evaluation form.

Criteria also help us identify the form and style of a transaction. Compare:

Give a sales talk *word for word*

with

Propose a product *in relation to the identified needs.*

("**Give a sales talk ...**" represents the stimulus-response style of selling. The salesperson delivers the message as prescribed by the company. "**Propose a product ...**" represents the need satisfaction style of selling. Salespeople using this style attempt to determine the customer's needs before proposing their product. Then the product is presented as a solution to the identified needs.)

Criteria enable all parties to judge the behavior contained in the training. Managers can see if it's relevant and consistent with the culture of the company. Developers can measure the students' competence with the desired behavior and students can decide if the training is relevant to their needs.

E. The Performance Time Component

It could be argued that time should be classified under criteria and not as a separate component. However, I suggest that time expressed in hours, minutes or seconds is applicable to every performance <u>that will be observed to measure learner competence</u>.

<u>Performance Time</u> is important for <u>measuring the student's competence</u> with the desired behavior. In our example, the sales talk must be given word for word in 6 minutes. If the student talks rapidly and gives the talk in 3 minutes, the result may be a confused prospect. On the other hand, if the student takes 10 minutes while he/she tries to remember the words, we introduce a new set of problems. While he meets the accuracy standard (word for word), the long time period indicates that he does not really know the material. Will prospects put up with his slow, halting delivery? The 6-minute time limit allows the instructor to determine that the student knows the material and can deliver it at an understandable pace.

<u>Performance Time</u> is also a major factor in <u>planning a course</u> of instruction, especially with regard to the length of the training. For example, assume that each student's performance will take 6 minutes and that each will be observed twice during the training. Further assume that each student will receive 10 minutes of feedback from the instructor and group. There are 20 students in the group. The length of each student's performance plus the time to discuss the performance, multiplied by the number of students and the number of performances to be observed yields the <u>Training Time</u> that must be allocated to performance and evaluation:

Performance Time	6	Minutes
<u>Discussion Time</u>	+ 10	
Sub Total	16	
<u>Number of Students</u>	× 20	
Sub Total	320	
<u>Number of Performances</u>	× 2	
Training Time (allocated to Performance)	640	Minutes

If the training day begins at 9:00 a.m. and ends at 5:00 p.m. with one hour for lunch and two 15 minute breaks, then there are 390 minutes of Training Time. To conduct this training program we can quickly calculate that we need almost two days to determine if the students can competently perform. If the explanation and demonstration phase of the training is 180 minutes, then we have a two and a half day course.

Effect of Performance Time

When you include the measurement of performance in your training design, you begin to look at time differently. The first issue is to separate <u>Training Time</u>, the time allocated for the training event, from <u>Performance Time</u>, that which is need-ed to observe each student's performance. A focus on measurement of perfor-mance will result in <u>Performance Time</u> being the principal determinant of the length of the training program.

A commitment to allow time for performance will revolutionize the training you conduct. It is only through the observation and measurement of student per-formance that you (the developer), and your organization determine the effec-tiveness of your training.

Too often managers responsible for training, or developers, will allocate time for the training event without considering the time for each student's perfor-mance. Such managers tend to view training as a "leap of faith." They "hope" that the training will solve the problem that motivated them to allocate resources: time, people and money.

Many developers and instructors believe that training is dynamic and, there-fore, put minimal emphasis on performance. This mode of thinking holds that the recipient of the message "puts it all together" at some future point and then is magically able to perform. This assumption is highly questionable and is rarely tested for validity by subsequent evaluation of the training.

Without performance, the manager, the developer and the instructor (who may also be the developer of the training) may not be able to determine if the student <u>understood</u>, <u>accepted</u> and <u>can competently use</u> the knowledge and skills con-tained within the training.

<u>Performance Time</u> will help you to make training decisions that maximize your organization's training investment.

F. The Performer Component

"A description of a performance you want **learners to be able to** exhibit before you consider them competent."

Another component and criterion for measuring the usefulness of an objective is derived from the phrase the **"learners to be able to."** It suggests that the objec-tive should contain the <u>job title of the performer</u> and the words <u>be able to</u>. Without this, the statement would be incomplete since it is a specific person who will be motivated to acquire the behavior described in an objective. For example, a doc-tor would not need to learn a sales talk word for word, but an insurance agent sell-ing door to door might.

Measuring the Performer Component

The following lists the criterion for measuring the usefulness of the Performer Component of a learning objective. To avoid any confusion caused by the similarity of the words "performer" and "performance," I have also shown the Performance Component:

Performer Component	Contains the **job title of the performer** and the words **"be able to"** immediately before the active verb.
Performance Component	Contains **the performance** to be exhibited. (Active verb[s] and the object of the verb describe <u>the desired behavior</u>.)

Here is an example of a statement with both components: *The developer will be able to plan a training module.* It is shown in relation to the criteria for measuring the Performer and Performance Component:

The developer will be able to	Contains the **job title of the performer** and the words **"be able to"** immediately before the active verb
plan a training module	Contains **the performance** to be exhibited. (Active verb[s] and the object of the verb describe <u>the desired behavior</u>.)

The Job Title of the Performer

Should we use the **job title of the performer** rather than the word "<u>student,</u>" "<u>participant</u>" or "<u>you</u>?" An effective way to focus on the learner's point of view is to see the learner within the context of the job you are training them to do, rather than as "students." Hence, the reason for stating the **job title of the performer** in the objective.

Another reason for stating the **job title of the performer,** relates to the role the learner will play in any simulation that you use to observe performance. For example, consider the objective for Part 1, the module of training in which you are participating.

Given a performance discrepancy that is caused by a lack of skill or knowledge on a subject that the instructional developer has mastered, **the developer** will be able to write a learning objective that contains performance, criteria, conditions and time components within 12 minutes which achieves an Effectiveness Rating of 10 (on a 10 scale) against prescribed criteria.

Notice the objective refers to you as a <u>developer</u>. Regardless of your actual job title, when you are writing learning objectives you are acting in the role of a developer.

This concept would also apply to a group of college students in a class on, for example, training program development. In the learning objectives for this course, I would refer to the students as "the developer or instructional developer," as this is the role they will be acting in when we observe them perform.

G. Learning Objective or Instructional Objective?

Bob Mager also raises another issue through the use of the phrase the **"learners to be able to."** He is suggesting that the objective be written from the learner's point of view, not the instructor's.

This raises a question. Should we refer to objectives used in a training program as Learning Objectives or Instructional Objectives? The term learning objectives suggests we are learner centered and concerned that the learner be able to perform. Conversely, if we use the term Instructional Objective we appear to be more teacher centered. The argument, however is eliminated by examining Mager's Principle, which is clearly learner centered.

"A description of a performance you want learners to be able to exhibit before you consider them competent."

What Is Learning?

"Learning is a change in the human disposition or capability that persists over a period of time and is not simply ascribable to processes of growth. The kind of change called learning exhibits itself as a change in behavior, and the inference of learning is made by comparing what behavior was possible before the individual was placed in the *learning situation* and what behavior was exhibited after such treatment. The change may be, and often is, an increased capability for some kind of performance. It may also be an altered disposition of the sort called *attitude or interest or value.* The change must have more than momentary permanence; it must be capable of being retained over some period of time. Finally, it must be distinguishable from the kind of change that is attributable to growth, such as a change in height or the development of muscles through exercise." (Gagne, 1965, pp. 2–3)

"There is remarkable agreement upon the definition of learning as being reflected in a change in behavior as the result of experience." (Haggard, 1963, p. 20) This idea is supported by Cronbach's statement "Learning is shown by a change in behavior as the result of experience." (Cronbach, 1963, p. 71)

Burton defines learning as follows: "Learning is a change in the individual, due to the interaction of the individual with his environment, which fills a need and makes him more capable of dealing adequately with his environment." (Burton, 1963, p. 7) In Burton's definition we also see the issues of <u>motivation</u> (fills a need) and <u>competence</u> (capable of dealing adequately).

Each of these theorists is suggesting that the only way we know that anything is actually learned is by observing a change in performance. Therefore, for our purposes, we will define learning as **"an observable change in behavior that persists over a period of time."**

What Is an Objective?

An objective is a noun that refers to the end of an effort or activity. Synonyms include: goal, aim, conclusion, mission, target, task, intent and design.

What Is a Learning Objective?

"A description of a performance you want learners to be able to exhibit before you consider them competent."

A learning objective describes the end of an activity that produces an observable change in behavior that persists over time. Mager stated that **"a (learning) objective describes an intended result of instruction, rather than the process of instruction itself."** This is particularly important.

The "intended result" that can be observed within the training event is evidence of a desired behavior. Therefore, the power of the words, **be able to,** in the structure of the learning objective. By using these words in combination with an active verb and the object of the verb, the statement will describe the desired behavior.

Does It Really Matter?

Consider the following commonly used prefaces to objectives: **"You will learn how to, you will understand or you will learn."** These statements omit the job title of the performer and are written from the instructor's viewpoint. The instructor is saying "you will learn, you will change," but nothing specific.

Consider the objective: **You will learn how to write an objective.** The verb is **learn** and the object of the verb is **how to write an objective.** The words **"learn how to"** imply that the training will be about writing objectives, but fails to state that you will be able to perform. Too often, training based on objectives containing any variation of the words **"learn how to"** tends to be long on explanation, but short on performance and evaluation.

Compare this to the statement: **The developer will be able to write a learning objective.** Now the verb is **write** (an observable performance) and the object of the verb is **a learning objective**—a written description of desired behavior. Training based on this objective will tend to be long on performance and evaluation— which is what you will find in Part 1. This does not imply that the explanation will be short. In fact, the explanation must be comprehensive in order to bring about skilled performance.

H. Concrete Language

Finally, we can look at Mager's Principle from a semantic viewpoint. As you recall, it reads **"A description of a performance you want learners to be able to**

exhibit before you consider them competent." Notice that it does not contain words subject to misinterpretation (e.g., "proper," "right," "successful" or "understand"). From this we can infer a sixth criterion. The objective should contain concrete, image provoking language.

Consider the following objectives from a conference workshop of one of the national training associations. I have highlighted each of the abstract words.

*Participants will **learn** how to **maximize impact** by designing and delivering training that makes **full** use of the trainee's **capabilities**.*

*Participants **learn** how to **greatly enhance basic** learning skills.*

How will the developer measure whether or not the student attending this seminar has, in fact, learned? We are not given a clue. The use of abstract words serves no purpose, except perhaps to "hype" the training.

The use of abstract words in learning objectives is a widespread practice. Developers seem to be stating the benefit of their offerings within their objectives. Unfortunately, this practice renders the objectives useless. Consider the following statements which appeared in a brochure I received after the words **"Here's what you'll learn how to write:"**

Questionnaires to conduct needs analyses
Detailed proposals to top management
Behavioral objectives
Detailed lesson plans that include methods and exercises
Case studies
Evaluation pieces
And more!

The key phrase is **"and more."** The above is a list of benefits, not a list of learning objectives. Notice that the list includes **"write behavioral objectives."** I think at this stage of Part 1 we can agree that these are not learning (behavioral) objectives.

I called the vendor and requested a set of learning objectives for the program. They replied by sending me another brochure. Included was a cover letter stating that the vendor's course "represents high quality education." My conclusion: this course has no objectives. I am confident that by attending it you would not learn very much about learning objectives.

I am not suggesting for a moment that sellers of training should not state the benefits of their training. I am underscoring that the benefits of a training program have no place in its learning objectives.

Abstract Words in the Performance Component

Abstract words are often found in the Performance Component masquerading as active verbs. Examples are words such as *demonstrate, learn, use* or *make*. Such words should be viewed with skepticism when they are used to describe interactive behaviors. For example:

*Use the **key elements** of Accelerated Learning.*

In this case the word <u>use</u> tells us very little and the words <u>*Accelerated Learning*</u> appear to be standing for a desired behavior that is not defined. For example, what would we observe when the instructor is using "Accelerated Learning?" Would he or she be talking faster? Would the students be learning faster? The objective, as written, tells us nothing. Compare the following:

Concrete Verbs	*Abstract Words Used as Verbs*
Plan	Understand
Write	Think
Organize	Appreciate
Conduct	Learn
Evaluate	Demonstrate knowledge
Analyze	Use
Select	Know
Differentiate	Acquire knowledge
Describe	Recognize
Calculate	Develop a knowledge
Score	Develop
Name	Comprehend
Identify	Grasp
Tighten	Become familiar with
Design	Employ
Mark	
Circle	
List	

Abstract Words and Criteria

Criteria provide us with a standard by which we can judge whether or not something occurred. Abstract words, such as those listed below, reduce the usefulness of criteria. Concrete words, on the other hand, enhance their usefulness.

Concrete Criteria	Abstract Words used as Criteria
Justified	Right
Obtain	Proper
Complement	Successfully
Criteria	Effectively
Reduces	Greatly enhance
Objectives	Maximize impact
Interactive	Enhance
Reach agreement on	High
Compare	Quality
Evaluate	Acceptable
Every	Suitable
Without reference to	Appropriate
Classify	Good
Detect	True
Identified needs	Specific

Abstract Words Referenced to Criteria

Frequently, it is necessary to use an abstract word in an objective. This occurs when the desired behavior requires some element of decision making. For example the word suitable is used in an objective where a financial counselor must select from one or more products.

> **Select a Suitable Investment:** <u>Given a narrative containing the content of a discovery interview, the client's financial statement and 6 investment products varying in risk,</u> the financial counselor will be able to **select and justify (in writing) a** *suitable* **investment product** *in relation to the client's risk tolerance and identified needs* within 20 minutes.

If the abstract word is linked or referenced to criteria the objective can be considered to contain concrete language. For example, "suitable in relationship to the client's risk tolerance and identified needs" is an example of linking the abstract word *"suitable"* to criteria, *"the client's risk tolerance and identified needs."*

Use of Asterisks and Parenthesis

Another technique that enables a learning objective to meet the Concrete Language Criterion involves the use of an asterisk (*). Consider the following objective developed to measure the competence of an automobile salesperson's ability to negotiate terms with a customer:

Negotiate Agreement: <u>Given the selected vehicle, the needs agreed upon, the customer's intended method of payment and a student acting as a customer,</u> the salesperson will be able to *negotiate agreement on acceptable terms in relation to dealer profit and finance guidelines* and the customer's responses* within 30 minutes.

(*Guidelines: <u>Profit</u>: A list containing the minimum acceptable profit based on make, model, year, inventory, availability and dealer incentives. <u>Finance</u>: Interest rates based upon term of loan and down payment.)

The developer of this objective was concerned that the words *"profit and finance guidelines"* required further clarification. The asterisk (*) is used to alert the reader that the term used will be clarified.

This objective also demonstrates referencing an abstract term to criteria. The word *acceptable* is linked to *dealer profit and finance guidelines* by the term <u>in relation to</u>.

The Optional 6th Component

The question now arises as to whether or not concrete language is a component of a learning objective or a criterion for measuring the usefulness of an objective.

Concrete language <u>is always a criterion</u> for measuring the usefulness of an objective. As stated earlier, abstract words appearing in the Performance or Criteria Component render the objective useless.

Concrete Language Criteria

Contains **concrete image provoking language** in both the performance (desired behavior) and criteria. Any abstractions are referenced to criteria.

Concrete language <u>is considered a component when</u> asterisks and parenthesis are used to define terms that are abstract or esoteric. The component definition is shown in the following.

Concrete Language Component

<u>Concrete Language</u>: **A definition or reference, <u>if applicable</u>, to any abstract word used in the Performance or Criteria Components.**

Experiencing Concrete Language

Concrete language refers to the use of verbs and nouns. Verbs are action words. You can see a person write, list, count or describe. Nouns refer to persons, places or things. The following objective (performance and criteria only) demonstrates the use of concrete language.

Prepare a survey instrument *that measures the learner's perception of the value* and effectiveness of a training event in relation to the program's learning objectives.*

(*Value: Perceived need, relevance, practicality and applicability.)

We can observe a person preparing a survey. Once it is completed, we can check to see if the survey contains the program's learning objectives. If it does contain the objectives, we can then determine if the objectives are used to measure the relevance and effectiveness of the training event. You can actually do this if you wish.

In App. C there is such a survey instrument. It's called a Student Evaluation of Training. Compare this form to the learning objective and determine if it meets the criteria contained within the above objective.

I will ask you to complete a Student Evaluation of Training and mail it to me when you complete Part 1.

The Optional 7th Component

Notice the words **"Select a Suitable Investment"** in the model objective below. This represents the <u>title of the objective</u>.

> **Select a Suitable Investment:** <u>Given a narrative containing the content of a discovery interview, the client's financial statement and 6 investment products varying in risk</u>, the financial counselor will be able to **select and justify (in writing) a** *suitable* **investment product** *in relation to the client's risk tolerance and identified needs* within 20 minutes.

I also refer to the title as an <u>advertising statement</u>, as it communicates in the shortest set of words the behavior to be brought about. The title gives the reader (who may be the decision maker who commissioned the development effort, an instructor, a student or a fellow developer) the ability to see the performance without having to read through the complex structure to find it.

In most cases, one would structure the title like a Performance Component (active verb and the object of the verb) and **boldface** it for the reader. Notice the similarity to the objective's actual Performance Component: **select and justify (in writing) a** *suitable* **investment product.**

The placement of this issue within the Concrete Language section is also significant. Because of their complexity, useful objectives tend to be a bit intimidating. The title gives the reader the opportunity to, metaphorically, see the forest without getting lost in the trees.

I. Components of a Learning Objective

At this point we can summarize the components of a learning objective as follows:

Principal Components:

1. <u>Performer</u>: **The job title of the performer and the words "be able to."**

2. <u>Performance</u>: **The desired behavior you want the learner to exhibit.**

3. <u>Performance Time</u>: **The time for the performance expressed in hours, minutes or seconds.**

4. <u>Criteria</u>: **The standard or standards by which you will measure the desired behavior.**

5. <u>Conditions</u>: **The situation under which the performance occurs, limitations imposed on the performer or non-implicit resources available to the performer.**

Optional Components:

6. <u>Concrete Language</u>: **A definition or reference, <u>if applicable</u>, to any abstract word used in the Performance or Criteria Components.**

7. <u>Title</u>: **A brief (3 to 5 word) description of the performance.**

Does Every Objective Require All Five Principal Components?

Numerous writers on the subject of learning objectives state that the Conditions and Criteria Components of an objective are only required when clarification is needed. Mager's Principle points in a different direction.

It suggests that one objective should describe the behavior you wish to observe to measure learner competence. In the literature, this has been referred to as a terminal objective. Therefore, any objective labeled with words such as Terminal, Core, Module or Program must contain all five components in order to be considered useful.

Other objectives can and should be used to identify units of knowledge and skill that enable the learner to perform the desired behavior. These other, or subordinate, objectives need not contain all components.

The absence of a terminal objective will constitute a significant flaw in the developer's objectives. The wisdom of a set of learning objectives is explained in the sections entitled The Hierarchical Structure of Objectives (page 56) and Measuring a Set of Learning Objectives (page 74).

J. Criteria for Measuring the Usefulness of an Objective

The following lists the six criteria that measure the presence or absence of the components which we derived from Mager's Learning Objective Principle. These criteria are applicable to an objective which is identified as the terminal behavior of a training event. Such objectives may be identified with the words Core, Terminal, Program or Module Objective:

Mager's Principle

"A description of a performance you want learners to be able to exhibit before you consider them competent."

To be considered a useful learning objective the statement must:

A. Contain the **job title of the performer** and the words **"be able to"** immediately before the active verb.

B. Contain **the performance** to be exhibited. (Active verb[s] and the object of the verb describe <u>the desired behavior</u>.)

C. Contain a fixed **time** limit for the performance.

D. Contain **criteria** to measure the desired behavior <u>at program's end</u>.

E. Contain **conditions** which describe the situation in which the performance occurs, limitations imposed or non-implicit resources.

F. Contain **concrete image provoking language** in both the performance (desired behavior) and criteria. Any abstractions are referenced to criteria.

K. Measuring the Desired Behavior

"A description of a performance you want learners to be able to **exhibit before you consider them competent.**"

In this next discussion we will look closely again at the words **"exhibit <u>before</u> you consider them competent"** in relation to the criterion for the Criteria Component of a learning objective; specifically, that it **contain <u>Criteria</u> to measure the desired behavior <u>at program's end</u>.**

The **intended result** of instruction is performance; the desired behavior you want the learner to exhibit. When should this performance be observed and measured? Consider this time line:

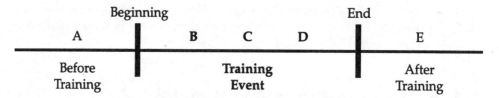

The words **"<u>before</u> you consider them competent"** suggest that the measurement of the student's competence with the desired behavior should come at or near Point D, the end of the training event. For example, if you were teaching claims adjustors to make claim decisions and wanted to test their skill and the effectiveness of your training, you would measure their performance by having them adjust a number of claims at Point D.

You could also measure the adjustor's performance at Point A, before the training program or at Point B, the beginning of the training. These would provide baseline measurements of the student's existing knowledge and skill. Measurement at Point C, in the middle of the event, would indicate the student's progress toward the stated objective. Measurement at Point E would be considered post training evaluation. This evaluation would measure the degree to which the student continues to use and maintain the skills learned in the training. <u>Measurement at Point D, within the context of the training event, is most important, for it is here that you determine both the student's skill and establish the facility for measuring the effectiveness of the training at Point E</u>. Stated another way, you can use the same evaluation process at Points D and E.

Training is effective to the degree that it produces a desired behavior that the learner continues to use after training. Hence, training effectiveness is a comparison between the competence measures at Point D, the end of training and Point E, after training.

Performance Evaluation Systems

To measure performer competence before, during and after a training event the developer must create a system to measure the desired behavior. An effective system consists of criteria to judge each component of the behavior, a scoring system, a rating scale and a formula for determining the rating.

The criteria for measuring the performance are derived from the Criteria Component of the learning objective. This relationship is shown in the following example.

Criteria to Measure the Usefulness of an Objective
in relationship to
the Criteria Component of the Learning Objective

Module Objective

Write a Learning Objective: Given a performance discrepancy that is caused by a lack of skill or knowledge on a subject that the instructional developer has mastered, the developer (reader) will be able to write a learning objective **that contains performance, criteria, conditions and time components** within 12 minutes which achieves an Effectiveness Rating of 10 (on a 10 scale) against prescribed criteria.

Criteria to Measure the Usefulness of an Objective
To be considered a useful learning objective the statement must:

A. Contain the **job title of the performer** and the words **"be able to"** immediately before the active verb.

B. Contain **the performance** to be exhibited. (Active verb[s] and the object of the verb describe <u>the desired behavior</u>.)

C. Contain a fixed **time** limit for the performance.

D. Contain **criteria** to measure the desired behavior <u>at program's end</u>.

E. Contain **conditions** which describe the situation in which the performance occurs, limitations imposed or non-implicit resources.

F. Contain **concrete image provoking language** in both the performance (desired behavior) and criteria. Any abstractions are referenced to criteria.

The Criteria Component (**bolded**) of the Module Objective (above) contains the principal components of a useful objective. <u>The presence of these components is also criteria for measuring an objective's usefulness. It either has them or does not</u>.

Notice that the Criteria Component contains only four components: **performance, criteria, conditions and time** and that each is described by a single word. Compare this to the **Criteria to Measure the Usefulness of an Objective** which contains six items. Each is written in such a way that it is possible to judge whether or not the objective being evaluated meets the standard. For example:

C. Contains a fixed **time** limit for the performance.

To meet this particular criterion the objective must contain a stated time and the time must relate to the performance of the student, not the instructor.

Criterion A, the Performer Component and criterion F, Concrete Language were not included in the Module Objective's Criteria Component. This demonstrates an important point. The learning objective does not need to contain all possible criteria. It should, however, contain the principal criteria. The developer, in creating the performance evaluation system, may discover additional components of the behavior that must be measured. These may be shown on the performance evaluation form only or they may result in a modification of the objective. Objectives often go through a series of modifications as the evaluation system and the content of instruction is written. People often refer to this process as that of developing a learning objective.

The next chapter will explain the use of the criteria in combination with a scoring system, rating scale and formula to measure the usefulness of learning objectives.

A Note to the Reader: The creation of the Performance Evaluation System is the step which logically follows the development of the learning objective. Once these two components of training are created, the developer has a specific direction for writing the program's content.

Chapter 8 goes into even greater depth on the structure and content of a Performance Evaluation System. It also provides examples of evaluation systems for a psychomotor and a sales behavior. This chapter may be referred to at any time. However, it will be most meaningful after the reader has mastered learning objectives and used the evaluation system described in Chaps. 3 and 5.

3

Measuring the Usefulness of Objectives

A. The Criterion Scoring System

In order to measure an objective with multiple criteria you must have a scoring system, rating scale and formula for determining the rating. The following is a system for evaluating criteria that make up an objective or, for that matter, any other component of the training process.

Criterion Scoring System		Effectiveness Rating	
10	Meets the Criterion	8.0 to 10	Effective
5	Questionable	5.0 to 7.9	Marginal
0	Does Not Meet or Not Evident	1.0 to 4.9	Ineffective
		0.0 to 0.9	Not Evident

The **Criterion Scoring System** is based on a ratio scale (Kidder, 1985, p. 61). This scale recognizes a true zero and contains values that can be added or multiplied. Since we are measuring each component of the objective against a criterion, we are able to say that the criterion is either met or not met by certain words and phrases in the objective being measured. This accounts for the 10 and 0 points of the scale.

The score of 5, (questionable), allows for skepticism. Skepticism is defined as "an attitude of doubt or suspended judgment." It would be wonderful if the world was black and white, all tens or zeroes. However, objectives are a combination of abstract symbols that stand for human behavior. On occasion, it may be difficult to state that the words in a particular objective do or do not meet one or more criteria. A "5" rating allows the evaluator to say, in effect, that there is some value to the words in the objective, but also some doubt about their satisfaction of a particular criterion.

Using the Criterion Scoring System

The use of the **Criterion Scoring System** is demonstrated by the following. Listed below are five statements, each containing the performance **"score a criterion."** Each is to be rated against the first Criterion for Measuring the Usefulness of an Objective: (Note: all six Criteria are shown for reference.)

   A. Contains the **job title of the performer** and the words **"be able to"** immediately before the active verb.

Practice Exercise 1

In this <u>Practice Exercise</u> you will decide if the component of the objective meets, is questionable or does not meet the criterion and award the appropriate score: 10, 5 or 0. You can check your answers on the next page.

____ 1. The developer will be able to **score a criterion.**

____ 2. The student will be able to **score a criterion.**

____ 3. The developer will **score a criterion.**

____ 4. The student will understand how to **score a criterion.**

____ 5. **Score a criterion.**

For Reference

Criteria for Measuring the Usefulness of an Objective

To be considered a useful objective the statement must:

A. Contain the **job title of the performer** and the words **"be able to"** immediately before the active verb.

B. Contain **the performance** to be exhibited. (Active verb[s] and the object of the verb describe <u>the desired behavior</u>.)

C. Contain a fixed **time** limit for the performance.

D. Contain **criteria** to measure the desired behavior <u>at program's end</u>.

E. Contain **conditions** which describe the situation in which the performance occurs, limitations imposed or non-implicit resources.

F. Contain **concrete image provoking language** in both the performance (desired behavior) and criteria. Any abstractions are referenced to criteria.

Solution to Practice Exercise 1

Listed in the following are my scores for each of the five statements. Scoring, in this instance, involves searching for two properties: the **job title of the performer** and the words **"be able to."**

 _10_ 1. The developer will be able to **score a criterion.**

 _5_ 2. The student will be able to **score a criterion.**

 _5_ 3. The developer will **score a criterion.**

 _0_ 4. The student will understand how to **score a criterion.**

 _0_ 5. **Score a criterion.**

     Statement 1 contains both properties.

     Statements 2 and 3 each contain only one property. The word "student" does not count in Statement 2, since it is not the **job title of the performer.** An effective way to focus on the learners is to see them within the context of the job you are training them to do, not as "students." In Statement 3 the words **"be able to"** are absent.

     Statements 4 and 5 contain neither.

Practice Exercise 2

Let's apply the scoring system to the <u>Performance Component</u> of the objective. Listed in the following are eight statements. Each is to be rated against the second Criterion for Measuring the Usefulness of an Objective:

    B. Contains **the performance** to be exhibited. (Active verb[s] and the object of the verb describe <u>**the desired behavior.**</u>)

     Again you will decide if the component of the objective meets, is questionable or does not meet the criterion and award the appropriate score: 10, 5 or 0. You can check your answers on the next page.

    ____ 1. Score a criterion.

    ____ 2. Reduce shoplifting in the store by December 31.

    ____ 3. Understand the principles of scoring a criterion.

    ____ 4. Appreciate the steps essential to planning a lesson.

    ____ 5. Demonstrate knowledge of scoring a criterion.

    ____ 6. Conduct a 5-day installation meeting (four-hour class with 30 students).

    ____ 7. Identify statements which contain a performance to be exhibited.

    ____ 8. Learn how to score a criterion and calculate an Effectiveness Rating.

Solution to Practice Exercise 2

_10_ 1. **Score** *a criterion.*

_0_ 2. Reduce shoplifting in the store by December 31.

_0_ 3. Understand the principles of scoring a criterion.

_0_ 4. Appreciate the steps essential to planning a lesson.

_0_ 5. Demonstrate knowledge of **scoring a criterion.**

_5_ 6. Conduct a 5-day installation meeting (four-hour class with 30 students).

_10_ 7. **Identify** *statements which contain a performance to be exhibited.*

_5_ 8. Learn how to **score** *a criterion* and **calculate** an *Effectiveness Rating.*

Statement 1 meets the criterion. It contains a verb, **score,** and an object of the verb, *a criterion,* which can be exhibited during a training program.

Statement 2 contains a result (business objective) not a performance that can be exhibited. Therefore, it is not a learning objective. To test for compliance with this criterion, ask: Can the performance be exhibited during the training?

Statements 3, 4 and 5 are classic examples of the use of an abstract word in the Performance Component. What will the student be doing to demonstrate an "understanding of the principles of scoring a criterion?" The same question can be asked with regard to the words "appreciate" and "demonstrate knowledge" in Statements 4 and 5, respectively

Statement 6 suffers from the same problem as 2, a performance that cannot be exhibited during training. How can 30 students demonstrate the activities in a 5-day installation? However, it does contain a performance, "conduct a 5-day installation meeting." Thus the rating of 5. Arguably, one could assign a score of "0" and be correct. However, a score of 10 is incorrect, since it does not meet the criterion of containing a performance that can be exhibited.

Statement 7 meets the criterion. It contains a verb, **identify,** and an object of the verb, *statements which contain a performance to be exhibited.* As evidenced by your involvement in the practice exercise, it can be exhibited during a training program.

Statement 8 contains the word "learn," a passive verb. What would the person be doing to demonstrate competence? Score a criterion, I suspect. Then, why not say so? Thus the rating of 5. The words "learn how" reduce the focus on the two performances: **score** *a criterion* and **calculate** an *Effectiveness Rating.* The words, "the student will learn how to …" are, in my opinion, passive and teacher-centered. Training based on teacher-centered objectives tend toward excessive lecture, limited performance and no evaluation.

B. A Word About the Score of 5— Questionable

Notice in the preceding two practice exercises that it was relatively easy to assign a value of 10 or 0. The score of 5 should be used when you are not sure that the component meets the criterion. Notice also that it would be difficult to be more precise than the value of 5.

C. The Effectiveness Rating

The **Effectiveness Rating** is derived by dividing the Total Score by the number of criteria. The Total Score is the sum of the Scores for each Criterion. In this sense, each criterion is assumed to have the same value. This suggests that each is important and that the absence of one or more decreases the usefulness of the objective. (See Using the System to Measure an Objective.)

Effectiveness Ratings

8.0 to 10	Effective
5.0 to 7.9	Marginal
1.0 to 4.9	Ineffective
0.0 to 0.9	Not Evident

Usefulness, in this case, means containing enough data to help a manager to decide if the training will produce the knowledge and skill trainees need. This "need" could be motivated by a problem which is interfering with their performance or the need for a new set of skills. This concept demonstrates the cause and effect relationship between training and the behavior contained in the training. It is the behaviors (knowledge or skills) produced by the training that enables the trainees to perform and, thereby, achieve the business objective.

The ratings of Effective, Marginal, Ineffective or Not evident indicate the likelihood of producing the desired behavior from a training program based on the rated objective. A rating of less than 10 indicates that the objective contains missing or flawed components. This enables corrections that either focus the training toward the desired behavior or increase its measurability.

D. The Performance Standard

The ability to calculate an **Effectiveness Rating** permits us to establish a **Performance Standard**. A **Performance Standard** is a benchmark for competent performance stated as a rating which is derived from a set of specific criteria. You will recall in the Solution to the Self Test, (page 511), the **Performance Standard** was identified as an optional component of a learning objective.

The **Performance Standard** for an objective written as the performance to measure your competence after completing Part 1 (training module) is a rating of 10 against the (6) Criteria for Measuring the Usefulness of an Objective identified on page 42. The concept is demonstrated on the next page in the segment entitled, Using the System to Measure an Objective.

The **Performance Standard** provides a criterion by which to judge the ability of each student to perform the desired behavior. It also enables the developer to measure the effectiveness of the training by calculating the average of the students' **Effectiveness Ratings.** For example, if 8 out of 10 students achieve an Effectiveness Rating of 10, the training can be said to have successfully brought about the desired behavior. Conversely, if 2 out of 10 students are successful, the training failed, not the students.

E. Using the System to Measure an Objective

Consider the following objective in relation to the six criteria. *The insurance agent will be able to give a sales talk word for word in 6 minutes.* This objective meets five of the six criteria.

Criterion Scoring System		*Effectiveness Rating*	
10	Meets the Criterion	8.0 to 10	Effective
5	Questionable	5.0 to 7.9	Marginal
0	Does Not Meet or Not Evident	1.0 to 4.9	Ineffective
		0.0 to 0.9	Not Evident

SCORE	COMPONENT		CRITERIA
<u>10</u>	*The insurance agent will be able to*	A.	Contains the **job title of the performer** and the words **"be able to"** immediately before the active verb.
<u>10</u>	*give a sales talk*	B.	Contains **the performance** to be exhibited. (Active verb[s] and the object of the verb describe <u>the desired behavior</u>.)
<u>10</u>	*in 6 minutes*	C.	Contains a fixed **time** limit for the performance.
<u>10</u>	*word for word*	D.	Contains **criteria** to measure the desired behavior <u>at program's end</u>.
<u>0</u>	Missing Component	E.	Contains **conditions** which describe the situation in which the performance occurs, limitations imposed or non-implicit resources.
<u>10</u>	There are no abstract words	F.	Contains **concrete image provoking language** in both the performance and criteria. Any abstractions are referenced to criteria.

50—Total Score

The Total Score is 50. To determine the rating divide the Total Score by 6, the number of criteria (50 ÷ 6 = 8.3). The **Effectiveness Rating** for this objective is 8.3 or effective.

F. Correcting a Flawed Objective

Measurement of objectives provides the developer with a guideline for making corrections to identified discrepancies. For example, consider the objective evaluated on the previous page.

> **Selling Insurance:** The insurance agent will be able to *give a sales talk word for word* in 6 minutes.

This objective is missing the Conditions Component. To achieve a 10 rating, we must state the conditions under which the behavior will occur. For example: "Given a student acting as a customer who does not object." The correctly stated objective would now read as follows:

> **Selling Insurance:** Given a student acting as a customer who does not object, the insurance agent will be able to **give a sales talk** *word for word* in 6 minutes.

The addition of the Condition Component enables us to visualize the situation in which the performance will take place. The student performing will be making a presentation to another student who will not offer any resistance.

Again, we are not suggesting that this is a desirable behavior for a salesperson. We are using it as an example of a learning objective which precisely describes behavior. In this case, an example of a stimulus-response behavior.

G. An Objective for a Complex Interactive Sales Behavior

The following is an example of a learning objective that achieves an Effectiveness Rating of 10 for a more complex, need selling, behavior with the added dimension of training complexity, a partial sales discussion.

> **Need Selling:** Given a narrative describing the need discovery phase of a previous contact and a student acting as the customer, the agent will be able to **continue the sales discussion** *and, based on the needs agreed upon, select and present a suitable insurance product* within 45 minutes.

In this case, the Condition Component tells us that the agent will be performing a partial sales discussion. The instructor will be providing him or her with the information that would have been gathered in a previous interview. The agent will have to review and use information provided in the narrative. This objective also demonstrates the use of referencing an abstract term "suitable" to a criterion "the need agreed upon."

A Note to the Reader: A complete discussion of the levels of complexity of learning objectives can be found on page 84. The preceding examples and those that follow illustrate and provide examples of complex behaviors that achieve an Effectiveness Rating of 10.

H. An Objective for a Complex Written Behavior

The following is the Module Objective for Part 1. It also meets all the criteria and achieves an Effectiveness Rating of 10. This example also demonstrates the optional **Performance Standard** Component (shown in plain text). As previously described, a **Performance Standard** is a benchmark for competent performance stated as a rating which is derived from a set of specific criteria.

Develop a Learning Objective: Given a performance discrepancy that is caused by a lack of skill or knowledge on a subject that the instructional developer has mastered, the developer (reader) will be able to **write a learning objective** *that contains performance, criteria, conditions and time components* within 12 minutes which achieves an Effectiveness Rating of 10 (on a 10 scale) against prescribed criteria.

I. An Objective for a Physical Skill

The next example is for a psychomotor skill, the tennis serve.

Execute a Tennis Serve: Given 10 balls on an indoor court, the player will be able to **serve the ball** *into the opponent's service court while exhibiting prescribed form 7 out of 10 times* at a speed of 50 MPH.

The objective may, at first glance, appear to be missing the component of Performance Time. In fact, Performance Time is stated; 50 MPH. In the case of a serve, time is measured as speed.

The criterion, "*7 out of 10 times,*" coupled with the Performance Time, "at a speed of 50 MPH," also establishes a Performance Standard for the serve.

J. An Objective for a Complex Interactive Consulting Behavior

The next example is even more challenging:

Problem Solving Meeting: Given a narrative containing information about the existing Finance and Insurance program containing one to three prob-

<u>lems, available reports, an evening (2 hours) to prepare and a student act-ing as the dealer</u>, the Account Manager will be able to **plan and conduct a problem solving discussion** *that reaches agreement on a measurable course of action* to solve the problem(s) identified which is/are justifiable based on the infor-mation provided and the dealer's response(s)* within 20 minutes. (*Examples: conduct a meeting, conduct training, prepare a forecast, evaluate the sales skills of the F&I Manager.)

This represents a problem solving behavior that is employed by a consultant in developing the profit potential of a car dealer's finance department. Notice in the Condition Component (<u>underlined</u>) that the developer is using case methodology to simulate reality in the classroom. Also notice the principal Criteria: the course of action agreed upon must be <u>measurable</u> and <u>justifiable</u> in relation to <u>both</u> the information provided and the responses of the student act-ing as the dealer.

The structure of the Condition and Criteria Components provide direction to the developer as to the resources that must be created for this program. In this sit-uation, a case must be constructed that has data to enable the student acting as the Account Manager to prepare for the meeting with the dealer. The student playing the role of the dealer must also have case information that enables him or her to respond to the Account Manager's recommendations. With this two part case, the developer can measure whether the Account Manager's course of action is justifiable in relation to the data given and the dealer's response. This also enables the developer to measure both the planning and conducting phases of the transaction.

The objective for the **Problem Solving Meeting** (above) reveals another tech-nique that enables a learning objective to meet the Concrete Language Criterion. Notice the words in parentheses below (which are abstracted from the above objective):

(*Examples: conduct a meeting, conduct training, prepare a forecast, eval-uate the sales skills of the F&I Manager.)

The developer of this objective was concerned that the words *"measurable course of action"* required further clarification. In this case, an asterisk (*) is used to alert the reader that the term used will be clarified.

K. Alternative Structure of a Learning Objective

A concern is often expressed with regard to the structure of the objectives used as models thus far. They appear to violate the rules of English. For example, the objective stated above contains 79 words and appears to be a run-on sentence. Its length and complexity tend to increase any reader's difficulty in understanding the result (behavior) that the instruction is designed to bring about.

The structure below is offered as an alternative method for expressing a learning objective. It consists of listing all 6 components found in the Criteria for Measuring the Usefulness of an Objective (see page 42) and attaching to each your description of the desired behavior. This structure is referred to as the Component Format.

Title: Problem Solving Meeting

Performer: The Account Manager will be able to.

Performance: **Conduct a problem solving discussion.**

Performance Time: Within 20 minutes.

Criteria: *That reaches agreement on a measurable course of action* to solve the problem(s) identified which is/are justifiable based on the information provided and the dealer's response.*

Conditions: <u>Given a narrative containing information about the existing F&I program containing one to three problems, available reports, an evening (2 hours) to prepare and a student acting as the dealer.</u>

Concrete Language: *Examples of measurable courses of action: conduct a meeting, conduct training, prepare a forecast, evaluate the sales skills of the F&I Manager.

An Algebraic Formula

The usefulness of a learning objective can also be expressed algebraically: A Useful Learning Objective = the sum of its components (Performer, Performance, Performance Time, Criteria, Conditions and Concrete Language) divided by 6.

L. Formats for a Learning Objective

The following formats will assist you in writing a useful learning objective. They will also be useful in analyzing any learning objective identified by its developer as a Core, Terminal, Program or Module Objective.

Option 1—Sentence Format

Title: Describe the Transaction

Given (insert the conditions), **the** (state the job title of the performer) **will be able to** (describe the performance) **that** (describe the principal criteria) **within** (state the time limit for the performance). (Define or reference, if applicable, any abstract words.)

Option 2—Component Format

Title: Describe the Transaction

Performer:	**The** (state the job title of the performer) **will be able to,**
Performance:	Describe the performance.
Performance Time:	**Within** (state the time limit for the performance).
Criteria:	**That** (describe the principal criteria). Note: The words **which, in relation to** or **based upon** can be substituted for **that.**
Conditions:	**Given** (insert the conditions).
Concrete Language:	Define or reference, if applicable, any abstract words.
Performance Std:	(optional) Describe the benchmark for competent performance as a rating derived from a set of specific criteria.

M. Evaluating Learning Objectives

The component structure is the basis for the evaluation system and therefore is particularly effective in analyzing learning objectives. It will be helpful to you in completing the exercises throughout Part 1. The procedure for evaluating is as follows:

1. Take the content of the objective and identify it according to any component part that is evident. This is accomplished by underlining, boxing, circling or using different colored highlighters. It can also be accomplished by writing the words next to the component (as shown above).

Develop a Learning Objective

Given a performance discrepancy that is caused by a lack of skill or knowledge on a subject that the instructional developer has mastered, the developer (reader) will be able to write a learning objective that contains performance, criteria, conditions and time components within 12 minutes.

_____ Performer

[_____] Performance

(_____) Performance Time

_____ Criteria

[_____] Conditions

2. Accept the writer's intent before scoring any component.

For example: A Condition of an objective states: <u>Given 4 hours of training by a qualified instructor</u>. I would identify it as the writer's intended Condition even though I know it will score "0" against Criterion "E."

The writer's intended "Condition" describes **the process of instruction** from the trainer's point of view. The reference to the length of the training program, 4 hours, is a limitation on the trainer. It is not a limitation on the performance we desire the student to exhibit.

N. Test Your Evaluation Skill—Task 4

Here is an opportunity for you to test your evaluation skill. Calculate the Effectiveness Rating for these objectives. *A suggestion: Identify the various components of the objective (by underlining or circling) before you attempt to score them.*

1. Given that the types of dinners served and the dining room atmosphere of the 94th Aero Squadron Restaurant are conducive to wine consumption, the servers will be able to suggest specific wines to customers and demonstrate knowledge of wine serving etiquette using the server manual as a guide.

2. You will learn how to write high level objectives in three domains: cognitive, psychomotor and affective.

3. As a result of this session, the developer will be able to classify learning objectives according to Bloom's Taxonomy.

Criterion Scoring System		*Effectiveness Rating*	
10	Meets the Criterion	8.0 to 10	Effective
5	Questionable	5.0 to 7.9	Marginal
0	Does Not Meet or Not Evident	1.0 to 4.9	Ineffective
		0.0 to 0.9	Not Evident

OBJ 1	OBJ 2	OBJ 3	
___	___	___	Contains the **job title of the performer** and the words **"be able to"** immediately before the active verb.
___	___	___	Contains **the performance** to be exhibited. (Active verb[s] and the object of the verb describe <u>the desired behavior</u>.)
___	___	___	Contains a fixed **time** limit for the performance.
___	___	___	Contains **criteria** to measure the desired behavior <u>at program's end</u>.

___ ___ ___   Contains **conditions** which describe the situation in which the performance occurs, limitations imposed or non-implicit resources.

___ ___ ___   Contains **concrete image provoking language** in both the performance and criteria. Any abstractions are referenced to criteria.

___ ___ ___   **Total Score**

___ ___ ___   **Effectiveness Rating (Total Score divided by 6)**

The solutions to this task are located on page 513.

O. Do You Need Help?

You are having difficulty if:

1. Your **Effectiveness Ratings** at this stage are more than plus or minus 1.5 points away from the model solutions.
2. Your criterion scoring contains excessive "5"s.
3. Your score for any criterion is opposite to the model solution.

Where are you having difficulty?

___ Identifying the components of an objective (Performance, Conditions, Criteria, Performance Time). If so, go to page 530. (Practice Exercise 3).

___ Evaluating the Performance Component. Go to page 534. (Practice Exercise 4)

___ Evaluating the Conditions Component. Go to page 539. (Practice Exercise 5)

___ Evaluating the Criteria Component. Go to page 543. (Practice Exercise 6)

___ Dealing with Abstractions. Go to page 547. (Practice Exercise 7)

If you are not having difficulty or you have completed any or all of the above Practice Exercises, go on and try evaluating the next five test items.

P. Test Your Evaluation Skill—Task 5

Here is another opportunity for you to test your evaluation skill. Calculate the Effectiveness Rating for the following objectives.

4. Given 12 or less salespeople in a setting that allows for 4 hours of relatively uninterrupted instruction time, the salesperson will participate in three in-class role play phone-ups that will result in a rating of 8.0 or greater on the Evaluation Sheet as scored by fellow salespersons.

5. Within three weeks, sales representatives should be able to use the total needs presentation visual to make presentations that will result in at least 5 fact-finding interviews and 2 sales per week.

6. The objective of the workshop is to acquaint people with the concepts, philosophies and methods of accelerated learning as applied primarily to corporate training, seed people's imagination in terms of the infinite possibilities for enhancing human learning and enable people to exercise more of their innate creativity in designing and delivering more effective training.

7. You will learn how to identify important problems worth solving; find the most likely cause of each problem; select practical solutions that will eliminate the causes; effectively implement your solutions; and prevent potential problems.

8. Given a list of tasks to be performed, population to be trained, time and resources available, participants will select an appropriate method of training for each task in relation to task selection criteria.

Criterion Scoring System		*Effectiveness Rating*	
10	Meets the Criterion	8.0 to 10	Effective
5	Questionable	5.0 to 7.9	Marginal
0	Does Not Meet or Not Evident	1.0 to 4.9	Ineffective
		0.0 to 0.9	Not Evident

OBJ 4	OBJ 5	OBJ 6	OBJ 7	OBJ 8	
___	___	___	___	___	Contains the **job title of the performer** <u>and</u> the words **"be able to."**
___	___	___	___	___	Contains **the performance** to be exhibited.
___	___	___	___	___	Contains a fixed **time** limit.
___	___	___	___	___	Contains **criteria.**
___	___	___	___	___	Contains **conditions.**
___	___	___	___	___	Contains **concrete language.**
___	___	___	___	___	**Total Score.**
___	___	___	___	___	**Effectiveness Rating** (Divide Total Score by 6)

The answers to this Self Test are located on page 516.

9. Test Your Writing Skill—Task 6

Now here is an opportunity to test your writing skill. In this case, you will correct the following objective:

> Given that the types of dinners served and the dining room atmosphere of the 94th Aero Squadron Restaurant are conducive to wine consumption, the servers will be able to suggest specific wines to customers and demonstrate knowledge of wine serving etiquette using the server manual as a guide.

One of the flaws in this objective is that it combines selling (suggesting) wine with serving wine. Suggesting wine is a knowledge based interactive behavior, while serving wine is primarily a psychomotor skill. The term psychomotor refers to a skill that requires a physical action involving the coordination of mental and muscular activity. While the total wine service involves both tasks, it is often desirable to separate them for instructional purposes. Therefore, the training design would involve two modules.

Your Task

Write two Modules Objectives that meet an **Effectiveness Rating** of 10. One for the suggesting segment and one for the serving segment.

My assumption is that you have some knowledge of wines and experience as a restaurant patron. This should enable you to develop the objective, even though you may not have sufficient knowledge or sales training skill to write the training program.

Suggesting Wine Objective

_____

_____

_____

Serving Wine Objective

_____

_____

_____

You will find the solution to these problems on page 522. On page 108 there is an example of *Expert Criteria* for evaluation of performance that relates to the serving objective. The role of the subject expert and the program developer in the identification of criteria for expert performance are discussed on page 103.

4
The Hierarchical Structure of Objectives

The **Hierarchical Structure** is the key to using objectives to structure training. Figure 4.1 contains precise definitions which position the Business, Core, Module and Unit Objectives according to a hierarchy. These are also the answers to question 3 of the self test, where you were asked to differentiate 4 types of objectives that are relevant to <u>structuring</u> a training program.

Figure 4.2 shows the Module and Unit Objectives for Part 1. This is an example of a set of objectives organized according to a **Hierarchical Structure.**

Figure 4.1. The Hierarchical Structure of Objectives

A. Result Objective: The results that the training program will bring about stated in units of sales or production.

B. Core Objective: Describes **<u>the desired behavior</u>** to be exhibited **<u>at the program's end</u>** to measure competence that relates to the Result Objective.

C. Module Objective: Describes <u>a desired behavior</u> to be exhibited **<u>during the program</u>** (within modules of the program, if modules are applicable) that relates to the Core Objective.

D. Unit Objective: Describes a **<u>unit of skill or knowledge</u>** to be exhibited **<u>during the module</u>** that relates to the Module's Objective.

Figure 4.2. Objectives of this Book

Module Objective

Write a Learning Objective: Given a performance discrepancy that is caused by a lack of skill or knowledge on a subject that the instructional developer has mastered, the developer (reader) will be able to write a learning objective that contains performance, criteria, conditions and time components within 12 minutes which achieves an Effectiveness Rating of 10 (on a 10 scale) against prescribed criteria.

Unit Objectives

To accomplish the Module Objective, the Instructional Developer will be able to:

1. Write a definition of a learning objective.

2. List 6 components of a useful objective.

3. List 6 criteria (standards) that would measure the usefulness of a Core, Terminal, Program or Module Objective.

4. Given 6 criteria, a Rating Scale and a learning objective, calculate the Effectiveness Rating of the learning objective with an accuracy of +/− 1.0 against the author's solution.

5. Differentiate between Core, Module and Unit Objectives.

6. Calculate an Effectiveness Rating for a set of learning objectives.

A. The Benefit of the Hierarchical Structure

The **Hierarchical Structure** is an organized ranking of a set of learning objectives that identifies the objective <u>containing the desired behavior that will be observed to measure learner competence</u> as the **Superior Objective** and which identifies the **Subordinate Objectives** that enable the learner to perform the desired behavior.

The **Hierarchical Structure** enables all of the material in a training program to be relevant to the achievement of one or more units of a business plan. The key to its structure is found within the <u>superior-subordinate</u> relationship in Fig. 4.3. This structure enables the developer to bring order and focus to the training being developed.

Consider, for a moment, the objectives for Part 1. The performance in the **Superior Objective** is to **write a learning objective.** It is identified by the term Module Objective. The term Unit Objectives is used to identify the **Subordinate Objectives.** They include: defining objectives, describing components, listing criteria, calculating Effectiveness Ratings, differentiation of the objectives within the Hierarchical Structure and rating a set of objectives. In identifying these as subordinate, we have stated that mastering them <u>will enable</u> the learner to carry out the writing task.

Figure 4.3. Hierarchical Structure of a Training Program

Business Plan
- Result Objective
- Core Objective(s)

Training Program
- Core Objective
- Module Objective(s)

Training Module
- Module Objective
- Unit Objective(s)

Training Unit
- Unit Objective
- Related unit(s) of knowledge and skill

Unit of Knowledge and Skill
- An idea, concept or procedure
- Related point(s)

Within the concept of the **Hierarchical Structure** each term has a special meaning. On the following page(s) I will explain the characteristics and relationships for Module and Unit objectives by making reference to this section of Part 1, which, as you have discovered is, in fact, a Training Module.

B. Terms with Special Meanings

Module Objective

The term Module Objective as used within the **Hierarchical Structure** assigns the objective four characteristics: Each is defined and illustrated in the following. A Module Objective:

1. **Describes the desired behavior which you intend to measure at the end of the training event.** This is critical. You will have the opportunity to measure your competence at the end of Part 1 by writing an objective. The competence performance (test) consists of a description of a situation where training is required. You

will write a learning objective to describe the desired behavior. Then you will have the opportunity to compare your answer with mine.

At the end of this training event, you will not be tested on any knowledge based items such as definitions of objectives or their components or the rating system. While these are important, the ultimate objective (goal, end, conclusion or aim) is your ability to write a learning objective. Except for the 4th objective (which follows), none of the other Unit Objectives contain Criteria.

> Given 6 criteria, a Rating Scale and a learning objective, calculate the Effectiveness Rating of the learning objective with an accuracy of +/− 1.0 against the author's solution.

This is not to say that you will not remember the components of an objective, the criteria for judging them or the rating method. It merely says that from the standpoint of this training event, they are a means to an end.

2. **Is related to, but subordinate to a Core Objective.** The writing of any learning objective can be an end in itself, since it is an observable and complete module of human behavior. However, learning objectives are a step in the instructional development process. Hence, a person who develops a training program uses this skill to achieve a higher purpose.

In some cases a Module Objective can be directly subordinate to the Result Objective in a Business Plan. For example, a business wants to conduct training on a section of employment law such as Sexual Harassment. This Training Module would not have to be connected to a Core Objective.

3. **Cannot stand alone.** It must have a set of Unit Objectives. (Refer to page 19, Objectives of Part 1.)

4. **It must meet all 6 criteria.** (See pages 65–67 for further explanation.)

Unit Objective

The term Unit Objective as used within the **Hierarchical Structure** assigns the objective four characteristics. A Unit Objective:

1. **Describes a unit of knowledge or skill.** Here, for example, the attempt is to meet the fifth Unit Objective: Differentiate between Core, Module and Unit Objectives. The <u>Training Unit</u> is entitled **The Hierarchical Structure of Objectives.**

2. **Is related to, but subordinate to a Module Objective.** Here the relationship is not as clear, since the Module Objective refers to the writing of a (single) learning objective, not a set of objectives. However, as you discover from the Unit Objectives on page 19, not all objectives have to contain the five principal components (Performer, Performance, Conditions, Criteria and Performance Time). Objectives 1, 2, 3, 5 and 6 contain only the Performance Component. Hence, the ability to "differentiate between Core, Module and Unit Objectives" is related to the skill of writing objectives.

Alternatively, we could have expressed the Module Objective as follows (Performance and Criteria only):

> Write a <u>set of Hierarchically Structured</u> learning objectives *that contain Performance, Conditions, Criteria and Performance Time components.*

The words "set" and "Hierarchically Structured" would have made the fifth Unit Objective (page 19) directly relevant to the Module Objective. On the other hand, it would have, in my opinion, added to your confusion. Additionally, I would have to measure your ability to write a set of objectives, making your task and mine more difficult. Besides, I have found that people rarely have trouble with Unit Objectives once they understand how to write a Core or Module Objective.

3. **Cannot stand alone.** It must have one or more related units of knowledge or skill. Consider this unit which begins on page 56, **The Hierarchical Structure of Objectives.** It contains the following units of knowledge:

A. The Benefit of the Hierarchical Structure (page 57)

B. Terms with Special Meanings (page 58)

C. Separating the Forest, from the Trees, Branches and Leaves (page 60)

D. The Business Plan and The Result Objective (page 63)

E. What Is a Core or a Module Objective? (page 65)

F. What Is the Difference Between a Core and a Module Objective? (page 66)

G. How Does a Module Objective Differ from a Unit Objective? (page 67)

H. Criteria for Measuring the Usefulness of a Set of Objectives (pages 68–69)

I. A Set of Objectives (page 69)

J. The Hierarchical Structure (A chart depicting relationships on page 72)

4. **It does not have to meet all 6 criteria** (See page 67 for further explanation)

Stated another way, the **Hierarchical Structure's** superior-subordinate relationship shows both the superior objective and the plan to reach that objective. This enables decision makers, trainers and students to readily see where the developer of training is going and the route to be taken.

C. Separating the Forest from the Trees, Branches and Leaves

The **Hierarchical Structure** also helps us to separate the "forest from the trees, branches and leaves." The Core Objective, metaphorically, is the forest. Each Module Objective is a tree. Each Unit Objective is a branch of the tree and each unit of knowledge and skill is a leaf. The <u>explanation of each unit</u> is the content of the leaf. The following two pages represent a leaf and its content.

Figure 4.4 shows the tree and its branches. Figure 4.5 is a list of all the units of knowledge in Part 1, or metaphorically, the leaves of the tree.

Does the list of **Units of Knowledge and Skill** in Fig. 4.5, by itself, communicate to the decision maker what the learner will be able to do with this information?

Now compare the list of **Units of Knowledge and Skill** to the **Module Objective** in Fig. 4.4. In a few words you are able to see what you will learn, the way you will be measured and the situation in which you will perform.

Learning Objectives are the means for describing training ends (desired behaviors) that increase the chance of achieving the business ends (results) that motivated the need for the training.

Figure 4.4. The Tree and its Branches

Module Objective—The Tree

Write a Learning Objective: Given a performance discrepancy that is caused by a lack of skill or knowledge on a subject that the instructional developer has mastered, the developer (reader) will be able to write a learning objective that contains performance, criteria, conditions and time components within 12 minutes which achieves an Effectiveness Rating of 10 (on a 10 scale) against prescribed criteria.

Unit Objectives—The Branches

To accomplish the Module Objective, the Instructional Developer will be able to:

1. Write a definition of a learning objective.

2. Describe (by listing) 5 components of a useful objective.

3. List 6 criteria (standards) that would measure the usefulness of a Core, Terminal, Program or Module Objective.

4. Given 6 criteria, a Rating Scale and a learning objective, calculate the Effectiveness Rating of the learning objective with an accuracy of +/− 1.0 against the author's solution.

5. Differentiate between Core, Module and Unit Objectives.

6. Calculate an Effectiveness Rating for a set of learning objectives.

Figure 4.5. The Leaves of the Tree

Units of Knowledge and Skill—The Leaves

- The Learning Objective Principle
- The Performance Component
- The Conditions Component
- Criteria and Performance Time
- The Criteria Component
- The Performance Time Component
- The Performer Component
- Learning Objective or Instructional Objective?
- Concrete Language
- Components of a Learning Objective
- Criteria for Measuring the Usefulness of an Objective
- Measuring the Desired Behavior
- Measuring the Usefulness of Objectives
- The Criterion Scoring System
- A Word about the Score of 5—Questionable
- The Performance Standard
- Using the System to Measure an Objective
- Correcting a Flawed Objective
- An Objective for a Complex Interactive Sales Behavior
- An Objective for a Complex Interactive Consulting Behavior
- An Objective for a Physical Skill
- The Hierarchical Structure of Objectives
- The Benefit of the Hierarchical Structure
- Terms with Special Meanings
- **Separating the Forest, from the Trees, Branches and Leaves**
- The Business Plan and Result Objective
- What is a Core or a Module Objective?
- What is the Difference Between a Core and a Module Objective?
- How does a Module Objective Differ from a Unit Objective?
- Criteria for Measuring the Usefulness of a Set of Objectives
- A Set of Objectives
- The Hierarchical Structure (A chart depicting relationships)
- Formats for Sets of Learning Objectives
- Measuring a Set of Learning Objectives
- Determining the Effectiveness Rating
- Importance of a Core or Module Objective
- Evaluation Forms for Sets of Learning Objectives
- Measuring the Objectives of Part 1
- A Set of Flawed Objectives
- Complexity and the Writing of Objectives
- Bloom's Taxonomy
- Use of Verbs to Describe Complexity of Behavior
- Describing a Complex Behavior
- Bloom's Taxonomy versus the Hierarchical Structure
- Training Process Objectives
- Training Process Expressed as Objectives
- A Formula for Success

D. The Business Plan and the Result Objective

The Business Plan and the Result Objective are the justification for the existence of a training program. An effective training program produces a desired behavior that can be used on the job; this is the justification for expending organizational resources (time and money). For example:

> A sales manager learns that a large number of salespeople are making cold calls on prospective clients. She knows that an effective sales interview takes two to three hours and that few prospects will have that kind of time available without prior notice. She also knows that the salespeople have access to a customer brochure that effectively tells the company's story, but because of its length, tends to be intimidating to most salespeople. She desires her salespeople to make appointments by phone.
>
> However, after switching the salesforce to making telephone appointments, she discovers, by listening to their calls, a discrepancy in their skills. The salespeople also report that they are having difficulty securing appointments. The manager decides to conduct training. Her Result Objective should be stated as a measurable result, i.e., obtain one confirmed appointment for each four contacts.
>
> Figure 4.6 contains the learning objective she prepared for the training program. Contained within the objective is a behavior that represents the solution to the problem. In this case, she has direct experience obtaining appointments and desires to transfer those skills to her salespeople.
>
> If she were hiring a training vendor, she should:

A. check their objectives to ensure that the behaviors they teach are compatible with those she feels are needed.

B. ask for evidence that demonstrates that the vendor's training program actually produced the desired results for other organizations.

Figure 4.6. Objective for Making Appointments

Making an Appointment: <u>Given a student acting as a prospect who received a letter and a customer brochure</u>, the seller will be able to **conduct a follow-up call** *that reaches agreement on the date, time, purpose, participants and prospect preparation (reads the customer brochure) for a formal sales interview which explores the mutual benefit of establishing a business relationship within 6 minutes.*

Optimally, the results a training program will bring about should be stated in units of sales or production. This permits post-training evaluation. In an optimal situation, the developer would observe the salespeople making phone calls on the job and determine if they were using the desired behavior to secure appointments. Assuming they were using the behavior and securing appointments in 3 out of 10 contacts the training would be deemed effective, since it brought about the desired result.

In many cases, Result Objectives related to training are stated abstractly (e.g., "to improve the number of interviews"). In these situations, the developer can measure the post-training effectiveness of the program by ascertaining baseline results data on the students prior to training. If the results data after training shows an increase and the developer is able to observe and measure the presence of the desired behavior learned in the training program on the job, the training can be considered successful.

A Case In Point

As part of a project for a large life insurance company, a developer conducted a post training evaluation of a video training program. This program had no stated learning objectives and the business objective was stated in terms of "an increase" rather than as measurable results. Agents were shown the 95-minute video at a salesmeeting. The video contained both product knowledge (75 minutes) and the technique for selling the product (20 minutes). However, there was no:

- Instructor manual to reinforce or support the video.
- Resources to conduct performance evaluation (criteria and rating scale for evaluating observed performance).
- Evaluation of the agent's performance.

The company's hypothesis was that watching the video would bring about acquisition of the behaviors depicted in a role played interview within the video. To determine if the agents had acquired the desired behavior the developer established criteria in relation to the role played interview. Agents were then observed in actual sales transactions. These agents exhibited none of the behaviors contained in the video. They also did not make many sales. Each appeared to be using a trial and error approach as there was no observable consistency in any one agent or between any two agents. The absence of objectives contributed to the ineffectiveness of the training program and business initiative.

Ineffectiveness, in this case, translated into the waste of approximately 1,000 man hours, the loss of the $100,000 spent on the video, agent frustration and the company's failure to achieve the business objective.

Summary

Training is the methodology employed to bring about a desired behavior in the student. The desired behavior is the methodology employed by the performer to bring about a desired result on the job. Stated as a principle:

Effective Training produces **Desired Behavior**
Desired Behavior *produces Results*

E. What Is a Core or a Module Objective?

A Core or Module Objective is an objective that meets Robert Mager's definition of a learning objective. It represents, from the organization's viewpoint, a unit of behavior that the student will use <u>on the job</u> to bring about the result that motivated the organization to conduct the training. From the developer's (trainer's) viewpoint it represents <u>the desired behavior</u> to be exhibited <u>at the program's end</u> to measure competence. This type of objective is also referred to as a program or Terminal Objective in the training literature.

For example: If a large company desires its developers of training to use learning objectives as the basis (foundation) of its training, it would conduct training on writing learning objectives. If the company had a person with expertise in its employ, it could develop the program internally. If it did not, contracting with a training vendor would be appropriate. In either case, the Module Objective for the course entitled **Writing Learning Objectives** would read as follows:

> **Write a Learning Objective:** <u>Given a performance discrepancy that is caused by a lack of skill or knowledge on a subject that the instructional developer has mastered</u>, the developer will be able to **write a learning objective** *that contains performance, criteria, conditions and time components* within 12 minutes which achieves an Effectiveness Rating of 10 (on a 10 scale) against prescribed criteria.

On the other hand, if the same large company wanted to train a group of researchers to evaluate the learning objectives used by its developers, the module objective for the course entitled **Evaluating Learning Objectives** would read as follows:

> **Evaluate a Learning Objective:** <u>Given 6 criteria, a Rating Scale and 10 learning objectives for a program or module of instruction</u>, the researcher will be able to **calculate the Effectiveness Rating of the learning objectives** *with an accuracy of +/– 1.0 against the developer's solution* within 70 minutes.

In the course on **Developing Learning Objectives** the focus is on writing an objective. Competence is measured by the student's skill in taking his or her technical knowledge and translating it into learning objectives that meet the six criteria. One does not really care if the student can evaluate objectives written by other developers of training, although this may be an unexpected benefit of the course.

In the course on **Evaluating Learning Objectives** the focus is on measurement. The final exam involves calculating Effectiveness Ratings for 10 learning objectives. One does not really care if the student can write an objective although, again, that may be a side benefit.

F. What Is the Difference Between a Core Objective and a Module Objective?

From a technical (criteria) standpoint there is no difference. Both must meet Robert Mager's definition of a learning objective and therefore all six criteria. From a practical standpoint, the Core Objective represents both a higher level of skill and in many cases a transaction with a broader scope.

For example, this section of the book, <u>Learning Objectives: The Foundation</u>, could be part of a program on "developing training programs." The Core Objective for such a program might read (**Performance** component and principal *Criteria* component only):

> **Plan, organize, conduct, evaluate and modify a training program** *which uses learning objectives to bring about a desired behavior at a prescribed competence standard.*

This program would have a module on developing learning objectives and one or more of the following modules:

1. Organizing an instructor guide.
2. Conducting the training.
3. Evaluating student performance.
4. Making modifications to training based on observed performance.
5. Conducting a Needs Analysis.

This concept can also be demonstrated with our tennis serve example. The serve could be a module of a program that taught the student how to **play the game of tennis.** Such a program could have the following modules:

1. The rules of the game.
2. Serving the ball.
3. Executing Ground Strokes
4. Playing with Advanced Strategy.

On the other hand, we may choose to enroll in a program that only focuses on the ability to serve. In such a case, we might desire to correct a performance discrepancy or increase our level of competence; such as, being able to serve the ball at 100 MPH with a first serve accuracy of 60 percent.

G. How Does a Module Objective Differ from a Unit Objective?

A Unit Objective describes a __unit of skill or knowledge__ to be exhibited __during the module__ which is relevant to the Module's Objective. This type of objective is also called a subordinate, enabling or knowledge objective. Figure 4.7 lists the Unit Objectives for Part 1.

The criteria for Unit Objectives are similar to those for Core and Module Objectives (refer to pages 68–69). But notice that criteria C, D and E (which follow) are optional (shown in parentheses as **if applicable**). Also notice that wording of the Performance criterion and Criteria criterion are changed. They now refer to "units of knowledge or skill" rather than the "desired behavior."

Criteria for Unit Objectives

A. Contains the **job title of the performer** and the words **"be able to"** immediately before the active verb. For convenience, a set of Unit Objectives can be prefaced with a statement such as "To accomplish the Module Objective, the (performer job title) will be able to:"

B. Contains a **performance** which describes __a unit of skill or knowledge__ to be exhibited.

Figure 4.7. Unit Objectives of Part 1

To accomplish the Module Objective, the Instructional Developer will be able to:

1. Write a definition of a learning objective.

2. List 6 components of a useful objective.

3. List 6 criteria (standards) that would measure the usefulness of a Core, Terminal, Program or Module Objective.

4. Given 6 criteria, a Rating Scale and a learning objective, calculate the Effectiveness Rating of the learning objective with an accuracy of +/− 1.0 against the author's solution.

5. __Differentiate between Core, Module and Unit Objectives.__

6. Calculate an Effectiveness Rating for a set of learning objectives.

C. Contains a fixed **time** limit for the performance. **(If applicable)**

D. Contains **criteria** to measure <u>the unit of skill or knowledge during the module</u>. **(If applicable)**

E. Contains **conditions** which describe the situation in which the performance occurs, limitations imposed or non-implicit resources. **(If applicable)**

F. Contains **concrete image provoking language** in both the performance (desired behavior) and criteria. Any abstractions are referenced to criteria.

In Fig. 4.7, objective 4 meets 5 of the 6 criteria (notice that time for the performance is missing). Objectives 1 through 3 and 5 are performance statements. They contain a verb and an object of the verb. They also contain concrete image provoking language. Abstract words such as *proper, appropriate, right, understand, learn, effectively* or *successfully* have been avoided. The prefacing statement, "to accomplish the Module Objective, the Instructional Developer will be able to," enables these Unit Objectives to meet the first criteria.

Unit Objectives represent the content of the training. While each is important, the elements of Performance Time, Criteria for measuring competence and Conditions under which the performance will occur are not always needed. We are not going to specifically test the student on each unit objective (although we can if it is desirable).

Following are the **Criteria for Measuring the Usefulness of a Set of Objectives.** This will enable you to compare and contrast the differences between Core, Module and Unit Objectives.

H. Criteria for Measuring the Usefulness of a Set of Objectives

Core or Module Objectives

To be considered useful, the statement must:

A. Contain the **job title of the performer** and the words **"be able to"** immediately before the active verb.

B. Contain **the performance** to be exhibited. (Active verb[s] and the object of the verb describe <u>the desired behavior</u>.)

C. Contain a fixed **time** limit for the performance.

D. Contain **criteria** to measure the desired behavior <u>at program's end</u>.

E. Contain **conditions** which describe the situation in which the performance occurs, limitations imposed or non-implicit resources.

F. Contain **concrete image provoking language** in both the performance (desired behavior) and criteria. Any abstractions are referenced to criteria.

Unit Objectives

To be considered useful the statement must:

A. Contain the **job title of the performer** and the words **"be able to"** immediately before the active verb. For convenience, a set of Unit Objectives can be prefaced with a statement such as "To accomplish the Module Objective, the (performer job title) will be able to:"

B. Contain a **performance** which describes <u>a unit of skill or knowledge</u> to be exhibited.

C. Contain a fixed **time** limit for the performance. **(If applicable)**

D. Contain **criteria** to measure <u>the unit of skill or knowledge during the module</u>. **(If applicable)**

E. Contain **conditions** which describe the situation in which the performance occurs, limitations imposed or non-implicit resources. **(If applicable)**

F. Contain **concrete image provoking language** in both the performance (desired behavior) and criteria. Any abstractions are referenced to criteria.

I. A Set of Objectives

A set of objectives can consist of a Module Objective and one or more Unit Objectives or a Core Objective and one or more Module Objectives. In the latter case, we would view the training program from the standpoint of the highest level and most holistic unit of behavior and the major skills that would enable the learner to exhibit this behavior. Figure 4.8 contains a Core and two Module Objectives.

Notice that the Core and Module objectives <u>each</u> achieve an Effectiveness Rating of 10 by meeting all six criteria.

Figure 4.9 shows a set of objectives for a training module. In this case they are the Module and Unit Objectives for Part 1. Notice that only the Module Objective meets all six criteria.

Summary

A set of objectives provides a clear outline for the decision maker, developer, instructor and learner of the program's content and, because of their structure, a basis to measure whether or not the training program was effective.

Figure 4.8. Objectives for a <u>Training Program</u>

Core Objective

Develop a Training Program: Given 10 hours of preparation and a group of developers acting as students, the developer will be able to plan, organize, conduct, evaluate and modify a training program which uses learning objectives to bring about a desired behavior at a prescribed competence standard within 120 minutes.

Module Objectives

To accomplish the Core Objective the Instructional Developer will be able to:

1. **Write a Learning Objective:** Given a performance discrepancy that is caused by a lack of skill or knowledge on a subject that the instructional developer has mastered, the developer (reader) will be able to write a learning objective that contains performance, criteria, conditions, and time components within 12 minutes which achieves an Effectiveness Rating of 10 (on a 10 scale) against prescribed criteria.

2. **Plan a Training Module:** Given a learning objective (rated 10) on an activity where the developer is a competent performer, **plan and document a training module** that identifies the criteria, rating scale, knowledge and skill objectives and resources needed to produce and measure the desired behavior within 4 hours.

Figure 4.9. Objectives for a <u>Training Module</u>

Module Objective

Write a Learning Objective: Given a performance discrepancy that is caused by a lack of skill or knowledge on a subject that the instructional developer has mastered, the developer (reader) will be able to write a learning objective that contains performance, criteria, conditions and time components within 12 minutes which achieves an Effectiveness Rating of 10 (on a 10 scale) against prescribed criteria.

Unit Objectives

To accomplish the Module Objective, the Instructional Developer will be able to:

1. Write a definition of a learning objective.

2. List 6 components of a useful objective.

3. List 6 criteria (standards) that would measure the usefulness of a Core, Terminal, Program or Module Objective.

4. Given 6 criteria, a Rating Scale and a learning objective, calculate the Effectiveness Rating of the learning objective with an accuracy of +/− 1.0 against the author's solution.

5. Differentiate between Core, Module and Unit Objectives.

6. Calculate an Effectiveness Rating for a set of learning objectives.

J. The Hierarchical Structure

The following table contrasts the three types of learning objectives used to structure a training program.

	Core	Module	Unit
Scope of performance	Desired behavior	Desired behavior	Unit of Skill or knowledge
Where observed	End of program	End of module	During module
Perspective	Forest	Trees	Branches
Components required	Performer Performance Conditions Criteria Time	Performer Performance Conditions Criteria Time	Performer Performance
Hierarchical relationship	Relevant to the Result Objective	Relevant to the Core Objective	Relevant to the Module Objective
Examples	**Develop a Training Program:** Given 10 hours of preparation and a group of developers acting as students, the developer will be able to plan, organize, conduct, evaluate and modify a training program which uses learning objectives to bring about a desired behavior at a prescribed competence standard within 120 minutes.	**Write a Learning Objective:** Given a performance discrepancy that is caused by a lack of skill or knowledge on a subject that the instructional developer has mastered, the developer (reader) will be able to write a learning objective that contains performance, criteria, conditions and time components within 12 minutes.	Differentiate between Core Module and Unit Objectives.

K. Formats for Sets of Learning Objectives

The following formats will assist you in writing a set of learning objectives for a **Training Program** or **Training Module.** They will also be useful in analyzing any set of learning objectives.

Training Program

Core Objective

Title: Describe the Transaction

Given (insert the conditions), **the** (state the job title of the performer) **will be able to** (describe the performance) **that** (describe the principal criteria) **within** (state the time limit for the performance). (Define or reference, if applicable, any abstract words.)

Module Objectives

To accomplish the Core Objective **the** (state the job title of the performer) **will be able to:**

\#. **Title: Given** (insert the conditions), (describe the performance) **that** (describe the principal criteria) **within** (state the time limit for the performance).

Training Module

Module Objective

Title: Describe the Transaction

Given (insert the conditions), **the** (state the job title of the performer) **will be able to** (describe the performance) **that** (describe the principal criteria) **within** (state the time limit for the performance). (Define or reference, if applicable, any abstract words.)

Unit Objectives

\#. (Describe the unit of knowledge or skill.) Add Conditions, Criteria and Performance Time as required.

5
Measuring a Set of Learning Objectives

The Effectiveness Rating of a <u>set of objectives</u> predicts the degree to which behavior is likely to change. Programs with Effectiveness Ratings of 8.0 or greater are likely to provide students with a set of skills that they will be able to use on the job and will employ methodology that is likely to transfer those skills. Such programs will make extensive use of performance (role play or simulation) with evaluation of performance against criteria.

Programs rated below 4.9 are not as likely to produce a set of observable behaviors. Such programs will often contain a potpourri of knowledge and skills. However, it is unlikely that the learner will be able to apply more than a few of the skills. These programs will tend to make less use of performance and evaluation type exercises. The learners will get something, but will it be enough to justify the cost of the training, travel, related expenses and the time spent? Programs rated between 5.0 and 7.9 are considered marginal.

A. Determining the Effectiveness Rating

The following is the formula for evaluating a set of objectives for a training program or module:

$$\frac{\text{Rating of the Superior Objective} + \text{Average of the Ratings of the Subordinate Objectives}}{2} = \text{Effectiveness Rating}$$

This formula is based on the Hierarchical Structure. It allocates 50 percent of the Effectiveness Rating to the Superior (Core or Module) Objective. Hence, a training program with no Core Objective and 6 Module Objectives rated at 10, 8, 8, 6, 5 and 5 respectively, would achieve an Effectiveness Rating of 3.5.

$$\frac{0 + [(10+8+8+6+5+5)/6]}{2} = 3.5$$

$$\frac{0 + (42/6)}{2} = 3.5$$

$$\frac{0 + 7}{2} = 3.5$$

B. Importance of a Core or Module Objective

By identifying the specific **"performance you want learners to be able to exhibit before you consider them competent"** the training program gains a powerful focus. While each of the modules may be important, the ultimate success of the training is that the student can now use these skills to meet the challenges of the job.

The skill you learn in Part 1 is a good example. If you learn how to write and measure objectives, your skill as a developer will increase. But to what degree? How will you make use of the objectives you wrote? Without additional training on how to use objectives at each step of the program development process you might write perfect objectives that are still underutilized.

However, Part 1 is a module of a training program that will enable you **to plan, organize, conduct, evaluate and modify a training program which uses learning objectives to bring about a desired behavior (at a prescribed competence standard).** By completing the remaining sections you will be able to put the objectives to work at each stage of the development process. The finished product is a training program that is driven by, and totally linked to, learning objectives.

C. Evaluation Forms for Sets of Learning Objectives

Figure 5.1 depicts the evaluation form for measuring the learning objectives for a Training Program. Notice that the criteria are the same for both the Core and Module Objectives.

Figure 5.2 is used for evaluating the objectives for a Training Module. Criterion B in the Module Objective refers to **the desired behavior** while Criterion B in the Unit Objectives refers to a **unit of knowledge or skill**. This is also true for

Figure 5.1. Evaluation Form for a Set of Learning Objectives—Training Program

PROGRAM: _____   DEVELOPER _____   DATE _____

Core Objective

A. Contains the performer job title and the words "be able to" before the active verb.

B. Contains a performance which describes the desired behavior to be exhibited.

C. Contains a fixed time limit for the performance.

D. Contains criteria to measure the desired behavior at program's end.

E. Contains conditions which describe situation, limitations or non-implicit resources.

F. Contains concrete language and any abstractions are referenced to criteria.

Total Score

Rating—(Divide Total by 6)

Module Objectives

A. Contains the performer job title and the words "be able to" before the active verb.

B. Contains a performance which describes a desired behavior to be exhibited.

C. Contains a fixed time limit for the performance.

D. Contains criteria to measure the desired behavior during the program.

E. Contains conditions which describe situation, limitations or non-implicit resources.

F. Contains concrete language and any abstractions are referenced to criteria.

Total Score

Rating—(Divide Total by 6) Group Rating—(Divide Total by # of objectives rated)

Total of Ratings (Core plus the Average Group Rating of the Module Objectives)

EFFECTIVENESS RATING (Total divided by 2)

	1	2	3	4	5	6		Average Group Rating

Criterion Scoring

10	Meets Criterion
5	Questionable
0	Does Not Meet or Not Evident

Effectiveness Rating

8.0 to 10	Effective
5.0 to 7.9	Marginal
1.0 to 4.9	Ineffective
0.0 to 0.9	Not Evident

Figure 5.2. Evaluation Form for a Set of Learning Objectives—Training Module

PROGRAM: _____ DEVELOPER _____ DATE _____

Module Objective

A. Contains the performer job title and the words "be able to" before the active verb.
B. Contains a performance which describes the desired behavior to be exhibited.
C. Contains a fixed time limit for the performance.
D. Contains criteria to measure the desired behavior at program's or module's end.
E. Contains conditions which describe situation, limitations or non-implicit resources.
F. Contains concrete language and any abstractions are referenced to criteria.

Total Score

Rating—(Divide Total by 6)

Unit Objectives

A. Contains the performer job title and the words "be able to" before the active verb.
B. Contains a performance which describes a unit of knowledge or skill to be exhibited.
C. Contains a fixed time limit for the performance.*
D. Contains criteria to measure the unit of knowledge or skill during the module.*
E. Contains conditions which describe situation, limitations or non-implicit resources.*
F. Contains concrete language and any abstractions are referenced to criteria.

Total Score

Rating—(Divide Total by 6) Group Rating—(Divide Total by # of objectives rated)

Total of Ratings (Module plus the Average Group Rating of the Unit Objectives)
EFFECTIVENESS RATING (Total divided by 2)

	1	2	3	4	5	6	Average Group Rating

Criterion Scoring

10 Meets Criterion
5   Questionable
0   Does Not Meet or Not Evident

*If applicable

Effectiveness Rating

8.0 to 10   Effective
5.0 to 7.9 Marginal
1.0 to 4.9 Ineffective
0.0 to 0.9 Not Evident

Criterion D. Also notice in the Unit Objectives section that Criteria C, Performance Time; D, Criteria to measure the performance; and E, Conditions, which describe the situation, are made optional by the words **"if applicable."**

Which Form Shall You Use?

A critical question: How do you know whether to evaluate the objectives as those of a *Training Program or Training Module*? I would use the following guidelines:

1. **Program Length and Content.** Generally programs lasting several days will list as objectives or as agenda items several subjects that are, in fact, modules of behavior, for example, Conducting a Selection Interview; Conducting One on One Training; Holding a Disciplinary Interview; or Preparing a Forecast. While each of these subjects are related to managing, they are also distinctly different behaviors that can be observed. A selection interview requires a different set of skills than a training session with one employee. Therefore, I would rate the objectives using the evaluation form for a *Training Program*. The Superior Objective would be a Core Objective. The Subordinates would be Module Objectives. This, of course, holds the set of objectives to the most rigorous standard as each must meet all 6 criteria.

By comparison, the objectives for Part 1 are clearly focused on the development of learning objectives. I would evaluate them using the evaluation form for a *Training Module*. The Module Objective would be the Superior Objective. The Subordinate Objectives would be Unit Objectives. In this instance, a less rigorous standard as the Unit Objectives need only contain a Performance Component, the words "be able to" and the job title of the performer. (The latter items can be generic to a set of Unit Objectives by the presence of the prefacing statement: To accomplish the Module Objective, the program developer will be able to....). Criteria, Conditions and Performance Time are optional.

2. **The Developer's Description of the Program.** In some cases, the developer will identify a unit of training as a Program or Module.

Evaluating a set of objectives as those of a Training Program holds the objectives to a higher standard. This is due to the fact that both the Superior and the Subordinate Objectives must meet all six criteria for a useful objective.

D. Measuring the Objectives for This Part

The objectives for this part are shown below in Fig. 5.3. We will use the Performance Evaluation Form for a Training Module to determine the Effectiveness Rating for this set of objectives. The Effectiveness Rating is shown in Fig. 5.4.

Figure 5.3. Objectives for a Training Module

Module Objective

Write a Learning Objective: Given a performance discrepancy that is caused by a lack of skill or knowledge on a subject that the instructional developer has mastered, the developer (reader) will be able to write a learning objective that contains performance, criteria, conditions and time components within 12 minutes which achieves an Effectiveness Rating of 10 (on a 10 scale) against prescribed criteria.

Unit Objectives

To accomplish the Module Objective, the Instructional Developer will be able to:

1. Write a definition of a learning objective.

2. List 6 components of a useful objective.

3. List 6 criteria (standards) that would measure the usefulness of a Core, Terminal, Program or Module Objective.

4. Given 6 criteria, a Rating Scale and a learning objective, calculate the Effectiveness Rating of the learning objective with an accuracy of +/- 1.0 against the author's solution.

5. Differentiate between Core, Module and Unit Objectives.

6. Calculate an Effectiveness Rating for a set of learning objectives.

Figure 5.4. Rating of Objectives in Fig. 5.3

Module Objective				Unit Objectives							
				1	**2**	**3**	**4**	**5**	**6**		
A	10		A	10	10	10	10	10	10		
B	10		B	10	10	10	10	10	10		
C	10		C	NA	NA	NA	NA	NA	NA		
D	10		D	NA	NA	NA	NA	NA	NA		
E	10		E	NA	NA	NA	NA	NA	NA		
F	10		F	10	10	10	10	10	10		Average Group Rating
	60	Total		30	30	30	30	30	30		
	10	Rating		10	10	10	10	10	10	10	

Total of Ratings   20

EFFECTIVENESS RATING   10

E. A Set of Flawed Objectives

The following objectives were abstracted from a training program offered as a 2-day workshop at the convention of one of the national training associations. The program, entitled the Program Development Workshop, contained the six objectives shown in Fig. 5.5. The training fee was $495. I have **bolded** the abstract words.

Figure 5.6 shows the completed evaluation form with the Effectiveness Rating for this set of objectives. In this case we have evaluated the objectives as those of a Training Program due to the program's scope (course development), content (needs analysis, objectives, design of materials, communication with subject experts) and length of the program (2 days).

The Effectiveness Rating for this set of objectives is 1.0. A rating of 1.0 suggests ineffective, unusable objectives.

Even if you challenge the hypothesis that objectives for a program or module must identify a Superior (Core or Module) Objective that represents the focus of the training, the rating for this set of objectives is 2.0 or ineffective. There is no <u>Performance Time</u>, no <u>Criteria</u> and no description of the situation in which your performance will occur (<u>Condition</u>). Considering the number of abstract words used, you can expect a lecture or controlled discussion that does not reach any definitive conclusions.

You might get something out of the potpourri of ideas that are offered. Human beings cannot help learning, but it is unlikely that you will gain any measurable skills from this program. I believe that I can say categorically, that you will not learn anything about writing learning objectives.

Figure 5.5. Program Development Workshop Objectives

You will learn how to:

1. Explain how to conduct two types of needs analysis.

2. Interact with subject matter experts to obtain **complete** and **accurate** information.

3. Write **high level** objectives in three domains: cognitive, psychomotor and affective.

4. Create criterion test items that accurately measure **high level** skills.

5. Choose instructional strategies that match the objectives and needs of the trainees.

6. Apply message design **principles** to design **dynamic** and **effective** training materials.

Figure 5.6. Rating of Objectives in Fig. 5.5

Core Objective			Module Objectives						
			1	2	3	4	5	6	
A	0	A	0	0	0	0	0	0	
B	0	B	10	10	5	10	10	5	
C	0	C	0	0	0	0	0	0	
D	0	D	0	0	0	0	5	0	
E	0	E	0	0	0	0	0	0	
F	0	F	10	0	0	0	10	0	
	0	Total	20	10	5	10	25	5	Average Group Rating
	0	Rating	3.3	1.6	0.8	1.6	4.1	0.8	2

Total of Ratings	2
EFFECTIVENESS RATING	1

F. Evaluating a Set of Objectives—Task 7

Here is an opportunity to test your evaluation skill. The objectives in Fig. 5.7 were abstracted from a book entitled How to Write Learning Objectives. Calculate the Effectiveness Rating for this set of objectives. In this exercise, you will calculate their rating both as a Training Module and Training Program. Use the evaluation matrixes in Figs. 5.8 and 5.9 on the following page.

Figure 5.7. Objectives from a Training Program

The reader will be able to:

1. Identify two characteristics of instructional objectives and name the three functions of an instructional objective.

2. Identify the three components of any given instructional objective.

3. Distinguish between acceptable and unacceptable statements of performance in a given set of objectives.

4. Determine whether the conditions component of an instructional objective is both concise and complete according to the criteria given in this section.

5. Determine whether the standards component in an objective is stated in an acceptable manner.

6. Given a task for which training is required, write a clear, complete instructional objective.

(Lutterodt and Grafinger, 1985)

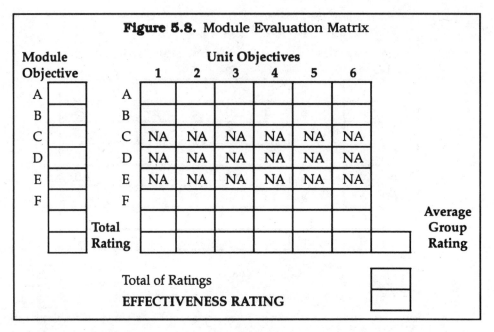

Figure 5.8. Module Evaluation Matrix

Now take the same set of objectives and calculate their Effectiveness Rating as a training program. This exercise will enable you to practice your skill in identifying components. It will also enable us to draw conclusions about the usefulness of these objectives and the flexibility of the evaluation system.

Refer to pages 524 through 527 for the solution to this exercise (Task 7).

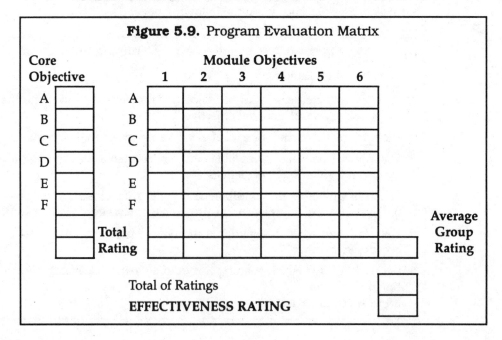

Figure 5.9. Program Evaluation Matrix

Evaluate the Set of Objectives You Wrote in Task 1

In Task 1 on page 17 you were asked to write a set of objectives for a training program on writing learning objectives. Use the **Evaluation Form for a Set of Learning Objectives—Training Module** (Fig. 5.2 on page 77) to calculate the Effectiveness Rating for the set of objectives you originally wrote. You should find a direct correlation between your **Objective Utilization Rating** (calculated on page 18) and the Effectiveness Rating of the objectives you wrote.

In my experience with the Self Test, people achieve a low Effectiveness Rating. As a general rule, it is difficult to write learning objectives for a performance that you are unable to perform. Additionally, the level of difficulty increases when the desired behavior relates to sales, management or teaching. These behaviors require describing the measurable outcomes of human interaction and decision making which are often difficult to express in words.

6
Complexity and the Writing of Learning Objectives

The challenge in writing useful objectives centers around three issues. The first is one's own knowledge of the subject matter. The second relates to the structure of the objectives. The third, and perhaps most challenging, is describing behavior using words at the appropriate level of complexity. This section will address the third challenge.

A. Classification of Objectives

Benjamin S. Bloom, edited the <u>Taxonomy of Educational Objectives, Book 1, Cognitive Domain</u> (Bloom, 1984) and <u>Book 2, Affective Domain</u> (Bloom, 1964) which represented eight years of work by a group of 34 college examiners. Bloom and his colleagues classified objectives into three areas:

1. **Cognitive:** Includes objectives that deal with the recall or recognition of knowledge and the development of intellectual skills and abilities.

2. **Affective:** "Objectives which emphasize a feeling tone, an emotion, or a degree of acceptance or rejection." (Bloom, 1964, p. 7) These objectives describe changes in interest, attitudes and values.

3. **Psychomotor:** "Objectives which emphasize some muscular or motor skill, some manipulation of materials and objects, or some act which requires a neuromuscular co-ordination." (Bloom, 1964, p. 7)

The word **taxonomy** refers to the science of classification, the laws and principles covering the classifying of objects. Bloom reports the following:

"After considerable effort and thought it became apparent that the objectives (and corresponding behaviors and evaluation materials) differed in complexity. An objective such as 'knowledge of specific facts' could be isolated and defined at one level of complexity. But at another level of complexity this objective became part of another objective such as 'the ability to apply principles. **At one point the 'knowledge of specific facts' was an end in its own right, <u>while at a later point it became a part of, tool for, or means to, a larger more complex objective</u>.**" (Bloom, 1964, p. 9) Note: Bolding and underlining is the emphasis of this author.

B. Bloom's Taxonomy

Bloom and his colleagues used this principle of complexity as the major ordering basis for objectives in the cognitive domain. The following are the six major classes of the Taxonomy:

1.00 Knowledge

2.00 Comprehension

3.00 Application

4.00 Analysis

5.00 Synthesis

6.00 Evaluation

The following are the definitions for each of the major classes. Listed below each is an example related to the objectives of Part 1.

1.00 Knowledge: The recall of information (i.e., terms, facts, ways and means, conventions (rules), trends, classifications, categories, criteria, methodology, principles, theories, etc. "For measurement purposes, the recall situation involves little more than bringing to mind the appropriate material." (Bloom, 1984, p. 201)

     e.g., Write a definition of a learning objective.

2.00 Comprehension: At this level the individual "can make use of the material without necessarily relating it to other material or seeing its fullest implications." (Bloom, 1984, p. 204) Observable behaviors include translation (paraphrase of the original material without distortion), interpretation (rearrangement of the material) and extrapolation (the ability to extend trends or tendencies beyond the given data to determine implications and conclusions).

     e.g., Describe (by listing) 6 criteria (standards) that would measure the usefulness of a Core, Terminal, Program or Module Objective.

3.00 Application:

"The use of abstractions (knowledge) in particular and concrete situations." (Bloom, 1984, p. 205) The application of knowledge to a new situation.

e.g., Identify Criteria in an Objective: <u>Given 3 learning objectives containing one or all of the components (performance, condition or criteria)</u>, the reader will be able to **identify (by underlining)** *correctly* **the words** *that are used as criteria in each* within 2 minutes.

4.00 Analysis:

"The breakdown of a communication into its constituent parts such that the relative hierarchy of an idea and/or the relationship between the ideas expressed are made explicit." (Bloom, 1984, p. 205) To breakdown knowledge into parts and show relationships among the parts.

e.g., Classify Objectives: <u>Given any objective in a subject area which you are familiar,</u> *in all instances* be able to **identify (label)** *correctly* **the performance, the condition, and the criterion of acceptable performance,** *when any or all of those characteristics are present.* (Mager, 1986, p. 3)

5.00 Synthesis:

Bringing together parts (elements, components) of knowledge to form a whole and build relationships for new situations.

e.g., Writing Learning Objectives: <u>Given a performance discrepancy that is caused by a lack of skill or knowledge on a subject that the instructional developer has mastered,</u> the developer will be able to **write a learning objective** *that contains performance, criteria, conditions and time components* within 12 minutes.

6.00 Evaluation:

"Judgments about the value of material and methods for given purposes. Quantitative and qualitative judgments about the extent to which material and methods satisfy criteria." (Bloom, 1984, p. 207)

e.g., Evaluate Learning Objectives: <u>Given 6 criteria, a Rating Scale and 10 learning objectives for a program or module of instruction,</u> the researcher will be able to **calculate the Effectiveness Rating of the learning objectives** *with an accuracy of +/− 1.0 against the developer's solution* within 70 minutes.

C. Use of Verbs to Describe Complexity of Behavior

In Fig. 6.1 is a list of verbs that can help you in the writing objectives. The list is arranged according to Bloom's Taxonomy. It should be noted that certain verbs, depending on meaning, may apply to more than one level.

Figure 6.1. Verbs to Describe Complexity of Behavior

1.00 Knowledge: The recall of information.

define	name	order
describe	recite	recognize
label	recall	record
list	relate	reproduce
match	repeat	state
arrange		underline

2.00 Comprehension: The translation, interpretation or extrapolation of knowledge.

arrange	explain	interpret
classify	express	locate
describe	identify	report
discuss	indicate	restate
sort	translate	extrapolate

3.00 Application: The application of knowledge to a new situation.

apply	practice	solve
choose	prepare	use
illustrate	schedule	demonstrate
operate	sketch	measure

4.00 Analysis: To break down knowledge into parts and show relationships among the parts.

analyze	diagram	question
appraise	discriminate	test
calculate	distinguish	differentiate
categorize	examine	compare
contrast	experiment	inventory
criticize		

5.00 Synthesis: Bringing together parts (elements, components) of knowledge to form a whole and build relationships for new situations.

arrange	design	prepare
assemble	formulate	propose
collect	manage	set up
compose	organize	synthesize
create	plan	write
construct	modify	conduct

6.00 Evaluation: Judgments about the value of material and methods for given purposes.

appraise	estimate	select
argue	evaluate	support
assess	judge	value
attack	predict	score
compare	rate	defend

D. Describing a Complex Behavior

The complexity of a behavior is reflected in the Performance and Criteria Components of the Learning Objective. Consider the following components for a course on **Developing a Training Program:**

Conditions:	Given a performance discrepancy that is caused by a lack of skill or knowledge on a subject that the instructional developer has mastered, 10 hours to prepare and a group of developers acting as students,
Performer:	the developer will be able to
Performance:	**plan, organize, conduct, evaluate and modify a training program**
Criteria:	which uses learning objectives to bring about a desired behavior at a prescribed competence standard.
Performance Time:	within 120 minutes.*

> * This relates to the conduct of the training not the time required for preparation and modification of the program.

The series of active verbs in the Performance Component (**plan, organize, conduct, evaluate and modify**) describe the complexity of the task of developing a training program. The verbs relate to the <u>synthesis</u> and <u>evaluation</u> levels of the Taxonomy. Compare these to **write a learning objective** and you immediately see that the task is more difficult.

This training program is also complex, since it involves two developers. Developer One is the person who wrote the above objective. Developer Two will be the person who will be evaluated on their ability to perform as described in the objective. Figure 6.2 depicts the relationships.

The Criteria Component of the objective for **Developing a Training Program** tells us that learning objectives written by Developer Two will be used to bring about a desired behavior at a prescribed competence standard. If Developer Two chooses to write a training program on selling an insurance product, then Developer Two's students would be insurance agents. These agents will use the new skills to sell insurance to their customers.

Stated another way, Developer One wants to observe the <u>teaching performance of Developer Two</u> as well as to <u>measure the effectiveness of the instruction by measuring the performance of the students performing as the agents</u>. This accounts for the Performance Time of 120 minutes. Measurement factors for Developer Two's program may include:

1. **Planning:** Learning Objectives, Performance Evaluation System, design of the program (agenda).

2. **Organizing:** Construction and content of the instructor guide, cases, practice exercises, job aids, etc.

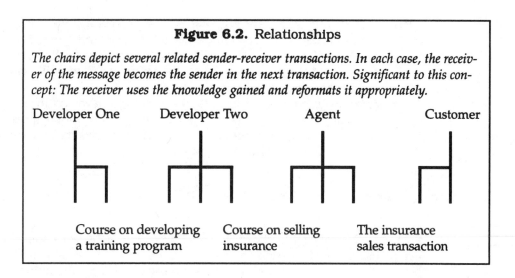

Figure 6.2. Relationships

The chairs depict several related sender-receiver transactions. In each case, the receiver of the message becomes the sender in the next transaction. Significant to this concept: The receiver uses the knowledge gained and reformats it appropriately.

Developer One   Developer Two   Agent   Customer

Course on developing   Course on selling   The insurance
a training program   insurance   sales transaction

3. **Conducting:** Teaching techniques, time management, relationship of Developer Two's plan to its actual execution.

4. **Evaluating:** The reliability of the evaluation form in measuring the behavior, the number of students who exhibit the desired behavior and the competence level each attains.

5. **Modifying:** Developer Two will be asked to prepare a narrative describing course modifications which are justified by the data obtained from the conduct of the program. (This would take into account both the developer's competence performance and the performance of the students being trained.)

The Condition's Component provides additional insight into behavioral complexity. In this case, the student will have 10 hours to prepare and will be teaching a group of fellow developers acting as students.

Now compare this to a sales behavior to handle inbound customer inquiries.

Obtaining an Appointment

Performer:	the salesperson will be able to,
Performance:	***conduct a telephone sales discussion.***
Performance Time:	Within 5 to 10 minutes.
Criteria:	that reaches agreement on the date, time and content of the next transaction in relation to the customer's needs and position in the decision making process.
Conditions:	Given a script and student acting as a prospect or customer who is making an inquiry by phone.

The Condition Component tells us that this is a relatively simple behavior. The salesperson is required to follow a script to obtain an appointment.

The Criteria Component suggests that evaluation will include understanding the customer's needs and position in the decision making process (with regard to the purchase). It will also include agreement on the specifics for the appointment. However, since the salesperson is aided by the script (which we will assume to be effective), the behavioral complexity is reduced.

The active verb, conduct, falls into the <u>Synthesis</u> level of the Taxonomy. However, the fact that the salesperson has the use of a script suggests that the <u>Application</u> level is probably more correct. The salesperson is *applying* knowledge; the behaviors contained within the script.

E. Bloom's Taxonomy Versus the Hierarchical Structure

Bloom and his colleagues stated that the **Taxonomy** "represents <u>something of a hierarchical order</u> of the different classes of objectives. As we have defined them, the objectives in one class are likely to make use of and be built on the behaviors found in the preceding classes on the list." (Bloom, 1984, p. 18) They stopped short of calling it a **Hierarchical Structure.**

As you recall, the **Hierarchical Structure** identifies one objective as the Superior Objective. All other objectives become subordinate to that objective. The Superior Objective is either a Core or Module Objective. This means that it identifies the desired behavior that will be observed to measure learner competence.

The Subordinate Objectives are the means to an end. They contain the knowledge, skills and behaviors that enable the learner to understand, accept and use the desired behavior.

Let's use a training module on learning objectives to demonstrate this subtle difference between the **Taxonomy** and the **Hierarchical Structure.** The Performance Component in the Superior (Module) Objective is **write a learning objective.** This relates to the <u>Synthesis</u> level of the Taxonomy. The verbs in the Subordinate (Unit) Objectives include **defining, describing, differentiating and evaluating (calculate Effectiveness Ratings).** These represent the full range of the Taxonomy's complexity levels. Refer to annotated Taxonomy on pages 85 and 86.

Evaluation of objectives, while at the highest level (<u>6:00 Evaluation</u>), is not the expected result (behavior) to be produced from the training. The training's effectiveness will be judged on the students' ability to write objectives at the end of the course and back on the job. Evaluation of objectives is used as a teaching strategy to bring about the writing skill.

F. Evaluation as a Teaching Tool

As shown in the preceding discussion, evaluation is both a tool for measuring and teaching. When students use criteria to measure their own and their fellow students performance they consider the desired behavior from a different viewpoint.

To evaluate you must be able to discriminate the subtle differences between expert, competent, marginal and ineffective performance. Each evaluation exercise reinforces the student's understanding of the behavior.

G. Competence Performance—Task 8

This is your opportunity to test your ability to write a learning objective that meets the performance standard for this book; a rating of 10 against the six criteria for a useful objective.

On the following pages are six problems representing a range of behaviors where training is required. Pick the one(s) that match your area of expertise and write a Module Objective or Core Objective.

You may construct your objectives using either of the following Sentence or Component Formats. As with all previous assignments, you can compare your answer to the author's on page 527.

Sentence Format

Title: Describe the Transaction

Given (insert the conditions), **the** (state the job title of the performer) **will be able to** (describe the performance) **that** (describe the principal criteria) **within** (state the time limit for the performance). (Define or reference, if applicable, any abstract words.)

Component Format

Title: Describe the Transaction

Performer:	**The** (state the job title of the performer) **will be able to,**
Performance:	Describe the performance.
Performance Time:	**Within** (state the time limit for the performance).
Criteria:	**That** (describe the principal criteria). Note: The words **which, in relation to** or **based upon** can be substituted for **that.**
Conditions:	**Given** (insert the conditions),
Concrete Language:	Define or reference, if applicable, any abstract words.

Problem 1—Meetings

You have been asked to conduct a training program for 12 sales managers that enables them to conduct effective meetings with their salespeople. The V.P. of Sales observes that the sales managers are not effective conducting meetings to solve problems and that they have difficulty getting people involved in meaningful discussions. You will have up to 2 full days to conduct the training and access to videotape recording equipment.

Problem 2—Financial Arrangements

You are to design a course for a group of salespeople on the preparation of a Retail Installment Contract. These salespeople sell consumer goods with a value between $500 and $1000. The finance arrangement will enable their consumers to finance their purchases.

The contracts must be 100 percent accurate. Any errors in calculation or description of the property will result in the finance company rejecting the contract. (Salespeople are not paid until the finance company accepts the contract.) The salespeople will use a <u>calculation chart</u> supplied by the finance company to calculate the required contract entries. These include the monthly payment, interest rate, total of payments and deferred payment price. The unpaid balance (cost of the goods purchased) is used to enter the <u>calculation chart</u>. Assuming the salesperson has completed a purchase order and uses a pocket calculator, the required calculations and contract can be filled out in 5 minutes.

Problem 3—Investment Advice

You are to teach a course to a group of financial advisors. These people must assist clients in selecting investments. The investments must be consistent with the risk tolerance, personal objectives and financial position of the client. The company's products range in risk from commodities, options, stocks, bonds, real estate, mutual funds and real estate investment trusts all the way to money market mutual funds and life insurance. The company that employs these financial advisors desires to maintain a long term relationship with each client. Sound advice is critical and most advice is put into writing. It takes approximately 30 minutes to write a written justification for a particular recommendation.

Problem 4—One on One Training

You have been asked to conduct training for a group of ten new managers who work with salespeople. These salespeople sell a range of intangible products. The managers must conduct individualized training for each salesperson based on their needs. Stated another way, the manager must correct the specific problem with each salesperson's performance. Most of the sales presentations used by the salespeople last about 5 minutes. The company prescribes a method it calls the One-on-One Training Technique, which it wants these new managers to use. The One-on-One method consists of contracting with the salesperson on the problem to be solved, having the salesperson conduct a sales discussion with the manager acting as the customer and discussing the salesperson's performance. This is followed by the manager acting as the salesperson and the salesperson acting as the customer. A discussion also follows the manager's "model" (demonstration). Finally, the salesperson is asked to perform again. The manager's objective is to measure the improvement in performance as a result of the session.

Problem 5—Selection Interview

You have been asked to conduct training for a group of 12 managers who conduct selection interviews. You plan to teach them a behavioral interviewing technique. Behavioral interviewing involves asking preplanned questions to obtain information from the candidate about how they have performed in the past in relation to job relevant selection criteria. The interviewer's objective is to collect two to three complete behavioral examples for each of 7 job criteria. A behavioral example is a measurable response that is similar to the components of a learning objective. The candidate describes the situation he/she faced, the action he/she took, and the result his/her action (behavior) produced. The interview is structured to cover 7 job relevant selection criteria and background information from two previous jobs within 60 minutes. An expert interviewer can achieve 21 behavioral examples. Acceptable performance is 14 behavioral examples. The interview guides that the manager will use were developed by a job analysis process.

Problem 6—Product/Contract Knowledge

You have been asked to conduct training for a group of 20 life insurance agents on a new life insurance policy. The company wants them to understand the benefits, exclusions and policy conditions. Product knowledge is very important and there is a concern that the agent not misrepresent the product when explaining any policy provision. Expert performance involves the ability to locate data within a policy and describe the policy's features, benefits, limitations and conditions. The agent must also be able to describe the policy's response (to pay or not to pay) in relationship to an event.

Note: The subject of this objective is technical knowledge of contracts. Hence, you may substitute "legal contract" for the words "life insurance policy."

7
Training Process Objectives

Effective Training produces **Desired Behavior**
Desired Behavior *produces Results*

Another class of objectives deals specifically with the methodology employed to bring about learning. These may be called Training Process Objectives. *A Training Process Objective is an objective which describes, from the learner's viewpoint, the behaviors the instructor will use to enable the learner to understand, accept and perform the desired behavior.* Here is an example:

- **Baseline Performance:** <u>Given a series of statements describing uses of learning objectives, a technical knowledge self test and a rating scale,</u> **determine behavioral needs** *in relationship to the module objective.*

This objective was designed to create an awareness in the reader of his or her need to learn about objectives. It was accomplished by giving the reader three tasks to perform: write a set of objectives, rate your use of objectives and test your actual knowledge (pages 17–18). The performance of these tasks enables the readers to **determine** their **behavioral needs** *in relationship to the Module (Part 1) Objective.* **Behavioral needs** refers to a performance discrepancy that is caused by a lack of skill or knowledge.

As evidenced by the fact that you are at this stage of the book, one could conclude that sufficient motivation has been created and sustained. This phase of the process could be classified as the motivation phase of the training process (see Fig. 7.1).

A. Training Process Expressed as Objectives

Each phase of the training process can be expressed from the learner's viewpoint using the components of a useful objective. For example, consider the demonstra-

---

Figure 7.1. The Training Process

- Introduction
- Motivation (Baseline Performance)
- Explanation
- Demonstration (Modeling)
- Performance (Practice Exercises)
- Evaluation (Competence Performance)
- Conclusion

---

tion (modeling) phase of the training process in a program that teaches an interactive sales or management behavior.

- **Model (before explanation):** <u>Given a model by the instructor,</u> **describe the structure of the desired behavior** *in terms of criteria* (as listed in the Performance Evaluation Form).

Assuming this objective followed the prefacing statement, **"the developer will be able to,"** one can see that it contains the Performer, Performance, Conditions and Criteria Components. Only the Performance Time is missing.

The **"Model (before explanation)"** objective communicates the fact that the instructor is going to demonstrate the behavior before explaining it. Then the instructor will use the demonstration to evoke a discussion of the behavior's structure. A variation of this technique was used on pages 20 through 38.

On page 19 I listed the Objectives of Part 1. This served two purposes. First, the objectives inform the reader of the knowledge and skill that will be acquired. Second, they are presented as a model of a useful set of objectives. In the section entitled the Learning Objective Principle, beginning on page 20, I discussed the structural components of a learning objective. Indeed, the Module Objective for Part 1 (page 19) contains all of the structural components. The discussion concludes on page 38 with the six <u>Criteria for Measuring the Usefulness of an Objective</u>. These criteria, of course, represent the structure of the behavior.

The modeling objective could also be written, if desired, as follows:

- **Model with Performance Evaluation (after explanation):** <u>Given a model by the instructor,</u> **evaluate the behavior** *using the criteria, rating scale and scoring system listed in the Performance Evaluation Form.*

In this case the instructor would hold his or her performance up as a model and allow the student to rate it using previously established criteria. This technique is particularly helpful to students, as they get to see expert performance and practice using the evaluation system. Such exercises have been used throughout this book, for example on page 46 (Using the System to Measure an Objective) and on page 78 (Measuring the Objectives for this Book). In the latter exercise, the reader uses the Evaluation Form for a Set of Objectives to measure this volume's learning objectives (see page 79).

The process of evaluation (Competence Performance) can also be expressed as a Training Process Objective written from the learner's viewpoint.

- **Competence Performance:** Given a problem or narrative describing a situation, **perform and evaluate performance** *using the criteria, rating scale and scoring system listed in the Performance Evaluation Form.*

This technique was used on page 55, in the section entitled Test Your Writing Skill—Task 6. Here the reader is given an objective containing a number of flaws (one false condition and criteria, two performances and several abstract words). The reader is asked to write two objectives, one for suggesting wine and another for serving wine, that contain all the components of a useful objective. The two model Module Objectives on page 522 enable the reader to compare and contrast their answers to the author's

This Training Process Objective was used again in the section entitled Competence Performance—Task 8 (pages 91–93). There the reader is given a series of narratives describing a desired behavior that will be the subject of a training program. The reader is asked to write a Core or Module learning objective that meets the performance standard for this book (an Effectiveness Rating of 10).

A slight variation of the **Competence Performance** objective is found in the objective for the **Practice Exercises** throughout the book. In each case, the reader is asked to evaluate a series of statements to determine if they meet the criterion under discussion. These exercises, which appear at various places in the book, were designed to help the reader build confidence and competence with measurement.

- **Practice Exercises:** Given a problem, **perform and evaluate performance** *using the criteria and scoring system.*

Even the Introduction (of a book or training program) can be expressed as a Training Process Objective written from the learner's viewpoint. In this case, no conditions or criteria are stated.

- **Introduction:** Identify issues which are relevant to the module's (Part 1's) learning objectives.

On pages 13–17, in the section, Foundation or Formality?, I raised three issues which are relevant to the subject of learning objectives. This included the absence of Available Training (on writing objectives), the lack of Consistency and Uniformity and the existence of a Raging Controversy about the need for predetermined objectives.

The conclusion of Part 1 is also based on a Training Process Objective. In this instance, the reader is asked to complete a Student Evaluation of Training form (App. C) and mail it to me on completion of Part 1.

B. Explanation of the Knowledge and Skills

The explanation phase of the training is described by its learning objectives. In Fig. 7.2 I have listed the section titles of Part 1 in relation to the objective which they achieve. (Refer to Table of Contents.) This is an example of linking the learning objectives to the content of the training program.

Figure 7.2. Learning Objectives for this Book Linked to Section Content

Module Objective

Write a Learning Objective: Given a performance discrepancy that is caused by a lack of skill or knowledge on a subject that the instructional developer has mastered, the developer (reader) will be able to write a learning objective that contains performance, criteria, conditions and time components within 12 minutes which achieves an Effectiveness Rating of 10 (on a 10 scale) against prescribed criteria.

Complexity and the Writing of Learning Objectives (Chap.6)
Performance Evaluation Systems (Chap. 8)
A Point of View (Chap. 9)

Unit Objectives

To accomplish the Module Objective, the Instructional Developer will be able to:

1. Write a definition of a learning objective.

   The Learning Objective Principle (Chap. 2)

2. List 6 components of a useful objective.

   The Learning Objective Principle (Chap. 2)

3. List 6 criteria (standards) that would measure the usefulness of a core, terminal, program or module objective.

   The Learning Objective Principle (Chap. 2)
   Measuring the Desired Behavior (Chap. 3)

4. Given 6 criteria, a Rating Scale and a learning objective, calculate the Effectiveness Rating of the learning objective with an accuracy of $+/- 1.0$ against the author's solution.

   Measuring the Usefulness of Objectives (Chap. 3)

5. Differentiate between Core, Module and Unit Objectives.

   The Hierarchical Structure of Objectives (Chap. 4)
   Training Process Objectives (Chap. 7)

6. Calculate an Effectiveness Rating for a set of learning objectives.

   Measuring a Set of Learning Objectives (Chap. 5)

Figure 7.3 lists the Training Process Objectives for Part 1 linked to the section titles of Part 1, the Tasks and the Practice Exercises.

Figure 7.3. Training Process Objectives Linked to Content

The developer (reader) will be able to:

- **Introduction:** Identify issues which are relevant to the Book's learning objectives.
Foundation or Formality?

- **Baseline Performance:** <u>Given a series of statements describing uses of learning objectives, a technical knowledge self test and a rating scale,</u> **determine behavioral needs** *in relationship to the module objective.*
Where do you stand? (A Self Test) Tasks 1 through 3.

- **Model (before explanation):** <u>Given a model by the instructor,</u> **describe the structure of the desired behavior** (as listed in the Performance Evaluation Form) *in terms of criteria.*
Objectives of Book One (page 19)

- **Explanation:** The learning objectives of Part 1. (Refer to Fig. 7.2.)

- **Model with Performance Evaluation (after explanation):** <u>Given a model by the instructor,</u> **evaluate the behavior** *using the criteria, rating scale and scoring system listed in the Performance Evaluation Form.*
Using the System to Measure an Objective
An Objective for a Complex Interactive Sales Behavior
An Objective for a Complex Behavior
An Objective for a Complex Interactive Consulting Behavior
Measuring a Set of Learning Objectives

- **Practical Exercise:** <u>Given a problem,</u> **perform and evaluate performance** *using the criteria and scoring system.*

1 & 2—Use of the Criterion Scoring System	5—Conditions Component
3—Classifying Components	6—Criteria Component
4—Performance Component	7—Concrete Language

- **Competence Performance:** <u>Given a problem or narrative describing a situation,</u> **perform and evaluate performance** *using the criteria, rating scale and scoring system listed in the Performance Evaluation Form.*
Test Your Evaluation Skill—Task 4 and 5
Test Your Writing Skill—Task 6
Evaluating a Set of Objectives—Task 7
Competence Performance—Task 8

- **Conclusion:** <u>Given a survey form and a rating scale,</u> **score the learning objectives achieved (or not) and value the program's success in meeting their identified needs.**
Student Evaluation of Training Form

C. Training Process Objectives in Relation to the Hierarchical Structure

Training Process Objectives are to be treated as Unit Objectives within the Hierarchical Structure. This means that they do not have to meet all 6 <u>Criteria for a Useful Objective</u>. Figure 7.4 demonstrates the training design for Part 1.

Notice that Training Process Objectives appear <u>before</u> and <u>after</u> the Unit Objectives (numbered 1 through 6). Also notice that following Unit Objective 4 there are three Training Process Objectives. This demonstrates conceptually the integration of modeling, practice and evaluation (competence performance) with the units of knowledge and skill.

The Competence Performance following Unit Objective 4 is labeled Competence Performance 1. Following Unit Objective 6, the same Training Process Objective is labeled Competence Performance 2. This indicates that the learner is given two opportunities to write learning objectives and receive feedback (provided in this book by the Criteria to Measure the Usefulness of Objectives and model objectives which present an answer for each exercise).

Figure 7.4. The Training Design for Part 1:
Integration of Learning and Training Process Objectives

Module Objective

Write a Learning Objective: <u>Given a performance discrepancy that is caused by a lack of skill or knowledge on a subject that the instructional developer has mastered,</u> the developer (reader) will be able to **write a learning objective** *that contains performance, criteria, conditions and time components* within 12 minutes which achieves an Effectiveness Rating of 10 (on a 10 scale) against prescribed criteria.

Unit Objectives and Training Method

To accomplish the Module Objective, the Instructional Developer will be able to:

- **Introduction:** Identify issues which are relevant to the module's (Part 1's) learning objectives.

- **Baseline Performance:** <u>Given a series of statements describing uses of learning objectives, a technical knowledge self test and a rating scale,</u> **determine behavioral needs** *in relationship to the module objective.*

- **Model (before explanation):** <u>Given a model by the instructor,</u> **describe the structure of the desired behavior** (as listed in the Performance Evaluation Form) *in terms of criteria.*

Explanation of the Knowledge and Skills:

1. Write a definition of a learning objective.

2. List 6 components of a useful objective.

Figure 7.4. *(Continued)* The Training Design for Part 1:
Integration of Learning and Training Process Objectives

3. List 6 criteria (standards) that would measure the usefulness of a core, terminal, program or module objective.

4. Given 6 criteria, a Rating Scale and a learning objective, calculate the Effectiveness Rating of the learning objective with an accuracy of +/- 1.0 against the author's solution.

- **Model with Performance Evaluation (after explanation):** <u>Given a model by the instructor,</u> **evaluate the behavior** *using the criteria, rating scale and scoring system listed in the Performance Evaluation Form.*

- **Practical Exercise:** <u>Given a problem,</u> **perform and evaluate performance** *using the criteria and scoring system.*

- **Competence Performance 1:** <u>Given a problem or narrative describing a situation,</u> **perform and evaluate performance** *using the criteria, rating scale and scoring system listed in the Performance Evaluation Form.*

5. Differentiate between Core, Module and Unit Objectives.

6. Calculate an Effectiveness Rating for a set of learning objectives.

- **Competence Performance 2:** <u>Given a problem or narrative describing a situation,</u> **perform and evaluate performance** *using the criteria, rating scale and scoring system listed in the Performance Evaluation Form.*

- **Conclusion:** <u>Given a survey form and a rating scale,</u> **score the learning objectives achieved (or not) and value the program's success in meeting their identified needs.**

D. Summary—Training Process Objectives

Training Process Objectives represent the methodology employed by the instructor to bring about the desired behavior contained within a Module or Core Objective. *They describe, from the learner's viewpoint, the behaviors the instructor will use to enable the learner to understand, accept and perform the desired behavior.* They can be integrated with the Unit Objectives to form a training design. Within the Hierarchical Structure, Training Process Objectives are treated as Unit Objectives in terms of the components of a useful objective that they must contain.

Training Process Objectives are the developer's tools for planning instruction. Therefore, I suggest they not be displayed with the Learning Objectives. As shown above, they are highly technical and when shown to students detract from the message conveyed by the Learning Objectives. The training methodology (role play, baseline performance, practice and competence performance) can and should be explained in an agenda.

Appendix F contains a complete training module for an interactive training session on Developing Learning Objectives. On page 436, the Training Method, you will notice that a time value has been assigned to each Unit and Training Process Objective. This enables the time for the training event to be linked directly to objectives.

8
Performance
Evaluation Systems

Mager's Principle
 "A description of a performance you want learners to be able to exhibit **before
 you consider them competent.**"

The ability to determine learner competence requires a system to measure performance (observed behavior). An effective system consists of criteria to judge each component of the behavior, a scoring system, a rating scale, a formula for determining the rating, instructions for calculating the rating and, for most situations, a role play case or problem which simulates the conditions under which the behavior is used.

This chapter deals with the evaluation of observed interactive behavior. Interactive behaviors are those that occur between two or more people who are working together to reach agreement on a course of action to achieve their goals. These behaviors are seen in sales, management, customer relations and training situations.

The measurement techniques are also applicable to cognitive behaviors such as writing and measuring a learning objective. Psychomotor skills such as serving wine or serving a tennis ball can also be measured using the techniques described in this chapter. In fact, the techniques are applicable to behavior at all levels of the taxonomy.

However, the testing of technical knowledge with multiple choice, true/false or matching type exercises is not addressed. The measurement of knowledge based behaviors has been adequately covered by other authors. The reader is directed to Bloom (1956) for examples of test items for a variety of knowledge based learning outcomes.

Listed on the following page are the learning objectives for this chapter. This is a departure from the structure of previous chapters. The content and methodology used in Chaps. 1 through 7 were driven by the objectives on page 19 for writing learning objectives. **We now build on that foundation and take the process to its logical conclusion: The measurement of the learner's competence, which is the result brought about by the objective and the instruction developed from it.**

A. Objectives for This Chapter

Module Objective

Evaluate Performance: Given a learning objective (rated 10) on an activity where the developer is a competent performer, the developer will be able to construct a Performance Evaluation System that measures interactive behaviors related to sales, management, training or customer relations transactions using *Expert Criteria* which produces a rating variation of no more than +/- 10 percent by two or more trained observers.

Unit Objectives

To accomplish the Module Objective, the reader will be able to:

1. Describe the role of the developer and the subject expert.
2. Describe the structure of a Performance Evaluation System.
3. Describe *Expert Criteria.*
4. Describe the relationship between the Learning Objective and the Performance Evaluation System.
5. Describe the use of the rating scale and scoring system in measuring the performer and the training.
6. Describe the structure of the evaluation form in relation to the formula and instructions for scoring.
7. Describe the process for developing a reliable Performance Evaluation System.
8. Describe a system for measuring an interactive sales behavior including the relationship between the learning objective, behavioral documentation and the structure of the evaluation form.
9. Describe the use of the performance evaluation form in measuring the desired behavior in relation to Needs Analysis, Competence Performance and Post Training Evaluation.

B. The Role of the Developer and the Subject Expert

Effective Training produces **Desired Behavior**
Desired Behavior *produces Results*

Training is the methodology employed to bring about a desired behavior in the student. The desired behavior is the methodology employed by the performer to bring about a result on the job. This concept implies that the development of training requires the efforts of two parties; the program developer and the subject expert. In some cases these are the same person. In other cases, a developer works on a team with one or more subject experts.

The developer is the architect of the training. Like an architect, a program developer designs the training and advises subject experts on the methodology that will enable students to acquire the new skills.

A subject expert is a person who can describe the criteria for expert performance. Generally, this is a person who has practical experience in the subject being taught. The optimum subject expert is a top performer who can describe the structure of a behavior or process and the reason behind each step. As a general rule, a developer should observe the subject expert performing on the job.

Listed below are the key questions to ask a subject expert. These enable the developer to translate the expert's skills into the components of a learning objective.

- What would we observe when a person is performing competently? Expertly? These become the criteria for expert performance. (See example on the following pages.)
- What background knowledge is essential, important or nice to know?
- What types of situations will a person be in when they use this behavior?
- What resources would they have available?
- How long should the performance take?
- To what standard, if any, shall the learner be held?

Once the objectives are written, the subject expert and the developer identify **any and all criteria** that they will use to measure the performance. They also create problems for the students to solve or role play cases that simulate the situation that the person faces on the job. Once these critical tasks are completed, the team can begin writing the training manual. Figure 8.1 depicts the relationship between developing the training and measuring learner competence.

C. *Expert Criteria*

Expert Criteria represent the observable behaviors (performance) of a person having knowledge and skill derived from training or experience that can be used to judge the performance of learners or performers. The term is derived from the following definitions:

- **Criteria:** Standards upon which a judgment or decision can be based.
- **Expert:** A person with special skill or knowledge representing mastery of a particular subject. Hence the term subject expert.

In Chaps. 1 through 7 you used *Expert Criteria* to evaluate learning objectives. The criteria, as you may recall from an earlier discussion (page 37), also represent the component structure of the behavior. This is an important point. The act of

Figure 8.1. Developing Training and Measuring Learner Competence

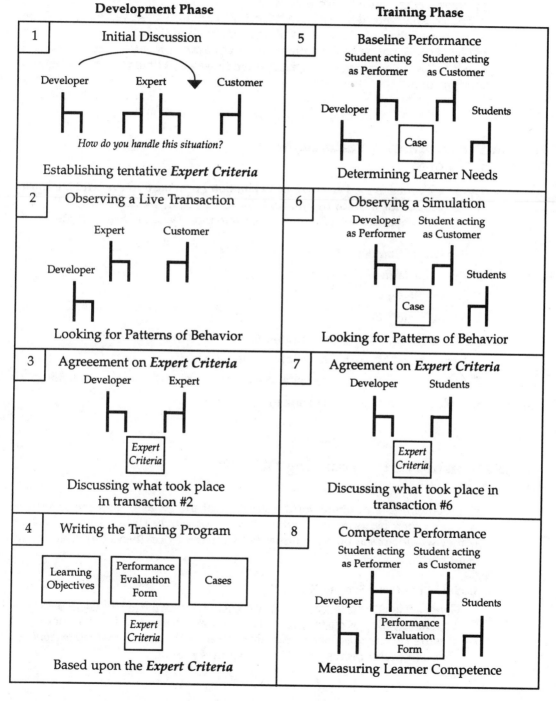

Development Phase — Training Phase

1. Initial Discussion — Developer, Expert, Customer — *How do you handle this situation?* — Establishing tentative *Expert Criteria*

5. Baseline Performance — Student acting as Performer, Student acting as Customer, Developer, Students, Case — Determining Learner Needs

2. Observing a Live Transaction — Expert, Customer, Developer — Looking for Patterns of Behavior

6. Observing a Simulation — Developer as Performer, Student acting as Customer, Students, Case — Looking for Patterns of Behavior

3. Agreeement on *Expert Criteria* — Developer, Expert, *Expert Criteria* — Discussing what took place in transaction #2

7. Agreement on *Expert Criteria* — Developer, Students, *Expert Criteria* — Discussing what took place in transaction #6

4. Writing the Training Program — Learning Objectives, Performance Evaluation Form, Cases, *Expert Criteria* — Based upon the *Expert Criteria*

8. Competence Performance — Student acting as Performer, Student acting as Customer, Developer, Students, Performance Evaluation Form — Measuring Learner Competence

evaluation simultaneously reinforces the desired behavior by bringing the criteria of expert performance to a conscious level.

The criteria were derived from Mager's Learning Objective Principle. They were refined through the process of using them to evaluate the performance of students participating in the author's program development classes. Criteria are effective (useful) when they are stated in such a way that limits the chance for misinterpretation.

D. The Structure of a Performance Evaluation Form

Figure 8.2 contains the Performance Evaluation Form used to evaluate the learning objectives for a **Training Module**. From this form we can identify the key structural components of a Performance Evaluation System. These include:

1. Behavioral Component.
2. *Expert Criteria.*
3. Scoring System.
4. Rating Scale.
5. Matrix for recording scores, ratings and the Effectiveness Rating.
6. Formula and Instructions for calculating ratings.
7. Identification of the performer and the rater (person doing the evaluation).
8. A place for comments (not shown).

E. Relationship of the Learning Objective to Criteria

The following is an example of the structure of the behavior and the criteria to measure expert performance for the following objective. These are shown below as they would appear on a Performance Evaluation Form (henceforth referred to as a PEF):

Module Objective—Serving Wine

Given a waiter's corkscrew, an unopened bottle of wine, a white towel and 2 students acting as customers, be able to **present, open and serve a bottle of wine** *following the 5-step procedure outlined in the server's manual, without error, and execute each step with finesse* within 4 minutes.

Figure 8.2. A Performance Evaluation Form

Evaluation Form for a Set of Learning Objectives—Training Program

Program _____ Developer _____ (7) Rater _____ (7) Date _____

Core Objective (1)

A. Contains the job title of the performer and the words "be able to" immediately before the active verb.
B. Contains the performance which describes the desired behavior to be exhibited.
C. Contains a fixed time limit for the performance.
D. Contains criteria to measure the (2) red behavior at program's end.
E. Contains conditions which describe the situation, limitations imposed or non-implicit resources.
F. Contains concrete image provoking language and any abstractions are referenced to criteria.

Total Score.
Rating—(Divide Total by 6) (6)

Module Objective (1)

A. Contains the job title of the performer and the words "be able to" immediately before the active verb.
B. Contains a performance which describes the desired behavior to be exhibited.
C. Contains a fixed time limit for the performance.
D. Contains criteria to measure the (2) red behavior during the program.
E. Contains conditions which describe the situation, limitations imposed or non-implicit resources.
F. Contains concrete image provoking language and any abstractions are referenced to criteria.

Total Score.
Rating—(Divide Total by 6) Group Rating—(Divide Total by # of Objectives rated) (6) (6)

Total of Ratings (Core plus the Average Group Rating of the Module Objectives)
Effectiveness Rating (Total divided by 2)

Criterion Scoring (3)

10 Meets Criterion
5 Questionable
0 Does Not Meet or Not Evident

Effectiveness Rating (4)

8.0 to 10	Effective
5.0 to 7.9	Marginal
1.0 to 4.9	Ineffective
0.0 to 0.9	Not Evident

(5)

1	2	3	4	5	6

Average Group Rating

Expert Criteria for Serving Wine

How effectively did the server:

____ **Present the wine:** Bottle is presented to ordering patron, label up and acceptance is ascertained.

____ **Cut the wrapper:** The waiter's corkscrew is opened prior to approaching the customer. The wrapper is placed in the waiter's apron. *All moves are smooth and crisp.*

____ **Open the bottle:** Bottle is placed on the towel on table in view of patron. Cork is removed *intact, in one motion,* and placed in front of the patron.

____ **Gain acceptance:** 3/4 inch is poured into ordering patron's glass. The corkscrew is closed and placed in apron pocket while patron samples. Acceptance is ascertained. *No wine is spilled and glass is not touched. No item is dropped or disturbed.*

____ **Serve the wine:** Permission is obtained based on time required for the wine to breathe. Wine is poured for female guests first, ordering patron last and served from right to left. Wine is poured to within 1 inch and the *action is finished with a twist of the bottle. No wine is spilled and glass is not touched. No item is dropped or disturbed.* Bottle is placed in the holder. Need for additional service is ascertained.

____ **Act professionally:** Attitude indicates a desire to please, actions are non-intrusive, responds to customer participation. Demeanor is both friendly and business like.

____ **Time:** Within 4 minutes. (Deduct 1 point for each 30 seconds of excess time)

____ Total Score

____ Effectiveness Rating (Divide the Total Score by 7)

In the above, the criteria shown in *italics measure the server's finesse.* Also notice that *acting as a professional* was identified as a desired part of the performance even though it was not shown in the objective. This is an example of identifying **any and all criteria** used to measure the performance.

F. The Structure of the Behavior

The example on the previous page enables us to discuss several key issues in the development of Performance Evaluation Systems. The first involves the derivation of the behavior's structure and the criteria to measure each component of the behavior. Notice that the Performance Component contains the following verbs: **present, open and serve a bottle of wine.** These establish the beginning and end of the transaction.

In this performance we can assume that the patron has ordered the wine since this transaction begins with the presentation of the selected wine. The transaction ends with the initial wine service. This means that we do not intend to observe or measure refilling patron wine glasses or ascertaining the ordering patron's desire for additional bottles of wine.

Both the Performance and Criteria Component provide direction as to the structure of the desired behavior. In the previous example, the Criteria Component of the learning objective referred to *"following the 5-step procedure outlined in the server's manual."* This provided the developer and the subject expert with the structure or components of the behavior. Shown in the following are the active verbs in relation to the structure of the behavior on the PEF.

Active Verbs in the Performance Component	*Components (Structure) of the Behavior on the PEF*
Present	Present the Wine
Open	Cut the wrapper
	Open the bottle
Serve	Gain acceptance
	Serve the wine

G. The Structure of the Criteria

The next key point involves the structure of each behavioral component. The criteria which follows the component enables us to judge if the performance is acceptable.

Component of Behavior	*Criteria*
Cut the wrapper:	The waiter's corkscrew is opened prior to approaching the customer. The wrapper is placed in the waiter's apron. *All moves are smooth and crisp.*

H. The Scoring System and Rating Scale

The Scoring System and Rating Scale are key components in the structure of the Performance Evaluation System. They provide a basis to both evaluate and discuss performance by causing the performer, fellow students and instructor to make judgments about the quality of the observed performance. The act of judging requires that each observer look carefully for the key criteria that represent expert performance.

Scoring Systems

In Chaps. 3 through 5 you used the Criterion Scoring System (10 - 5 - 0) to judge each component of a Learning Objective. This system is based on using precisely stated criteria that enable you to judge that something is or is not acceptable or is questionable. The Criterion Scoring System is most applicable to judging written materials.

Criterion Scoring System

10   Meets the Criterion

5   Questionable

0   Does Not Meet or Not Evident

Judging an interactive behavior where the performer exhibits confidence and finesse in relation to criteria requires a broader scale. The system that I have found to be most useful is a 5-point scale based on the numbers 0 to 4.

The 0-4 Scoring System

Scoring		Description of Performance
4	Expert	Performs with *finesse & confidence* and meets <u>all</u> criteria.
3	Effective	Performs with *confidence* and meets <u>75 percent</u> of the criteria.
2	Marginal	Performs *mechanically* <u>or</u> meets <u>50 percent</u> of the criteria.
1	Ineffective	Performs *mechanically* <u>and</u> meets <u>less than 50 percent</u> of the criteria.
0	Not Evident	None of the criteria met.
N	Not Applicable	The criterion is not applicable to the problem.

The key to the 0-4 Scoring System is true zero: not evident. This enables the scale values to be added and multiplied. Another benefit of 5 points is the ability to differentiate expert performance from effective performance.

A score of zero, **Not Evident,** means that a desired component of the behavior has not been exhibited. If the component of the behavior is evident, then we use the criteria to determine the level of competence. This leads to a score of 1, 2, 3 or 4.

Importance of Whole Numbers in Scoring

Only whole numbers are used in scoring. This encourages the observer to make a firm decision and to justify that decision with the criteria. If you allow 1/2 point ratings (e.g., 3.5) you have created an 8-point scale. In many cases, there are not enough sub criteria to differentiate 8 levels of competence. The following criteria and discussion demonstrate the principle.

> ___ **Open the bottle:** Bottle is placed on the towel on table in view of patron. Cork is removed *intact, in one motion,* and placed in front of the patron.

A score of 4 indicates that the performer met all criteria. A score of 3 could be justified by the omission of any component. For example, the server placed the cork in his or her apron rather than in front of the patron. The server's failure to remove the cork in one motion could justify a score of 2, especially if uncorking required two or more moves. Breaking the cork might also justify a score of 2. A score of one would be justifiable if the server made all of the above errors including failure to place the bottle on the towel. A score of 0 could only occur if the server was unable to remove the cork.

The Effectiveness Rating

The **Effectiveness Rating** describes the overall competence of the performance. It is <u>derived</u> by dividing the total of the scores for each evaluated component by the number of components. The following is an example:

The 0-4 Rating Scale

Rating	Description	Description of Performance
3.6–4.0	Expert	Performs with *finesse and confidence* and meets <u>90 percent</u> of the criteria.
3.0–3.5	Effective	Performs with *confidence* and meets <u>75 percent</u> of the criteria.
2.0–2.9	Marginal	Performs *mechanically* <u>or</u> meets <u>50 percent</u> of the criteria.
1.0–1.9	Ineffective	Performs *mechanically* <u>and</u> meets <u>less than 50 percent</u> of the criteria.
0.0–0.9	Not Evident	*Unable to perform.*

Notice that the Rating Scale uses fractional numbers and provides a range of ratings (i.e., 3.6 to 4.0). The range permits us to recognize the competence of the performance while simultaneously identifying a strength or discrepancy in one or more components.

The use of the 0-4 Rating Scales can be demonstrated by the following description of a pilot's performance when landing an airplane. My friend Rick demonstrated expert performance in 95 percent of the landings he made. This was discernable from the fact that he would land on the runway numbers with total smoothness. In other words, the airplane's wheels scuffed along the ground before he let the full weight of the airplane settle upon them. It was an impressive performance, and you could not feel the landing.

My landings scored "effective" most of the time. I could land within the first third of the runway without bouncing. Occasionally, they would score "marginal." This occurred when the airplane bounced once or twice. Rarely were they "ineffective": that is multiple bounces or a loss of control or wandering off the runway. An interesting note: Under this system a loss of control resulting in a crash landing would receive a score of "not evident."

Measuring the Performer and the Training

The following Matrix of Performance (Fig. 8.3) shows the scores and ratings for a wine service performance of six performers. The Effectiveness Rating for performer "A" was calculated by dividing the total score by six, the number of scored components. The group rating is calculated in a similar manner.

The matrix also enables the instructor or developer to identify potential problems with the training. The group rating of 2.1 for **opening the bottle** suggests that the students require additional practice. This is confirmed by the fact that 4 of the 6 students scored 2 or below. By comparison, the group rating and component scores for **gaining acceptance** tell a different story. In this case 4 of the 6 students successfully performed. Two appear to have forgotten this important step in the wine service.

Figure 8.3. Matrix of Performance

A	B	C	D	E	F	Component	Group
4	4	3	3	4	3	Present the wine	3.5
4	4	3	2	4	2	Cut the wrapper	3.1
3	3	2	1	2	2	Open the bottle	2.1
4	4	4	4	0	0	Gain acceptance	2.6
3	4	2	4	3	3	Serve the wine	3.2
4	4	2	4	4	3	Act professionally	3.5
4	4	4	4	4	3	Time	3.8
26	27	21	22	20	16	Total Score	21.8
3.7	3.9	3.0	3.1	2.9	2.3	Effectiveness Rating (divide by 7)	3.1

I. Formula and Instructions for Calculating Ratings

In the previous example each of the components for serving wine is of equal value. Hence, the scores for each component are added together and inserted in the space labeled Total Score. The rating is derived by dividing the total score by 6 since each component is of equal value.

Figure 8.4 demonstrates weighting. If the developer desires to reinforce any portion of the behavior, then that component is isolated and a separate rating is

---

Figure 8.4. A Weighted Performance Evaluation Form

Expert Criteria for **Serving Wine**

How effectively did the server:

_3_ **Present the wine:** Bottle is presented to ordering patron, label up and acceptance is ascertained.

_2_ **Cut the wrapper:** The waiter's corkscrew is opened prior to approaching the customer. The wrapper is placed in the waiter's apron. *All moves are smooth and crisp.*

_1_ **Open the bottle:** Bottle is placed on the towel on table in view of patron. Cork is removed *intact, in one motion,* and placed in front of the patron.

_4_ **Gain acceptance:** 3/4 inch is poured into ordering patron's glass. The corkscrew is closed and placed in apron pocket while patron samples. Acceptance is ascertained. *No wine is spilled and glass is not touched. No item is dropped or disturbed.*

_4_ **Serve the wine:** Permission is obtained based on time required for the wine to breathe. Wine is poured for female guests first, ordering patron last and served from right to left. Wine is poured to within 1 inch and the *action is finished with a twist of the bottle. No wine is spilled and glass is not touched. No item is dropped or disturbed.* Bottle is placed in the holder. Need for additional service is ascertained.

_14_ Total Score

_2.8_ Rating (Divide the total score by 5)

_4_ **Act professionally:** Attitude indicates a desire to please, actions are non-intrusive, responds to customer participation. Demeanor is both friendly and business like.

_6.8_ Total Ratings

_3.2_ Effectiveness Rating (Divide by 2)

obtained. In the case below, **act professionally** now represents 50 percent of the Effectiveness Rating as compared to 17 percent in the previous example.

By treating **Act Professionally** as a separate rating (since the score of 4 was not added and divided) the overall Effectiveness Rating increased from 3.0 to 3.2. At the same time, the ability to isolate the rating for the psychomotor skill from the interactive behavior enables the instructor and student to determine the precise areas of learner competence. The learner above needs to work on the skill of using a waiter's corkscrew to cut the wrapper and open the bottle.

A Complex Example of Weighting

The PEF for measuring a Set of Learning Objectives (Fig. 8.6) visually demonstrates the structure of a matrix for recording the scores and ratings in relation to the formula for calculating the Effectiveness Rating. (See Fig. 8.5.)

Figure 8.5. Formula for the Effectiveness Rating

$$\frac{\text{Rating of the Superior Objective} + \text{Average of the Ratings of the Subordinate Objectives}}{2} = \text{Effectiveness Rating}$$

Instructions for Scoring and Rating

The instructions for calculating ratings must be shown on the PEF. Figure 8.7 shows the instructions for calculating the rating for the Core and Module Objectives as well as the instructions for calculating the overall Effectiveness Rating. In this case the ratings for the Core and Module Objectives are added together. Their sum is the **total of ratings**. The **total of ratings** is then divided by 2 to obtain the overall Effectiveness Rating.

It is desirable to show the scoring system and rating scale on the form.

J. Developing a Reliable Evaluation System

"A reliable measure is one that has a small error component and, therefore, does not fluctuate randomly from one moment to the next." (Kidder, 1985, p. 45) This is a must for a Performance Evaluation System and a critical part of the development process.

For purposes of evaluating observed interactive behavior or measuring written components of training, such as learning objectives, a rating error of less than 10 percent in relation to the subject expert's is desirable. Rating errors greater than 10 percent will tend to produce arguments by the trainees which detract from a productive discussion and evaluation of the performance.

Figure 8.6. PEF Reflecting the Formula

Evaluation Form for a Set of Learning Objectives—Training Program

Program_____ Developer _____ Rater _____ Date _____

Core Objective

A. Contains the job title of the performer and the words "be able to" immediately before the active verb.
B. Contains the performance which describes the desired behavior to be exhibited.
C. Contains a fixed time limit for the performance.
D. Contains criteria to measure the desired behavior at program's end.
E. Contains conditions which describe the situation, limitations imposed or non-implicit resources.
F. Contains concrete image provoking language and any abstractions are referenced to criteria.
Total Score.
Rating—(Divide Total by 6)

Objective #

	1	2	3	4	5	6

Module Objectives

A. Contains the job title of the performer and the words "be able to" immediately before the active verb.
B. Contains a performance which describes the desired behavior to be exhibited.
C. Contains a fixed time limit for the performance.
D. Contains criteria to measure the desired behavior during the program.
E. Contains conditions which describe the situation, limitations implied or non-implicit resources.
F. Contains concrete image provoking language and any abstractions are referenced to criteria.
Total Score.

Rating—(Divide Total by 6) Group Rating—(Divide Total by # of Objectives rated)

Average Group Rating

Total of Ratings (Core plus the Average Group Rating of the Module Objectives)
Effectiveness Rating (Total divided by 2)

Criterion Scoring

		Effectiveness Rating	
10	Meets Criterion	8.0 to 10	Effective
5	Questionable	5.0 to 7.9	Marginal
0	Does Not Meet or Not Evident	1.0 to 4.9	Ineffective
		0.0 to 0.9	Not Evident

Figure 8.7. Structure of a Performance Evaluation Form

Evaluation Form for a Set of Learning Objectives—Training Program

Program_____ Developer _____ Rater _____ Date _____

Core Objective

A.
B.
C.
D.
E.
F.
Total Score.
Rating—(Divide Total by 6)

Objective #

	1	2	3	4	5	6

Module Objective

A.
B.
C.
D.
E.
F.
Total Score.
Rating—(Divide Total by 6) Group Rating—(Divide Total by # of Objectives rated)

Average Group Rating

Total of Ratings (Core plus the Average Group Rating of the Module Objectives)
Effectiveness Rating (Total divided by 2)

Criterion Scoring

		Effectiveness Rating	
10	Meets Criterion	8.0 to 10	Effective
5	Questionable	5.0 to 7.9	Marginal
0	Does Not Meet or Not Evident	1.0 to 4.9	Ineffective
		0.0 to 0.9	Not Evident

It should be emphasized that the achievement of a reliable system is a process. It begins with having a group of subject experts using the proposed PEF to measure actual or simulated performance. This will produce an initial set of ratings and in all probability rating errors greater than 10 percent. It is at this point that the developer, working in combination with the subject experts, modifies the criteria or the formula for calculating the rating. Then the process is repeated with a revised form. Another performance is observed, ratings are compared and, where necessary, criteria modified. The process continues until a rating error of 5 percent or less is achieved (among the experts).

For example, in a study on the influence of alcohol on the victims and perpetrator's of crimes, trained observers rode with police and recorded data. However, they could not give breathalizer tests. Hence, an instrument was devised to measure levels of intoxication from the <u>visual symptoms exhibited by subjects</u>. To develop the instrument, criteria were established and the ratings obtained were validated against breathalizer data. The subjects were people in emergency rooms who volunteered to take a breathalizer. The process resulted in a highly reliable instrument that was then used by trained observers in the study.

The next step is testing with a group of students. In this case the evaluation form is used to measure their performance. Expect some problems at this juncture. Again, it will be necessary to make a few adjustments to the criteria.

The criteria in the evaluation you used to measure learning objectives were developed by the process described above. My students and I often debated rating errors at great length. In many cases, we negotiated the language of each criterion to achieve the desired measurement. The result of this effort produced a reliable instrument. I am confident that if you have read this far, your Effectiveness Ratings on the sample objectives were within plus or minus 10 percent of those given as model ratings.

Getting the "Bugs" Out

A "bug" is defined as an unexpected defect, fault, flaw or imperfection. A "bug" in a computer system causes the system to fail or to produce flawed data. Computer vendors attempt to correct these "bugs" before they deliver the system to their customers.

A "bug" in a performance evaluation system detracts from the discussion of the performance. Instructors and students waste time debating the criteria or fairness of the system. Therefore, the goal is to remove as many flaws before using the system with a group of students.

The scoring system holds the key to debugging a system. This is due to the fact that the overall Effectiveness Rating is derived from the scoring of the individual components of the behavior. By making the criterion for each of the components sufficiently precise, the resulting Effectiveness Ratings will be within the 10 percent tolerance.

The rule for discussing scoring variance is to concentrate on the area of greatest variance. Therefore, with a 10 - 5 - 0 scale, ask the raters who rated the performance 10 and 0 to justify their ratings.

Consider the scores obtained for the evaluated objective in Fig. 8.8. Important: Notice that the criterion for the Performer Component is flawed. Also notice that the group score is dramatically different than the developer's score.

In this case, the vagueness of the criterion for the Performer Component has resulted in a sizable variance. Three raters say that the statement contains a usable Performer Component, while three say it does not. This suggests that the criterion for the Performer Component is flawed. Additionally, the 5 score in the Performance Component is justified by rater "F" and the developer by the fact that the passive statement "learn how to score" is not an observable performance.

By correcting the flawed criterion "written from the student's point of view" to "contains the job title of the performer and the words 'be able to' immediately before the active verb" we eliminate the ambiguity. Now the Performer Component of the evaluated objective must meet the three tests contained within the criterion. (See Fig. 8.9.)

As a result, the scores for the Performer Component all change to zero as the evaluated objective does not contain the words "be able to" or the job title of the performer. The discussion also results in a correction to the scores for the Performance Component.

Figure 8.8. Score Obtained as the Result of a Flawed Criterion

<u>Evaluated Objective</u>

You will learn how to score a criterion

<u>Criteria</u>

Performer: Written from the student's point of view.

Performance: Contains **the performance** to be exhibited. (Active verb[s] and the object of the verb describe <u>the desired behavior</u>.)

<u>Obtained Scores</u>

A	B	C	D	E	F	Component	Group	Developer
10	10	0	0	0	10	**Performer**	5.0	0.0
10	10	10	10	10	5	**Performance**	9.2	5.0

Figure 8.9. Score Obtained with the Corrected Criterion

<u>Evaluated Objective</u>

You will learn how to score a criterion

<u>Criteria</u>

Performer: Contains the **job title of the performer** and the words **"be able to"** immediately before the active verb.

Performance: Contains **the performance** to be exhibited. (Active verb[s] and the object of the verb describe <u>the desired behavior</u>.)

<u>Obtained Scores</u>

A	B	C	D	E	F	Component	Group	Developer
0	0	0	0	0	0	**Performer**	0.0	0.0
5	5	5	5	10	5	**Performance**	5.8	5.0

Rating Variance and the 0-4 Scoring System

The 0-4 Scoring System is particularly effective for discussing performance based on score variation. In the following example the developer's score is 3.0. Two raters match the developer's score and two fall within one point. Rater "E" is two points below the developer's and three points from Rater "A." Discussion would start with rater "E" and then move to rater "A."

Example Ratings

A	B	C	D	E	Component	Group	Developer
4	3	3	2	1	**Act Professionally**	2.6	3.0

Using Rating Variance

If we are in the process of debugging the performance evaluation system with subject experts, the focus of the discussion should concentrate on insuring that the criterion contains sufficient detail to enable any rater to state that the performance does or does not meet it. The developer and subject experts should observe and score performances until the rating errors are minimal.

During a discussion with students using a tested system, the discussion will concentrate on the observer's justification of their rating. In this case, the criteria rarely change. It should be noted that scoring errors (and the resulting rating errors) will decrease as the students gain experience with the evaluation system and competence with the desired behavior.

Clarification of *Expert Criteria*

Occasionally, it is necessary to supplement *Expert Criteria* with examples of ratings. Consider the following objective for a sales performance:

> **Probing to Discover Need:** <u>Given a data gathering form with preplanned questions and a student acting as a customer,</u> the salesperson will be able to **discover needs** *through the use of probing questions that relate to the benefits of one or more products* within 15 minutes.

The company was concerned that its salespeople would have difficulty asking probing questions. The concern was justified by the fact that the salesforce had been selling the company's products using a canned sales presentation. Salespeople had not been trained to discover needs through questioning. The company was also introducing a more sophisticated line of products.

To measure this performance, the developer created a case for each student playing the role of the prospect. The case contained the answers to every preplanned question that the salesperson would ask. It also contained supplementary information that the prospect could give if he or she were asked a probing question. For example the preplanned question on the data gathering form asks: "What is your most important goal?" The answer on the prospect case for a 30-year-old single female reads:

IMPORTANT GOAL: Emergency funds and retirement:
[GIVE ONLY IF PROBED]

A. Realizes that she will have to accumulate money to provide for her retirement.

B. Has not considered the specific amount to be saved or the details of her retirement.

C. Has saved $5,000 after 6 years of working.

The *Expert Criteria* for this performance reads as follows:

> **Probing to Discover Needs:** Used indirect questions and waited for answers. Probing was relevant to the customer's response and the benefits of the company's products. Paraphrase and body language demonstrated active listening. Discovered 90 percent of the supplementary information.

The following scale was developed to clarify the scoring of the probing component:

4	Expert	Used indirect questions and waited for answers. Probing was relevant to the customer's response and the benefits of the company's products. Paraphrase and body language demonstrated active listening. Discovered 90 percent of the supplementary information.
3	Effective	Mostly asked indirect questions and waited for most answers. Most questions were relevant to the customer's response and company's

products. Listening is evident, but paraphrase or body language is not always appropriate. Discovered 70 percent of the supplementary information.

2	Marginal	Direct questions outnumber indirect questions or few demonstrations of active listening. Discovered less than 50 percent of the supplementary information.
1	Ineffective	Mostly asked direct questions—No demonstration of active listening. Discovered less than 30 percent of the supplementary information.
0	Not evident	No questions asked or probing is inaccurate and lacks focus. Supplemental information not discovered.

A Final Word

The process of producing a reliable performance evaluation system is challenging. Expect a number of revisions and you will not be frustrated. The payoff for producing a reliable system is considerable. Performance can be evaluated both during training and on the job. This enables the developer to validate (test the effectiveness of) the training and to conduct needs assessments.

Most importantly, student learning is greatly enhanced. The process of evaluating performance with *Expert Criteria* reinforces, with each evaluation, the desired behavior. Students who are able to distinguish the components of the behavior in themselves and others are progressing down the road to becoming experts.

K. Measuring a Complex Sales Behavior

As the complexity of the behavior increases so does the complexity of the Performance Evaluation System. On the following pages we will consider an interactive telephone sales behavior focused on obtaining a 2-hour appointment with a prospective customer. The product is a consulting service which provides sales and management training to enable an organization to develop its people. The customer is the Chief Executive Officer, Chief Training Officer or Director of Human Resources. (See Fig. 8.10.)

Notice that the criteria for this sales behavior is described in great detail and that the performance includes sales resistance. The following resources are needed to produce and measure this behavior:

1. **Performance Evaluation Form:** Refer to Fig. 8.11. Notice that the Interview Structure represents the structure of the behavior. (This is often referred to as a task analysis in the literature.)

2. **Behavioral Documentation:** Figure 8.12 contains a detailed outline of the sales behavior. This document represents a key stage of the development process that leads to the Expert Criteria. It also can be used as a resource during the training process.

Figure 8.10. Objective for a Complex Sales Behavior

Make an appointment: <u>Given background information and a student acting as a prospect who was sent a pre-solicitation,</u> the salesperson will be able to **conduct a telephone interview** *that reaches agreement on the date, time, participants and customer preparation* for a formal sales interview based on the prospect's needs and experience with training vendors* within 12 minutes and **respond to** 2 *instances of* **resistance.**

**All participants read the customer brochure.*

---

3. **Role Play Cases:** Both performer (salesperson) and the student acting as the customer will need information to simulate a realistic transaction. Refer to Fig. 8.16.

    A. Salesperson Role: This will consist of a narrative containing information about the prospective client which is referred to in the Condition Component of the Objective.

    B. Customer Role: This will consist of a narrative describing the customer's situation along with specific information that relates to the sales transaction. Also included would be one or two specific objections to be raised during the transaction. A useful case also provides parameters for acceptance or rejection of the salesperson's proposition.

Relationship of the Learning Objective to the Expert Criteria

Close examination of the Performance Evaluation Form reveals three measurement areas each of which leads to an Effectiveness Rating. Each area has a direct relationship to the learning objective. These areas include:

1. **Interview Structure:** This represents the component structure of the behavior in a linear sequence. Notice that each component is stated as a criterion rather than specific words or phrases. This structure enables the performer to use individual personality and style to meet the criterion while still exhibiting the overall strategy of the subject expert(s). Refer to Fig. 8.11.

Performer:	the salesperson will be able to
Performance:	**conduct a telephone interview**
Criteria:	*that reaches agreement on the date, time, participants and customer preparation* for a formal sales interview based on the prospect's needs and experience with training vendors.*
	**All participants read the customer brochure*

2. **Response to Resistance:** This represents a 6-step process for addressing resistance. In this case, the salesperson will respond to one or two customer objections. The structure of the form permits independent measurement of each response and a summation of effectiveness through the Rating. Refer to Fig. 8.11.

Performance: **respond to** 2 *instances of* **resistance**

Criteria: *based on the prospect's needs and experience with training vendors.*

3. **During and After the Transaction:** This represents behaviors that occur frequently throughout the sales transaction. They include relationship building, questioning, probing, paraphrase and control of time. Refer to Fig. 8.11.

Performance Time: within 12 minutes

The Effectiveness Rating for the total performance is derived by dividing the sum of the *Ratings* calculated for each area by three, the number of areas. This is referred to as the *Overall Rating* on the form.

L. Behavioral Documentation

Figure 8.12 is an example of documentation that describes, in detail, the desired behavior. The *Expert Criteria* on the Performance Evaluation Form were derived from this document. The document itself is the answer to the developer's question to the subject expert:

What would we observe when a person is performing competently? Expertly?

If the development process has been carried out as described in Fig. 8.1, then the finished behavioral document would represent the patterns of behavior that the developer identified when observing the subject expert in actual transactions with a customer. In this case, listening to both sides of the telephone conversation.

Notice the frequency with which contracting, questioning, probing and paraphrasing behaviors are used. This particular transaction requires the salesperson to use a high level of interactive skills. By studying the documented behavior, the developer can identify both the linear structure (flow) and the key components of the behavior. This will lead to training program content that addresses both.

This particular behavior is based on sending the customer a cover letter and a detailed customer brochure that provides an overview of the company's services to the customer. The salesperson's phone call follows several days later. Also notice the algorithmic structure of the behavior (**shown as bolded lines of text**). The customer may or may not have read the materials or have knowledge of the company or may have had a positive or negative experience with the company (referred to as TQT Associates).

Figure 8.11. Performance Evaluation Form for a Sales Behavior

Expert Criteria for Making Appointments

_____   _____   __/__/__
SALESPERSON   RATED BY   DATE

<u>Interview Structure</u>: Rate for content and relevance to the situation.

_____ Contracted for time and questions at the start of the contact.

_____ Determined if customer has received and read the brochure.

_____ Determined reaction to the brochure or familiarity with the company.

_____ Determined customer's experience with company or other training and development companies.

_____ (If applicable) Explained briefly the mission and services of the company.

_____ Offered to meet for the purpose of exploring the mutual benefits of a relationship.

_____ Obtained commitment on the date, time, purpose and participants.

_____ Contracted with the customer to read the brochure prior to the meeting.

_____ *Total and divide by 9*   *RATING* _____

<u>Response to Resistance</u>: Rate for content and relevance to the situation.

OBJ 1   OBJ 2

_____   _____ **Acknowledgment:** Paraphrase is used to demonstrate understanding of the customer's concern. Response is spontaneous.

_____   _____ **Contract Established:** Permission is obtained to ask questions or to explore the stated concern.

_____   _____ **Need Discovery:** Questions and probes are used to discover the customer's needs, issues or relevant facts. Most "needs" discovered.

_____   _____ **Need Awareness:** Questions and/or explanation result in agreement by the customer that there is a problem to be solved.

_____   _____ **Need Fulfillment:** Benefit(s) of a formal sales interview is/are relevant to the need established or concern expressed. Explanation is complete.

_____   _____ **Agreement Reached:** Questions are asked to measure understanding or, if applicable, acceptance.

_____   _____ *Total and divide by 6 or 12*   *RATING* _____

Figure 8.11. *(Continued)* Performance Evaluation Form for a Sales Behavior

<u>**During the Transaction**</u>: Rate frequency and appropriateness of observed salesperson behaviors.

_____   **Relationship Building:** The salesperson displayed a concern for the customer's needs, allows the customer to speak without interruption (or interruptions are excused).

_____   **Questioning:** Open ended questions (except probes) are posed to discover needs and create awareness.

_____   **Probing to clarify need:** Short questions, nonthreatening and relevant to the customer's response.

_____   **Paraphrase (to demonstrate active listening):** Spontaneous, in the salesperson's own words and appropriate to the customer's response. Acknowledgment is sought.

<u>After the Transaction</u>:

_____   **Time:** Completed within 12 minutes. Lower score for excess time.

_____   *Total and divide by 5*   *RATING* _____

OVERALL RATING (Add ratings and divide by 3)   _____

SCORING		**OVERALL RATING**	
4 Expert	Performs with *finesse &* *confidence* and meets <u>all</u> criteria.	3.6 to 4.0	Expert
		2.7 to 3.5	Effective
		1.8 to 2.6	Marginal
3 Effective	Performs with *confidence* and meets <u>70 percent</u> of the criteria.	0.9 to 1.7	Ineffective
		0.0 to 0.8	Not Evident
2 Marginal	Performs *mechanically* <u>or</u> meets <u>50 percent</u> of the criteria.		
1 Ineffective	Performs *mechanically* <u>and</u> meets <u>less than 50 percent</u> of the criteria.		
0 Not Evident	None of the criteria met.		
N Not Applicable	The criterion is not applicable to the problem.		

Figure 8.12. Sales Behavior and Algorithm

- Make contact, introduce self, TQT Associates and contract for time.
- Ask if customer has read the Customer Brochure.

A. **Has read:**

  - Ask for customer's reaction: What was your reaction to TQT Associates and our services?
  - Listen, take notes and clarify interests or reservations.

B. **Has not read:**

  - Ask if the customer has the Customer Brochure.
  - Ascertain customer's familiarity with TQT Associates.
  - Listen, take notes, paraphrase and clarify customer's knowledge of TQT Associates.

    1. **No knowledge of TQT Associates:**

       - Briefly describe the TQT Associates program.
       - Contract for questions.
       - Ascertain experience with training and development firms. Have you ever worked with a training and development firm? What firm? What was your experience?
       - Listen, take notes and clarify customer's experience with T&D firms.

    2. **Familiar with TQT Associates:**

       - Contract for questions.
       - Ascertain experience with TQT Associates. What was your experience with TQT Associates? When?
       - Listen, take notes, clarify customer's experience with TQT Associates.

         a. **Positive Experience:** Ascertain why customer is not a client.

         b. **Negative Experience:** Explain briefly how TQT Associates has changed.

       - Ascertain experience with training and development firms. Have you ever worked with a training and development firm? What firm? What was your experience?
       - Listen, take notes and clarify customer's experience with T&D firms.

Figure 8.12. *(Continued)* Sales Behavior and Algorithm

- Offer to meet to explore the mutual benefits of establishing a relationship.
- *Schedule an appointment—Offer to meet at TQT Associates.*

  A. **Has Customer Brochure (but has not read)**
  - Ask customer to read the Customer Brochure prior to the meeting.
  - Explain Benefit: This enables us to discuss and explore the benefits of a relationship in the most time efficient and productive manner.
  - *Ask for a commitment to read the Customer Brochure.*

  B. **Has disposed of Introduction Letter and Customer Brochure.**
  - Offer to send the customer the Customer Brochure prior to the meeting.
  - Explain benefit: This enables us to discuss and explore the benefits of a relationship in the most time efficient and productive manner.
  - *Ask for a commitment to read the Customer Brochure.*

M. Case Structure

In order to measure behavior you have to be able to observe performance. To accomplish this within the context of a training program the developer must simulate the conditions of an actual transaction in the classroom. This is commonly referred to as role playing or behavioral simulation.

The Condition Component of the learning objective (Fig. 8.13) states the developers intention to utilize behavioral simulation through the words "a student acting as a customer who was sent a presolicitation." The need for a role play case is evident from the words "a narrative containing information about a prospective customer."

Figure 8.13. Objective for a Complex Sales Behavior

Make an appointment: Given background information and a student acting as a prospect who was sent a pre-solicitation, the salesperson will be able to **conduct a telephone interview** *that reaches agreement on the date, time, participants and customer preparation* for a formal sales interview based on the prospect's needs and experience with training vendors* within 12 minutes and **respond to 2 instances of resistance.**

*All participants read the customer brochure.

The "narrative" (refer to seller role in Fig. 8.16) provides the performer (student acting as the salesperson) with the information he or she would have in a transaction with an actual prospect. This puts the performer into the situation and enables him or her to use the behavior to achieve the objective.

Importance of the Customer Role

The Role Play Case (Fig. 8.14) is the key to an effective behavioral simulation. The case consists of two roles: a Seller Role and a Customer Role. While both are important, the "customer role" is the critical component in producing a behavior that can be measured.

Without a defined customer role, a behavioral simulation can be unproductive and frustrating to all parties. This can occur in a number of ways. The student acting as the customer can play the role of an extremely difficult customer or play the customer in an unrealistic manner. This overly aggressive portrayal frustrates the student acting as the salesperson, as he or she is prevented from effectively using the skills learned. If the "customer" is too easy, the student playing the salesperson loses the opportunity to use the skills. Inaccurate customer portrayal also frustrates the developer's attempt to measure learner competence. Figure 8.15 lists criteria for a useful case.

Figure 8.16 provides examples of Seller and Customer Roles which meet the case criteria. These form the case for the behavioral simulation of making an appointment, the desired behavior described by the learning objective (Fig. 8.10 on page 121).

Figure 8.14. Major Components of a Role Play Case

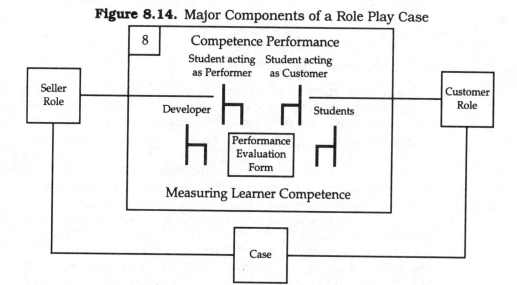

Figure 8.15. Case Criteria

A. Contains a synopsis which provides the student playing the receiver (prospect, customer, worker, manager) with an overview of the receiver's role.

B. Contains relevant data to be provided to the sender (seller, supervisor, manager) by the receiver in the normal course of the interview and, if applicable, data to be provided if the sender probes.

C. Contains one or more objections, questions or issues to be raised by the receiver to produce the behavior to be observed and, if applicable, non verbal cues.

D. Contains instructions to the receiver which indicate when the objection(s), question(s), issue(s) or non verbal cue(s) is/are to be inserted into the transaction.

E. Provides guidelines for the acceptance or rejection of the proposition (if applicable) by the receiver.

F. Contains a narrative that provides the sender (seller, supervisor, manager) with the situation and relevant background information.

The Seller Role provides background information that enables the student acting as the seller to conduct the transaction. The student is expected to use the behavior outlined in Fig. 8.12 to obtain the appointment. The developer and observing students would use the Performance Evaluation Form (Fig. 8.11) to evaluate the performance.

N. Validation of Training

Validation is comparing the results you expect against the results you get. In sales training this means using a systematic approach to measure the effectiveness of the training program and the effectiveness of sales behaviors being taught. Validation helps maximize the investment made in the development of training.

The process involves observing salespeople in actual selling situations and recording data about the transactions observed. This behavioral data is then analyzed and conclusions are drawn.

The analyzed data provides management with an informed basis for making decisions that have a high potential for improving results. It also provides program developers with a sound basis for making changes to the training. Optimally, all changes in training methodology or content, especially sales behaviors, should be dictated by the data obtained from validation in relationship to the objectives to be achieved.

Figure 8.16. Example Role Play Case

Customer Role—Mr. Smith

Situation: You are the CEO of Green Motors. You recently received a cover letter and customer brochure from TQT Associates, a company selling training and development services. You have read the letter. You have not read the brochure (although you still have it in your possession).

Background: Green Motors is a large multi franchise dealership employing over 100 salespeople and managers (in 6 locations). Green Motors is struggling through a recession and sales are down. Historically, you have experienced high salesforce turnover which you attribute to poor management and lazy, unmotivated salespeople. You do not currently employ a training and development company. You have not been impressed by the training programs you have attended or purchased over the last 18 years.

Resistance: Give resistance when the salesperson asks you about your experience with training companies.

1. "Training works great in the classroom but not on the job." Use an analogy. "Vince Lombardi's plays worked perfectly on the locker room blackboard, but it's another matter on the field. The opposition's knowledge and skills reduce the play's effectiveness to 1 in 5."

2. "How much does your service cost?" Your objective is to get the price and tell the salesperson that you feel the cost does not justify the value.

Role Play Parameters. Agree to an appointment and to read the customer brochure if:

1. The salesperson remains focused on the transaction objective—to get an appointment.

2. Responds with empathy to your concern that training only works in the classroom.

3. Does not quote the company's fee.

4. Explains the value of getting together from your point of view.

5. Avoids selling any particular service.

Seller Role

Situation: You have targeted Mr. Smith, the CEO of Green Motors as a potential client. Green Motors is located in a market where you have a number of clients. However, you were unable to get a referred lead to Mr. Smith. Therefore, you mailed him the pre-solicitation package consisting of a cover letter and customer brochure.

Background: Green Motors is a large multi franchise dealership employing over 100 salespeople and managers (in 6 locations). You are aware from your discussions with people in the industry that the Green organization has a reputation for high salesforce turnover.

Both training methodology and sales behavior can and should be validated. Validation of a sales behavior confirms that the methodology being employed actually produces the desired sales results. Desired, in this instance, means producing a sale(s) of sufficient value to justify the time invested. Validation of training confirms that the methodology employed in the training program produces the desired behavior in the salesperson.

The question arises as to whether sales data can achieve the same end. **Sales data alone do not indicate whether the sales behaviors taught in the training produced the sales.** Sales data only suggest that the training could have produced the sales. Results can be related to other factors such as product, price or competition.

Sales data are fine when the results are acceptable. But when poor sales or increased salesforce turnover or lowered incomes or customer dissatisfaction occurs, the sales data—by itself—does not reveal the problem or problems being experienced. For example, are the unacceptable results attributable to the product, the market, the sales behavior, the training, the competition, the compensation package or the management support system or a combination of these factors?

Without behavioral feedback and/or competitive data the leader must make assumptions as to the "cause" of the unacceptable results. Decisions based on such assumptions are often flawed. Subsequent sales data can lead to further incorrect assumptions and more ineffective decisions. Decision making solely on sales data is a "trial and error" approach to solving problems.

Hence, the process of validation produces data upon which informed decisions can be made by leaders and developers to solve problems. It also produces training which can transfer effective sales behaviors. The ability to transfer effective sales behavior is the key to helping people achieve greater productivity, and through their efforts achieve organizational objectives.

What Is a Validation Study?

A validation study measures the effectiveness of the training in a representative population. Effectiveness is defined as producing a desired behavior that impacts sales results and persists over time.

What if the Sales Behavior Persists?

When the desired behavior persists after training it can be safely assumed that the behavior is being reinforced. Reinforcement occurs when the interaction with customers is productive and when they buy in a sufficient quantity to justify the time and effort spent. It can also be reasonably assumed that the training was effective when the desired behavior is observable in the population sampled.

What if the Sales Behavior Does Not Persist?

If the behavior does not "pay-off," in other words, prospects fail to buy, the behavior is likely to diminish and finally extinguish. The question then must be answered: "Is the training methodology flawed or is the desired behavior at fault, or, are other factors influencing the seller's results?"

When training is developed for a <u>validated sales behavior</u> (explained in the following) and the behavior is not evident or marginally observable in the population, it can reasonably be assumed that the training methodology is flawed. Hence, methodology changes such as increasing the time spent on role play and performance evaluation would likely produce greater persistency of the behavior. Evidence of the improvement can and should be measured by subsequent validation.

However, when training is developed for a sales behavior that <u>has not been validated</u> and the behavior is not evident or marginally observable in the population, both the training methodology and the behavior should be suspected. Actions to correct the problem are dependent on the state of training developed. For example:

A. If the desired behavior **has not been observed** <u>and performance evaluated in a classroom situation</u> against a set of criteria, the training should be modified to include role play and evaluation activities. Subsequent validation will confirm if the problem is corrected.

B. If the desired behavior **has been observed** <u>and performance evaluated in a classroom situation</u> against a set of criteria, then the sales behavior should be validated.

How Do You Validate a Sales Behavior?

Validation of the sales behavior can be accomplished by observing subjects **who exhibit the prescribed behavior, using it in live sales interviews.** A Performance Evaluation Form must be constructed to record the components of the behavior and prospect response. Data obtained will substantiate the effectiveness of the behavior or identify the flaws. If the behavior is flawed, modifications should be made and the behavior retested. This process should continue until the behavior is deemed to produce satisfactory results.

O. Competence Performance

The competence performance for this chapter is optional. If you desire to test your skill at writing *Expert Criteria* (the core skill in creating a Performance Evaluation System), you can. **Appendix D,** *The Training Effectiveness Evaluation System,* contains criteria for 35 components of the training process. To practice, you select a component where you feel that you are a subject expert and write a set of *Expert Criteria. Then you compare your answers to those listed in* **The Training Effectiveness Evaluation System.**

9

A Point of View

A set of learning objectives can reveal a great amount of information about training and the behavior contained within the training. This includes:

- The content and style of a desired behavior.
- The knowledge, skills and behaviors contained within the training.
- The developer's knowledge of the topic.
- The likelihood that the learner's behavior will change and therefore an indication of the effectiveness of the training.
- The methodology employed to bring about the desired behavior.
- The assumptions of the instructor (developer).

You will recall (on page 47) that we were able to distinguish between stimulus response and need selling behaviors from the words used in the Performance, Conditions and Criteria Components. Compare the two Module Objectives below. They represent two behaviors for the same activity.

Stimulus Response

> **Selling Life Insurance:** <u>Given a student acting as a customer</u>, the agent will be able to **give a sales talk** *word for word* in 15 minutes.

Need Selling

> **Selling Life Insurance:** <u>Given a student acting as a customer</u>, the agent will be able to **conduct a sales discussion** *that reaches agreement on a suitable insurance product in relation to the needs agreed upon* within 45 minutes.

Each of the above objectives achieves an Effectiveness Rating of 10 against the six Criteria for Measuring the Usefulness of a Learning Objective. From the developer's view these objectives are a foundation to structure their training.

From the students' view, the behavior contained in the objective is a foundation that will enable them to use themselves to accomplish a goal. As the student, which behavior would you want to acquire? Which is more likely to be growth producing?

Which training program would you, as the life insurance company manager, prefer to invest your company's money in? Which behavior is more likely to bring about long term relationships with your customers? Which behavior is more likely to be used by your salesforce after the training event?

The behavioral content and structure of the objectives enables all parties to make <u>prudent</u> decisions about the training. (Prudent is defined as skill and good judgment in the use of resources.)

A. The Assumptions of the Instructor (Developer)

The original name for this book was **Learning Objectives: Foundation or Formality?** This title was based on the premise that a useless objective is a formality, an established form or procedure that is required or conventional. Considering the fact that approximately 95 percent of the training advertisements I receive contain objectives, the majority of which are ineffectively structured, one could reasonably conclude that they are a formality.

Many people were upset over the use of the word formality. They argued, and I agreed, that few people consider objectives a formality. People take objectives seriously. Unfortunately, their flawed structure renders many objectives useless. While not intended as such, their uselessness makes them ineffective and a mere formality in the design and delivery of training.

A synonym for formality is ceremony. "Ceremony refers to an act prescribed by convention." From the words "prescribe" and "prescription" we derived the following meanings:

- To lay down a rule.
- To lay down as a guide.
- To specify by authority.
- To designate or order the use of a remedy.
- The act of laying down authoritative rules or directions.
- A written direction for therapeutic or corrective action.

Notice the authoritarian tone of the preceding definitions. Now consider the structure of the following alleged learning objectives:

You will learn how to sell life insurance effectively.

You will understand how to write effective objectives.

You will improve your ability to sell life insurance to customers.

Each of these statements achieves an Effectiveness Rating of "0," meaning that there is no evidence of any of the components of a useful objective.

In many cases, training which I evaluated containing objectives with the common prefacing phrases **"you will learn how to"** and **"you will understand"** or **"to improve"** turned out to be lecture oriented, lacking evaluation procedures and generally ineffective.

Now consider the word "prescription." What do you associate with the word "prescription?" My first thought is the field of medicine. Who prescribes medicine? A doctor. Why does the doctor prescribe medicine? Because the patient is sick. Could the flawed objectives above and throughout this book be written by well meaning people who see their students as "sick patients"?

A 1988 survey of 45 Fortune 500 companies showed that while all of them used some form of participant reaction form, only 30 percent used measures of learning (testing) and only 15 percent used measures of behavior. (Brandenburg & Shultz, 1988) Brandenburg's 1982 survey also found that post training evaluation was the least used measure of training effectiveness. He stated then that the "most used evaluative techniques, regardless of the criticisms heaped upon them, are the 'smile' indices, i.e. questionnaires and comments. Cognitive and performance-based outcome measures are used less often." (Brandenburg, 1982)

This continued emphasis on "smile indices" indicates that developers (doctors) of training are concerned that the patient liked the medicine. It also suggests that these "doctors" didn't check to see if the patient got well.

B. Theory X Versus Theory Y

The structure of these objectives suggests that many developers of training hold the traditional views of direction and control which McGregor labeled as "Theory X." He states that "behind every managerial decision or action are assumptions about human nature and human behavior." [Douglas McGregor, *The Human Side of Enterprise* (McGraw-Hill, Inc.: New York, 1960, pp. 33-34, 47-48)] I suggest that the same thing can be said of training decisions. McGregor's "Theory X and Y" are shown in Fig. 9.1.

Thomas Kramlinger building on the work of McGregor developed the following **Instructor Assumptions about Students.** He reasoned that training decisions based on these assumptions are observable as two styles of teaching which he labeled Theory X and Y. He referred to Theory X as the lecture and testing methods of education. Theory Y is identified as an interactive style that "… generates an atmosphere of trust and creativity in the classroom and results in greater internalization of the people-skills being taught." (Kramlinger, 1975)

Kramlinger's Instructor Assumptions about Students

Theory X

1. They cannot be trusted to pursue their own learning.

2. Presenting material to them is the same as learning.

Figure 9.1. McGregor's Assumptions About Human Nature

Theory X

1. The average human being has an inherent dislike of work and will avoid it if he can.

2. Because of this human characteristic of dislike for work, most people must be coerced, controlled, directed or threatened with punishment to get them to put forth adequate effort toward the achievement of objectives.

3. The average human being prefers to be directed, wishes to avoid responsibility, has little ambition, wants security above all.

(McGregor, 1960, pp. 33–34)

Theory Y

1. The expenditure of physical and mental effort in work is as natural as play or rest.

2. External control and the threat of punishment are not the only means for bringing about effort toward organizational objectives. Man will exercise self direction and self control in the service of objectives to which he is committed.

3. Commitment to objectives is a function of the rewards associated with their achievement.

4. The average human being learns, under proper conditions, not only to accept but to seek responsibility.

5. The capacity to exercise a high degree of imagination, ingenuity and creativity in the solution of organizational problems is widely, not narrowly, distributed in the population.

6. Under the conditions of modern industrial life, the intellectual potentialities of the average human being are only partially utilized.

(McGregor, 1960, pp. 47–48)

---

3. They build factual knowledge brick by brick.

4. Truth is known; they must merely be convinced to accept it.

5. Creative/mature people develop from passive learners.

6. Evaluation means judging and being judged by experts.

Theory Y

1. People can learn and want to learn for their own growth.

2. People commit their energies to what they perceive is relevant.

3. Self evaluation is primary. Judgment by others is secondary.

4. Truth is discovered through participation in formulating the problem, from drawing on personal experience, in searching for resources, by suggesting alternatives and contrasting them and in testing options and accepting the consequences.

5. Asking relevant questions is the primary role of the teacher. (Kramlinger, 1975)

I believe that learning objectives written in accordance with Mager's Principle and evaluation based on pre-agreed upon criteria are totally consistent with Theory Y. Both Kramlinger and McGregor identify commitment to objectives as a foundation of human motivation. Useful learning objectives enable all parties to determine if the knowledge, skills and behaviors contained in the training are relevant to the learner's needs and compatible with the organization's culture.

I also believe that <u>an interactive learning environment is essential</u>. Knowledge, skills and behaviors being taught must be tested in situations that simulate the circumstances in which they will be used. The statement of objectives in behavioral terms, coupled with modeling and evaluation, encourage such an environment. Through this process, the behavior contained within the training is determined to be either practical and usable or wishful thinking.

C. The Training Process and Kramlinger's Theory Y

Kramlinger's 4th "Theory Y" Assumption also points toward and provides a road map for the interactive learning environment.

4. **Truth is discovered through participation in formulating the problem, from drawing on personal experience, in searching for resources, by suggesting alternatives and contrasting them and in testing options and accepting the consequences. (Kramlinger, 1975)**

Formulating the Problem (Problems to Solve).   I have found that discussions with learners regarding the problems they are experiencing with the knowledge and skills to be taught extremely helpful. Through this discussion we jointly discover that there are discrepancies that they want to fix. The technique even works when learners have limited or no experience. Often, they can anticipate problems they are likely to encounter when using the desired behavior described by the learning objective.

A Note to the Reader: Task 2 on page 17 where you rated your use of objectives is my way of operationalizing the above technique (Problems to Solve) in a book version of a training program. If we were together in a formal training session, I would have begun the session by asking you to describe the problems that you have experienced when using learning objectives in the design and delivery of training.

Drawing on Personal Experience (Baseline Performance). The baseline performance technique referred to on page 94 is a method of operationalizing this component of Kramlinger's Assumption. A baseline performance allows the learners to use themselves and their experience to solve the problem. The technique, when used effectively, creates strong learning motivation as people discover discrepancies in their knowledge and skills that are preventing them from achieving their goals. Effective use of the technique involves structuring a problem that is within the learner's capacity to solve and which relates to the event's learning objective. The observed performance will reveal the learner's behavioral strengths as well as discrepancies in the learner's knowledge and skill.

In Searching for Resources (Modeling). The instructor's examples and models provide a powerful resource for the learner. Modeling enables the learner to observe the ideas and techniques in use. Effective use of this technique requires that the instructor use the techniques contained within the behavior to solve a problem.

Suggesting Alternatives and Contrasting Them (Discussion). The discussion of issues evolving from the student's performance and the instructor's model are essential to understanding and acceptance of a new form of behavior. Through these discussions ideas are tested and, in some cases, new and more effective techniques emerge as the group (instructor and learners) use their problem solving skills.

McGregor's Theory Y Assumption 5

> "The capacity to exercise a high degree of imagination, ingenuity and creativity in the solution of organizational problems is widely, not narrowly, distributed in the population." (McGregor, 1960, p. 48)

Testing Options and Accepting the Consequences (Performance and Evaluation). Use of the desired behavior in behavioral simulations which replicate, to the extent possible, the conditions under which the performer will use the behavior is essential for determining understanding, acceptance and competence. As previously discussed, performance with evaluation according to pre-agreed upon criteria is also essential for measuring the effectiveness of the training event and to determine if the behavior persists after training (post training evaluation).

Theory Y assumptions, useful objectives and the techniques of baseline performance, modeling, discussion, performance and evaluation result in the <u>discovery of truth</u>; knowledge and skills that people can take from the classroom and apply on the job.

A Final Word

Training is not an end in itself. It is a means to an end; the learners' acquisition of knowledge and skills that help them and their organizations reach their goals. The next section on *Training Effectiveness Evaluation* will enable you to use the objective writing and measurement skills you gained in Part 1 to bring about effective training.

And a Request

I would like to measure both your satisfaction with Part 1 and your skill in writing learning objectives. The Student Evaluation of Training form located in App. C will allow me to measure your satisfaction with the training. To measure your skill in writing objectives, I need to see a "before" and "after" sample. Therefore, please send me a set of objectives that you rewrote after reading this book. Mark the new objectives "After" and the originals "Before." Also indicate if you would like me to comment on your objectives. (Be sure to include a return address.) Send these documents to:

Lester T. Shapiro, CFP
c/o McGraw-Hill
11 West 19th Street
New York, NY 10111

PART 2

Training Effectiveness Evaluation

The Key to Maximizing the Return from Your Training Investment

10
Overview of the System

The *Training Effectiveness Evaluation System* enables any person or organization to achieve total quality in the training they purchase, conduct or manage. The system consists of *The Total Quality Training Standards, Guidelines for Meeting the Standards* and *Expert Criteria to Measure the Standards*. The system is based on Learning Objectives and the performance evaluation methodology described in Part 1. Used individually or in combination, they enable any person involved with training at any level within the organization to:

- **Predict the likelihood that the training and the behavior contained within the training will be effective.**
- **Make modifications to existing training that increase its effectiveness.**
- **Develop training that produces an observable change in learner behavior that persists over time.**
- **Make cost-effective training decisions.**

Listed below are the learning objectives for Part 2:

A. Learning Objectives of Part 2

Module Objective

Evaluate Training: Given a training program's documentation or its learning objectives, the reader will be able to calculate an **Effectiveness Rating** for a training event with an accuracy of +/− 10 percent of the author's solution using five **standards of training effectiveness and criteria to measure each** within, depending on the depth of measurement, 20 to 120 minutes.

Unit Objectives

To accomplish the Module Objective, the reader will be able to:

1. Describe five **standards of training effectiveness** in relation to Learning Objectives.
2. Describe the hierarchical relationship of standards and criteria.
3. Describe the need for standards.
4. Describe techniques for meeting each *Standard.*
5. Describe the procedure for determining the Effectiveness Rating of any training program or module with the *Standards.*
6. Describe the strategy, process and resources required to implement and monitor training effectiveness using the *Total Quality Training Standards.*
7. Describe the process for conducting a *Training Effectiveness Survey.* (App. B)
8. Describe the strategy, process and use of data acquired from the *Student Evaluation of Training.* (App. C)

Result Objectives

The ability to evaluate training, the behavior previously described in the Module Objective, <u>coupled with the ability to enable all developers of training to write learning objectives and evaluate performance (the subject of Part 1)</u> will enable the:

Chief Executive Officer to increase productivity and results through cost effective management, administrative and sales training programs that produce measurable behavioral outcomes that can be linked to the results produced.

Chief Training Officer to bring about organizational training effectiveness. Depending on the size of the organization, this can be accomplished in one to five years.

Any person with a training responsibility to plan, organize, conduct, evaluate and modify training that brings about a desired result in relation to the desired behavior described in the learning objectives for the training event.

Any purchaser of training to select a program that is likely to bring about the knowledge and skills required to correct an identified performance discrepancy and be consistent with the culture of the organization.

The Method

First I will provide a brief overview of the *The Training Effectiveness Evaluation System.* Then we will look at the need for standards, *Guidelines for Meeting the Standards* and the strategy, process and systems required to implement the *Total*

Quality Training Standards in an organization. Then you will use the *TQT Standards* to evaluate the training module on learning objectives that you experienced in Part 1. For additional practice, you will evaluate a sample training module called *Interaction by Design*.

B. What Are Training Standards?

Training standards represent a set of criteria. As such, they permit a judgment to be made with regard to the effectiveness of a training methodology in relation to the **desired behavior** described in a learning objective.

Standards are established by authority, custom or general consent. The authority, so to speak, for the following training standards is the concept that **learning is an observable change in behavior that persists over time which can be described by a learning objective and measured by criteria**. It is also based on the practical reality that an organization's resources should be committed to training when the problem to be solved is related to knowledge or skill discrepancies evident in one or more employees' performance.

Total Quality Training Standards

To achieve training effectiveness, the initiative should contain:

1. Learning Objectives which describe the **desired behavior(s)** to be exhibited during the training program. (Learning Objectives)
2. Evidence of a performance discrepancy in relation to the **desired behavior** resulting from a lack of skill or knowledge. (Needs Analysis)
3. Examples or models of the **desired behavior** during the training program. (Modeling)
4. Evaluation of student performance of the **desired behavior** to determine competence during training. (Performance Evaluation)
5. Evidence that the **desired behavior** has persisted after training and is linked to results. (Post Training Evaluation)

The preceding *Standards* apply to any event which is designed to improve organizational results through the enhancement of knowledge or skills.

The *Total Quality Training Standards* permit an organization to achieve the highest level of effectiveness without interfering with an individual developer's style. For example, a developer can conduct the explanation phase of their training with a lecture, if that is desired or appropriate. The Standards do not dictate a particular communication style.

However, they do require that the communication be effective as evidenced by *Standards 4* and *5* (Performance Evaluation and Post Training Evaluation).

Standard 4 requires that the developer observe and evaluate performance. This provides the critical feedback that <u>indicates</u> whether or not learning has taken place during the training event. *Standard 5* is the ultimate test. It <u>proves</u> that learning has taken place by providing documented evidence that performers are using the desired behavior to bring about results on the job.

The *Standards* also prescribe certain key program activities. If, for example, the instructor is teaching a class on learning objectives, he or she must be able to show model objectives to the students. The same thing is true of a class on conducting negotiations. *Standard 3* (Modeling) requires **examples or models of the <u>desired behavior</u> during the training program.**

Standard 4 requires performance and evaluation. To meet this *Standard*, the developer must establish criteria to measure the performance, allocate time to observe it and, in many instances, create a case to bring about the behavior.

Standard 2 (Need Analysis) insures that any training purchased or conducted is related to an identified performance problem. *Standard 5* enables us to determine if the problem that motivated the expenditure of organizational resources has been resolved. *Standard 5* also connects the desired behavior contained within the training to results produced on the job.

The Learning Objectives required by *Standard 1* ensure that the training is measurable by requiring the desired behavior to be described.

There is considerable support in the literature for the *Standards*. For example:

- *Standard 1:* "The specification of training content by behavioral objectives is now regarded as a 'core' concept in training development and practice." (Morrison, 1991, p. 2)

- *Standards 2 and 5:* "A skill is a solution to a problem and the view is taken that skill acquisition is best understood if the nature of the problem to be solved is understood." (Morrison, 1991, p. 44)

- *Standard 3:* "Behavior Modeling training programs have proven to be particularly effective for inculcating supervisory skills." (Morrison, 1991, p. 271)

- Standard 4: "Practising with knowledge of results provided by an instructor, either directly or through some automatic scoring device, is one of the most effective ways of acquiring a skill." (Morrison, 1991, p. 31) "While overall achievement may be reduced to a single score, this may not be useful if it does not enable the learner to identify specific aspects of performance which should be modified." (Morrison, 1991, p. 37) This supports evaluation of performance based on specific criteria.

C. The Hierarchical Structure of Measurement

A <u>standard</u> is defined as something established by authority, custom, or general consent as a model or as a rule for the measure of quantity, weight, extent, value or quality. The word "criterion" is a synonym for standard. A <u>criterion</u> is defined as a standard upon which a judgment or decision can be based. The word "criterion" applies to anything that is used as a test of quality whether formulated as a principle or not. The word "standard" is a synonym for criterion.

How Does a Criterion Differ from a Standard?

The Hierarchical Structure's superior-subordinate relationship is the key to understanding the relationship between standards and criteria. A standard is the equivalent of a Superior Objective. Criteria are the equivalent of Subordinate Objectives. This principle can be demonstrated by the *Standard* for learning objectives (Fig. 10.1) and the *Expert Criteria* to measure that *Standard.*

The reader should immediately recognize that the criteria in Fig. 10.1 are the Criteria for Measuring the Usefulness of a Set of Learning Objectives for a Training Module from Part 1.

Each criterion can also be measured by a set of subordinate criteria. Figure 10.2 contains the criterion for the Performance Component for a Module Objective and three subcriteria that can be used to test for performance.

D. The Training Effectiveness Evaluation System

Learning Objectives, TQT Standards, Guidelines for Meeting the Standards and the *Expert Criteria to Measure the Standards* create a system that can be simultaneously used to evaluate and develop training. Think of the system as an iceberg or as a four power microscope (see Fig. 10.3).

Learning Objectives represent the tip of the iceberg or the low power lens. A useful set of objectives quickly communicate the desired behavior, the end result of the training event, and the knowledge and skills that will enable the student to perform. They enable any person evaluating training to quickly assess the quality of a training program.

Just below are the *TQT Standards.* The five *Standards* communicate to all parties involved in the training process the fundamental characteristics of quality training. They link the <u>desired behavior</u> described in the learning objective (one of the five Standards) to the methodology that will bring about the desired behavior in the student. From an evaluation standpoint this represents a medium power lens.

Below the *TQT Standards* are the *Guidelines for Meeting the Standards.* These are particularly helpful to the occasional trainer in developing a program or the manager in evaluating the effectiveness of a program. The guidelines represent the high power lens. By comparing the methods employed to those suggested in the guidelines, the evaluator is able to more accurately assess effectiveness.

Below the guidelines are the *Expert Criteria to Measure the Standards,* the super power lens. This tool provides the specific criteria to measure 37 compo-

Figure 10.1. Relationship of a Standard to Criteria

Standard 1

Learning Objectives which describe the <u>desired behavior(s)</u> to be exhibited during the training program.

Expert Criteria to Measure the Standard

Module Objective

To be considered useful the statement must:

A. Contain the **job title of the performer** and the words **"be able to"** immediately before the active verb.

B. Contain **the performance** to be exhibited. (Active verb(s) and the object of the verb describe <u>the desired behavior</u>.)

C. Contain a fixed limit of **time** for the performance.

D. Contain **criteria** to measure the desired behavior <u>at program's end</u>.

E. Contain **conditions** which describe the situation in which the performance occurs, limitations imposed or non-implicit resources.

F. Contain **concrete image provoking language** in both the performance (desired behavior) and criteria. Any abstractions are referenced to criteria.

Unit Objectives

To be considered useful the statement must:

A. Contain the **job title of the performer** and the words **"be able to"** immediately before the active verb. For convenience, a set of Unit Objectives can be prefaced with a statement such as "To accomplish the Module Objective, the (performer job title) will be able to:"

B. Contain a **performance** which describes <u>a unit of skill or knowledge</u> to be exhibited.

C. Contain a fixed limit of **time** for the performance. **(If applicable)**

D. Contain **criteria** to measure <u>the unit of skill or knowledge during the module</u>. **(If applicable)**

E. Contain **conditions** which describe the situation in which the performance occurs, limitations imposed or non-implicit resources. **(If applicable)**

F. Contain **concrete image provoking language** in both the performance (desired behavior) and criteria. Any abstractions are referenced to criteria.

Figure 10.2. Relationship of a Criterion to Subcriteria

Performance Component Criterion

B. Contains **the performance** to be exhibited. (Active verb(s) and the object of the verb describe <u>the desired behavior</u>.)

Subordinate Criteria

To test for a Performance, the statement must contain:

1. An active (action) verb and the object of the verb.
2. Describe the behavior of the student, not the instructor.
3. Be observable during the training event. (Can you observe the student performing the desired behavior in the classroom?)

Figure 10.3. A Layers of Depth Evaluation Model

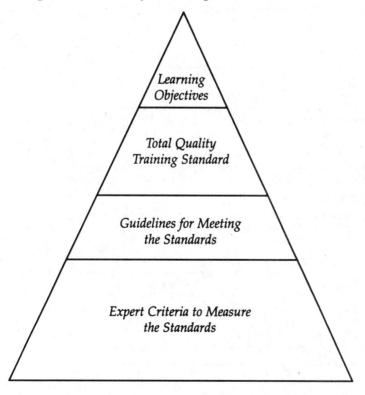

nents of the training process. These criteria can be used by the evaluator to determine the usefulness of each program component. They can also be used by a developer as a guideline to structure any needed component.

E. Evaluating a Training Program Using The System

Figure 10.4 demonstrates the relationship between the *TQT Standards* and the *Expert Criteria to Measure the Standards*. To determine if a program meets the *Standard,* the evaluator can examine each of the program's components which are relevant to the *Standard.*

For example, consider *Standard 4—Evaluation of student performance to determine competence during training.* If the developer (vendor) states that there is student performance, then the evaluator would want to look at the documented program components to determine the quality of the performance evaluation process.

The first level of this examination is the mere presence of the component. The fact that a program contains a performance evaluation form, a performance standard, cases, a time allocation for the performance and prescribed methodology for its evaluation <u>provides an indication</u> that the program is likely to meet the *Standard.* Evaluation at this level is useful when comparing a number of training programs offered by different vendors.

Figure 10.4. Relationship of *Training Standards* to Program Components

Total Quality Training Standard	Program Component
Learning Objectives which describe the <u>desired behavior(s)</u> to be exhibited during the training program.	04. Program Objectives—Core & Module 05. Module Objectives—Module and Unit
Evidence of a performance discrepancy in relation to the <u>desired behavior</u> resulting from a lack of skill or knowledge (Needs Analysis)	01. Performance Analysis 02. Needs Analysis 03. Major Assumptions
Examples or models of the <u>desired behavior</u> during the training program.	11. Interactive Behavior Documentation 12. Instruct'l Method: Behavior Modeling
Evaluation of student performance of the <u>desired behavior</u> to determine competence during training.	06. Performance Standard 07. Performance Evaluation Form 08. Performance Time Allocation 09. Role Play Cases 10. Performance Evaluation Method
Evidence that the <u>desired behavior</u> has persisted after training and is linked to results. (Post Training Evaluation)	15. Validation of the Desired Behavior 16. Post Training Evaluation 17. Student Evaluation of Training

If the evaluator wishes to measure the quality of any or all of the components, then the evaluator would use the *Expert Criteria to Measure the Standards.* (App. D). Take, for example, a program's Performance Evaluation Form. Figure 10.5 shows the *Expert Criteria* to measure a Performance Evaluation Form. The reader will recall that these criteria were identified in Chap. 8 as the Structural Components of a Performance Evaluation Form (page 106).

Figure 10.5. Relationship of a Component to *Expert Criteria*

Program Component	*Expert Criteria*
07. Performance Evaluation Form	A. Contains the component structure of the desired behavior including, if applicable, any repeating behaviors (paraphrase, probing, illustrating, etc.).
	B. Contains Expert Criteria: A precise description of the behavior which can be observed and measured for each component or repeating behavior. (Weight by 5)
	C. Contains a Scoring System: A numeric rating which links to a one or two word description of the performance and, if applicable, <u>criteria</u> to judge levels of achievement on a scale which starts at "0." The scoring is appropriate to the performance being judged.
	D. Contains a Rating Scale: A numeric rating which links to a one or two word descriptive label (i.e., effective, marginal, ineffective) and an overall description of the performance on a scale which starts at "0."
	E. Contains a matrix for recording scores, any interim rating and the overall Rating.
	F. Contains a formula and instructions for calculating the Overall Rating.
	G. Identifies the performer and the person doing the evaluation.
	H. Provides space to record specific observations or critical incidents.
	Determine rating by adding the score for each criterion and dividing by 12

F. Scoring and Rating

The **Criterion Scoring System** (below) is used to score each *Standard,* each guideline for meeting a *Standard* or the *Expert Criteria* for measuring program components. As you recall from Chap. 8, Criterion Scoring (10 - 5 - 0) is most appropriate for judging written materials. The system is based on the idea that a component of something is or is not acceptable or is questionable in relation to a precisely stated criterion. If the component is missing, then the score is 0.

Criterion Scoring System

10	Meets the Criterion
5	Questionable
0	Does Not Meet or Not Evident
N	Not Applicable

The **Effectiveness Rating** is derived by dividing the Total Score by the number of criteria. The Total Score is the sum of the scores for each criterion adjusted for any weighting. This system is based on the idea that the whole, a training program or any of its components, is the sum of its parts. Weighting enables the system to identify the most critical components.

The following is a description of the overall Effectiveness Rating derived from measuring a program's components in relation to the *TQT Standards:*

Training Effectiveness Rating Scale

Rating		Description
8.0–10.0	<u>Effective</u>	Program produces or is likely to produce the desired behavior.
5.0–7.9	<u>Marginal</u>	Program appears to be missing components that would insure the student's acquisition of the desired behavior.
1.0–4.9	<u>Ineffective</u>	Unlikely to produce a desired behavior <u>that can be observed on the job</u> or <u>that can be linked to results</u>.
0.0–0.9	<u>Not Evident</u>	No structured training program exists. The likelihood of producing a desired behavior that can be observed on the job falls between uncertain and nil.

Disregard the rating when Post Training Evaluation links the desired behavior to productivity and/or results.

G. The Value of Rating

In the example in Fig. 10.5, Criterion "B," *Expert Criteria,* is weighted by a factor of five (5). Thus the maximum score is 120 (rather than 80) and the divisor is 12 instead of 8. Therefore, if the evaluation form being rated lacked *Expert*

Criteria but contained all other components, the Effectiveness Rating would be 5.8, a marginal rating.

Does the Effectiveness Rating really describe the usefulness (effectiveness) of the component being rated? Here is an example. A colleague of mine complained that a Performance Evaluation Form he was using to evaluate telephone sales behavior was not performing. He felt that the ratings being produced by the PEF were too high in relation to the student performance he observed. Close examination of the PEF revealed that the form contained the component structure of the behavior and flawed criteria (see Fig. 10.6). Instead of being standards to judge performance, the alleged criteria turned out to be justifications for each behavioral component. Therefore, criterion "B" was scored zero.

Additionally, the form used Criterion Scoring (10 - 5 - 0) rather than 0-4 Scoring. Criterion Scoring tends to produce higher ratings as there are only two levels; Questionable and Meets Criteria. The 0-4 system provides four levels for any evident behavior; ineffective, marginal, effective and expert. To score a 4 on any component, the performer must exhibit both finesse and confidence in addition to meeting each test in the criterion. As a result, we scored criterion "C" as 5 since the scoring was not appropriate to the performance being judged.

The PEF also lacked space to record observations (criterion "H"). The resulting score was 55 as the form met all other criteria. This produced an Effectiveness Rating of 4.6. (an ineffective rating). Arguably, the form was not totally ineffective. It was performing, albeit, to some degree. The key point is the rating accurately reflected the fact that there was a flaw in the design of this particular PEF. Most importantly, the specific flaws were identified by the rating process.

Correcting the PEF involved changing the scoring system from 10 - 5 - 0 to 0-4 and restructuring the criteria. An example of restructured criteria is shown in Fig. 10.7.

The restructured criteria enables the observer to use the 0-4 Scoring System to judge performance. For example, a pause would justify a score of 3 if all other factors were present. A long pause plus phrasing the question as *"where are you calling from?"* might justify a score of 2. Asking the customer *"can I have your number please?"* in addition to the aforementioned, might warrant a 1. Failure to ask for the customer's phone number would receive a 0.

After the changes were made, my colleague reported that the Effectiveness Ratings of student performance reflected the actual competence observed. In addition, there was increased reliability (smaller gaps in student rating error). He

---

Figure 10.6. Flawed Criteria

Behavioral Component	*Alleged* Criteria
Not pause before asking where they are calling from:	*To avoid interruption, does not pause before the next question.*

Figure 10.7. Restructured Criteria

Behavioral Component   *Criteria*

Request the phone number
- *Asked if customer was calling from home or work.*
- *Did not pause after "setting the stage."*
- *Number is requested with an open question. (i.e., "What's the number there?")*

also noticed that the level of competence on a second performance exceeded those he had previously observed. We attributed the improvement to the reinforcement which occurs through the rating process. The new PEF caused the students to focus on the factors that are present in expert performance.

Conclusion

In the above example, the ratings being produced by a PEF did not reflect student competence. This caused us to use the *Training Effectiveness Evaluation System* to find and correct the problem.

From the *Expert Criteria* for Measuring a PEF (Fig. 10.5), we derived an Effectiveness Rating that indicated a flawed form. The process also identified the specific flaws. By correcting them, the Effectiveness Rating of the PEF increased (Fig. 10.8). This suggested that the revised PEF should produce more accurate ratings of student performance, which is what occurred.

From this we can conclude that the *Expert Criteria* for Measuring a PEF and the resultant Effectiveness Rating are valid since, in both instances, the rating predicted the performance of the PEF in measuring student performance.

Figure 10.8. Effectiveness Rating Versus PEF Usefulness

TIME FRAME	RAT'G	PEF's RATING OF STUDENT'S PERFORMANCE
Before Evaluation	4.6	Does not reflect competence level
After Correction	9.1	Reflects competence level

11
Total Quality Training Standards

A. The Need for Training Standards

In 1982 Brandenburg found that "no universally accepted model for evaluation of training exists, nor are there generally accepted modes of operation or behavior." The NSPI 1993 Conference program, while focused on performance technology, contains no mention of any effort to explore or adopt universal training standards.

Several organizations have independently attempted to produce training standards. Yet none have achieved wide acceptance. One, for example, is the American National Standards Institute (ANSI). ANSI's Guidelines for the Application of ANSI/ASQC ... to Education and Training Institutions (1993) provides a broad set of standards. Two are similar to *Standards 3 and 4.* There is also a reference to "performance objectives." However, ANSI does not provide specific guidelines for meeting their standards.

Why has the training field been reluctant or unable to establish such standards of effectiveness? I suggest part of the answer lies in Malcolm Knowles' observation:

> "Behaviorists insist that objectives are meaningless unless they describe terminal behaviors in very precise, measurable, and observable terms.... Theorists who see learning as a process of inquiry expressly (and sometimes vehemently) reject the idea that there should be pre-set or prescribed objectives at all." (Knowles, 1973, pp. 126–129)

Bloom, in the forward to the <u>Taxonomy of Educational Objectives</u>, speaks to the problems associated with the creation of the taxonomy.

> "One of the first problems raised in our discussions was whether or not educational objectives could be classified. It was pointed out that we were attempting to classify phenomena which could not be observed or manipulated in the same concrete form as the phenomena of such fields as the physical or biological sciences, where taxonomies of a very high order have already been developed.

There was some concern expressed in early meetings that the availability of the taxonomy might tend to abort the thinking and planning of teachers with regard to curriculum, particularly if teachers merely selected what they believed to be objectives from the list provided in the taxonomy." (Bloom, 1984, pp. 5–6)

Bloom and his colleagues did agree that "educational objectives stated in behavioral terms have their counterpart in the behavior of individuals" and that such behaviors can be observed, described and classified. (Bloom, 1964, p. 5)

The resulting taxonomy succeeded in classifying objectives according to levels of complexity. However, it made no progress with regard to the component structure of the objectives. This is apparent in the model objectives contained in manuscript. "Illustrative Educational Objectives" from three levels of the taxonomy are shown in Fig. 11.1.

As shown, these objectives have no consistency in their structure. Example A contains none of the components of a useful objective. Examples B and C contain only a Performance Component (bolded). The Performer, Conditions, Criteria and Performance Time Components are not evident.

The inability of developers of education and training to agree on the need for objectives or their structure also explains, to some degree, the absence of universal standards.

The Consequences

The absence of training standards, evaluation methods and leadership results in duplication of effort, ineffective programs and inappropriate programs. This wastes an organization's resources and sacrifices the profits that motivated the training effort in the first place.

Mary F. Cook stated in an article that appeared in <u>Management Review</u> "Many companies are spending millions of dollars on nontraditional employee training programs—programs that some call cults." (Cook, 1988, p. 42) She referred to these programs as "New Age" training and cited the following examples:

Figure 11.1. "Illustrative Educational Objectives"

A. Knowledge of Methodology (1.20): "Knowledge of scientific methods for evaluating health concepts." (Bloom, 1964, p. 74)

B. Analysis of Elements (4.10): "Ability to **distinguish a conclusion from statements which support it.**" (Bloom, 1964, p. 146)

C. Judgments in terms of External Criteria (6.20): "The ability to **identify and appraise judgements and values that are involved in the choice of a course of action.**" (Bloom, 1964, p. 192)

- Werner Erhard repackaged EST, a two weekend, $300 program that taught people in the 1970s to get "it," into a new two weekend and one weeknight program called Forum. Forum promises to provide participants with a decisive edge in their ability to achieve. The program costs $525 per participant.

- The Church of Scientology has "two subsidiaries that specialize in training and consulting with corporations. Despite rumors that brainwashing and thought control techniques are used, some companies foot the bill for their employees to take this training."

- "The California Public Utilities Commission launched an investigation into Pacific Bell's 'Krone training' program (officially known as Leadership Development). Employees being 'Kroned' are taken through a series of mental exercises. They are taught to think about six essentials of organizational health—expansion, freedom, identity, concentration, order and interaction—and relate them to the demands of the workplace. Some Pacific Bell employees say the training is a dangerous form of mind control. They complained to the utilities commission that these exercises are based on the teachings of Georges Gurdjieff, a controversial Armenian philosopher and mystic. Public watchdog groups were angry when they found out that PacBell intends to spend $47 million dollars on Krone training." (Cook, 1988, pp. 42–43)

Cook goes on to say:

> "Many companies, desperate to increase productivity and employee commitment, are buying non-traditional training programs and asking (sometimes insisting) that employees participate. In some cases, employees refusing to participate have been fired. Disgruntled employees are filing suit under these circumstances, and government regulations to control abuses are likely to follow.
>
> Many corporations may not intentionally create a 'Big Brother' atmosphere. In fact some executives have no idea their managers are buying these so-called thought control programs.
>
> **Training budgets are often dispersed and decentralized, so that various work sites can buy the programs they feel are needed for their particular groups.** Executives need to wake up to how employee training needs are being met." (Cook, 1988, p. 43)

Cook's observation that executives need to "wake up" deserves comment. Would their participation result in more effective training decisions? Being an executive does not confer training expertise. Thus, their participation, by itself, is not likely to increase the effectiveness of training decisions.

Common Training Errors

Over the years I have observed, evaluated and documented numerous examples of ineffective training. Common to these cases was the absence of learning objectives, needs analysis, modeling and any attempt to measure whether anybody learned anything. A few examples:

1. **Cutting out Performance Time:** A life insurance company spent over $500,000 to retrain 500 experienced agents. The agents, who were accustomed to selling small ($5,000) life insurance policies using a 10-minute canned sales talk, were trained to sell a new product that could meet any customer's need, using a 60-minute sales interview. The Chief Operating Officer arbitrarily cut the length of the training program from six days to four days. This resulted in the elimination of the performance and evaluation activities. As a result, agent understanding, acceptance and competence with the new techniques were not measured.

A year later, a combination needs analysis and post training evaluation was undertaken. Three trained observers evaluated 17 agents in 81 actual sales transactions using a reliable performance evaluation system. The study revealed that the desired behavior, the 60-minute sales interview, was not evident in the performance of the salespeople observed. Result: Lost sales, reduced agent incomes and agent terminations as high as 60 percent, following the introduction of the new product and sales system.

2. **Buying a used car without a test drive:** In 1985 a company purchased a training program on communication for managers. The cost was $5,500 for the instructor manual and initial license fee. Materials for each participant cost $100. The program was purchased solely on the representations of the vendor's salesperson. The instructor, charged with conducting the program, was not provided with facilitator training or an opportunity to see the program conducted by an experienced trainer. The instructor manual turned out to be extremely flawed and required extensive rewriting. Several years later, only 133 of a targeted 1,000 managers had been trained.

3. **Training for its own sake:** A senior manager contracted with a college professor for a training program on strategic leadership. The audience was to be the most senior managers in a large diversified corporation.

The program contained neither objectives nor criteria for measuring learner competence. Also, the planning methods being taught were not something that the senior manager himself practiced. A three day test program conducted with a group of senior managers within his division was aborted after two days. The program was scrapped and approximately $50,000, representing development costs was lost.

4. **Wasted effort:** A large company produced three different videos to accomplish the introduction of a complicated benefits program. Each was produced independently and each contained a different communication/selling style. One was a sales talk by a manager who told the employees they needed the optional protection. One backed the "proverbial hearse up to the door" to cause people to buy optional coverage. The third contained learning objectives in its design and a communication style based on need selling. It enabled people to make decisions about

the optional coverages by showing examples and providing helpful information. The total cost of $100,000 to produce three videos did not include employee time spent on development. This duplication of effort wasted approximately $60,000.

5. **Anybody can train:** A common error involves using managers as trainers. Decision makers assume that because a person is a manager he or she is also an effective developer of training. It is also thought that the manager is a role model who knows how to perform. In almost every instance where this technique is applied, I have observed the absence of learning objectives, modeling and performance evaluation methodology. For the most part leaders and managers do not have the time to prepare or the knowledge to develop effective training.

Here is a classic example. A senior vice president's late arrival and failure to consider that the manager who began conducting the session in his absence "might" have been effective, resulted in an embarrassing situation. The senior vice president spent the next 2 hours recovering the exact same ground as the manager. Neither the students nor the manager mentioned the obvious redundancy. This incident also suggests that authority reduces the level of participation.

Each of the preceding situations resulted in a loss to the organization. Internal development costs, fees paid to vendors for material and licensing, wages to trainers and travel expense are the obvious hard dollar costs. However, there are other significant costs associated with ineffective training. These involve lost productivity and lost opportunity. An ineffective training program reduces the chance that sought after productivity or profits will be realized. They also cause a loss of current productivity. Instead of attending training, the same employees could have been productive on the job.

Another consequence of ineffective or inappropriate training is lowered morale and lowered expectations regarding future training. In many cases, employees would prefer to stay at their jobs and use the time to meet their objectives.

B. Using Training Standards in an Organization

Total Quality Training Standards enable managers, developers and trainers to approach training projects with a common language and establish guidelines that assist all parties in achieving the greatest return from the investment made in training.

Senior Managers who utilize training to achieve results within their business unit can use the Standards to determine the relevance and effectiveness of their unit's training programs. To accomplish this, the manager requires each developer or instructor to justify how their programs meet the Standards.

Each developer scores their program according to the *TQT Standards.* Then they write a brief narrative describing the methodology they employ to meet the *Standard.* Instructions for evaluating a program using the *TQT Standards* are explained in the next section.

Following this, the manager and developer meet to discuss any needed changes. These might include increasing the program's time allocation for student performance or providing the developer with time required to create any missing components.

TQT Standards are also helpful in the development of new training. For example, consider an employee who is given the responsibility to conduct training who is not a professional trainer or program developer. An employee can use the Standards and the *Guidelines for Meeting the Standards* (which follow) to develop their program. The guidelines are, in effect, a training program on performance based training.

The Standards are also relevant to the people being trained. When they are published and distributed within the organization they create an expectation with regard to the quality of the training event. Students attending training know they will be asked to perform. Furthermore, they know they will be evaluated with regard to their competence. The Standards insure that the training will have clear objectives and that instructors are prepared to demonstrate effective techniques for the students.

Finally, the *TQT Standards* are a tool that enables a Chief Executive Officer or Chief Training Officer to bring about organizational training effectiveness. This is particularly important in a large organization where training dollars are spent by business unit managers who may have limited expertise or time to make cost effective training decisions. The concluding section of this chapter contains a detailed outline for implementing the *TQT Standards*.

C. Guidelines for Meeting the Standards

Following are guidelines for meeting each *Standard*. Included for each is the rationale for the *Standard* and suggested methods for meeting it. The guidelines for each *Standard* are scored with the Criterion Scoring System. Hence, each relevant guideline can receive a score of 10 - 5 - 0. In this case, the derived rating results in a precise score for each Standard that can be between 0 and 10.

Rating precision for any *Standard* can also be increased by rating the program's components using the *Expert Criteria to Measure the Standards* found in App. D (see Fig. 10.4, Relationship of *TQT Standards* to Program Components).

Note: During the planning phase, which is referred to as "Before Training," the employee is referred to as "the developer." When conducting training, which is referred to as "During Training," the employee is referred to as "the instructor."

Justification of Ratings

Evaluation accomplishes two objectives simultaneously. First, it enables us to determine if the time and money invested is likely to yield a return, in other words, increased performance. Second, it identifies the program's strengths and, if applicable, any improvement opportunities.

The maximum benefit occurs when the person or group performing the evaluation writes a brief narrative describing how the program meets or does not meet the *Standard.* The depth of the evaluation dictates the length and detail of the justification. (See Fig. 11.12 on page 187 for an example of a rating with justifications.)

The Effectiveness Rating

Figure 11.2 contains the *TQT Standards,* a matrix for recording scores and the formula for calculating the Effectiveness Rating. The Effectiveness Rating is derived by totalling the score for <u>each *Standard*</u> and dividing by 5. A description of the Effectiveness Rating is shown in Fig. 11.3.

D. Meeting Standard 1—Learning Objectives

Learning Objectives which describe the <u>desired behavior(s)</u> to be exhibited during the training program.
This standard is met as follows:

1. Before Training: The developer:
   a. **Writes the Module Objective: Given** (insert the conditions), **the** (state the job title of the performer) **will be able to** (describe the performance) **that** (describe the principal criteria) **within** (state the time limit for the performance).

Figure 11.2. Evaluation Matrix

	Total Quality Training Standards	SCORE or RATING
1	Learning Objectives which describe the <u>desired behavior(s)</u> to be exhibited during the training program.	
2	Evidence of a performance discrepancy in relation to the <u>desired behavior</u> resulting from a lack of skill or knowledge. (Needs Analysis)	
3	Examples or models of the <u>desired behavior</u> during the training program.	
4	Evaluation of student performance of the <u>desired behavior</u> to determine competence during training.	
5	Evidence that the <u>desired behavior</u> has persisted after training and is linked to results. (Post Training Evaluation)	
	TOTAL (Divide by 5)	
	EFFECTIVENESS RATING	

Figure 11.3. Training Effectiveness Rating Scale

Rating		Description
8.0–10.0	<u>Effective</u>	Program produces or is likely to produce the desired behavior.
5.0–7.9	<u>Marginal</u>	Program appears to be missing components that would insure the student's acquisition of the desired behavior.
1.0–4.9	<u>Ineffective</u>	Unlikely to produce a desired behavior <u>that can be observed on the job</u> or <u>that can be linked to results</u>.
0.0–0.9	<u>Not Evident</u>	No structured training program exists. The likelihood of producing a desired behavior that can be observed on the job falls between uncertain and nil.

Disregard the rating when Post Training Evaluation links the desired behavior to productivity and/or results.

    b. **Writes the Unit Objectives.**
       (1) To accomplish the Module Objective, **the** (state the name of the learner) **will be able to:**
       (2) Describe the performance.
       (3) Add Conditions, Criteria and Performance Time as required.
    c. **Organizes the Learning Objectives into a plan or agenda** that includes the sequence of events and training time allocated to each objective. (Refer to the example on page 436 of App. F.)
2. During Training: The instructor at:
    a. Program Introduction: Displays the objectives and reaches agreement with the students on the relevance of the objectives to their needs.
    b. Program Conclusion: Reviews the objectives with the students to determine if they have been achieved.

Rationale: Objectives provide the basis for:

1. *(Before Training) Conducting a needs analysis, determining program content, selecting instructional techniques and allocating time and resources.*
2. *(During Training) Focusing student effort toward the acquisition of the desired behavior and assessing the program's success in meeting its objectives and, as a direct result, the student's needs.*
3. *(After Training) Evaluating the program's success in terms of its impact on productivity. Refer to* **Standard 5.**

Refer to Part 1 for a full explanation of Learning Objectives.

E. Meeting Standard 2—
Needs Analysis

Evidence of a performance discrepancy in relation to the <u>desired behavior</u> resulting from a lack of skill or knowledge.

This standard can be met in one of two ways or disregarded:

1. Before Training: The developer collects behavioral data on the performance of the population targeted for training. In general, the developer collects this data by getting as close to the performance in question as is practically and economically feasible. *A report should contain the data collected, its analysis and the conclusions drawn.* The following are examples of data collection methods listed in order of effectiveness:

   a. Observing performers on the job.
   b. Have performers respond to simulated situations.
   c. Surveying employees or customers of the performer using a reliable survey instrument.
   d. Interviews or surveys with the immediate manager(s) of the performers to identify the problems the performers are experiencing.
   e. Interviews or surveys where performers describe the problems they are experiencing.

2. During Training: The developer or instructor can (in order of effectiveness):

   a. <u>Give the students problems to solve</u> (before giving the answer) that reveal their present competence with the knowledge or skills to be taught. This produces a baseline performance.
   Note: Requires the creation of pre-class assignments, cases or practice exercise, etc. prior to conducting training.
   b. Ask the students to <u>describe their perceived</u> knowledge or skill discrepancies or the problems they are experiencing in a given area.
   c. Discuss performance discrepancies identified in a Need Analysis (if one was conducted).

3. Disregarding this *Standard:* It may not be feasible to conduct a needs analysis in a situation where a new product or procedure is introduced. In such cases, Post Training Evaluation, once completed, will indicate the desired behavior's impact on results and will identify any discrepancies in performance. In this instance, Post Training Evaluation serves as a needs analysis and basis for modification of the training. Refer to *Standard 5.*

Rationale:

1. *Needs analysis focuses the training on the knowledge and skills needed to perform by identifying the actual discrepancies in current performance.*

2. *Learning occurs most effectively when the student perceives a problem and wants to clear up his or her own uneasiness about the problem.*

What Constitutes Evidence of a Performance Discrepancy?

It depends primarily on the size of the population to be trained, the potential training investment and the degree to which the population's needs are understood. A large population and a significant training investment justifies more extensive needs analysis.

For example, consider a performance problem in a group of 500 life insurance agents operating nationwide. Assume that these agents had been previously trained to conduct a 60-minute sales interview and that their sales per agent were substantially below expectations. Further assume that an analysis of the group's performance suggests that the performance problem is related to knowledge and skill rather than systemic factors; i.e., compensation, accountability, product, competition or the sales system being employed.

What would constitute reasonable evidence to justify a retraining program and what should be the training's focus? Should the company retrain the agents on the original sales interview or focus only on the phases that are not competently utilized? Is the problem really related to a discrepancy in knowledge and skill? Should the new program be internally developed or purchased from a vendor? How many agents should be observed?

The answer to these questions will be based on the conclusions drawn from the data collected. Hence, the accuracy of the data collection method is the key to making the most cost effective decision. Listed below, in order of effectiveness, are the needs analysis methods identified on the previous page.

Observing Performers on the Job

Actually, this can be broken down into three techniques: Unobtrusive observation, observation by a nonparticipating observer and observation by a participant in the transaction. Each has advantages and disadvantages. Where applicable, we will assume that the observer will rate the performer against a set of *Expert Criteria* contained within a Performance Evaluation System.

Unobtrusive observation has the distinct advantage of revealing performance discrepancies without any possible distortion induced by the observation process. Unfortunately, setting up such an environment is extremely difficult and expensive.

On the other hand, observation by a nonparticipating observer who is able to use the Performance Evaluation System is far more feasible and the optimal method. When this method is used, the observer accompanies the salesperson and is introduced to the customer as an observer. During the transaction observations are recorded on the PEF. The observer can also record critical incidents. These can be particularly helpful in creating role play cases to simulate real world experience during the training program.

My experience with this method suggests that there is minimal distortion created by the observation process. Salespeople will conduct the interview using their existing skills. The argument that they will try to perform as they believe they are supposed to perform is invalid. When time has passed and certain skills have not been used, the salesperson is unlikely to use them. In fact, he or she may be unable to competently use the "desired behavior(s)."

Nonparticipating observers need to be trained on the use of the Performance Evaluation System. This can be be accomplished by having them rate video taped performances and by discussing their ratings. This training increases rating reliability by minimizing observer drift and bias.

Data produced by the nonparticipating observer can be augmented with survey data. In one project, we had the salesperson and the customer complete surveys that explored each participant's perception of the sales transaction; the salesperson's perception of his or her effectiveness and the customer's perception of the salesperson's effectiveness.

The third technique involves observation by a participant in the transaction, often referred to as a <u>participant observer</u>. In a sales situation the participant observer would be called a "shopper." This technique has the greatest potential for distortion. This is due to the participant observer's:

1. Level of skill. The participant observer can induce distortion in the salesperson's performance by his behavior. For example, by asking a particular question, the salesperson may address an issue that he would not ordinarily have brought up.

2. Personal bias and emotion.

3. Buying motivation. A salesperson may sense that the participant observer is not really a customer for the product or service.

4. Delay in recording their observations. The participant observer must record their ratings after the transaction is completed.

A technique used by an agency that hired "shoppers" to evaluate car salespeople demonstrates the complexity and expense in solving the inherent problems with this method. The agency advertised for customers who were in the market to purchase a vehicle. These people were paid a fee ($100) for contractually agreeing to engage in a sales transaction with three of the agency's clients. Since, the "shoppers" were actually in the market, this element of the distortion factor was reduced. However, the reliability of the data is still reduced due to the fact that the "shopper" is not a trained observer of expert performance.

Assessment Programs

Having performers respond to simulated situations is commonly known as an assessment program. This method has several advantages. These include observation by a trained observer, the use of a reliable Performance Evaluation System and scheduling efficiencies. Therefore, the data collected represents observed, rather than perceived, performance discrepancies. The technique has the obvious disadvantage of being a simulation, a role play as opposed to an actual selling situation. The effectiveness of the assessment methodology is increased by the skill of the people playing the customers, their consistency and the realism built into the role play cases.

When an assessment program is carried out during the training event it is called a "baseline performance." Effectiveness is reduced when the customer role(s) is played by other salespeople rather than "trained role players." (See Needs Analysis During Training.)

Survey and Interview Techniques

<u>Surveying prospects or customers of the performer</u> using a reliable survey instrument offers several advantages. Surveys can be conducted by mail or, if desired, by phone and data can be collected quickly at a relatively low cost. The advantage and disadvantage to the technique is the type of data. At best, the data represents perceived rather than observed performance discrepancies. Its strength is the fact that the data represents a customer's perception rather than a manager's perception. In effect, the customer's perception is more valid than the manager's since it is he or she who ultimately makes the buying decision.

Data collected by <u>survey of the performer's manager</u> has all of the advantages of surveying prospects and customers. When the surveys are combined with interviews of managers who have observed the salespeople in actual transactions, the value of the data is increased. In such cases, the managers are asked to describe the performance discrepancies they observed. These critical incidents provide data that supports and substantiates the survey data. Again, the critical incidents may also be useful in constructing role play cases for use during the training program.

Data collected by surveying and <u>interviewing the performer</u> also represents perceived rather than observed performance problems. Here again, effectiveness can be increased by having the salespeople describe specific incidents.

Needs Analysis During Training

In many cases it is simply not practical to conduct a needs analysis prior to conducting training. For example, the population to be trained is very small, time does not allow it, the cost is prohibitive or there is reasonable certainty that the performance problem is due to a discrepancy in performers' skill or knowledge.

In such cases, the need analysis can be carried out during the training program. The techniques below can be used individually or in combination.

1. Give the students problems to solve (before giving the answer) that reveal their present competence with the knowledge or skills to be taught. This produces a baseline performance.

2. Ask the students to <u>describe their perceived</u> knowledge or skill discrepancies or the problems they are experiencing in a given area.

Asking the students to discuss the problems they are experiencing has many benefits. First, there is the general confirmation of the need for training by the group. Second, the process identifies the problems the group is experiencing. In some cases, problems may surface that were unanticipated in the training design. This may result in changes to future programs and, where feasible, adjustments to the program in progress.

Giving the students problems that reveal their present competence with the knowledge or skills was referred to earlier as a baseline performance. This technique is similar to assessment programs. A simulation is conducted where one or more students acts as the performer. The instructor and the group observe and discuss specific problems. The benefit of a baseline performance is its ability to reveal actual as opposed to perceived performance problems.

The technique, however, has obvious limitations, time being the most critical. Assuming the performance is 15 minutes, assessment of a group of 20 students could take well over <u>one day</u> if each received 10 minutes of evaluation.

Evaluation with a Performance Evaluation System is also somewhat restricted. In order to have the students judge themselves and their peers with the PEF, they have to be able to recognize the characteristics of expert performance. Hence, the instructor has to teach the structure of the behavior prior to the baseline performances. This tends to distort the performance since the students will often try to perform according to the *Expert Criteria.*

The other disadvantage is repetition of student errors. After one or two baseline performances, the range of performance discrepancies has generally been discovered. Hence, there is very little gained by having each student do a baseline performance.

In fact the greatest benefit of baseline performance is its ability to bring about learning motivation in the group. However, this can often be accomplished by having as few as two students participate in a baseline performance. Even though only two perform, the group participates vicariously. The non-performing students compare what they have done or would have done in the same situation to the performance of the student observed.

Based on a 15-minute performance with an equal amount of time for evaluation, the time required for two baseline performances is approximately <u>one hour</u>.

Needs Analysis and Motivation to Learn

The following demonstrates the use of needs analysis during training and its impact on the student's motivation to learn.

I was asked to conduct a two-day training program with a group of 12 consultants on techniques for conducting interactive meetings. These consultants introduced a system for handling telephone sales transactions in car dealerships. The first step in their installation process involved a meeting with the client dealer's sales management team. The manager of the consultants was concerned that his people were not maximizing the opportunity created by meeting with the client's management team. His concern was related to his own experience. He personally had difficulty, on occasion, controlling these meetings and had observed his consultants having the same problems.

Since there were only 12 consultants (students) and the manager had first hand knowledge of their problems, I elected to conduct my needs analysis as an integral part of the training. Specifically, by asking the group to describe the problems they were experiencing when conducting these meetings and by conducting a baseline performance. (This met guidelines B 1 and 2.)

As expected, the consultants knew that something was not right. The group readily agreed on the following problems (see Fig. 11.4) in a discussion that took about 16 minutes.

Following this we conducted a baseline performance, part of which involved having a consultant conduct a simulated 80-minute management team meeting. In structuring this exercise we attempted to maximize learning motivation and minimize time. Time, in particular, was a significant issue. We did not want each consultant to conduct a simulated meeting as this would have taken two days just for the performance. Discussion of the problems experienced would have added another day. We also knew there was a high probability that each consultant would experience similar problems.

The solution involved a two-phase baseline performance. In the first phase, the consultants outlined their meetings. Then they transferred the outline to a flip chart page which was hung on the wall. Each consultant was given an opportunity to explain how he or she conducted the meeting. This exercise created a significant level of need awareness. The consultants discovered that while there were many similarities, there were a few differences in the way they approached this meeting.

In the second phase, we conducted the simulated meeting. Five of the consultants acted as a group of managers while the remainder acted as observers. We had carefully developed a case with specific roles for each person playing a manager including the issues each would raise during the meeting. Half of the con-

---

Figure 11.4. Perceived Performance Problems

1. Difficulty handling resistance to certain aspects of their telephone sales system.

2. Difficulty getting the managers to actively participate in the meeting.

3. Not maximizing the opportunity to build a relationship with the management team.

4. A sense that, for whatever reason, many managers did not understand or accept the benefits of the system.

sultants volunteered to conduct the meeting. One consultant, who we shall call Bob Smith, was given the opportunity to perform.

The simulated meeting lasted exactly 60 minutes. When it was over we conducted a discussion which focused on the problems experienced (Fig. 11.5) and the validity of the exercise. All of the consultants, including Bob Smith, readily agreed that our case had simulated the types of problems they commonly encountered. This discussion lasted a full hour.

Most important, to a person, the consultants admitted that they would have experienced many of the same problems that Bob Smith encountered. The two-phase baseline performance had created a vicarious learning experience for the other 11 members of the group. Having outlined and verbally explained their meetings, they knew that they would have run into similar problems. The common excuse, "That's not the way I do it," had been removed.

The combination of listing perceived problems and identifying actual performance discrepancies brought about a high level of awareness and a desire to correct these problems. The process was accomplished in 2.5 hours which included 15 minutes to set up the simulated meeting. The rating for *Standard 2* is shown in Fig. 11.6.

Appropriateness Baseline Performance

When students have no background or experience with the desired behavior, it may be desirable to forgo a baseline performance. For example, consider a group of new employees who will be trained to sell a complex product in a lengthy (60-minute) sales interview. Little is to be gained by having them perform, as they do not understand the product.

Figure 11.5. Observed Performance Problems

1. Lack of an agenda. The management team did not know where the consultant was heading. This contributed to a loss of control.

2. Excessive one way communication despite a statement at the beginning of the meeting soliciting the managers' active participation.

3. A tendency to react ineffectively to questions and objections. His responses resulted in a win-lose transaction which did not build his relationship with the management team.

4. A loss of control as a result of reacting ineffectively to the resistance.

5 A significant degree of inconsistency between Bob Smith's outline and the actual flow of the meeting.

6. Failure to cover all of the relevant meeting content.

7. Failure to reach clear agreements with the management team.

Figure 11.6. Scoring for **Standard 2**

__10__ 1. Give the students problems to solve (before giving the answer) that reveal their present competence. A baseline performance.

__10__ 2. Ask the students to describe their perceived knowledge or skill discrepancies or the problems they are experiencing.

__10__ 3. Discuss performance discrepancies identified in a Need Analysis.

__30__ Total Score

__10__ Rating and score for **Standard 2** (Total Score divided by 3).

In cases where there is no baseline performance the instructor should model the behavior early in the program. In the above example (complex product and lengthy sales interview), the students would have the opportunity to see the entire transaction from the customer's viewpoint. They also gain an overview of the knowledge and skills that they will have to learn in order to perform competently. This overview is referred to as *whole versus part learning*. Once a person has a view of the whole, they can focus on learning the fine points of each part as they know how it all fits together.

However, in a situation where the person could use their existing knowledge and skills, even though they have no prior experience, a baseline performance can and should be used. This is especially true when the length of the performance can be limited to 10 or 20 minutes. In these cases, the instructor and students can gain considerable insight into the needs that must be met.

For example, transactions which involve the management of people lend themselves to baseline performance. Even though the trainee never managed people, they have been managed. These experiences with superiors, teachers and parents have shaped their concepts of management. Without any training, they will use the knowledge and people skills they have acquired to accomplish their goals. Baseline performances in these situations add to the challenge of the training program and significantly increases participation and learning motivation.

The same is true when teaching training skills or sales skills. Again people have formed strong concepts from prior experiences and will use their knowledge and skills to solve a problem.

In a course I developed on claims adjustment we used multiple baseline performances. In this program, we had students with no prior experience making claim decisions from day one. To accomplish this, we sequenced 40 cases ranging from relatively simple to highly complex. Each case (claim) was, itself a baseline and competence performance at the same time. Competence was measured by inserting issues that had been previously taught while simultaneously introducing new issues that required them to use their judgment and problem solving skills. As the course progressed, the adjustor's ability to make accurate claim decisions on new situations got stronger. This led to higher on the job productivity and less time running to supervisors with questions. Also fewer claims required readjusting after quality checking.

Students in a life insurance course learned to select and recommend the appropriate type and amount of life insurance in much the same way as the adjustors learned to adjust claims. Once they mastered the product line, they were given cases containing information about each prospect's financial situation. They had to select and recommend the amount of coverage and type of product before the "school" solution was given.

Another key point—baseline performance does not have to occur at the beginning of the training program. It can be used at any time during the training. For example, a new technique can be presented to the group in the form of a problem. The simple question, "How would you handle this?" can produce vignettes of behavior from several of the trainees. The performance helps the group discover their existing knowledge and skills, produces learning motivation, aids the trainee's understanding of the the skills contained in the course and makes the training more interesting for all parties.

F. Meeting *Standard 3*—Modeling

Examples or models of the <u>desired behavior</u> during the training program.
This standard can be met as follows:

1. Before Training: Depends on the type of behavior to be exhibited:
    a. Knowledge based: The developer can <u>prepare</u> sample problems and solutions.
    b. Interactive: The developer can either:
        (1) <u>Prepare</u> for a live demonstration:
            (a) <u>Create</u> cases and materials for a behavioral simulation (role play).
            (b) <u>Insure</u> that the instructor can competently demonstrate the desired behavior in a role play.
        (2) <u>Produce</u> a video of the desired behavior.
            (a) Optimal: The complete behavior is shown along with, if applicable, responses to typical questions and objections.
            (b) Questionable: The behaviors modeled are incomplete, frequently interrupted or do not show responses to resistance.
2. During Training: The instructor can:
    a. Depends on the type of behavior to be exhibited:
        (1) Knowledge based: Show example problems and solutions; e.g., the preparation of a tax return in relation to a case.
        (2) Interactive: <u>Conduct</u> a demonstration of the desired behavior in a role play simulation.
    b. Discuss the relevance, importance and structure of each of the units of knowledge and skill that enables the student to perform the desired behavior.

Rationale:

1. *People commit their energies to that which they perceive as relevant.*

2. *Examples and models provide graphic illustrations which permit the student to structure and compare the desired behavior to his or her own experience.*

The Power of Modeling

Modeling in combination with discussion of the model and performance evaluation brings about understanding, acceptance and the ability to use the desired behavior. Modeling enables the student to see the desired behavior used to solve a problem and creates a frame of reference that helps the student identify the components of expert performance.

During the training program on <u>Conducting Interactive Management Meetings</u>, the author acted as the consultant and conducted a simulated meeting. (See pp. 167–169) The same students who acted as managers in the baseline performance, acted as the managers in the model meeting. The case remained the same.

This process enabled the students to observe how expert behavior could eliminate or mitigate the problems Bob Smith had experienced during the baseline performance. It also helped them realize that these problems were caused by a lack of key skills and the knowledge that enables their usage. The model meeting lasted 90 minutes.

During the next four hours, the group explored the relevance, importance and structure of each of the techniques that they had observed in the model. At the conclusion of this discussion, we evaluated both the baseline performance and the model in relation to the *Expert Criteria* in the Performance Evaluation Form. As expected, the model received a 3.8 (on a 4.0 scale), indicating the presence of almost all the components of expert performance. The baseline's rating of 1.8 (ineffective) confirmed that most of the components of expert performance were missing.

The above example demonstrates several key techniques to enhance the effectiveness of behavior modeling. The first is the use of a case to simulate, to the extent possible, the issues that the student actually faces on the job. The second involves the use of a baseline performance prior to the model to create motivation. The discussion of the model and the use of a performance evaluation system further reinforce the behavior. Each technique is discussed in the following.

Discussion of the Model

People will accept and use new behaviors if they understand them and feel that the effort required to make the change will result in a sufficient pay-off. Hence, the guideline that the instructor discuss the relevance, importance and structure of each unit of skill or knowledge.

Discussing the structure of the behavior is critical. Structure refers to the component parts of the behavior. Figure 11.7 shows the structure of a behavior for making appointments with prospects who have received a sales brochure prior to a contact. After the instructor has modeled this behavior in a simulation, she should determine, through questioning, the degree to which the students were able to identify the components.

The process of listening to the students' interpretation of the behavior they observed serves two purposes. First, discussion by the students further reinforces the behavior as they put words to what they observed. Secondly, the instructor receives feedback that indicates the degree to which the students were able to identify the components of expert performance.

Student understanding is also enhanced by discussing the relevance and importance of each component. For example, consider component 1 which requires the salesperson to "contract for time and questions at the start of the contact." Contracting for time can be accomplished with a question to the prospect such as: "Am I taking you away from anything important?" Contracting for questions is accomplished with the question: "Do you mind if I ask you a few questions?" The contracting step depicted above enables the salesperson to start a relationship based on courtesy and respect for the prospect and his or her time. Discussion of these techniques and the motives (the "why") behind each reinforces the student's understanding of the component and leads to understanding and acceptance of the behavior as a whole.

Relevance, Applicability and Practicality

Discussions of any behavior or its components should address the issues of relevance, practicality and applicability. Relevance implies that desired behavior will

---

Figure 11.7. Structure of a Telephone Sales Behavior

<u>Interview Structure</u>: Rate for content and relevance to the situation.

1. Contract for time and questions at the start of the contact.
2. Determine if the customer has received and read the brochure.
3. Determine the customer's reaction to the brochure or her familiarity with the company. (If applicable, determine the customer's experience with company or other training and development companies.)
4. (If applicable) Explain briefly the mission and services of the company.
5. Offer to meet for the purpose of exploring the mutual benefits of a relationship.
6. Obtain a commitment on the date, time, purpose and participants for a formal sales interview. (If applicable, contract with the customer to read the brochure prior to the meeting.)

enable the students to solve the problems they face. Practicality is the degree to which the skills are usable by the student. Applicability relates to the idea that the desired behavior will be used often enough to justify the time invested in learning the skill. While the difference between relevance, practicality and applicability are subtle, each must be explored if acceptance is to occur.

For example, consider a course on interviewing and selecting prospective employees from the standpoints of relevance, practicality and applicability. Assume the course is attended by managers whose need for people varies greatly. Some experience high turnover and must recruit two to three people per month for a single position while others look for one or two persons in a year for a variety of positions. Now further assume that the course teaches the principles of selection rather than a particular system. Emphasis is placed on using preplanned behavioral questions derived from a sophisticated job analysis technique. This enables each question to be directly related to a key performance factor for the position. In our example, we will assume that the techniques are modeled and that the structure of each technique is thoroughly explored.

Participants are likely to find the desired behavior highly relevant as the techniques presented are directly related to the selection of the most suitable employee(s). However, from a practicality standpoint, the techniques are questionable. Most managers do not possess the time to conduct a sophisticated job analysis for each position, even when the job analysis techniques are thoroughly understood.

The desired behavior is also questionable from an applicability standpoint. The managers who interview and select one or two times per year will tend to find that they will have forgotten many techniques as a result of infrequent use. Also the fact that the job analysis must be completed for each position will further reduce their motivation to learn and use the techniques.

Does this really happen? Consider the experience of a training company that taught the principles of effective employee selection to managers who <u>interviewed frequently for one type of sales position</u>. They discovered, through post training evaluation, that few of the managers actually used the techniques on the job. As a result, they reformulated the desired behavior contained in their program into a system. They provided the managers with interview questions and an organized structure for explaining the job. Managers who received training on the system tended to use the desired behaviors to a significantly greater degree than those who learned only the principles.

Modeling with Performance Evaluation

When a desired behavior can be performed in a reasonable time frame (less than 30 minutes) it is often desirable to <u>model the behavior a second time</u> and have the group evaluate the performance using the *Expert Criteria* in the Performance Evaluation Form. This second model provides a powerful reinforcement of the behavior while simultaneously teaching the students how to use the performance evaluation system. It also sets the standard for Expert Performance (as measured by the rating scale).

As previously discussed, the process of evaluating performance with *Expert Criteria* reinforces, with each evaluation, the desired behavior. Students who are able to distinguish the components of the behavior in themselves and others are themselves progressing down the road to becoming experts.

The second model also reinforces the desired behavior in two other significant ways. These involve the learning principles of frequency and recency. Frequency holds that the points that are repeated the greatest number of times are more likely to be learned. A second model of the desired behavior meets this criteria. The principle of recency holds that the items at the end of a list, or points made at the end of a transaction, are best retained. When the second model is followed by evaluation of student performance, it increases the likelihood of competent performance.

The second model also helps the student "put it all together." When this model follows an explanation of the structure of the behavior, the students again see the desired behavior as a whole in context with the problem(s) that it is designed to solve.

Preparing the Group for the Model

To maximize the effectiveness of the model, the group must be prepared. This involves giving the students observing and those participating in the simulation one or more tasks to perform.

The observers should outline the flow of the behavior. (See Fig. 11.7.) They should also record any techniques that are used to facilitate the process. Such techniques include: contracting, transitions, questioning, probing, supporting, paraphrasing, complimenting and interrupting. Critical events that effect the outcome of the transaction should also be recorded.

Students acting as the customer, employee or manager can also be given an observation task in addition to their assigned role. They can be asked to comment on their reaction to the behavior being demonstrated. In some cases, they can also take notes on its structure. Notes help them recall the key components and take part in the discussion. This is especially important in long transactions. However, note taking is only appropriate when notes would be taken in the "real life" situation.

For example, students acting as managers in our model management team meeting were given the same task as the observers (i.e., to outline the structure of the behavior). This was appropriate since managers, in a real life situation, would be taking notes on the consultant's message.

Modeling and Motivation to Learn

Gary M. Grikscheit, Harold Cash and W.J.E. Crissy in The Handbook of Selling (1981, p. 23) suggest that a customer makes a buying decision when the product or service being sold fulfills his or her needs. Their Need Satisfaction Theory is illustrated below. The horizontal axis of the diagram represents time; the vertical axis represents the participation of the salesperson and customer. The process is divided into three phases: *Need Discovery, Need Awareness* and *Need Fulfillment*.

During *Need Discovery* the salesperson asks questions and listens to the customer. The salesperson's goal is to get the customer to talk about their needs. This phase is completed when the salesperson and customer agree on the needs. As the process moves into the *Need Awareness* phase, the salesperson's participation increases as he helps the customer understand those needs. This phase is completed when they agree on a problem to be solved. *Need Fulfillment*, the third phase, ends when they agree on the solution. Notice that the salesperson's participation increases significantly in this phase, as he explains the product or service (see Fig 11.8).

This theory also applies to training. In a training setting, the student is the customer and the instructor in the salesperson The desired behavior is the product being sold. The student makes a buying decision when she accepts the new behavior.

The discussion of problems being experienced and the baseline performance represents the *Need Discovery* phase (shown by the time line beneath Fig. 11.9). The instructor's role is to conduct the discussion and set up the simulation. The discussion of the baseline performance completes the discovery phase and moves the process into the awareness phase. Through discussion, the instructor helps the students identify the flaws in their current behaviors. The model by the instructor completes the *Need Awareness* phase and, as shown by the time-line, is also part of the *Need Fulfillment* phase. The fulfillment phase is completed by the explanation of the model. During this phase the instructor should thoroughly discuss the structure of the behavior and the importance (the "why") behind each unit of knowledge and skill. Notice that the instructor's participation increases during this phase, as she points out the subtleties in each component of the behavior.

Figure 11.8. Cash and Crissy's Need Satisfaction Theory

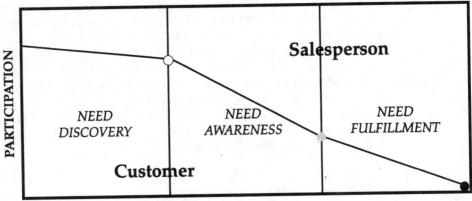

Reprinted with permission from *The Handbook of Selling* by Gary M. Grikscheit, Harold C. Cash and W.J.E. Crissy, © 1981 John Wiley & Sons, Inc. (Figure 11.9 is adapted with permission of the publisher)

Figure 11.9. Need Satisfaction Theory Applied to Training

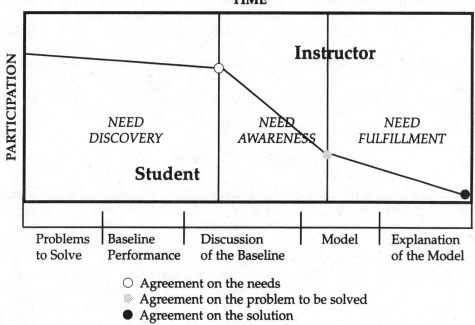

○ Agreement on the needs
▨ Agreement on the problem to be solved
● Agreement on the solution

   The model (demonstration of the desired behavior) also creates learning motivation which is why it is shown as part of the awareness phase. The model enables the student to see the gap between their current behavior and expert performance. In short, it brings about awareness of a solution to the problem and motivates the student to understand the component parts of the behavior.

Relationship of Baseline Performance to Modeling

The opportunity to experiment with one's own behavior in a baseline performance enables the student to identify their own strengths and weaknesses. It also helps the student appreciate expert performance. Without a baseline, the subtle components of expert behavior may be overlooked or the student may think that he uses them when, in fact, he does not.

   Quite often the difference between effective performance and marginal performance is extremely subtle. For example, consider a leader's response to an issue raised during a meeting which requires a certain amount of foundation to be established before it is discussed.

   Marginal performance occurs when the leader provides an immediate answer, but fails to determine the respondent's motivation. This often results in a loss of control. The untimely answer causes other questions and issues to be raised. The problem is exacerbated when the answer provided is explained poorly. In the latter case, the performance would be classified as ineffective.

Expert performance would involve the use of one or more techniques that enable the leader to present the proposal in the most logical and favorable sequence. These include contracting, paraphrasing and questioning. They help the leader to acknowledge and understand the respondent and, when appropriate, reach agreement on the timing of the answer. Used effectively, they enable the leader to bring the meeting to a successful conclusion.

Modeling: "One Picture Is Worth a Thousand Words"

I observed a salesperson conduct an 8-hour training session on the sale of a training service to a group of 10 sales managers each of whom worked for a sister company. The objective was to enable these managers to market the training service to their client base.

The instructor (salesperson) spent the entire time period explaining each of the pages of a lengthy sales presentation book, which he handed out one page at a time. The program, as presented, received an <u>Effectiveness Rating</u> of "0" (zero). There were no Learning Objectives (*Standard 1*), no needs analysis prior to training, no agreement of the problems to be solved and no baseline performance (*Standard 2*), no modeling of the sales interview (*Standard 3*), and no performance by the managers (*Standard 4*).

What could this "occasional trainer" (salesperson) have done to increase training effectiveness? I suggest that he could have set up a case (situation) and conducted a model sales interview. The sales interview for the training service could run 70 to 100 minutes depending on the client's receptivity. This would have enabled the managers to see the sales presentation book used within the context of the sales interview. If the model were coupled with a discussion of the structure of the interview and other relevant issues, *Standard 3* would have been fully met. The model and discussion would have used up approximately 3 hours of training time.

Training effectiveness would also have been increased by preparing a set of learning objectives (a possible score of 10), the absence of which contributed to the instructor's ineffective performance. Also, a brief discussion with the managers about the problems they perceived they would experience in selling the training service would have created some degree of learning motivation and earned a score of 5. Thirty to 40 minutes of training time would have been absorbed by this activity.

With the modifications listed above, a total score of 25 (out of 50) would have resulted in an Effectiveness Rating of 5.0. The instructor would still have had at least 4 hours to explain the content of the sales presentation book. Although, in all probability, the need for such explanation would have been alleviated by the model.

The need for a formal training program could have been eliminated by having each manager observe the salesperson conduct interviews with potential clients. However, the logistics of scheduling 10 managers to observe actual interviews, the cost of airfare and other obstacles (such as prospects who break their appointments) rendered this approach impractical. If it were practical, the manager would be able to observe the transaction and, at its conclusion, discuss it with the salesperson.

In a situation where there is limited time, modeling of the desired behavior with discussion of the model, may be the fastest and most efficient way to communicate the message.

Video Versus Live Modeling

Which is more desirable, a videotaped model or a live model performed by the instructor? I prefer live modeling by a person who is perceived by the group as a role model (i.e., a successful salesperson, if the topic is selling, or a manager, if the topic is management).

Videotaped models suffer from a number of problems, each of which tends to reduce their effectiveness. Videotape is expensive. In 1992 when this book was written, video production costs could easily reach $2,000 per minute. As a result of the investment, developers tend to make the videos "too perfect." Scripting, for example, makes the performance flawless. However, this often leads the students to sit back and say that the situation is not realistic.

Another problem involves camera angles and cuts. Directors, to increase the drama, focus the camera on the person speaking. Unfortunately, this reduces or eliminates the student's observation of the person listening to the message. As a result, the nonverbal reaction to the message is lost.

Video, once produced, is difficult and expensive to change. As a consequence, the desired behavior produced on video tends to be etched in stone. Unfortunately, some of the techniques depicted may be flawed. This forces instructors to work around or worse, defend the flawed techniques. In either case, the erosion of relevance tends to reduce the student's learning motivation or increase training time.

An example: A video was produced to depict a 60-minute sales interview. The video was completed before training program development commenced. During the training's development, significant flaws were discovered in a sales aid that organized the salesperson's presentation. As a result, substantial modifications were made to the sales aid, but not to the video. When the training commenced, the videotaped model did not depict the greatly improved sales aid. Significant time was lost in explaining the differences in performance brought about by the new sales aid. In effect, students had to unlearn parts of the depicted behavior.

Live modeling by a competent instructor who is also a competent performer eliminates these problems. The latest, most up-to-date, techniques and materials can be used. Also the student will view both the sender and the receiver simultaneously. Most important, the transaction will be human. There will be minor errors, and depending on the question or objections raised by the person who plays the receiver, (customer or employee) opportunities for the instructor to respond spontaneously.

Live modeling has its drawbacks. These involve the fear of performing in front of a group, controlling the situation in which the performance occurs and modeling ineffectively. Instructor fear of losing control and the potential for embarrassment caused by inability to respond, tends to inhibit some from live modeling. Preparation is the solution. The instructor who engages in live modeling needs to practice the desired behavior prior to conducting the training. Also, cases need to be prepared. Cases, as you recall from Chap. 8, help the student playing the role of the receiver to simulate a realistic situation.

In summary, any model which demonstrates expert performance in relation to a believable situation is going to increase student learning and training effectiveness. When students can say, as was the case in the class on <u>Conducting Initial Management Team Meetings</u>, that reality had been brought into the classroom, effectiveness is increased. Complete transactions also increase effectiveness. Behaviors that are incomplete or out of context make it more difficult for the student to see how the techniques being taught are used.

G. Meeting *Standard 4*— Performance Evaluation

Evaluation of student performance of the <u>desired behavior</u> to determine competence during training.

This standard can be met as follows:

1. Before training the developer can:
   a. Provide adequate time during the program for each student to perform the desired behavior. Two or more performances are optimal.
   b. Establish *Expert Criteria* to measure the desired behavior.
   c. Establish a rating scale to measure levels of competence.
   d. Create an Evaluation Form to record ratings and comments.
   e. Establish a performance standard. A minimum level of competence by which the success of both the student and course can be evaluated.
   f. Create cases (if applicable) to simulate situations likely to be encountered on the job.
2. During training the instructor can:
   a. Employ methods to permit the students to evaluate their own performance.
      (1) Have students identify both strengths and improvement opportunities.
      (2) Use criteria, evaluation forms and the rating scale to measure competence.
      (3) (Interactive Behaviors): Videotape the performance. This allows the student to see the performance rather than to recall it from memory.

b. Observe, evaluate and comment on student performance.

c. Insure that multiple performance and evaluation takes place (if time is allocated).

Rationale: Evaluation of performance allows both the student and instructor to determine if learning has taken place. Stated another way, we discover that the student has acquired the desired behavior if he or she is able to perform at a reasonable level of competence. Evaluation also increases the student's learning motivation by creating accountability for the acquisition of the desired behavior.

Note: The criteria, rating scale and evaluation form can be used to measure the desired behavior on the job. Refer to **Standard 5** (Post Training Evaluation).

Evaluating the Evaluation Method

Figure 11.10 contains a system for approximating the Criterion Score for performance and evaluation. The system considers both the quality of the evaluation method and the number of students who perform.

For example, a score of 10 is achieved when all students perform the desired behavior, more than once, and receive evaluation by the instructor (and the group) using established criteria. Additionally, the requirement for a performance standard dictates that numerical scoring and rating be used.

When all the students are evaluated, the instructor (or the developer of the training program) has empirical evidence of training effectiveness. Assuming that 8 of 10 performer's ratings are at or above the performance standard, the training would be considered successful. On the other hand, if only two of the 10 performed to standard, then the event would have to be considered ineffective as the students were unable to perform.

Consider the methodology that earns a score of 3.0, having the students perform in unsupervised teams with no structure provided for feedback. In this case, the instructor has no way of determining if learning has taken place. Additionally, the lack of structure for the evaluation process reduces the effectiveness of the feedback that students receive (or minimally suggests that it will be uneven). Even if 100 percent of the group performs, the Criterion Score for **Standard 5** does not deserve more than a score of 3.0. On the other hand, if only 20 percent of the group performs, then the Criterion Score would be .6. The score would suggest that the performance and evaluation within this particular training program was gratuitous.

Practical Problems with Time and Resources

You may argue that *Standard 4* is unrealistic especially for long performances with large groups. For example, consider a group of 20 students in a program

Figure 11.10. Short-Cut Criterion Scoring for **Standard 4**

Procedure to calculate Criterion Score:

1. Select the **SCORE** based on the **EVALUATION METHOD EMPLOYED** (below).
2. Multiply the **SCORE** by the percentage of the group that performs.

   Example: Evaluation Method Employed equals 8.0. Percentage of students performing equals 90 percent. **Final Criterion Score: 7.2 (8.0 × .9)**

SCORE	EVALUATION METHOD EMPLOYED
10.0	The student performs the desired behavior more than one time* with formal evaluation using pre-agreed upon criteria. Ratings obtained are compared to a performance standard. Performance is observed and evaluated by the instructor.
	*The first performance provides a baseline to measure from. The second shows improvement and competence. The third is a clear measure of competence.
8.0	Same as above except the student's performance is formally evaluated one time using pre-agreed upon criteria in relationship to a performance standard.
6.0	Performance is observed and evaluated by the instructor. During the evaluation the student, group and instructor identify strengths and weaknesses.
5.0	Students perform the desired behavior. This is followed by an evaluation of their performance based on criteria. However, the instructor **does not** observe or evaluate their performance.
4.0	Students perform and receive unstructured feedback by the instructor and group. There is no evaluation against criteria to measure competence.
3.0	Students perform the desired behavior in unsupervised teams with unstructured feedback or criteria for measuring competence.
0.0	Students do not perform the desired behavior.

teaching a behavior that requires 20 minutes to perform. Assuming each student receives 15 minutes of feedback, the performance time of 700 minutes for just one exercise is considerable.

Add videotaping to this exercise and the time problem is exacerbated. For example, if the training facility had five cameras and recorders, the group could be taped in 80 minutes (4 teams of 5 performers). Therefore, the total exercise would require 810 minutes, or, depending on the length of the training day, approximately two days.

30	Set-up time for the exercise
80	Videotape the performance
400	Performance Time (20 students × 20 minutes)
300	Evaluation Time (20 students × 15 minutes)
810	Total Time for One Exercise

The problem can be solved by having multiple instructors during the performance and evaluation segment. For example, a total of 4 instructors can complete the evaluations of 20 performances in 175 minutes if each evaluates 5 students.

30	Set-up time for the exercise
80	Videotape the performance
100	Performance Time (**5** students × 20 minutes)
75	Evaluation Time (**5** students × 15 minutes)
285	Total Time for One Exercise

VideoLab—Another Solution

To address the time problem, I designed a concept called VideoLab. VideoLab is a facility with a number of cubicles, each equipped with a VCR and a monitor. This enables students to simultaneously review their performances. To ensure meaningful feedback, each student views their own performance with a partner using a PEF containing *Expert Criteria.*

A VideoLab with 10 cubicles would enable 20 students to evaluate their performance in 70 minutes. Evaluation accuracy is increased by having the group review one student's performance before using the VideoLab. This sets a standard for the evaluation process. The time including videotaping is greatly reduced:

30	Set-up exercise
80	Videotape the performance
35	Group evaluation of one student's performance
35	Replay and evaluate 1st 10 performances
35	Replay and evaluate 2nd 10 performances
215	Total Time for One Exercise

Additionally, the instructor is required to observe and participate in the evaluation of two student performances while the group is in the VideoLab. This provides some degree of accountability for competent performance, since no one knows whose performance will be observed. The three performances evaluated by the instructor provide an indication of training effectiveness.

My use of the words, "some degree" and "indication," reflect the Criterion Score for *Standard 5* using the "short-cut system." On the "Evaluation Method Employed" scale (Fig. 11.10) the VideoLab methodology earns a score of 5 (marginal). The Criterion Score is also 5 due to the fact that 100 percent of the students receive evaluation.

A score of 6 can be justified by the fact that the instructor leads the group through the evaluation of one student's performance and observes two additional performances. These three performances receive a score of 8 on the "Evaluation Method Employed" scale (Fig. 11.10). However, the Criterion Score is reduced to 1.2 by the fact that only 15 percent of the students are evaluated (3 out of 20). I would be reluctant to score the VideoLab method beyond 6 (marginal), since the instructor (or developer) only has data that suggests rather than confirms that learning has occurred.

VideoLab is actually a structured practice session rather than evaluation of student competence. The opportunity for the student to observe their own performance on video and evaluate it with the *Expert Criteria* tends to increase competence to a greater degree than a practice session without the use of video. This is evident from the higher ratings achieved when a VideoLab exercise precedes the instructor's evaluation of the student's performance.

Performance and Learning Motivation

Motivation is increased when the student is held accountable for acquiring the desired behavior. Motivating factors include evaluation of the student's performance by the instructor and reporting of his or her competence (with the desired behavior) to the student's manager.

If the student's manager were also the instructor, the student would be motivated to perform at his highest level of competence. The student would perceive that future employment, promotion or compensation decisions could be effected by the manager's satisfaction with the student's performance. As a result, the student concentrates harder and puts in more practice time. Motivation is also increased when the student is competing with peers.

When an instructor conducts the training, the instructor is acting on behalf of the student's manager. However, in many cases, the group is composed of people sent by different managers. If you eliminate evaluation of performance and reporting of the student's competence, you substantially reduce the student's motivation to learn the desired behavior.

Douglas McGregor's Theory Y assumption 3 (McGregor, 1960, p. 33) states that **"commitment to objectives is a function of the rewards associated with their**

achievement." Evaluation, based on preagreed criteria, coupled with performance reporting increases the student's commitment to the objectives. The rewards (continued employment, future promotion, increased compensation or choice assignments) are related to the achievement of the objective. In a training situation, demonstrating competence with the desired behavior represents achievement of the objective.

Precise Scoring for *Standard 4*

To calculate a precise score for *Standard 4* (see Fig. 11.11), determine a rating for each component of the program using the *Expert Criteria* in App. D.

An example of calculating the precise score for *Standard 4* is found on page 198 (see Fig. 11.19).

H. Meeting *Standard 5*— *Post Training Evaluation*

Evidence that the <u>desired behavior</u> has persisted after training and is linked to results.

This *Standard* requires evaluation of on-the-job performance. To meet this *Standard* the developer must collect behavioral data on the population trained that demonstrates the program's impact on results in relation to *Standard 1* (Objectives), *Standard 3* (Modeling) and *Standard 4* (Performance and Evaluation). In other words, we observe the worker using the knowledge and skills contained in the training.

Figure 11.11. Scoring *Standard 4* with *Expert Criteria*

_____ 06 Performance Standard

_____ 07 Performance Evaluation Form

_____ 08 Performance Time Allocation

_____ 09 Role Play Cases

_____ 10 Performance Evaluation Method

_____ Total Score

_____ Tentative Rating (Divide total by the number of applicable components)

__%__ Percentage of Students Performing

_____ Rating

<u>**The process uses the same techniques as those employed in a needs analysis**</u>. The developer collects data by getting as close to the performance in question as is practically and economically feasible. A written report is prepared based on the data. *The report should contain the data collected, its analysis, the conclusions drawn and an action plan for correcting, if applicable, performance discrepancies identified.* The following are examples of data collection methods in order of effectiveness:

A. Observing performers on the job.

B. Having performers respond to simulated situations.

C. Surveying employees or customers of the performer using a reliable survey instrument.

D. Interviews or surveys with the immediate manager(s) of the performers to identify the problems the performers are experiencing.

E. Interviews or surveys where performers describe the problems they are experiencing.

Rationale: Post Training Evaluation proves that:

A. *The discrepancies the training sought to correct have, in fact, been corrected or*

B. *The desired behavior that the training was designed to bring about is being used by the performers to produce results or*

C. *The problem persists. In this case, the process acts as a needs analysis and provides data for modification of the training or the desired behavior.*

Without such a study, any increase in productivity may be the result of other factors such as management's institution of accountability, minimum performance standards or pay incentives to motivate performance. It could also be the result of altered attitudes rather than from specific employment of the techniques taught. Post Training evaluation proves that the organization is getting the most from its training investment.

I. Evaluation of a Program with *TQT Standards*—An Example

Figure 11.12 shows the Effectiveness Rating for the program entitled <u>Conducting Interactive Management Meetings</u> referred to throughout this chapter. The Effectiveness Rating of 7.8 suggests that the desired change in the behavior of these consultants during management team meetings has occurred and is likely to persist. Also listed is a justification for each rating.

Figure 11.12. Rating for the Training Program

Program Name: _Conducting Interactive Management Meetings_

Program Length: _2_ Days, Vendor Fee: $_N/A_ Student Materials Cost: $_N/A_

Training Vendor Name: _Not Applicable—Internally developed_

Decision Maker: _Bart Smith_

Developer: _Les Shapiro_ Development Date: _July, 1992_

Instructor(s): _Les Shapiro_

Students' Job Title: _Consultants_ Average Class Size _12_ Students

Evaluated by: _Les Shapiro_ Evaluation Date: _July, 1992_

	Total Quality Training Standards	SCORE or RATING
1	Learning Objectives which describe the <u>desired behavior(s)</u> to be exhibited during the training program.	10
2	Evidence of a performance discrepancy in relation to the <u>desired behavior</u> resulting from a lack of skill or knowledge. (Needs Analysis)	10
3	Examples or models of the <u>desired behavior</u> during the training program.	10
4	Evaluation of student performance of the <u>desired behavior</u> to determine competence during training.	4
5	Evidence that the <u>desired behavior</u> has persisted after training and is linked to results. (Post Training Evaluation)	5
TOTAL (Divide by 5)		39
EFFECTIVENESS RATING		7.8

Figure 11.12. *(Continued)* Rating for the Training Program

Justification of Ratings
Describe briefly how the training program meets each **Standard**.

1. Learning Objectives which describe the <u>desired behavior(s)</u> to be exhibited during the training program.

   The program is based on a set of learning objectives (see Fig. 11.13). These fully meet the criteria for a useful set of objectives. **Rating: 10**

2. Evidence of a performance discrepancy in relation to the <u>desired behavior</u> resulting from a lack of skill or knowledge. (Needs Analysis)

   Students are asked to describe the problems they are experiencing when conducting management team meetings. This is followed by having each outline the structure of their meeting. A baseline performance is then conducted where one student conducts a simulated meeting. This is followed by a thorough (1 hour) discussion of the problems experienced during the simulation. **Rating: 10**

3. Examples or models of the <u>desired behavior</u> during the training program.

   The instructor acts a consultant and conducts a simulated management team meeting. This is followed by a 4-hour discussion where the group explores the relevance, importance and structure of each of the techniques that they had observed in the model. Each student is provided with a copy of the meeting Guide which was used to conduct the simulated meeting. **Rating: 10**

4. Evaluation of student performance of the <u>desired behavior</u> to determine competence during training.

   Six (of the 12) consultants conducted a simulated management team meeting using the new skills. Each received an evaluation based on *Expert Criteria* contained in a Performance Evaluation Form. (See Fig. 11.14.) The score of 4 is based on the fact that 50 percent of the group performed one time (see Fig. 11.10). **Rating: 4**

5. Evidence that the <u>desired behavior</u> has persisted after training and is linked to results. (Post Training Evaluation)

   A survey was conducted with the group during a subsequent training program conducted 60 days later. Sixty percent of the group reported that they had conducted an initial management team meeting using the meeting guide which they had received. Ninety percent reported using a meeting agenda at all meetings they conducted. This was a key unit objective and a technique the group had not previously used. **Rating: 5**

Figure 11.13. A Set of Objectives for Conducting an
Initial Management Team Meeting

Module Objective

Conduct an Initial Management Team Meeting: Given information about the dealership obtained from the sales interview and a group of 5 students acting as the management team, the consultant will be able to conduct an interactive installation meeting that reaches agreement on the benefits and process of installing the company's system in relation to the goals and challenges facing the client's organization.

Unit Objectives

To accomplish the Module Objective, the Representative will be able to:

A. **Use of Agenda:** Describe the structure of the meeting and use of the agenda.

B. **Establishing Need Awareness:** Describe techniques for bringing about perceptual and behavioral awareness of problems associated with generating appointments, follow-up and telephone prospecting.

C. **Explaining the Solution:** Describe the process of explaining the systems, *Expert Criteria* for Sales and Management Behaviors, training and follow-up that the Company provides.

D. **Obtaining Commitments:** Describe the process for reaching agreement on an action plan to install the program including definition of the roles of the parties and documentation.

E. **Use of the Meeting Guide:** Describe the structure and use of the meeting guide.

F. **Respond to Resistance:** Describe the process of responding with a response that explains the benefit in relation to the customer's concern. (Use of issues list and contracting.)

J. Practice Exercises—Evaluation with *TQT Standards*

Exercise 1

You are to evaluate Part 1, Learning Objectives, The Foundation, as a module of training using the *TQT Standards* and the *Guidelines for Meeting the Standards*. Rate each *Standard* using the Criterion Scoring System (10 - 5 - 0) and write a brief justification describing how the training module meets or does not meet the *Standard*. Then compare your answer to mine (see Fig. 11.15).

	Total Quality Training Standards	SCORE or RATING
1	Learning Objectives which describe the <u>desired behavior(s)</u> to be exhibited during the training program.	
2	Evidence of a performance discrepancy in relation to the <u>desired behavior</u> resulting from a lack of skill or knowledge. (Needs Analysis)	
3	Examples or models of the <u>desired behavior</u> during the training program.	
4	Evaluation of student performance of the <u>desired behavior</u> to determine competence during training.	
5	Evidence that the <u>desired behavior</u> has persisted after training and is linked to results. (Post Training Evaluation)	
TOTAL (Divide by 5)		
EFFECTIVENESS RATING		

Exercise 2

A second exercise is also provided. In this case you will evaluate a 105-minute training module (App. E) entitled *Interaction by Design* that I submitted to the National Society for Performance and Instruction (NSPI) for delivery at their 1995 convention. You may assume that approximately 75 people will attend the program. Again, you can compare your ratings and justifications to mine. (See Fig. 11.16.)

I would suggest that you study the content of this module closely as it describes the structure and techniques that bring about discussion toward predetermined conclusions. This structure is also found in the Instructor Guide for a two-day training module entitled *Developing Learning Objectives* that is provided in App. F. This guide can be used in combination with Part 1 to teach people in your organization to write useful learning objectives. (See section "K," Implementing Standards in an Organization.)

**Figure 11.14. *Expert Criteria* for Conducting the
Initial Management Team Meeting**

_____   _____   __/__/__
          LEADER   RATED BY   DATE

Structure of the Meeting: How <u>effectively</u> did the salesperson:

_____ **Control the dealer introduction:** Dealer is provided with
Introduction Guideline. Dealer's comments are brief (less than 3 minutes) and dealer does not go into unnecessary detail.

_____ **Use the agenda:** Followed as outlined. Agreement on agenda is
solicited before preceding. Time objectives are achieved.

_____ **Establish need awareness:** Discussion of perceived problems is interactive. Baseline and Model tapes are played. Discussion of tapes are
interactive. Flip chart is used to record responses. [29 minutes]

_____ **Explain the System:** Explanation of system is complete. System
Diagram is used effectively. Benefits are interactively discussed. [30
minutes]

_____ **Explain the start-up process:** Explanation of start-up training and
ongoing procedures is complete. Anticipated problems are identified
interactively. Each problem is explored interactively and solutions are
identified. [23 minutes]

_____ **Establish roles and expectations:** Roles are assigned and initial objectives are established for names, numbers, appointments, show-ups
and sales. [6 minutes]

_____ _Total and divide by 6_   _RATING_ _____

Response to Resistance: Rate for content and relevance to the situation.

_____ **Acknowledgment:** Paraphrase is used to demonstrate understanding
of the person's concern. Response is spontaneous.

_____ **Contract Established:** Permission is obtained to ask questions or to
explore the stated concern or, if applicable, to postpone discussion.

_____ **Need Discovery/Awareness:** Questions and probes are used to discover needs, issues or relevant facts.

_____ **Need Fulfillment:** Benefit(s) presented is/are relevant to the need
established or concern expressed. Explanation is complete.

_____ **Agreement Reached:** Questions are asked to measure understanding
or, if applicable, acceptance.

_____ _Total and divide by 5_   _RATING_ _____

Figure 11.14. *(Continued)* ***Expert Criteria*** for Conducting the Initial Management Team Meeting

<u>During the Transaction</u>: Rate frequency and appropriateness of observed leader behavior.

_____ **Questioning:** Open-ended questions (except probes) are posed to the group to start discussion(s) and to elicit responses from group members.

_____ **Paraphrase (active listening):** Spontaneous, in the leader's own words and appropriate to the participant's response.

_____ **Probing:** Short, nonthreatening and relevant to the participant's response.

_____ **Participation:** Is <u>brought about and guided by the leader</u> and:

- All members participate.

- Participant responses are sentence-paragraph.

- Begins within 1 to 2 minutes and is continuous.

_____ **Use of the Flip Chart:** Conclusions are recorded interactively. Flip chart contains a title and writing is legible.

_____ **Time:** Control of time. 85 to 90 Minutes.

_____ *Total and divide by 6*   RATING _____

OVERALL RATING (Add Ratings and divide by 3) _____

SCORING:

4	Expert	Performs with *finesse and confidence* and meets <u>all</u> of the criteria.
3	Effective	Performs with *confidence* and meets <u>70 percent</u> of the criteria.
2	Marginal	Performs *mechanically* <u>or</u> meets <u>50 percent</u> of the criteria.
1	Ineffective	Performs *mechanically* <u>and</u> meets <u>less than 50 percent</u> of the criteria.
0	Not Evident	None of the criteria met.
N	Not Applicable	The criterion is not applicable to the problem.

OVERALL RATING		
	3.6 to 4.0	Expert
	2.7 to 3.5	Effective
	1.8 to 2.6	Marginal
	0.9 to 1.7	Ineffective
	0.0 to 0.8	Not Evident

Figure 11.15. Solution to Exercise 1 Evaluation of Part 1

Program Name: Learning Objectives. The Foundation (These ratings also apply to the Training Module "Developing Learning Objectives" in Appendix F)

Program Length: 2 Days, Vendor Fee: $ N/A Student Materials Cost: $ N/A

Training Vendor Name: Aon Corporation

Decision Maker: Steve Taylor—Vice President Professional Development

Developer: Les Shapiro Development Date: 1979

Instructor(s): Les Shapiro

Students' Job Title: Program Developers or Instructors Average Class Size 12 Students

Evaluated by: Les Shapiro Evaluation Date: July, 1992

	Total Quality Training Standards	SCORE or RATING
1	Learning Objectives which describe the desired behavior(s) to be exhibited during the training program.	10
2	Evidence of a performance discrepancy in relation to the desired behavior resulting from a lack of skill or knowledge. (Needs Analysis)	10
3	Examples or models of the desired behavior during the training program.	10
4	Evaluation of student performance of the desired behavior to determine competence during training.	10
5	Evidence that the desired behavior has persisted after training and is linked to results. (Post Training Evaluation)	0
	TOTAL (Divide by 5)	40
	EFFECTIVENESS RATING	8.0

Justification of Ratings

1. Learning Objectives which describe the desired behavior(s) to be exhibited during the training program. **Rating: 10**

   A set of Learning Objectives for Part 1 are displayed on page 19. These fully meet the Criteria for Module Objectives.

Figure 11.15. *(Continued)* Solution to Exercise 1
Evaluation of *Part 1*

2. Evidence of a performance discrepancy in relation to the **desired behavior** resulting from a lack of skill or knowledge. (Needs Analysis) **Rating: 10**Readers are provided with a pretest that enables them to measure their technical knowledge of learning objectives in relation to the way they currently use objectives. This occurs prior to beginning the explanation of the subject. Additionally, the Effectiveness Ratings for a number of objectives from actual training programs demonstrate that few developers are writing effective objectives and that there is no consistency in the structure of objectives. Other data suggest that these developers are unaware of the discrepancy in their ability to use objectives.

3. Examples or models of the **desired behavior** during the training program. **Rating: 10**

   Part 1 contains numerous examples of Core, Module and Unit Objectives which meet the defined criteria. The Effectiveness Rating is also provided for many of the model objectives.

4. Evaluation of student performance of the **desired behavior** to determine competence during training. **Rating: 10**

   The book (training module) is structured as programmed learning. Readers are provided with a series of exercises that enable them to measure their understanding of each concept presented. Problems increase both in terms of complexity and level of difficulty. *Expert Criteria* enable them to judge the competence of model objectives provided and those which they develop. The performance evaluation form contains a scoring system, rating scale and instructions for calculating an Effectiveness Rating. The Performance Standard is stated on page 19 as a rating of 10.

5. Evidence that the **desired behavior** has persisted after training and is linked to results. (Post Training Evaluation) **Rating: 0**

   No data is provided to demonstrate that people who read Part 1 applied the skill and rewrote the objectives of their programs.

   The reader's perception of the program's relevance, effectiveness and the writer's competence is measured by a survey (the Student Evaluation of Training). However, a survey of the reader's perception does not meet the previously stated *Standard.*

Figure 11.16. Solution to Exercise 2 Evaluation of *Interaction By Design.*

Program Name: Interaction By Design

Program Length: .25 Days, Vendor Fee: $ N/A Student Materials Cost: $ N/A

Training Vendor Name: Aon Corporation

Decision Maker: National Society for Performance and Instruction (NSPI)

Developer: Les Shapiro   Development Date: June 1992

Instructor(s): Les Shapiro

Students' Job Title: Program Developers or Instructors Average Class Size 75 Students

Evaluated by: Les Shapiro   Evaluation Date: July, 1992

	Total Quality Training Standards	SCORE or RATING
1	Learning Objectives which describe the <u>desired behavior(s)</u> to be exhibited during the training program.	8.3
2	Evidence of a performance discrepancy in relation to the <u>desired behavior</u> resulting from a lack of skill or knowledge. (Needs Analysis)	5
3	Examples or models of the <u>desired behavior</u> during the training program.	10
4	Evaluation of student performance of the <u>desired behavior</u> to determine competence during training.	0
5	Evidence that the <u>desired behavior</u> has persisted after training and is linked to results. (Post Training Evaluation)	0
	TOTAL (Divide by 5)	23.3
	EFFECTIVENESS RATING	4.7

Justification of Ratings

1. Learning Objectives which describe the <u>desired behavior(s)</u> to be exhibited during the training program. **Rating: 8.3**

   The Module Objective (see Fig. 11.17) is missing Performance Time and the Conditions under which the performance will occur (see following ratings). The content of the module is directly linked to the objectives.

Module Objective			Unit Objectives						
			1	2	3	4	5	6	
A	10	A	10	10	10	10	10	10	
B	10	B	10	10	10	10	10	10	
C	0	C	N	N	N	N	N	N	
D	10	D	N	N	N	N	N	N	
E	0	E	N	N	N	N	N	N	
F	10	F	10	10	10	10	10	10	
	40		30	30	30	30	30	30	
	6.6	Rating	10	10	10	10	10	10	10

Average Group Rating

Total of Ratings	16.6
EFFECTIVENESS RATING	8.3

2. Evidence of a performance discrepancy in relation to the **desired behavior** resulting from a lack of skill or knowledge. (Needs Analysis) **Rating: 5**

Students are asked to describe their perception of the problems they experience when trying to interact with a group. There is no baseline performance to determine their skills in relation to the module objective. The developer lists a number of performance problems which are related to the module objective. However, there is no data to indicate the incidents of these problems in the training population.

3. Examples or models of the <u>desired behavior</u> during the training program. **Rating: 10**

The program is a model of the interactive process. On the sixth page of the guide (App. E) the group is asked to identify the specific skills that enabled the instructor to bring about discussion toward a conclusion. Additionally, the guide which is handed to the group (App. E) is a behavioral model of a guide structure that facilitates interaction.

4. Evaluation of student performance of the <u>desired behavior</u> to determine competence during training. **Rating: 0**

Students are not provided with the opportunity to plan an interactive module of training or to use the plan to conduct a session. There is also no Performance Evaluation Form for evaluating the planning process. The exercise on writing questions, while a key component of the behavior, is not evaluated.

5. Evidence that the <u>desired behavior</u> has persisted after training and is linked to results. (Post Training Evaluation) **Rating: 0**

No data is provided to demonstrate that students who participate in this 105-minute program will be able to use the skills.

Figure 11.17. Flawed Module Objective

Developers of training will be able to **plan an** *interactive inductive* **discussion** *that reaches agreement on a predetermined conclusion* within 15 percent of the planned time.

Commentary on the Solution to Exercise 2

Interaction By Design receives a <u>marginal rating</u> (4.7). In other words, the program appears to be missing components that would ensure the student's acquisition of the desired behavior. The evaluation process has identified that there is an opportunity to increase effectiveness by providing time for performance and evaluation.

This illustration also supports that learning objectives are the tip of the iceberg, a point I made earlier. You can often spot flaws in the training design by evaluating the program's or module's learning objectives. Notice that the discrepancies which caused the Module Objective's 6.6 rating (see page 196) relate to the problems identified as a result of rating the module against the Standards. The Module Objective is shown in Fig. 11.17. (**Performance is bolded** and the *criteria are shown in italics.*)

The absence of a Condition Component and the flaw in the statement of Performance Time relate to the absence of performance and evaluation in the program's design. "Within 15 percent of the planned time" does not state a fixed limit of time for the performance. Rather it states a criterion to judge the effectiveness of the planning (i.e., the ability to hit one's time estimate within plus or minus 15 percent). The absence of a fixed time limit in the objective also relates to the lack of performance and evaluation in the training design.

The 105-minute time constraint and class size of 75 people effectively inhibit the use of performance and evaluation. However, suppose the program were modified as reflected by the Module Objective that follows. (<u>Conditions are underlined</u>, **Performance is bolded**, *criteria are shown in italics* and the Performer and Performance Time are shown in plain text.)

Corrected Module Objective

> <u>*Given a subject, 60 minutes to prepare and a group of students acting as participants,*</u> the developer of training will be able to plan and **conduct a** 20-minute *interactive inductive* **discussion** *that reaches agreement on a predetermined conclusion* within 15 percent of the planned time.

If 15 people performed, one time, and received an evaluation against pre-agreed criteria (a method that rates an 8), the score for *Standard 4* (using short-cut scoring) would be 1.6 (since only 20 percent of the group performed). The increase in the score for *Standard 4* would have a minimal impact on the Effectiveness Rating. Therefore, it would rise to from 4.7 to 5.0 as shown in Fig. 11.18.

However, the inclusion of performance would have a dramatic impact on training time. Based on 20 minutes for each performance and the same amount of time for the evaluation, a time allocation of 600 minutes would be required just to conduct the exercise with 15 participants. Now the module requires 705 minutes, or more than one training day.

Figure 11.18. Revised Effectiveness Rating

	Total Quality Training Standards	SCORE or RATING
1	Learning Objectives which describe the <u>desired behavior(s)</u> to be exhibited during the training program.	8.3
2	Evidence of a performance discrepancy in relation to the <u>desired behavior</u> resulting from a lack of skill or knowledge. (Needs Analysis)	5
3	Examples or models of the <u>desired behavior</u> during the training program.	10
4	Evaluation of student performance of the <u>desired behavior</u> to determine competence during training.	1.6
5	Evidence that the <u>desired behavior</u> has persisted after training and is linked to results. (Post Training Evaluation)	0
TOTAL (Divide by 5)		24.9
EFFECTIVENESS RATING		5.0

If the scoring for *Standard 4* was based on the *Expert Criteria for Measuring the Standards,* the score would decrease slightly. (Assume that there is no stated performance standard, no report to the participant's manager and no time allocated for a second performance. All other criteria are met). (See Fig. 11.19.)

Two Views of Performance and Evaluation

The Rating of 1.4 for *Standard 4* (Fig. 11.19) suggests that there is limited benefit from having 15 students perform. The Tentative Rating of 7.1 suggests methodology that is close to effective. Which is correct?

Figure 11.19. Scoring *Standard 4* with *Expert Criteria*
(see App. D for Criteria)

3.3	06	Performance Evaluation and Standard
10	07	Performance Evaluation Form
5	08	Performance Time Allocation
NA	09	Role Play Cases
10	10	Performance Evaluation Method
28.3		Total Score
7.1		Tentative Rating (Total Score divided by 4)
20%		Percentage of Students Performing
1.4		Rating for *Standard 4*

From the developer's viewpoint, having 20 percent of the group perform provides an indication of training effectiveness. If 15 people performed at or above the performance standard, then the developer (instructor) would have evidence that suggests that the training was effective. Justification, if you will, for the 7.1 Rating (8.0 on the short-cut scale).

The purchaser of the training may have a different viewpoint. Eighty percent of the group did not have the opportunity to practice the desired behavior and receive feedback. Evaluation, in addition to measuring competence also reinforces the desired behavior. Competent performance increases the participant's confidence, thus increasing the likelihood that the desired behavior will be used on the job.

The addition of 600 minutes for performance and evaluation would increase the Effectiveness Rating from 4.7 to 5.0 (using either the short-cut method [1.6] or the *Expert Criteria* scoring method [1.4]) from the training purchaser's viewpoint. It would also increase, as stated earlier, the total time required from 105 minutes to 705 minutes, or more than one training day.

Given the time constraint and class size, the *TQT Standards* suggest that *Interaction By Design,* as structured, delivers some degree of effectiveness. However, it will probably fall short in terms of changing the participant's behavior. On the other hand, training conducted at the NSPI conference's concurrent sessions is designed to expose participants to new ideas. Those who wish, can pursue acquisition of the skills by participating in further training.

K. Implementing *Total Quality Training Standards*

TQT Standards can bring about organizational training effectiveness in any size organization. A successful implementation requires the support of the Chief Executive Officer, a modest commitment of resources and the leadership of a training professional who has the ability to use learning objectives and the evaluations systems described in this book. The following is a strategy for implementing the *Standards* and measuring their impact.

1. Identify the *Professional Development Team* Leader: This should be a training professional with demonstrated leadership skills and the ability to use learning objectives and *The Training Effectiveness Evaluation System.*
2. Form a *Professional Development Team:* The team should be composed of people who have experience with the use, design and delivery of training. This would include senior training developers, training managers and business unit managers. Their mission is to:
   a. Adopt a set of measurable standards. The Standards in this book may be used as a model.
   b. Set a target date for meeting the organization's goal of training effectiveness.

     c. Inventory the training programs being conducted by or for the organization. This provides the basis to conduct a *Training Effectiveness Survey.*

     d. Conduct the initial *Training Effectiveness Survey* (see step 6) to establish the company's baseline Effectiveness Rating.

     e. Conduct a follow-up *Training Effectiveness Survey* to measure progress.

     f. Act as a resource to the organization.

A key decision involves the size of the team. To ensure a dialogue that reaches consensus, consider a limit of 10 or 12 people.

3. <u>Inventory the training programs being conducted by or for the organization</u>. This can be done by a survey of each business unit. The survey should be sent to the business unit manager who will, in all likelihood, delegate the task to training personnel.

Request: Program Name, Program Owner (i.e., the decision maker who controls the program's use) Developer or Vendor Name, Length, Instructor Names, Student Job Titles, Average Class Size and any Fees Paid for participant material or for consultants to conduct the program.

4. <u>Announce the *Training Standards*</u>. This should be done by the Chief Executive Officer. In the announcement memo (Fig. 11.20) the CEO:

     a. Gives recognition to the individual members of the *Professional Development Team.*

     b. Establishes a time frame for meeting the Standards.

     c. Announces the *Training Effectiveness Survey.*

5. <u>Provide managers, developers and trainers with an explanation of the Standards and procedures for the survey</u>. Refer to Fig. 11.21, Announcement of the Survey and the booklets: *Total Quality Training Standards*, **What They Are and How They Can Be Met ("Guide")** and the *Training Effectiveness Survey* (See App. A and B).

6. <u>Conduct a *Training Effectiveness Survey:*</u> Procedure:

     a. Managers assign the evaluation task to their training personnel.

     b. Developers and trainers use the "Guide" and "Evaluation Form" to evaluate their program(s).

     c. Managers review the results with their developers and trainers.

     d. Managers send the Evaluation Form to the *Professional Development Team* <u>along with a copy of the program's learning objectives</u>.

7. <u>Analyze and act on the data</u>. Surveys are collected and analyzed by the *Professional Development Team:* The team uses the results to:

     a. Identify business units with opportunities to make immediate changes that could increase effectiveness and results.

     b. Spot programs that may be wasting resources (time and money).

     c. Determine a "baseline" **Effectiveness Rating** for each program. This allows measurement of progress toward the organization's training effectiveness goal.

Figure 11.20. Announcement Memo

DATE

TO: All Managers

FROM: Chief Executive Officer

SUBJECT: *Training Standards*

I am pleased to announce (insert organization's name) *Training Standards.* These were developed by the *Professional Development Team,* a team of senior training officers representing all units of the organization. The team consists of:

- Name (Team Leader), Company or unit
- Name, Company or unit
- Name, Company or unit
- Name, Company or unit
- Name, Company or unit
- Name, Company or unit
- Name, Company or unit
- Name, Company or unit

This team was charged with the responsibility to create a set of guidelines that can assist managers and developers of training in making training decisions that increase the effectiveness of our personnel.

I would like to thank the members of the team for their work in developing the Standards. I believe that their contribution will significantly enhance the professional development of our employees.

Over the next 5 years it is my goal to have all training programs meet the attached Standards. Therefore, if you are responsible for the development of training or manage a training function you will want to work closely with the *Professional Development Team.* The team will help you ensure that your training is contributing to the achievement of your business goals.

The process will start with a *Training Effectiveness Survey.* You will receive a full explanation of it from the *Professional Development Team.*

CEO

Figure 11.21. Announcement of the Survey

DATE

TO: All Managers

FROM: Team Leader of the *Professional Development Team*

SUBJECT: *Training Effectiveness Survey.*

Recently you received a memo from (CEO's name) announcing (insert organization) *Training Standards*. These were developed by a team of senior training officers representing all parts of the organization. The Standards provide guidelines that you and your training staff can use to make effective training decisions; decisions that have a high likelihood of increasing the effectiveness of our personnel.

The goal is to have all programs meet these standards over the next ___ years. This time period recognizes that change is a gradual and evolutionary process. It also recognizes that resources have to be prioritized and that, in many cases, programs that do not currently meet the standards cannot be "fixed" overnight.

The first step in our ___ year mission was to compile an inventory of all training courses offered to our employees or clients. Next, we need to compare each of these courses with the *Training Standards*. For this, we need your help in completing the attached survey. The data from this survey will benefit us in the following ways. These include:

1. Promoting a dialogue between managers, developers and trainers.
2. Providing a "baseline" measurement that will permit us to assess our progress toward the goal.
3. Determining if your business unit is getting the most from its training investment.
4. Revealing opportunities to make immediate changes that could increase effectiveness.
5. Permitting the *Professional Development Team* to prioritize and allocate resources.

Also enclosed is a booklet which explains the Standards. Included are examples of training methods that meet each *Standard* and the reason behind each. The booklet includes instructions for evaluating programs, a rating scale and evaluation form.

The task of evaluating each program should be assigned to the developer or trainer responsible for the program. In addition to completing the evaluation form, you should have that person justify to you how their programs are meeting the Standards.

Figure 11.21. *(Continued)* Announcement of the Survey

If you have questions or need assistance with the survey contact myself (phone number). (If applicable) The *Professional Development Team* is available to help you assess your current training programs and future training needs.

Attached is a list of the programs to be surveyed. The completed evaluation forms should be forwarded to (Team Leader's Name) by (insert target date).

_____

8. Measure each program's learning objectives. This provides a needs analysis on the quality of objectives and acts as a cross-check to measure the accuracy of the ratings produced by the Survey. Over time, the most accurate measurement of an organization's training effectiveness will be the usefulness of each program's learning objectives.

9. Conduct training for the organization. Principal modules:
   a. Developing Learning Objectives. Appendix F contains a complete instructor guide for a two-day program. Appendix G contains a Participant Workbook for the course.
   b. Meeting Training Standards. This program should focus on measuring performance with criteria, scoring and rating.

10. Promote the *TQT Standards:* Articles can be published in the organization's newsletter that demonstrate the benefits and use of the Standards.

11. Conduct a follow-up *Training Effectiveness Survey* and act on the data. See items 6 and 7.

12. Remeasure each program's learning objectives. This provides a post training evaluation on the quality of objectives and acts as a cross-check to measure the accuracy of the ratings produced by the Survey.

13. Monitor Training: Install the *Student Evaluation of Training* survey in each training program where useful learning objectives have been developed. Refer to App. C.

Learning Objectives and Organizational Training Effectiveness

Learning objectives are the key to successfully using *Total Quality Training Standards* in an organization. As already stated, the most accurate measurement of an organization's training effectiveness will be the usefulness of each program's learning objectives.

Learning objectives are the foundation for change. The act of writing a Superior Objective which contains the five principal components causes the developer or instructor to focus on performance (desired behavior), the criteria to judge it, the circumstances under which it will occur and the time needed to produce and measure it. This leads to training strategies that are performance oriented.

Instructors who observe performance get immediate feedback on the effectiveness of their training. This leads them to make changes in their methodology to ensure that the student's performance meets the *Expert Criteria* which they derived from their learning objectives.

Additionally, the use of the *Student Evaluation of Training* survey in each training program supports the desired change. This is because a significant part of the survey rates the training in relation to its learning objectives. Students consistently rate objectives which are not reached as zero and down rate those which are not adequately addressed. As a result, learning objectives cannot be form without substance. The instructor cannot show the group a set of objectives and then teach something else.

Learning objectives enable a manager to effectively manage a training project. From project inception, a set of learning objectives enables the manager to see the training before it is conducted and to negotiate resources. During production of instructor guides and materials, the manager can measure the degree to which they are likely to meet the objective. During the test phase, the manager can have the developer or subject expert exhibit the behaviors. These can be measured with the *Expert Criteria* in the Performance Evaluation System, which as you recall, are derived from the principal criteria in the learning objective. During the training phase, the manager can monitor performance in relation to the objectives by reviewing the ratings achieved by students. If ratings begin to go down from a previously established average, it may indicate that changes have been made to the training which reduced its effectiveness. Finally, students' satisfaction and their perception of the degree to which objectives are achieved is monitored by the *Student Evaluation of Training.*

Finally, learning objectives, as we have discovered, are a behavior which can be learned and practiced at a high level of skill. Appendix F contains an Instructor Guide that you can use to bring about competence with learning objectives in your organization and, through the objectives, organizational training effectiveness.

12
Purchasing Training

A. Conventional Wisdom

Costly mistakes are commonly made in the purchase of training. These occur as a direct result of the organization's inability to determine the quality of a vendor's offering and the decision-making strategy they employ.

For example, consider the following scenario. A group of senior executives determine that the supervisors within their company need training in communication skills. They believe that this training will enhance supervisor effectiveness, improve teamwork and lead to greater productivity. The executives decide that a two- to three-day program which can be implemented on a timely basis by a cadre of human resources personnel would be appropriate. The population to be trained consists of 2,000 supervisors and managers. The task is assigned to one of the executives or most commonly, the senior human resources manager who we will refer to as the purchaser.

Since there are numerous programs available in the market, the purchaser decides to purchase a program from a training vendor rather than develop one internally. The overall initiative is expected to cost approximately $1 million. This includes:

- Vendor materials $200,000 (around $100 per student).
- Instructors' salaries plus travel and expenses: $200,000.
- Manager salaries $600,000 (6,000 worker days at $100 per day).

If you were the purchaser, how would you go about selecting a vendor? I have posed this question to numerous groups. These are the typical answers:

- Narrow the field to three or four vendors.
- Attend and evaluate the programs yourself.
- Have several subordinates attend and evaluate the programs.
- Contact other users and ask for their evaluation of the program they use.
- Seek advice from in-house training staff.

- Hire a consultant.
- Rely on the vendor's representations.
- Conduct a test with a representative group of managers and have them evaluate the program.

What's Wrong with This Picture?

Consider, if you will, all of the previous actions in light of this question: What is being evaluated, the effectiveness of the presenter or the effectiveness of the training?

Most decisions regarding training effectiveness are actually decisions about the presenter's effectiveness. In other words, a reliance on people's subjective opinions (smile indices) rather than data linking the behavior contained within the training to results produced on the job.

People attending a training program will be influenced by factors such as the instructor's style, visual aids, organization of materials and relevance. An instructor who is enthusiastic, articulate and able to get group participation will get high marks. However, these factors do not guarantee that behavioral change will take place or that the training will solve the problem.

B. Do They Really Need Training?

All too often, companies commit resources (time and money) without determining if training is the appropriate solution to the problem. A problem related to human performance can be caused by a lack of skill or knowledge. In such cases, training is an appropriate solution since effective training brings about a desired behavior in the students.

However, performance problems can also be related to other factors. These involve such issues as the structure of the system, compensation, accountability, performance standards and the suitability of the people selected to perform the job. In these cases, training may not solve the problem. The process of determining whether or not training is the appropriate solution to an identified performance problem is called needs assessment.

The Problem

Training decisions made from the top of the organization for people several layers below can be inaccurate with regard to their needs in the absence of behavioral data. Furthermore, any form of management or leadership training which is mandated by top management, but not attended by them is likely to be unsuccessful. This is caused by their failure to use (model) the behaviors contained within the training program. The absence of behavior modeling results in the classic contradiction: "Do as I say, not as I do." (See Fig. 12.1.)

Figure 12.1. Management Hierarchy

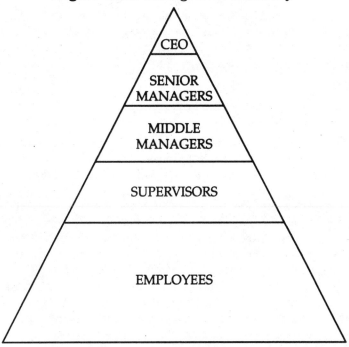

As a general rule, information with regard to problems facing the organization is communicated to the Chief Executive Officer by the senior managers. The senior managers may have formed their opinions from information received from the middle managers, from observations of the supervisors with employees or from conclusions drawn from situations in which they became involved. Unfortunately, a significant degree of distortion occurs as this message is communicated up the ladder. (See Fig. 12.2.)

Figure 12.2. Communication of the Problem

| CEO | Sr. Manager | Managers | Supervisor | Employee |

Distortion occurs as each person conveys the interpretation

The Solution

The key to maximizing the return on a training investment involves a process of identifying and verifying the need for training. This analysis or assessment process contains two phases. This first phase is called Performance Analysis. The second is called Needs Analysis.

C. Performance Analysis

In this phase, the top managers identify the disparity between what the subjects (managers and supervisors) of the proposed training are doing and what is desired. In other words, they consider the performance discrepancies or gaps in the **desired behavior** and the present behavior.

The most effective method for describing the discrepancy is to define the **desired behavior** using the Performance, Performance Time, Criteria and Conditions Components used to construct a Program or Module Objective. Then, the actual performance can be described within the same structure. The gap becomes immediately apparent.

A successful performance analysis involves hypothesizing the cause of the disparity against a number of factors. These include the knowledge and skills that the group is lacking, the system(s) in which they work, compensation structures, accountability, performance standards and the selection system used to determine employee suitability. Before preceding with training, the top managers need to decide if the performance problem is solely behavioral. To accomplish this they must consider performance factors relevant to motivation. Key questions include:

- Are employees held accountable for the performance?
- If they are held accountable, are they rewarded or punished for:

    —Correct performance?

    —Nonperformance?

- Does the system create obstacles to the desired performance?

At a minimum, this process will either confirm the training need or point in another direction. Too often training is prescribed as the cure for a performance problem that is not related to the performer's knowledge or skill. Such problems can be remedied by changing the system, accountability, compensation, etc. If the problem is related to the performers' knowledge and skill, then the identification of the performance problem will be useful in the selection of a training vendor. Also, it will help identify systemic changes that will bring about or support the desired behavior and results.

D. Needs Analysis

The second phase is called Needs Analysis. A Needs Analysis provides reasonable evidence that confirms or denies the hypothesized cause of a performance problem by getting as close as possible to the transaction in question. The concept is demonstrated in Fig. 12.3. Needs Analysis Methods were discussed in the guidelines for meeting *Standard 2* (page 163).

In Fig. 12.3 the CEO would actually observe managers in transactions with their employees. In that way, he or she would have first hand information in the quality of these transactions. Effectively, the person conducting the needs analysis is acting on behalf of the CEO. In a perfect world, this person would observe a number of manager-employee transactions. However, such observations are not always feasible. Figure 12.4 lists other methods for conducting the needs analysis. The score or rating assigned to each, reflects its value in relation to how close it gets to the "end user transaction."

It should also be noted that the method used to evaluate evidence of a problem can also be used to conduct the Post Training Evaluation.

E. A Selection Process Based on *TQT Standards*

The following is a selection process which uses the *Total Quality Training Standards* to evaluate one or more vendors' training programs:

1. Conduct a <u>Performance Analysis</u> to determine if there is, in fact, a performance problem related to a behavioral discrepancy. In the process of describing the gap in performance, you will identify one or more modules of desired behavior. These descriptions represent a preliminary set of learning objectives.
2. Conduct a <u>Needs Analysis</u> to confirm or deny the identified performance problem. Remember, the optimal needs analysis methodology utilizes a Performance Evaluation System to measure performer competence in relation to a desired behavior.

Figure 12.3. Concept of Needs Analysis

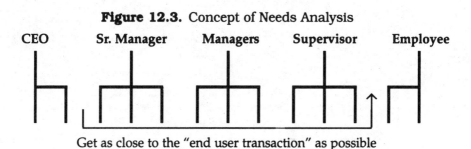

Get as close to the "end user transaction" as possible

Figure 12.4. Ranked Methods of Needs Analysis to
Determine the Need for Supervisory Training

RATING	TECHNIQUE
10	Unobtrusive observation of the supervisor by a trained observer in a transaction with an employee with rating against criteria.
9	Observation of the supervisor with rating against criteria by a trained, nonparticipating, observer.
8	Observation of the supervisor in a simulated situation with rating against criteria by a trained observer. Also known as an Assessment Program.
7	Survey of target population using a reliable instrument completed by the employee of the supervisor, the supervisor on him or herself and the supervisor's manager.
6	Interview or focus groups which describe specific incidents in addition to perceived needs. Maximum effectiveness occurs when a number of supervisors, employees and managers are involved.
5	Evaluations made from random observations of performance on the job. Maximum effectiveness occurs when there are written descriptions of deficiencies observed.
4	Surveys or interviews with the managers where they describe their perception of their supervisor's needs.
3	Interviews with senior managers where they describe their perception of the supervisor's needs.
2	Survey with the middle managers regarding desire for training for the supervisors in specific areas, such as by ranking the importance of job skills or selecting from a menu of subjects for training.
1	Survey with senior managers regarding desire for training in specific areas for the supervisors (using method rated as 2 above).
0	Assumption made by senior managers based on results data alone unsubstantiated by behavioral data collected from observation, surveys or interviews with the supervisors. In effect no needs analysis was conducted.

You may decide to have a consultant or the selected vendor conduct a needs analysis. If so, you will want to ensure that the methodology employed in the analysis produces useful information about the needs of the targeted population. In such cases, you would use the *Expert Criteria* for measuring needs analysis methodology found in App. D.

3. **Write a set of learning objectives that you believe describes the behavior(s) that are likely to bring about the desired results and the knowledge and skills that will bring about those behaviors. This set of objectives will provide a powerful basis to compare vendor offerings.**

4. Request that each vendor provide:
   a. Learning Objectives.
   b. Performance Evaluation Form(s).
   c. Behavioral documentation.
   d. Post Training Evaluation data.
   e. A detailed agenda.
   f. The number of people attending the program or the recommended class size.
   g. The Instructor Guide or Manual: This is necessary when the program is to be facilitated by employees of your organization who will be certified by the vendor to conduct the training.

5. Measure each program using the *TQT Standards*.
   a. **Learning Objectives:**
      (1) Determine if the vendor's learning objectives are relevant to the desired behavior by comparing them to the preliminary set of learning objectives which you developed. (See step 3.)
      (2) Evaluate these as a set of Program or Module objectives with the **Expert Criteria** in Part 1 or in App. D.
   b. **Performance Evaluation Form:** Look for behavioral components, *Expert Criteria*, a scoring system, a rating scale and the formula for calculating the rating. Answer the question: What performance(s) is the learner held accountable for? How is the performance measured?
   c. **Behavioral compatibility:** Look at the structure of the behavior or process for helping the person develop their own approaches. Is it linear or algorithmic? Ask yourself: Is the learner likely to continue to use what they have learned? Is the behavior compatible with your culture?
   d. **Post Training Evaluation Data:** Can the vendor provide post training evaluation data that demonstrates learner use of the behavior contained within the training on the job. The question you want to answer: Does the desired behavior persist over time? Is there pretraining and post training data?
   e. **Agenda:** This should show the time for the program's content and training activities. An agenda which shows Learning Objectives and Training Process Objectives in relation to time is optimal (See App. F page 436 for an example). Rate the program against:
      (1) *Standard 2:* Are the students given an opportunity to describe their needs? Is there a baseline performance?

      (2) *Standard 3:* Will the desired behavior be modeled?

      (3) *Standard 4:* Is there evaluation of student performance?

  f. **Number of people attending the program or recommended class size.** Determine mathematically the total time needed for the performance and evaluation process (including feedback to the learner). The key questions:

      (1) Is there adequate time to evaluate student performance?

      (2) Is the proposed training student-centered and performance oriented or an instructor-centered lecture?

  g. **Instructor Guide or Manual (if applicable):** You can use the *Expert Criteria* (in App. D) to measure the usefulness of the instructor guide by evaluating each of the guide's components.

6. Record the ratings on a matrix: Fig. 12.5 contains a matrix for comparing a number of programs. In this matrix, the relevance of the learning objectives, the compatibility of the behavior and the organization of materials are judged along with the *Total Quality Training Standards.*

Other key factors such as program cost, vendor reputation and consumer recommendations can also be added to the matrix or considered as separate issues.

This process will ensure that the behavior contained within the training will be relevant to the needs of the population and that the program's methodology will bring about the desired behavioral change.

Figure 12.5. Program Evaluation Matrix

Program / Selection Criteria	A	B	C	D	E
Relevance of Objectives					
Behavior Compatability					
Training Standards — Learning Objectives					
Training Standards — Needs Analysis					
Training Standards — Modeling					
Training Standards — Performance Evaluation					
Training Standards — Post Training Evaluation					
Instructor Guide & Materials					
Total Ratings					
Effectiveness Rating					

PART 3

Program Development

A System for Designing and Delivering Effective Training

13
Developing
Effective Training

A. Introduction to Part 3

In Part 2 we examined the process of <u>evaluating training</u> using five *Standards* of training effectiveness. Now we will look at the process of <u>designing and delivering effective training</u> using the same *Standards*.

The process of designing and delivering effective training involves the same factors that are used for evaluating the effectiveness of a training program. The reader will recall that the process of writing a useful Superior Learning Objective and evaluating a Superior Learning Objective's usefulness are essentially the same. When evaluating a Superior Learning Objective you determine the degree (using the Criterion Scoring System's 10 - 5 - 0 scale) that the written statement meets six criteria, each representing an identifiable component of a Learning Objective. When writing an objective, we ensure that the statement we have written contains a Performer, Performance, Performance Time, Criteria, Conditions and Concrete Language Component. In effect, the act of writing a learning objective involves the simultaneous act of evaluation.

In this book we will use the *Total Quality Training Standards* as the foundation for designing and delivering effective training. The learning objectives follow.

Core Objective

Develop a Training Program or Module: Given a performance discrepancy that is caused by a lack of skill or knowledge on a subject that the instructional developer has mastered, the developer (reader) will be able to **plan, organize, conduct, evaluate and modify a training program or training module** *which uses objectives and interactive inductive learning to bring about a desired behavior at a prescribed competence standard* within +/− 15 percent of the planned time.

Module Objective

To accomplish the Core Objective, the reader will be able to:

A. **Construct an Instructor Guide:** Given a set of objectives for a Training Module, a job aid (Module Planner) and time to prepare, **write an Instructor Guide Unit** *that enables an instructor to conduct a discussion of the units of knowledge and skills* within +/− 15 percent of the planned time.

B. **Conduct a Discussion:** Given an Instructor Guide Unit and a group of students, **conduct a discussion** *using the prescribed TECHNIQUE in the Instructor Guide and guide the group to the prescribed RESULT* within +/− 15 percent of the allotted time.

Organization of Part 3

Part 3 consists of three Chapters. In Chap. 13, Planning Effective Training, we will examine the development process for a Training Module. Then we look at the more complex process of developing a Training Program consisting of multiple Training Modules. You will find that the knowledge and skills you acquired in Parts 1 and 2 (learning objectives, *Total Quality Training Standards,* Performance Evaluation Systems and Cases) enable you to easily understand and perform the tasks in the Program Development Process. The following are the unit objectives for this chapter.

Unit Objectives

The reader will be able to:

1. Describe the process of developing a Training Module in relation to the *Total Quality Training Standards.*

2. Differentiate the program development process for a Training Module from that of a Training Program.

3. Describe the relationship between the learning objectives, Training Modules and the Master Training Design for a Training Program.

4. Describe nine uses of an Instructor Guide.

5. Describe the learning objectives and procedure for certifying instructors.

6. Describe four resources that can be used to monitor training effectiveness, program content and the quality of program delivery.

Chapter 14, *Interaction by Design,* focuses on the training program's explanation component. In this chapter we examine the structure, organization and logic for Instructor Guides which enable an instructor to conduct a discussion of the units of knowledge and skill. We also explore the differences between the lecture style and the interactive inductive (*Guided Discovery*) style. This leads to the introduction of an *Optional Sixth Training Standard* dealing with the structure and content of Instructor Guides.

Chapter 14 illustrates how a program's content can be directly linked through the structure of the guide to its learning objectives. Introduced are practical techniques for time management and a job aid, called the Module Planner, that organizes your program development efforts.

Finally, in Chap. 15 we examine the process of conducting a discussion which reaches agreement on a predetermined conclusion. This particular chapter is written in the Instructor Guide format discussed in Chap. 14. This enables you to experience, to the extent possible in a book, the interactive inductive process.

Part 3 fulfills the promises made in the introduction to the **Training Effectiveness Handbook** (page 9). Specifically, the knowledge and skills that follow will enable you to:

- Plan, organize, conduct, evaluate and modify training that brings about measurable results.

- Bring about change in an organization through effective training.

- Negotiate the time and resources needed to produce training that impacts results.

- Enable people to acquire skills that will help them achieve their and their organization's goals.

- Manage the overall training function including internal program development and assessment of new training projects.

- Evaluate instructor performance using objective measurements.

- Bring about training effectiveness in an organization of any size.

B. The Training Design/Agenda

The *Total Quality Training Standards* can be used as the foundation for developing effective training. This is accomplished by structuring the Training Design/Agenda in relation to *Standards* as shown in Fig. 13.1.

In the *Total Quality Training Design* the instructor begins the program by presenting the *learning objectives and Agenda* to the group. Assuming the objectives meet the criteria for a useful objective, *Standard 1* is fully met.

This is followed by a discussion of the *Problems to be Solved*. This provides the group and the instructor with an understanding of the group's needs and, as a by-product, begins to build learning motivation. Following this, the instructor conducts one or two *Baseline Performances*. These *Baseline Performances* help the group identify specific performance discrepancies that may be preventing them from bringing about the results they desire. Learning motivation, as discussed earlier, is enhanced by the *Baseline Performance*, which also, depending on the size of the group, acts as an accurate needs analysis. These activities enable the training to meet *Standard 2*.

Figure 13.1. The *Total Quality Training Design*

To achieve training effectiveness, the initiative should contain:

1. Learning objectives which describe the **desired behavior(s)** to be exhibited during the training program.
2. Evidence of a performance discrepancy in relation to the **desired behavior** resulting from a lack of skill or knowledge.
3. Examples or models of the **desired behavior** during the training program.
4. Evaluation of student performance of the **desired behavior** to determine competence during training.
5. Evidence that the **desired behavior** has persisted after training and is linked to results.

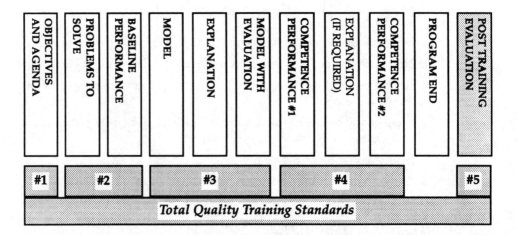

Following the *Baseline Performance(s)* the instructor *Models* the desired behavior for the group. Then they discuss the techniques and the rationale behind the techniques they observed in the *Model*. This is referred to as the *Explanation Component* in the Training Design. A second *Model* enables the group to use the Performance Evaluation Form to evaluate the instructor's *Model*. This sets the standard for expert performance while enabling the group to practice using the evaluation system. *Standard 3* is met by these activities.

Standard 4 is met by the two *Competence Performances*. *Competence Performance*, as shown by Fig. 13.6 (page 000), involves evaluation with the Performance Evaluation Form. Notice that an *Explanation Component* is inserted between the two performances. This indicates that the developer of the training should allocate time to review certain techniques and issues that may not be fully understood. These, of course, are discovered from the first set of student performances.

Standard 5 is met by *Post Training Evaluation.* Again, Fig. 13.6 shows that the same Performance Evaluation System used to measure the desired behavior during the training program can be used to measure it on the job.

Design or Agenda?

Figure 13.1 (page 218) also raises a question. Is this a Training Design or a Training Agenda? The answer depends on your point of view. If you are in the process of developing the program, the steps represent your Training Design. They allow you to view the process that you will use to bring about the desired behavior in your students. They also permit you to allocate time and determine the resources you will need for each component.

If you are the instructor conducting the program or the student participating in the program, Fig. 13.1 represents the Training Agenda. At the start of the program, it enables the instructor to communicate the flow of the program and the program's principal activities to the students. From the students' view, the agenda shows them the plan for their acquisition of the desired behavior.

A technique that I have found particularly effective involves reversing the presentation of the objectives and agenda with the discussion of the problems the group wishes to solve. By placing the objectives after the discussion of problems, the group discovers that the planned learning objectives specifically meet its needs.

C. Estimating Time and the Training Design

Accurate time estimates are facilitated by the Training Design's component structure. This is particularly true as it relates to the components that involve performance. Time required is determined by applying a formula (see Fig. 13.2). For example, the time for a Competence Performance involving all students can be calculated by multiplying the number of performances by the sum of the Performance Time plus the time needed to discuss or evaluate each student's performance. Add to this the time for setting up the exercise, briefing the players and videotaping the performance, if applicable, and you have an accurate estimate for these components of the program.

Time estimates can also be made for the **Objectives and Agenda, Problems to Solve** and **Program End** components. **Problems to Solve** could range from as little as 10 minutes to as much as 40 minutes depending on the complexity of the challenges facing the students. The review of the **Objectives and Agenda** should run approximately 10 to 20 minutes. Time, in this case, will be dictated by the number and complexity of the objectives and the activities in the agenda. A **Program End** based on reviewing the problems that the group wished to solve and completion of the Student Evaluation of Training (App. C) would take no more than 30 minutes (approximately 15 minutes each).

Figure 13.2. Time Allocation for Program Components
Involving Performance

BASELINE and COMPETENCE PERFORMANCE

_____   Briefing and set-up before performance.

_____   Preparation: If not completed preclass or as homework.

_____   Taping of performance (if applicable).

_____   Performance or (replay): ____ minutes per student (x) ____ observed.

_____   Discussion/Evaluation: ____ minutes per student (x) ____ observed.

_____   **Total Time Required.**

MODEL and MODEL WITH PERFORMANCE EVALUATION

_____   Briefing and set-up before performance.

_____   Performance Time for the instructor's Model.

_____   Evaluation using the PEF or, if a Model without evaluation, discussion time.

_____   **Total Time Required.**

D. Program and Module Introductions

Objectives and Agenda and **Problems to Solve** are generally considered part of a Program or Module Introduction which includes a segment for relationship building. The time required for the introduction of the students and the instructor will depend on a number of factors. These include the instructor's familiarity with the group, the length of the training program and the degree to which the program involves group participation, performance and evaluation.

When the instructor is new to the group and group participation in discussion and performance type exercises (Baseline and Competence Performances) is desired, the time allocation should be lengthened. The format for this type of introduction can be stated as a set of Training Process Objectives[*] in which the program's introduction is viewed as a separate Module. (See Fig. 13.3.)

This type of introduction is designed to build a trust relationship, allow the students to describe their experience, build a firm learning contract and proactively address concerns regarding role play type exercises. Figure 13.4 shows time estimates for such an introduction based on the assumption that the group will consist of 12 students who will work together for four days.

_____

[*]Refer to Chap. 7, Training Process Objectives.

Figure 13.3. Format Objective for a Program or Module Introduction

Module Objective

The student will perceive a nonthreatening environment which will permit participation in discussion, problem solving and role play activity focused on the program's learning objectives.

Unit Objectives

To accomplish the Module Objective the student will be able to:

A. Make a personal introduction which is relevant to the program's learning objectives (i.e., background, experience with the topic under discussion, expectations and reservations).

B. Identify the problems they wish to solve with regard to the topic being trained.

C. Reach agreement on the program's learning objectives.

D. Describe the content and activities of the program.

E. Describe the benefits of performance and evaluation.

The 5-minute allocation for "Benefits of Performance and Evaluation" involves discussion of the benefits of performing in role play situations. Such a discussion is often necessary as a small number of students may have had previous negative experience with role play exercises. These negative experiences could be due to people's natural hesitance to perform in front of a group, participation in unrealistic exercises and the perceived or real threat of embarrassment. An open discussion of these issues can often alleviate student anxiety.

Figure 13.4. Time Estimates for a Standard Program Introduction

__40__ Introductions: _3_ minutes for each student (×) _12_ students plus _4_ minutes for the instructor's introduction.

__30__ **PROBLEMS TO SOLVE.**

__20__ **OBJECTIVES AND AGENDA.**

_5_   Benefits of Performance and Evaluation.

__95__ Total Time Required.

When the instructor knows the group, has worked with them in role play exercises and has a trust relationship, the time factor can be greatly reduced. In Fig. 13.5, the instructor only asks the group to discuss their experience with the topic under discussion. Personal information and background data can be eliminated as can the discussion of the benefits of performance and evaluation. In this case the time is cut in half.

Figure 13.5. Time Estimates for a Modified Program Introduction

_0___   Introductions: _0_ minute for each student (×) _12_ students plus _0_ minutes for the instructor's introduction.

_30__   **PROBLEMS TO SOLVE.**

_20__   **OBJECTIVES AND AGENDA.**

_0___   Benefits of Performance and Evaluation.

_50__   Total Time Required.

Time estimates for the Explanation component of the instruction are based on the Unit Objectives. If an Instructor Guide is written, the time for each Unit Objective can be estimated based on the number of units of knowledge and skill and activities that will be used to bring about understanding of each. This will be discussed in greater detail later in Chap. 14.

E. The Program Development Process

Program development is a problem solving process. It starts with the identification of a problem related to a discrepancy in one or more performer's knowledge and skill. This is followed by the development of learning objectives and the resources that will be used to bring about the student's performance of the desired behavior during the training event. The process ends when evidence confirms that the desired behavior is used by learners on the job.

The process involves a planning phase and an implementation phase and is applicable to the development of both Training Programs consisting of a number of Modules and a stand-alone Training Module. This is evident in Steps 2, 5 and 7 which reflect the broader scope of the Training Program.

The applicability of each of the following steps is explained in the section entitled "Levels of Program Development." (See page 235.)

Planning Phase

Step 1.   **Prepare an Analysis of Learner Needs (Performance Analysis):** Determine if there is, in fact, a performance problem related to a lack of knowledge or skill. This is accomplished by making a list of observed or hypothesized performance problems.

In the process of describing the gap in performance, you will identify one or more modules of desired behavior. Also consider any systemic factors that may be contributing to the lack of performance such as a lack of accountability, poorly structured compensation or policy, procedures and systems that create obstacles to the desired performance.

Step 2.   **Write the learning objectives:**

A. Program: Write a Core Objective and one or more Module Objectives.

B. Module: Write a Module Objective and one or more Unit Objectives.

Step 3.   **Construct the Performance Evaluation Form(s):** Identify *Expert Criteria* to measure the desired behavior(s).

Step 4.   **Conduct a Formal Needs Analysis (if required):** Observe performers on the job to confirm or deny the identified performance problem. Use the Performance Evaluation Form (Step 3) to measure their competence.

Observers should also identify points in the transaction where problems occur. This will provide excellent data for the construction of role play cases or problems.

Step 5.   **Construct the Training Design:**

A. Program: Construct a <u>Master Training Design</u> for the overall program. (See Fig. 13.9.)

B. Module: Estimate the time needed to achieve each component of the Training Design in Fig. 13.1.

Step 6.   **Construct Cases and/or Problems:** These will be used to bring about the desired behavior during the various phases of the training. As shown in Figs. 13.6, 13.7 and 13.8, the cases are used in a Baseline Performance, Instructor Models and each Competence Performance.

Step 7.   **Write the Instructor Guide (if required):**

A. Program: Prepare an Instructor Guide for *each Module of the Program.* (Refer to Fig. 13-7.)

   1. Describe the Unit Objectives that enable the learner to perform the desired behaviors described in *each Module Objective.*

   2. Follow the procedure in "B" below for *each Module.*

B. Module:

   1. Arrange the Unit Objectives to achieve optimal reinforcement and teaching efficiency.

   2. Identify the units of knowledge and skill, specific training methods and other resources (i.e., references or handouts) needed to bring about an understanding of each Unit Objective.

Figure 13.6. Development Process for a Training Module

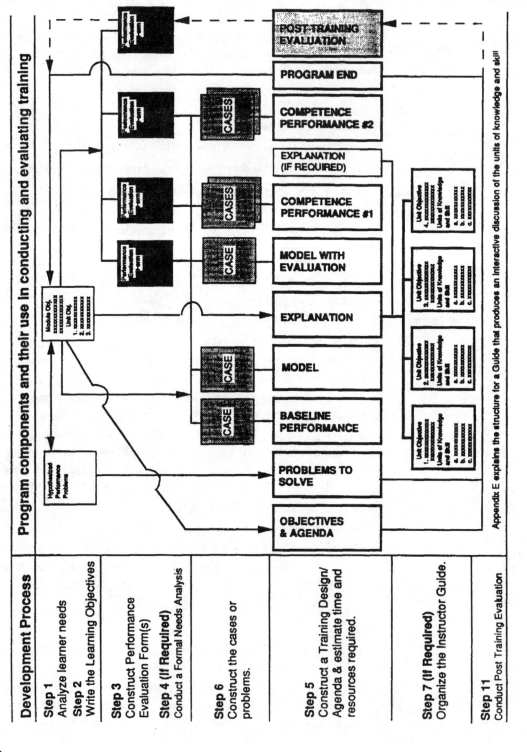

Appendix E, *Interaction by Design*, and App. F, *Developing Learning Objectives*, are examples of Instructor Guides that enable an instructor to conduct an interactive discussion of the units of knowledge and skill. Chapter 14 contains a detailed explanation of the guide's structure.

Step 8.   **Organize the Training Manual (if required):** Place the learning objectives, Training Design, Instructor Guide(s), Cases, Performance Evaluation Forms, program resources and the Student Evaluation of Training in a binder.

Implementation Phase

Step 9.   **Conduct or Test the Program or Module:** Determine effectiveness by measuring the observed behavior against the criteria and performance standard.

Step 10.   **Modify the Program or Module (if required):** Revise learning objectives, *Expert Criteria,* Cases, specific training methods and other resources based on observed performance.

Step 11.   **Conduct Post Training Evaluation:** Determine if the desired behavior is evident in the performer's on the job performance. The Performance Evaluation System can be used for this purpose.

Step 12.   **Certify Instructors (if required).**

Step 13.   **Monitor the Training (if required):** Measure student perception of training effectiveness, review Effectiveness Ratings of observed student performance and measure instructor competence.

Planning and Organizing a Training Module

Figure 13.6 shows the planning and organizing steps in the development process for a Training Module in relation to the program components used to conduct the program and evaluate the desired behavior.

In the diagram, the hypothesized performance problems leads to the formulation of the Module Objective. The Unit Objectives are then derived from the Module Objective, thus forming a set of hierarchically structured objectives.

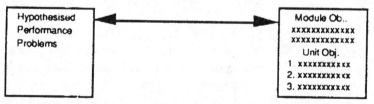

The double arrow between the Hypothesized Performance Problems and the Module Objective symbolize the gap between desired and present performance. It also stands for the fact that the learning objectives represent, at least, in part, the solution to the performance problem. Other solutions such as compensation, accountability and systemic changes are not shown in this model. (<u>Analyzing Performance Problems</u> [Mager & Pipe, 1984] provides an outstanding discussion on the use of performance analysis to address performance problems with solutions other than training.)

The Module Objective's Performance and Criteria Component forms the basis for the Performance Evaluation System as shown by the PEFs and cases in the following diagram. Its Condition Component creates the framework for the cases or problems. These key program resources then link directly to the Baseline Performance, Modeling and Competence Performances that they facilitate.

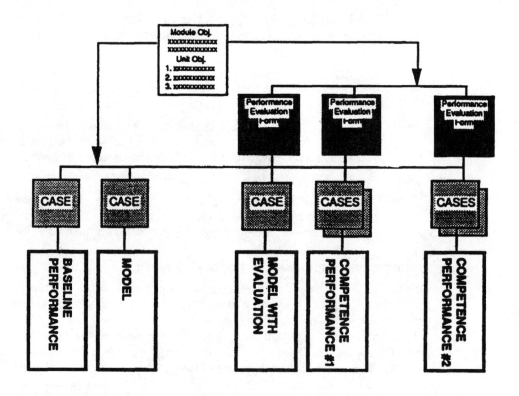

The diagonal line from the learning objectives leads to the first step in the Training Design. The review of the Objectives and Agenda establishes the contract between the students and the trainer. This line also leads from the Objectives and Agenda to the Program End and then back to the set of Objectives.

Essentially the line leading from the Program End back to the learning objectives symbolizes the fact that at the conclusion of the training event, the instructor should determine the degree to which the students perceive that the objectives have been achieved. This can be accomplished by discussion or by the use of the Student Evaluation of Training system contained in App. C.

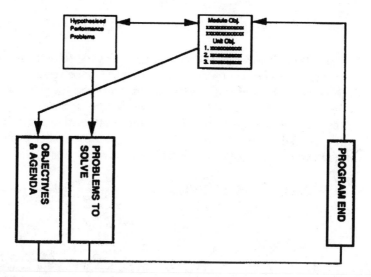

Notice, also, the line connecting the Hypothesized Performance Problems to the Problems to Solve. One technique for meeting Standard 2, Needs Analysis, involves inviting the students to discuss problems they are experiencing in relation to the training being conducted. This serves as a verification that the program is, in fact, designed to address the problems students are concerned about. It also can identify problems that were not foreseen in the development process. As stated earlier, these "new problems" may lead to modification of future programs or, in some cases, be addressed in the program being conducted. The line leading from Problems to Solve to Program End symbolizes that an instructor, at the program's conclusion, can invite students to discuss how effectively the training addressed their needs.

The line leading from the Unit Objectives to the Explanation symbolizes the relationship between the Unit Objectives and the units of knowledge and skill. These form the Training Units which are then organized in an Instructor Guide.

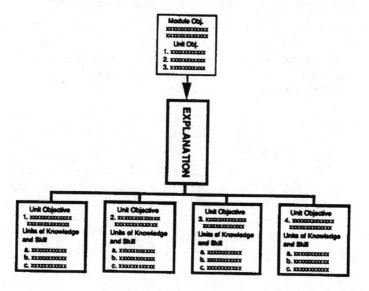

Finally, the illustration shows that the PEF used to measure student competence with the desired behavior at program's end can be used to measure it on the job. If the desired behavior is evident in students' on the job performances, then the training was effective and in all likelihood the performance problems that motivated the need for the training will have been resolved or mitigated.

Figure 13.6 shows that all components of the training program can be directly linked to a hierarchical set of learning objectives.

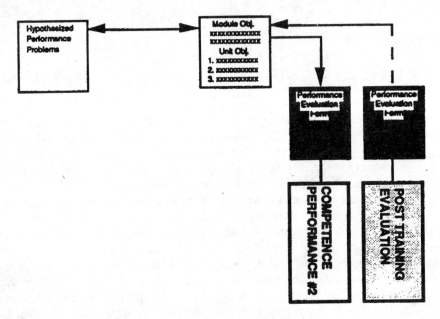

Planning and Organizing a Training Program

Figure 13.7, the <u>Development Process for a Training Program</u>, shows the <u>planning and organizing steps</u> in relation to the program components used to conduct the program and evaluate the desired behavior contained within the Core Objective. While similar to the process for developing a Module (Fig. 13.6), it differs in four significant ways:

Step 2:   The scope of the learning objectives. A Core and one or more Module Objectives versus a Module and one or more Unit Objectives.

Step 5:   A <u>Master Training Design</u> organizes the modules of the program in relation to the performance of the desired behavior in the Core Objective. As shown in Fig. 13.8, each module of the program has its own Training Design. A practical version of a <u>Master Training Design</u> is shown in Fig. 13.9 on page 231. The use of this key development tool is explained in the next section.

Figure 13.7. Deveopment Process for a Training Program.

Program components and their use in conducting and evaluating training

POST-TRAINING EVALUATION

PROGRAM END

COMPETENCE PERFORMANCE #2 — CASES

EXPLANATION (IF REQUIRED)

COMPETENCE PERFORMANCE #1 — CASES

MODEL WITH EVALUATION — CASE

EXPLANATION

MODEL — CASE

BASELINE PERFORMANCE — CASE

PROBLEMS TO SOLVE

OBJECTIVES & AGENDA

INTRODUCTIONS (IF REQUIRED)

Core Objective / Module Objectives A. B. C.

Hypothesized Performance Problems

MODULES OF THE PROGRAM

Development Process
Step 1 Analyze learner needs
Step 2 Write the Learning Objectives
Step 3 Construct Performance Evaluation Form(s)
Step 4 (If Required) Conduct a Formal Needs Analysis
Step 6 Construct cases/problems to measure the performance of the Desired Behavior in the Core Objective.
Step 5 Construct a Master Training Design & estimate time and resources required.
Step 7 Develop the Modules of the Program
Step 11 Conduct Post Training Evaluation

229

Figure 13.8. Module Development as Part of a Training Program

Program components and their use in conducting and evaluating training

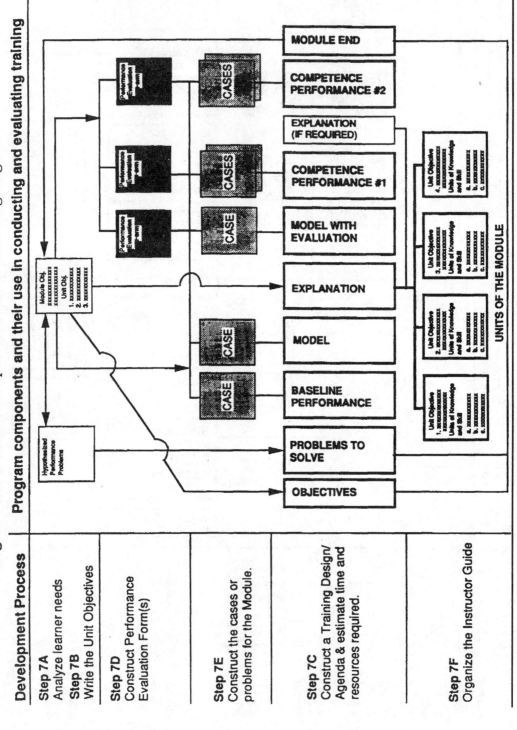

Figure 13.9. Master Training Design—Selling Annuities

Monday, Day 1	Tuesday, Day 2	Wednesday, Day 3	Thursday, Day 4	Friday, Day 5
Preclass: Compare and contrast 4 types of annuity products (H) 01: Pgm Introduction, Objectives & Agenda (F1) — 105 02: Product Differentiation Pre-Class Assignm't (H) — 95 03: Baseline Performance — 50 04: Model Interview (Core) — 110 05: Contracting Segment (A) — 60 06: Contracting Resistance (A) — 30 Homework A. 30 Questions on Fixed Annuity B. Practice for Role Play	07: Competence Performance Contracting with sales resistance (A) — 120 08: Data Gathering (B) — 120 09: Annuity Programs (D) — 30 10: Fixed Annuity (G) — 180 Homework A. Tax Assignment B. Practice for Role Play	11: Competence Performance Contracting and Data Gathering (A + B) — 180 12: Establishing the Retirement Need (C) — 120 13: Tax Considerations (I) — 85 14: Variable Annuity (G) — 75 Homework A. Product Selection Exercises B. Practice for Role Play	15: Competence Performance Establishing the Retirement Need (C) — 120 16: Product Selection (D) — 90 17: Product Explanation and Close (E) — 60 18: Illustrating Investment Results — 120 Homework A. Read Estate Tax Chapter B. Practice for Role Play	19: Competence Performance Product Explanation and Close (E) — 120 20: Common Objections (F) — 120 21: Calculating Retirement Income (C) — 120 22: Estate Taxes #1 (D) — 60 23: Ownership & Estate Consideration (D) — 60 Homework A. Product Selection Exercises B. Practice for Role Play C. Retirement Income Exercises

Monday, Day 6	Tuesday, Day 7	Wednesday, Day 8	Thursday, Day 9	Friday, Day 10
24: Competence Performance Response to Sales resistance (F) — 195 25: Immediate Annuity (M) — 120 26: Sales Interview Immediate Annuity (Core) — 30 27: Retirement Plans (D) — 120 Homework A. Read Social Security P26-59 B. Practice for Role Play	28: Competence Performance Sales Interview for Fixed Annuities with Resistance (Core) — 195 29 Social Security (I) — 180 Homework A. Estate Tax Assignment B. Practice for Role Play	30: Competence Performance Sales Interview for Variable Annuities with Retirement Income Calculation and Sales Resistance (Core) — 225 31: Wills (D) — 60 32: Estate Taxes #2 (D) — 120 33: Gift Taxes (D) — 60 Homework A. Read: Administrative Procedure Manual B. Practice for Role Play	34: Competence Performance Sales Interview with Product Selection and Estate Factors with Resistance (Core) — 240 35: Bank Products (D) — 60 36: Administration (K) — 60 37: Code of Conduct (L) — 30 Homework Practice for Role Play	38: Competence Performance Sales Interview with Product Selection, Retirement Income Calc., Estate Factors and Sales Resistance (Core) — 300 39: Weekly Sales Report (K) — 60 40: Service Center Operation (K) — 60 41: Program Conclusion (F3) — 30

Step 6:   A "set of cases or problems" is prepared to measure the performance of the desired behavior specified in the Core Objective. Each module of the program would also have its own set of cases (problems) as shown in Fig. 13.8.

Step 7:   A Training Program is made up of one or more Training Modules.

Notice that the Explanation Component of the Training Program is composed of the program's Module and Unit Objectives. These are arranged in a logical sequence to bring about understanding, acceptance and the ability to use the desired behavior contained within the Core Objective.

Figure 13.8, Module Development as part of a Training Program, shows that each module requires the preparation of PEFs, Cases and a Training Design. Notice that each module's Explanation Component is composed of the Unit Objectives and the units of knowledge and skill. These, as stated previously, form the content of the Instructor Guide.

In Chap. 4, The Hierarchical Structure of Objectives, we identified Core and Module Objectives as Terminal Objectives that describe the desired behavior you intend to measure at the end of the training event. Both represent, from the organization's viewpoint, a unit of behavior that the student will use on the job to bring about a desired result and both must meet all six criteria of a useful objective. From a practical standpoint, the Core Objective represents both a higher level of skill and, in many cases, a transaction with a broader scope. This is demonstrated by the learning objectives in Fig. 13.10.

F. The Master Training Design

The Master Training Design represents the overall plan for developing the program. It is the product of a number of critical decisions. These include:

1. The number of performances and students to be observed and evaluated.
2. The flow of the program's content (Module and Unit Objectives).
3. The time estimated for each module of the program.
4. The planned preclass, prediscussion and homework assignments.

An effective design shows the modules of the program and the time allocated to each module on a matrix. This provides a comprehensive overview of the program on a single document. Specifically identified are the times allocated to Competence Performances and, if applicable, homework assignments. A useful design also links each module or unit of the program to the learning objective from which it was derived. Figure 13.9 is an example of a Master Training Design for a sales training program on selling annuities. Figure 13.10 shows the learning objectives for this program.

Figure 13.10. Objectives for a Sales Training Program

Core Objective

Selling Annuities: <u>Given a student acting as a referred prospect with money to invest</u>, the agent will be able to **conduct a** *5-phase* **sales interview** *that reaches agreement on an appropriate annuity product (single or flexible premium, Immediate or Deferred or Fixed or Variable) in relation to the needs agreed upon and the client's risk tolerance* **and respond to 2 to 3 customer questions or concerns** within 60 minutes.

Selected Module Objectives (A-J)

To accomplish the Core Objective the agent will be able to:

A. **Contract with the prospect:** <u>Given a student acting as a referred prospect with money to invest,</u> **conduct a contracting transaction** *that describes the interview process and obligations of the parties* within 5 minutes.

B. **Gather Data:** <u>Given a student acting as client who has agreed to participate,</u> **conduct an interview** *that accurately* discovers the client's goals, assets, liabilities, cash flow and risk tolerance using the Client Data Form* within 15 minutes.

   *90 percent of available information is obtained.

C. **Establish the Retirement Need:** <u>Given a completed Client Data Form and a student acting as a client,</u> **conduct a discussion** *that reaches agreement on the amount of any additional capital needed for retirement and an optimal funding strategy in relation to the client's cash flow and stated goals* within 15 minutes.

D. **Select a Product:** <u>Given a Client Data Form, and established retirement need,</u> **select and justify an appropriate annuity product and premium** *that achieves the capital needed in relation to the client's payment capacity, stated goals, Social Security benefits and, if applicable, retirement and estate plan* within 5 minutes.

E. **Explain the Product:** <u>Given a student acting as a client and an illustration of Projected and Guaranteed Values,</u> **conduct an** *interactive* **explanation of the features, benefits, limitations and tax consequences,** *without misrepresentation,* within 10 minutes.

F. **Respond to Resistance:** <u>Given a student acting as a client and information on the stage of the interview,</u> **respond to a question or concern with a response** *that acknowledges the client's concern, determines the nature of the concern, addresses the concern and measures the client's comfort with the response* within 10 minutes.

G. **Fixed and Variable Annuity:** <u>Given an annuity policy and a series of questions,</u> **explain the contract** *by citing the appropriate contract provisions, without misrepresentation, and obtain a score of 70 percent correct responses on a pre-discussion assignment.*

Figure 13.10. *(Continued)* Objectives for a Sales Training Program

H. **Product Differentiation:** <u>Given product specification booklets and a blank "product comparison matrix,"</u> **compare and contrast the features of the Single Premium Deferred Annuity to the Flexible Premium Deferred Annuity, Immediate Annuity and Variable Annuity.**

I. **Social Security:** <u>Given a Social Security manual and client information,</u> **calculate benefits for client and spouse and demonstrate the impact of reduced Social Security upon the death of either prospect.** *Criteria: Score 70 percent correct on a 10 question test* within 40 minutes.

J. **Taxation of Annuities:** Describe the tax consequences associated with the purchase, holding and surrender of a tax deferred annuity in relation to a client's estate plan.

Format Objectives

F1. **At program start:** Perceive a non-threatening environment which will permit participation in discussion, problem solving and role play activity focused on the program's learning objectives. To accomplish this the students will be able to:

    a. Make a personal introduction which is relevant to the program's learning objectives.

    b. Identify the problems they wish to solve with regard to selling annuities to referred prospects.

    c. Reach agreement upon the program's learning objectives and agenda.

    d. Describe the benefits of performance and evaluation.

F2. **Baseline Performance:** Determine their needs in relationship to the stated (Core) objective. (Baseline Performance)

F3. **At the program's conclusion:** State the learning objectives achieved (or not) and value the program's success in meeting their identified needs.

The Master Training Design changes during the development process. At the outset of development, the placement of modules and the time allocations assigned to each are estimates based on the developer's knowledge and experience. As the Instructor Guide for each module is developed the level of abstraction is reduced as the Unit Objectives and units of knowledge and skill are identified. Time allocations become more concrete as training methodology is chosen for each element of program content.

As a consequence, modules may be relocated and their time allocations lengthened or shortened. These changes may also necessitate a change to the program's length. The Master Training Design enables the developer to communicate these changes to the decision maker(s). When questions arise, the completed Instructor Guide(s) can be used to justify the proposed changes.

The following should be noted on The Master Training Design in Fig. 13.9:

1. The group is composed of 12 salespeople who have an insurance license and some experience selling life insurance and annuity products.

2. There are 450 minutes of teaching time in each day. (8:30 a.m. to 5:30 p.m. with 90 minutes allocated for lunch and breaks.)

3. Each module of the program is cross referenced to a learning objective.

4. Product knowledge (knowledge) and sales techniques (skills) are integrated.

5. Competence Performance for each module of the sales behavior occurs on the day after its units of knowledge and skills are explained.

6. Each module of the program has its own Training Design.

7. The Competence Performances increase in complexity.

A supplementary narrative (Fig. 13.11) can also be used to clarify key issues in the Master Training Design. This is shown in the following matrix which shows the allocation of performance and evaluation time for an 11-day sales training program on a tangible big ticket product.

G. Levels of Program Development

The degree of preparation and documentation needed in the planning phase and the scope of activities in the implementation phase for a training program or module is related to a number of factors. These include:

1. The complexity of the learning objectives and the length of the program.

2. The size of the population to be trained.

3. The number of times that the program will be conducted and, if applicable, the intervals between programs.

4. The time available for the planning phase.

5. Whether or not the developer of the training is a subject expert who is able to model the desired behavior.

6. Whether or not the training will be conducted by instructors who were not part of the development team.

7. Whether or not other instructors who will conduct the program are subject experts or competent performers.

8. Degree of standardization desired.

Figure 13.11. Example of a Supplementary Narrative

Performance and Evaluation Time

Performance	Day	Before Group					In Teams						Briefing	Grand Total
		Perf Time	Eval Time	Time/Perf.	# Perf Eval.	Sub Total	Perf Time	Eval Time	Time/Perf.	# Perf Eval.	Sub Total	# in Team		
Establish Relationship	2	2	10	12	4	48	2	8	10	2	20	3	10	78
Relationship + Need Disc.	3	10	15	25	4	100	10	15	25	2	50	3	10	160
Product Explanation	4	15	15	30	4	120	15	15	30	2	60	3	10	190
Relationship to Prod. Expl.	5	25	20	45	12	540*	NA	NA	NA	NA	NA	NA	10	550*
Product Demo	7	15	15	30	4	120	NA	NA	NA	NA	NA	NA	10	130
Obtain Commitment	6	2	5	7	12	84	NA	NA	NA	NA	NA	NA	10	80
Negotiate Agreement	9	40	20	60	2	120	35	15	50	1	50	4**	15	185
Explain Lease Option	9	12	13	25	2	50	12	5	17	2	34	2	10	94
Negotiate Agreement	10	40	20	60	2	120	35	15	50	1	50	4**	15	185
Commitment + Negotiate	11	40	20	60	12	720*	NA	NA	NA	NA	NA	NA	15	735*

*Requires 2 Instructors.
**Students act as salesperson, customer and manager. The student evaluated before the group acts as the team leader and principal observer.

The Occasional Trainer

When the developer of training is the subject expert and the sole instructor, the level of preparation, documentation and scope of implementation are reduced. Consider, for example, a supervisor who is called upon to conduct training for a group of 30 employees on a skill (desired behavior) that he possesses. We will refer to this developer as an "Occasional Trainer." In this case, we will assume that our "Occasional Trainer" supervises a group of 12 customer service representatives and that he has observed them handling customers.

His objective is to construct a one-day program to bring about understanding, acceptance and the ability to use one or more customer service behavior(s). Since the program will be conducted infrequently and our "Occasional Trainer" will be the sole instructor he will need to:

Step Number	Program Development Step
1	Prepare an Analysis of Learner Needs. He can make a list of the performance discrepancies that he has observed.
2	Write a Module Objective and one or more Unit Objectives.
3	Construct a Performance Evaluation Form.
5	Construct a *Total Quality Training Design.*
6	Construct cases to simulate the type of situations the representatives will encounter so that he can evaluate their performance.
9	Conduct the program and measure learner competence.
11	Conduct Post Training Evaluation. He can observe customer service representatives on the job and measure their competence with the desired behavior using the same Performance Evaluation Form with which he measured their competence during training.

Because of his familiarity with the needs of the population to be trained, he will not need to conduct a needs analysis. Therefore, Step 4, conducting the Formal Needs Analysis, is eliminated. However, he will still meet *Standard* 2, Needs Analysis, by discussing the problems that learners are experiencing and by conducting a Baseline Performance during the training program.

Step 7, the construction of an Instructor Guide, may or may not be required. The executive who commissioned the training project may want the supervisor to prepare a guide. The guide structure shown in Apps. E and F enables the executive to see the training on the printed page. This would help in determining if the content was appropriate.

The Instructor Guide also facilitates an orderly transfer of the training program from one instructor to another. This is an important point. The time required to develop the training and the experience gained by our supervisor while conducting it are lost if he leaves the company. A detailed guide eliminates the need for subsequent instructors to "reinvent the wheel." It also facilitates the training of future instructors (which is referred to later in this chapter as Instructor Certification). From a management viewpoint, the production of an Instructor Guide ensures program continuity and eliminates duplication of effort.

If our "Occasional Trainer" desires to conduct an interactive discussion of the units of skill or knowledge, he would be advised to prepare a guide similar to those in Apps. E and F. An in-depth explanation of the Instructor Guide and the process for conducting a discussion to a conclusion is contained in Chaps. 14 and 15.

Large Scale Projects

The Program Development Process increases in complexity when training is conducted for a large population by a number of instructors. In these cases, the developer of training must construct:

A. A program or module that brings about understanding, acceptance and the ability to use the desired behavior.

B. An Instructor Guide(s) that can be used by multiple instructors.

Program length and the complexity of the learning objectives will also impact the complexity of the development process. Consider the following examples:

A. Example 1: A Training Module on the selection and use of a fire extinguisher for a population of 5,000 employees as part of safety training. Estimated length: 60 minutes.

B. Example 2: A Training Program on the selection and recommendation of an insurance product which is appropriate to the customer's needs where both sales techniques and product knowledge must be taught. Estimated length: Two weeks. Population: 100 people per year in groups of 12.

C. Example 3: A Training Program on management skills for managers and supervisors where the instructors are not able to model the desired behavior. Program length: 40 hours. Population: 1,000 in groups of 20.

These projects will involve all of the steps in the Program Development Process. The remaining sections of this chapter discuss elements of the Program Development Process related to planning, implementation and monitoring of large scale projects.

H. The Program Development Team

Large scale training projects usually require one or more subject experts who actively participate in the development of the program. I refer to this group as the program development team. Depending on the size of the project, members of the team may also act as instructors. Programs involving large populations may also require a number of instructors who are not part of the development team. In most cases, these instructors have to be trained to conduct the program (see section L, Instructor Certification).

Large scale projects require that a person be designated as the program developer (developer). The developer is the leader of the program development team and acts as the conduit between the team and the executive responsible for the program. The developer can be a subject expert or a specialist assigned to the project.

The developer must be able to write useful learning objectives, construct a reliable Performance Evaluation System, formulate a training design that meets the *Total Quality Training Standards* and write an Instructor Guide that can be used by the instructor team. Essentially, the developer needs the skills that are discussed in this book.

The developer has the following responsibilities. During the:

- planning phase (Steps 1 through 8), the developer secures the resources, actively leads the team through the development process and reports the team's progress in building the Training Manual.

- implementation phase (Steps 9 through 12), the developer is responsible for conducting the test, making appropriate post-test modifications, organizing Post Training Evaluation and reporting the results. The developer is also responsible for training the instructor team.

- the monitoring phase (Step 13), the developer observes instructors to assure the quality of program delivery. The developer also facilitates the process of collecting, adopting and implementing needed changes.

At each stage, the developer must ensure that all people involved in the program have the latest copy of the Training Manual.

I. Communication During Development

Communication is essential in large scale training projects as considerable organizational resources are expended. At each stage, the executive responsible for the program and others with a vested interest (i.e., the department manager who will interface with the trainees) must be able to monitor the program's content, its compatibility with organizational culture and the company's ability to support the finished product.

At the outset of development, a contract or set of specifications should define the finished product. This can be accomplished by submitting key program components to management for approval as they are completed. These documents can then be organized into a set of Program Specifications. Such a document is useful in communicating changes during the development process and orienting new instructors during certification. Figure 13.12 contains a model set of Program Specifications.

Figure 13.12. Contents of Program Specifications

A. Major Assumptions. (Refer to *TEES* 03)

B. Learning objectives (Core and Module). (Refer to *TEES* 04)

C. Performance Evaluation Forms. (Refer to *TEES* 07)

D. Master Training Design. (Refer to *TEES* 18 and Section F of this Chapter)

E. Instructor Certification Plan. (Refer to *TEES* 24 and Section L)

TEES refers to *The Training Effectiveness Evaluation System's Expert Criteria* for Measuring the *Total Quality Training Standards.* Appendix D.

As previously stated, the learning objectives represent the core program development document. Useful learning objectives reveal the program's content, cultural direction and training method. In order to build the objectives, the developer must make a set of assumptions (Major Assumptions) about the learner's needs, the experience they bring to the table, the anticipated program length, class size and the equipment available (such as videotape resources). These factors will have a significant impact on the content of the learning objectives and the training methodology employed.

Example: You cannot reach a Core Objective with a 60-minute Performance Time Component if the program is limited to two days with classes of 20 students. Assuming 390 minutes of time available for teaching (9:00 a.m. to 5:00 p.m. with 90 minutes for lunch and breaks) the Performance Time of 1,200 minutes, by itself, exceeds the 780 minutes available.

The second major communication tools are the Performance Evaluation Forms developed for each observed performance. These enable decision makers to examine the *Expert Criteria* that will be used to judge learner competence. Since substantial program content focuses on the how and why behind each criterion, the decision makers can "see" the desired behavior and provide input as necessary.

The other key communication tools are the Master Training Design and the Instructor Guide. The Master Training Design enables the decision makers to view the Program's agenda and time allocation for instruction and performance. Depending on the detail provided, the Master Training Design can also show the number of students evaluated in each Competence Performance.

J. Importance of the Instructor Guide

As we have seen, the Instructor Guide plays an important role in the development of a training program. In this discussion, I summarize the benefits of a detailed Instructor Guide. These include:

1. **Management review:** Managers can check the relevance, accuracy and completeness of a program's content by using a detailed guide. Managers can also judge a program's compatibility with the organization's culture and its effectiveness in relation to the *TQT Standards* without having to attend the program. For example, a *three day* program could be reviewed in less than *three hours* with a detailed guide.

Developing Learning Objectives (App. F) is an example of a detailed Instructor Guide. This guide was the basis for Part 1. By comparing its content to Part 1's, the reader can judge its relevance, accuracy and completeness.

2. **Negotiation of resources:** A program's learning objectives permit the manager and developer to make decisions with regard to time, money and personnel. However, these decisions are based on abstract statements that represent the end product of the training program. In the process of writing the guide, the developer identifies the specific knowledge and skills that will bring about the desired behavior described by each objective. The developer also identifies the activities and resources needed to achieve each. This, in almost all cases, affects time allocations. As time estimates become more precise, the developer and manager can agree on needed changes to the program's length, objectives or number of attendees.

3. **Time saving:** The guide enables the developer, if the developer is the instructor, to replicate the program for future groups. The guide eliminates the need to reinvent the program each time it is conducted.

4. **Duplication of effort:** In every organization people change positions or leave. When this occurs, and the program is not documented, the program leaves with the person. As a result, someone has to redevelop the program. The redevelopment project represents a duplication of effort.

5. **Program continuity:** Sometimes an instructor cannot complete a training program. The existence of a detailed Instructor Guide permits another person, who has been certified as an instructor, to take over with no loss of continuity. The guide permits the instructor, who cannot continue, to communicate precisely to the new instructor where he is in the program. This eliminates the new instructor covering old ground or not covering key units or modules that are essential to the student's ability to understand, accept and use the program's skills. Consider the model guide in App. F. If I asked you take over the program on page 000, you would know precisely what I had covered with the group.

6. **Multiplication of trainers:** When training is documented with an Instructor Guide, the developer can train one or more persons to conduct the program. This process, which is referred to as Instructor Certification, increases the number of people who are qualified to teach the program. Certification has two significant benefits. The first deals with the issues of time, duplication of effort and program continuity discussed above. The second deals with the organization's development of people. Training experience, especially that which involves the use of

group facilitation skills, contributes to an employee's growth and value to the organization. I will discuss the certification process later in this chapter.

7. **Program quality:** A detailed Instructor Guide facilitates accountability for the delivery of quality training. A manager observing an instructor conduct the program with a copy of the guide can determine the degree to which the instructor delivers or departs from the prescribed program. This is particularly important when training is developed to impact the performance of a large number of people and is to be conducted by a number of instructors on a decentralized basis.

8. **Basis for program modifications:** A detailed Instructor Guide creates a vehicle for making and communicating changes to a program. Despite a thorough development effort involving testing and Post Training Evaluation to measure effectiveness, changes are inevitable. As time passes instructors will find better, more effective or more time efficient ways to achieve one or more of the program's learning objectives. These changes can be reflected in replacement pages to the Instructor Guide, approved, if appropriate by the manager responsible for the program, and communicated to other certified instructors. Such changes are also necessitated by changes to internal policy, the product or service, the market and/or other factors such as competition. These changes can often be communicated quickly and efficiently as replacement pages to an existing guide.

9. **Use of an interactive style:** Another aspect of quality involves the communication style used to conduct the training. In my experience, the structure of the Instructor Guide has a direct impact on the instructor's ability to facilitate discussions. A guide structure for interactive training and techniques for conducting discussions are explained in Chaps. 14 and 15.

K. Testing, Modifying and Post Training Evaluation

Once the Instructor Guide is completed, the program is ready for testing. Programs should be tested with a representative group of students. In other words, a group whose previous training, experience and needs closely parallels the original assumptions made and whose number is within 10 percent of the projected average class size. This provides the developer with the most accurate data on the:

- Time required to conduct the program. Can the program be accomplished within the planned time frame?

- Relevance, appropriateness and sequence of the content (units of knowledge and skill). Is the material organized to bring about student understanding, acceptance and ability to use the desired behavior?

- Students' competence with the desired behavior. Are they able to perform at or above the desired Performance Standard?

- Reliability of the Performance Evaluation System. Are Overall Ratings at program end within +/− 10 percent of the instructor's ratings?

- Students' perceived satisfaction with the program. Do they see the knowledge and skills learned as practical solutions to the problems they face or will face on the job?

Following the initial test, modifications will undoubtedly need to be made. These modifications will be dictated by the answers to the above questions. A second test of the program, again with a representative group, will indicate the degree to which problems have been corrected.

Post Training Evaluation should be undertaken, whenever possible, before instructors are certified and before the program is implemented. This is particularly important when the desired behavior(s) are new to the organization. Refer to Meeting *Standard 5* for an explanation of the procedure for conducting a Post Training Evaluation and *Standard 2* (Needs Analysis) for an explanation of appropriate methodology.

A Training Program is ready for wide scale implementation and the certification of instructors when:

A. It produces student performance of the desired behavior in the classroom at the prescribed Performance Standard.

B. The desired behavior is observable in the student's on the job performance and rated at or above the desired Performance Standard.

C. You have determined that the training can be conducted within the planned time frames using the Instructor Guide. Chapters 14 and 15 provide a detailed explanation of techniques for developing usable Instructor Guides.

L. Instructor Certification

Instructor Certification is the process of training instructors who are capable of using the approved Instructor Guide to produce the requisite behaviors as measured by the *Expert Criteria* in the Performance Evaluation System. Certification ensures that the resources invested in writing, testing and Post Training Evaluation are not wasted. It also ensures program continuity and effectiveness. The process requires a number of decisions. These include the:

- Selection of the Instructor Trainees and the Certifying Instructor
- Procedures to be followed during certification
- Learning objectives for the certification process and the
- Time frame in which the process is accomplished

Again, the Instructor Guide and Performance Evaluation System should be fully "debugged" before you attempt to certify instructors.

Instructor Trainee

An Instructor Trainee should be a competent performer on the subject being trained, have the desire to teach and be willing to demonstrate the desired behavior(s) in front of a group. This is especially important when training involves interactive communication skills.

He or she should also be a role model. By role model, I mean a person who has performed successfully with regard to the subject that they are training and who reflects the values of the organization (i.e., dress, speech, manner, etc.). Successful on the job performance is especially critical. Students will tend to disregard the ideas of an instructor who they feel has not performed.

The optimal candidate is a person who has attended the training and then successfully used the skills on the job. This, of course, is not possible with the initial group of Certified Instructors.

Certifying Instructor

Before a person can certify instructors he or she must first be a Certified Instructor who has experience conducting the course. The first Certifying Instructor is usually the member of the Program Development Team who conducted the program through the testing and modification process. As a general rule, a minimum of three programs should be conducted before certification is attempted. This would include the initial test program, the second test after modification and a third program which proved that the Instructor Guide was performing effectively.

Subsequent Certifying Instructors should be experienced Certified Instructors. A standard should be set for the number of programs conducted and the Certified Instructor's competence with the Instructor Guide, the desired behavior(s) and the Performance Evaluation System.

Learning Objectives for the Certification Process

The certification process can be viewed as a set of learning objectives which describe the desired behavior the Instructor Trainee must exhibit before she is considered competent to conduct the training program. These behaviors include the ability to conduct the program using the Instructor Guide, model the desired behavior, evaluate student performance and conduct discussions. Figure 13.13 provides a model set of certification objectives for a training program that uses behavior modeling.

Figure 13.13. Instructor Certification Objectives

Core Objective

Conduct the Training Program: Given a group of students, the Certified Instructor will be able to conduct the training program using the approved Instructor Guide within 15 percent (plus or minus) of the prescribed time frames and produce the desired behavior at the stated Performance Standard.

Module Objectives

To accomplish the Core Objective, the Instructor Trainee will be able to:

A. **Conduct a discussion:** Given an Instructor Guide Unit and a group of students, conduct a discussion using the prescribed technique in the Instructor Guide and guide the group to the prescribed Conclusion within 15 percent (plus or minus) of the planned time. (See Chaps. 14 and 15.)

B. **Model the desired behavior:** Given a case, demonstrate (MODEL) each behavior contained within the program and achieve an Overall Rating of 3.6 on each.

C. **Evaluate student performance:** Given a student performance (on videotape), conduct a performance evaluation using the Performance Evaluation Criteria and Form within the time frame defined for the exercise and which identifies at least 70 percent of the errors noted by the <u>Certifying Instructor</u>.

D. **Set up a behavioral simulation:** Given an Instructor Guide's performance Module or Unit, appropriate cases and a group of students, set up and conduct a role play exercise including briefing and student performance within the stated time frame.

E. **Use media in a discussion:** Demonstrate the use of the flip chart, overhead projector and whiteboard to produce the illustration or frame defined in the Instructor Guide while interacting with the group.

F. **Set up the classroom:** Given a checklist and the location of program materials, organize the handouts and other materials required to conduct a training session and set up the classroom.

G. **Demonstrate the use of the following equipment:**

   1. Videotape Recorder.

   2. Overhead projector including identification of appropriate markers.

   3. Flip Chart including identification of appropriate markers.

H. **Describe the training program:** Given the Training Design and any Training Module, describe the instructional intent of the module and its specific relationship to other modules which continue the learning process on that subject.

The Certification Procedure

To become certified, the Instructor Trainee participates in a series of activities that develop the confidence and finesse needed to effectively facilitate the program. These include participation in three training programs, training on the program itself and observation of a number of trainees on-the-job after they have completed training. The main activities are defined in the following six-phase process.

To accomplish the Instructor Certification Objectives (Fig. 13.13), the Instructor Trainee:

A. **Phase 1:** Participates in a training program conducted by the Certifying Instructor, without reference to the Instructor Guide and participates in all role play and performance evaluation exercises as the performer (salesperson, manager, etc.).

B. **Phase 2:** Receives training on the structure of the guide, the logic of the Training Design and, if the program is structured for group discussions, training on conducting discussions. These activities are specifically related to Module Objectives A and H.

C. **Phase 3:** Observes a training program conducted by the Certifying Instructor, with reference to the Instructor Guide, and participates in all role play and performance evaluation exercises as the performer. The Instructor Trainee must achieve an Overall Rating of 3.6 on all performances. During this program the Instructor Trainee should co-teach a few segments of the program.

D. **Phase 4 (If the Instructor Trainee's performance of the desired behavior does not meet the Performance Standard):** Performs each behavior that will be modeled and receives evaluation by the Certifying Instructor.

E. **Phase 5:** Co-teaches under the supervision of the Certifying Instructor. The Instructor Trainee takes over greater responsibility as the course progresses. The Instructor Trainee receives daily performance evaluation on his use of the Instructor Guide, modeling and effectiveness in evaluating performance.

F. **Phase 6 (Post Training Evaluation):** Evaluates the on-the-job performance of at least six students who have completed the training program. The Instructor Trainee acts as a non-participating observer and evaluates their performance using the Performance Evaluation System. (To eliminate bias, the Instructor Trainee should observe students who he did not train.)

Notice the emphasis on performance and evaluation of the desired behavior in the early stages of the process and on conducting the program in the latter stages.

Developing Competence with the Instructor Guide

If we view the certification process in relation to a Training Design that meets the *Total Quality Training Standards*, Phase 1 is the equivalent of the Model. The

Instructor Trainee experiences the activities in the program and observes the group's response. This creates an understanding of how she will be expected to perform.

Phase 2 represents the Explanation Component. The explanation of the training program's learning objectives, Training Design, Performance Evaluation System and guide structure represent the units of knowledge and skill that enable the Instructor Trainee to competently facilitate the program. Appendix E, Interaction by Design, App. F, Developing Learning Objectives, and Chap. 15, Guiding a Discussion to a Conclusion, provide you with a set of tools for accomplishing this phase of the certification process.

Phase 3 is the equivalent of the Model with Performance Evaluation. Here the Instructor Trainee observes the Certifying Instructor with a copy of the Instructor Guide. In this way the Instructor Trainee can measure the degree to which the Certifying Instructor competently uses the Instructor Guide. Having the Instructor Trainee's conduct of a few segments of this training program provides a baseline measurement of her skill with the guide. Optimally, these performances should be videotaped and reviewed prior to Phase 5.

Phase 4 is required when the Instructor Trainee's competence with the desired behavior is below standard. Maximum effectiveness is achieved by performing the desired behaviors on videotape and then reviewing the taped performances with the Certifying Instructor.

Training which meets the *Total Quality Training Standards* places high emphasis on the instructor's ability to model and evaluate the desired behavior (Fig. 13.14). Without these skills, instructors will be unable to effectively conduct the program. **Instructor Trainees who are not confident with modeling tend to lengthen other segments of the training in an attempt to creatively avoid performing in front of the group.** If the Certifying Instructor allows this to occur, the training time allocated to Competence Performance gets sacrificed and with it training effectiveness.

Phase 5 is a series of Competence Performances. During this phase the Certifying Instructor measures the Instructor Trainee's ability to use the Instructor Guide within the time allocations. The standard of plus or minus 15 percent of the planned time is a guideline that I have found reasonable when a program is designed for active student participation in discussion and performance.

Figure 13.14. Components Involving Performance or Evaluation

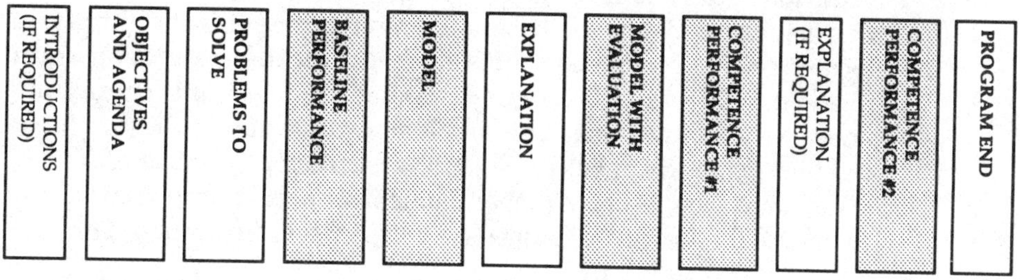

Phase 6 is Post Training Evaluation. By evaluating students (who have completed the training) performing on the job, the Instructor Trainee gains first hand knowledge of the program's effectiveness. The data collected in the process helps the organization to measure training effectiveness. This is particularly true when the Instructor Trainee uses the Performance Evaluation Form designed to measure the desired behavior in the Terminal Objective at the end of the training program. These observations also identify weakness in the training or in the desired behavior itself. Hence, Phase 6 activities also represent a needs assessment.

The suggestion that the Instructor Trainee observe students trained by other Certified Instructors eliminates the potential for bias induced by selective perception (seeing only what you want to see). An Instructor Trainee will want to see his or her students performing at or above the performance standard. As a consequence he or she may overlook performance discrepancies that should be reported to the developer or manager of the training.

Coaching During Certification

Certification has two objectives. The first is to enable the students to competently perform the desired behavior. The second is to enable the Instructor Trainee to competently facilitate the program. Both must be achieved for the process to be considered a success. This effectively requires that the Certifying Instructor walk a fine line as it relates to his or her coaching during the program.

The main problem is excessive intervention by the Certifying Instructor. Excessive intervention tends to confuse the students. They begin asking themselves "Who should they pay attention to?" This can lead to relationship tension if the group feels that the Certifying Instructor is demeaning the Instructor Trainee. Excessive intervention also tends to erode the Instructor Trainee's confidence in herself and reduces the Certifying Instructor's ability to measure the Instructor Trainee's facilitation skills.

The need for excessive intervention and the problems it causes are exacerbated by three issues. These involve the program's stage of development, the Instructor Trainee's modeling skills and the role established by the Certifying Instructor at the program's start. We will look at them one at a time.

The difficulty with certifying instructors on an untested program is determining the cause of problems which occur during the program. Is the problem related to the Instructor Trainee's use of the guide, the guide itself or the group (i.e., is their background knowledge inhibiting progress)? If the Certifying Instructor does not have confidence in the guide's content, organization and time allocations, he will have difficulty determining the cause of the problem and will be more likely to intervene. The problem is controlled by testing, modifying and retesting the program before beginning Instructor Certification.

The consequences of not preparing the Instructor Trainee to effectively model will jeopardize the Instructor Trainee's credibility with the group. Phases 1, 3 and 4 of the Certification Process are specifically designed to eliminate the problem by providing three opportunities to evaluate the Instructor Trainee's ability to competently perform <u>each</u> behavior that they will later have to model for a group of students.

Finally, the Certifying Instructor must establish his coaching role during the program introduction. The group should understand that they are actually participating in two training programs. One that enables them to learn the knowledge and skills they will need to perform successfully on the job and one that enables the Instructor Trainee to competently facilitate the program. They should expect the Certifying Instructor to interrupt from time to time. The co-teaching approach defined in Phase 5 further reduces the relationship tensions that occur when the Certifying Instructor, the authority figure, intervenes. When the Certifying Instructor is viewed as both a coach and a co-teacher, the group is more likely to accept his active interventions.

M. Monitoring Training

Prudent investors in stocks and bonds continually monitor the financial performance of their investments. Similarly, organizations must also monitor the performance of their training programs. This can be accomplished by the program developer, the training manager or the executive who uses the program to increase the effectiveness of personnel within his or her business unit. The primary vehicles for monitoring program effectiveness are the Performance Evaluation System, the Student Evaluation of Training Survey, the Instructor Guide and the Training Manual. Each provides special insight into program effectiveness, program integrity and the competence of the instructors in meeting their student's needs.

The Student Evaluation of Training Survey

The Student Evaluation of Training Survey (App. C) reveals the students' perception of training effectiveness. It measures the degree with which learning objectives are achieved, the value of the skills to the student, the effectiveness of the training methodology and the competence of the instructor. The ratings are a measure of customer (student) satisfaction. These can be summarized and reported for each group that completes the program. (Refer to the Student Evaluation of Training Summary Analysis in App. C.)

Ratings obtained by a Certified Instructor can be compared to the ratings of the instructor team or to the ratings established during the test programs or, once established, to the Certified Instructor's historical average. Ratings which fall below the established norms indicate problems with the Certified Instructor's facilitation skills or with the program's ability to meet current needs.

Performance Reports

A summary of the ratings obtained from student performances of the desired behavior provides meaningful insight into training effectiveness. At the most basic level, the absence of ratings indicate that performance or the number of performances did not occur. For example, when class sizes are allowed to exceed the planned group size, performance time is affected and some or all student performances are eliminated.

A drop in performance ratings may indicate a significant deviation in the Certified Instructor's explanation of the knowledge and skills or his or her failure to competently model the desired behavior. Any significant drop should trigger an action by the training manager. These ratings can also be compared to established norms.

For example, users of the previous systems observe a drop in both student satisfaction and student competence when classes exceed their planned size or when training time is arbitrarily changed (without appropriate changes to the learning objectives and *Expert Criteria*).

Certified Instructors should be restricted from making unilateral changes to the Performance Evaluation Forms or the Student Evaluation of Training Survey. Changes to these instruments destroy the manager's ability to monitor their performance.

The Instructor Guide

The Instructor Guide provides the tool for determining if the program is being conducted as designed. Certified Instructors can be observed by the developer, the training manager or another Certified Instructor with a copy of the guide. If the guide is as detailed as those found in Apps. E and F, it is possible to determine if the program is being conducted as it was originally designed.

The Training Manual

The Training Manual is a tool for organizing, controlling and monitoring the training program. It consists of the following documents:

- Program Specifications
  - —Major Assumptions
  - —Learning Objectives
  - —Master Training Design
  - —Instructor Certification Plan
- Performance Evaluation Form(s)
- Instructor Guide(s)
- Student Evaluation of Training Survey

- Cases

- Resources (handouts, reference materials, etc.)

- Revision Record and Revision Memos

To ensure program integrity, procedures are established for making modifications. Proposed changes to the Instructor Guide, cases and other materials should follow a prescribed review process. Once the changes are accepted, replacement pages are distributed to the Certified Instructors by the the training manager. These are then filed in the Training Manual.

A Revision Record should be included in each Training Manual (see Fig. 13.15). This enables the training manager to determine, at a glance, if the Certified Instructor's manual contains the latest updates.

Figure 13.15. Revision Record

REVISION RECORD			
From time to time you will receive updated materials. These should be inserted in your Training Manual according to the instructions in each Revision Memo. Record the Revision Date and Date Inserted below. Record the page numbers of pages revised or file the Revision Memo behind this page.			
#	**Revision Date**	**Date Inserted**	**Page Numbers of Pages Revised**
1	1-25-92	2-2-92	3.1 to 3.29, 5.7, 5.10, 6.16
2	3-13-92	3-23-92	See Revision Memo
3			
4			
5			
6			
7			
8			
9			
10			
11			
12			
13			

14

The *Guided Discovery* System

A student's ability to perform a desired behavior is related to the instructor's ability to bring about his or her understanding of an underlying set of knowledge and skills. This is the focus of the explanation phase of the Training Design. Here the student examines the desired behavior in depth, and learns the "how and why" that make it work. This enables the student to judge whether the desired behavior will help solve the problems faced on the job.

This chapter introduces *Guided Discovery;* a teaching style which uses objectives and interactive inductive learning to bring about one or more desired behaviors in the student. The system is based on a guide structure and communication style which enables an instructor to conduct a preplanned discussion of the program's units of knowledge and skill. The resultant feedback allows the instructor to tailor the message to the student's needs.

In effect, the student's ability to perform is related to the instructor's ability to communicate.

Listed in the following are the learning objectives for this chapter:

A. Objectives for This Chapter

Module Objective

Construct an Instructor Guide: Given a set of objectives for a Training Module, a job aid (Module Planner) and time to prepare, the developer (reader) will be able to *write an Instructor Guide Unit that enables an instructor to conduct a discussion of the units of knowledge and skills* within +/− 15 percent of the planned time.

Unit Objectives

To accomplish the Module Objective the reader will be able to:

1. Describe the benefits of active participation and the factors that tend to limit participation (especially with regard to the Explanation Component of the Training Design).

2. Describe the interactive-inductive (*Guided Discovery*) style and contrast it to the lecture style.

3. Describe the structure of an Instructor Guide Panel (the guide's most basic component) in relation to the principle: **Questions must be <u>preplanned</u> and <u>relevant to the Conclusion</u> you wish your students to reach and a part of the Instructor Guide.**

4. Describe the structure of an Instructor Guide Panel, Unit and Module in relation to the Hierarchical Structure of Objectives.

5. Differentiate between a question, task, task question and spontaneous secondary question and describe the most appropriate use of each.

6. Describe the process for determining time allocations for a training program or module and define <u>estimated,</u> <u>actual</u> and <u>replicated</u> time.

7. Describe techniques for using inductive process where the student has limited knowledge of the subject matter under discussion.

8. Describe the structure, organization and use of the Module Planner.

B. Getting Active Participation

How many times have you heard trainers say "This is not going to be a lecture," and then proceed to lecture their way through the material? The stated objective or request for active participation usually comes in the opening statement of the training. It represents a sincere desire on the part of the instructor to involve the group in meaningful discussion. The instructor realizes that there are significant benefits. Among these are:

- The training program tends to be more interesting for both the students and the instructor.

- Student responses indicate understanding and acceptance of the ideas under discussion.

- The process builds a trust relationship between the instructor and students. As trust builds, students become increasingly willing to express and challenge ideas. Trust also increases the student's willingness to participate in role play type exercises.

- The instructor often gains new insight by listening to the student's viewpoint. People bring a wealth of experience and problem solving skills to the table.

- Flawed concepts are often uncovered through the discussion process resulting in constant improvement to the program's units of knowledge and skill.

- Students have to listen more actively. The flow of information comes from the group rather than from the instructor in the front of the room.

- When the training is on the use of interactive communication skills, the effective use of discussion techniques by the instructor acts as a behavioral model that reinforces the skills under discussion. This is particularly important in sales, management, customer relations or "train the trainer" training programs.

Despite these significant benefits and the instructor's desire, many programs turn out to be a lecture. In other cases, there is some degree of participation, but it tends to be participation for its own sake rather than an honest attempt to reach agreed upon conclusions. In these cases, student responses tend to be limited to one or two words or a few sentences.

The question then arises, why do instructors, who sincerely desire participation, find themselves lecturing or getting limited participation? The answer involves human nature (more specifically student and instructor behavior in relation to human needs), flawed assumptions about interactive process and the absence of techniques that bring about participation.

For example. I attended a 105-minute training session at the NSPI Conference on training techniques where the instructor stated "I want you to interrupt, I want this to be participatory." This session also turned out to be 95 percent lecture. However, within this instructor's statement ("I want you to interrupt") we can see a flawed assumption. He believes that participation is brought about by the students as a result of their interest or desire for greater understanding of the ideas he is presenting rather than by specific actions on his part.

The absence of techniques that facilitate interaction also contribute to the dichotomy between the desired participation and the resulting lecture. These involve practical problems such as time limitations in relation to content to be covered or a classroom set up which is not conducive to participation. For example, consider a room set up classroom style (see Fig. 14.1). This arrangement restricts eye contact within

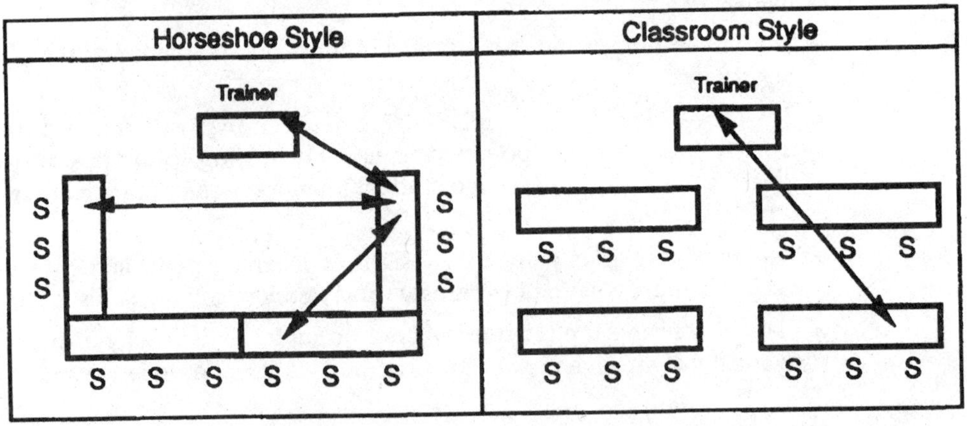

Figure 14.1. Eye Contact Between Participants as a Result of Classroom Arrangement

the group. Students' ability to observe fellow students in successful transactions tends to foster participation. Hence, when participation is desired, a conference or horseshoe arrangement is more likely to support the process.

The real inhibitors to active participation center around issues of control. Instructors, in many cases, fear that they will lose control if they allow people to participate. This is not a totally irrational fear. Once an instructor opens a subject up for discussion, there is the risk that the students will arrive at an answer that is considerably different than the one intended. In fact, one or more students could hold a viewpoint that is considerably different than the one held by the instructor and may be able to defend that viewpoint articulately.

The instructor's fear of being "shot down," upstaged or discovered to be lacking accurate knowledge in a group situation acts as an obstacle to group interaction. This includes the potential for a loss to the instructor's self-esteem or a perceived threat to personal security. The challenge by the students could call into question, publicly, the integrity of the material or the competence of the instructor. The consequence of instructor failure in a training situation could result in being passed over for a promotion or worse, a loss of job.

The handling of dissonant ideas or responses that are incorrect or incomplete pose another challenge for the instructor. If not handled effectively, student participation will also diminish. People experience a loss of self esteem or a threat to their job security when they are exposed as lacking knowledge or judgment.

Continuity of an interactive discussion also poses challenges for the instructor. Keeping the discussion focused on the desired objectives requires the instructor to listen, make judgments with regard to the direction of the discussion, deal with student responses that are often incorrect, incomplete or dissonant (out of harmony) with the instructor's. This requires the instructor to competently use facilitation skills involving paraphrase, probing and the use of questions. These, like most skills, evolve from continued practice. To become an expert swimmer you must first get in the water. Instructor avoidance of active participation or use of tightly controlled participation does not allow these expert facilitation skills to develop.

Planning and organization of materials also plays a significant role in whether or not group participation is achieved. As a general rule, I have found that the sequence of materials for a lecture is decidedly different than the sequence for a discussion. This is also true with regard to the use of visual aids. For example, a blank pad of paper on a flip chart is essential to interactive process. It allows an instructor to record student responses and as a by-product measure the degree to which their responses are on target. In a lecture format, an overhead projector, prepared flip chart pages or handouts containing an outline of the material are more commonly used.

In particular, the use of questions poses one of the greatest challenges. Knowing the right question to ask requires that the instructor actively listen to the responses. It is difficult to both listen to students, deal with their responses and plan the direction of the discussion. Many times instructors come to the class with an outline of the material they plan to cover rather than a set of questions they plan to ask.

There is also some degree of resistance to active participation by students. Students fear that the instructor may try to put them on the spot or trap them into giving "wrong" answers. This potential for embarrassment acts an inhibitor to participation. Another, and even more significant inhibitor, is resistance to change. Students will resist active participation in discussion and role play exercises to avoid having their ideas or behaviors held up to scrutiny by the instructor or the group.

Finally, there is the fear of failure and the potential consequences of having that occur in a classroom setting among one's peers, subordinates or superiors. The old adage, "To be silent and thought a fool is better than to open one's mouth and confirm it," works to inhibit active participation.

C. Group Participation and the Training Design

Active participation is brought about by the instructor as a direct result of the structure of the Training Design, the structure of the Instructor Guide, the use of techniques that facilitate discussion and, most important, the developer's recognition of the need for two way communication. Essentially, the developer/instructor must receive student feedback to measure the student's understanding, acceptance and ability to use the skills contained within the training.

A Training Design that meets the *Total Quality Training Standards* (Fig. 13.1) produces extensive student participation throughout the program. This, in turn, provides the feedback that indicates the degree to which the students are able to perform the desired behavior.

Figure 13.1. The *Total Quality Training Design*

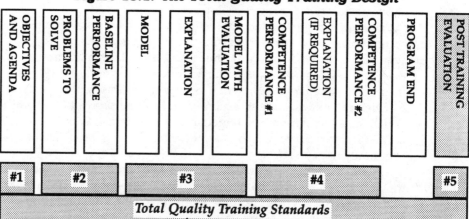

The Importance of Feedback During the Explanation Component

Important in the Training Design (Fig. 13.1) is the Explanation Component. It is during this phase of the program that the instructor communicates the essential units of knowledge and skill that enable the student to perform the desired behavior.

It might be helpful to contrast the Training Design in Fig. 13.1 to a conventional lecture with no evaluation of student performance. Effectively the lecture represents the Explanation Component of the design. It is my position that despite the thoroughness of preparation, the cleverness of the visual aids and the articulateness of the instructor, the message, in many cases, does not get through. Unfortunately, the lecturer never realizes this unless the student's ability to use knowledge and skills has been measured.

In fact, my movement toward the interactive inductive (*Guided Discovery*) training style came about as a direct result of observing student performance after I had lectured. I would observe students who were marginally able or unable to use the skills I was teaching. Unfortunately, by the time I became aware of this (toward the end of the program) there was little time to correct the problem.

By changing to the interactive style during the Explanation Component I was able to get constant feedback that enabled me to gauge understanding and acceptance. This feedback allowed me to make adjustments to the message that helped the student understand, and, most importantly, indicated to me that I was communicating effectively.

Perception and Cognition

There are a number of psychological factors that influence a person's interpretation of a message. It was a very basic understanding of two of these factors, perception and cognition, that helped me realize the need for two way communication. Consider the following characteristics of the perceptual process:

1. Perception is subjective. No two people perceive (see) the same object, event or message in the same way.

2. Perception is selective: People see that which they want to see or that which they are prepared to see.

3. Perception is influenced by past experience and needs. People interpret an object, event or message in light of their past experience, knowledge, prejudices and their needs.

"There is evidence that the past experience of a person influences his perception of objects and situations. If the needs and past experiences of the customer (student) and salesperson (instructor) differ so will their understanding of the proposition." (Cash and Crissy, 1966, Vol. 1, p. 21) While Cash and Crissy were referring to sales, their statement has direct application to teaching—especially in a business setting. The word "proposition" means something offered for consideration or acceptance. I suggest that the desired behavior contained within a training program and the knowledge and skills that bring about the ability to use that behavior must be both considered, understood and accepted by the student. If this does not occur, then the training must be considered ineffective since little or no change is likely to occur.

Two-way communication is the key to ensuring that the student's perception and subsequent interpretation of the message is the same as the instructor's.

"Cognition is an element influencing the interpretation of a message. It relates to a person's store of knowledge. A thought has inputs from the past and the present. Those from the past emerge into consciousness from memory. Those from the present come from perception." (Cash and Crissy, 1966, Vol. 7, p. 15) Knowledge is stored as abstract words and symbols. Cash and Crissy go on to say that "the thought process has a peculiar property called reification. This comes from the Latin words *res* and *facio* which mean thing and make. The mind abhors abstractions. It translates each incoming abstract word to a concrete image, usually from previous experience. For example, purity might be converted to soap, virgin, white, etc. This property of the thought process suggests the importance of avoiding abstract terms in the sales interview (training session). Rather the salesperson (instructor) should use concrete image provoking language. Examples and comparisons abound in an effective presentation. When an abstract word cannot be avoided, it may be desirable to define it or illustrate it in order to avoid misunderstanding." (Cash and Crissy, 1966, Vol. 7, p. 16)

Again, two-way communication is essential to ensuring that the message is interpreted by the student in the same way that it was sent by the instructor. By asking questions and listening, the instructor is able to gauge the student's level of understanding and acceptance of the message.

D. Inductive Process: An Elegant Short-Cut

One way to overcome the communication problems created by perception and cognition is through the use of questions <u>which are asked before the answer is given</u>. When an instructor asks such a question, he learns the students' interpretation of the question and their knowledge of the subject. This enables the instructor to respond directly to the students' needs. He or she can reinforce correct answers, explore areas of confusion and explain that which is not known or understood.

In effect, a question which is posed to the group before the answer is given produces a student response which is the equivalent of a Baseline Performance. As illustrated in Fig. 14.2, the instructor discovers what the student knows and does not know (Need Discovery). Notice that in the Need Discovery phase the instructor spends the balance of the time listening. The instructor then has the option to

Figure 14.2. Inductive Process (***Guided Discovery***)

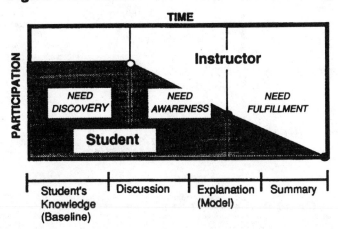

question further, explain or a combination of both. This is illustrated as the Need Awareness phase. In this phase, the instructor and students are interacting as shown by their equal participation. The instructor's explanation of the unit of knowledge is the equivalent of the Model Component of the Training Design. This provides the answer to the question that challenged the student. The instructor's detailed explanation of the unit of knowledge and summary represents the Need Fulfillment phase of the transaction.

This reversal of the communication process allows the instructor to tailor his or her message in direct relation to the students' needs as reflected by their responses.

Contrasted to a Lecture

Consider for a moment the classic lecture (see Fig. 14.3). The instructor communicates the message and then asks if there are any questions. In many cases, the students have none or just a few.

Why? I'm sure you have had this experience and can fill in your own answers. I suggest that the phrase "are there any questions?" is a request for participation. It asks, in effect, do you understand the message I just communicated?

In many cases, students do not want to indicate that they did not understand in front of their peers or superiors. Others may feel they understood the message. However, student questions to the instructor are not an indicator that the student understood or accepted the message. They merely indicate student interest in the topic presented, disagreement or a desire to clear up a point which was misunderstood. Their participation through their questions at the end of the lecture does not suggest that they understood or accepted the points that were not questioned.

Figure 14.3. The Classic Lecture

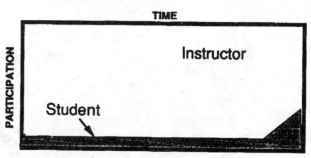

It should also be noted that the instructor's response to the students' questions produces a continuation of the lecture. Again, the instructor's final request for questions is not a request to the students for an explanation of their understanding of the message.

The timing of the lecturer's request for questions also contributes to the lack of response. In most cases, it comes toward the end of the session when people want to leave.

Motivation and Participation

Inductive questioning also creates learning motivation. "Motivation is one of the most important keys to learning. It is doubtful that any organism learns unless it is impelled by a need, faced with a problem or lured by a reward." (Goldenson, 1970, p. 687) When a question (we will assume the subject under discussion is relevant to the student's needs) is asked before the answer has been given, the student is challenged to use existing knowledge and problem-solving skills. This relates to being "impelled by a need or faced with a problem." In most cases, a sense of unease or need is created by the act of answering. This is especially true when the student(s) perceive(s) that the answer(s) is/are partially correct or incomplete. There is also a need by the student to know how well he or she performed in responding to the question. This relates to being lured by a reward. The reinforcement of the student's answer by the group and by the instructor, who is seen as an authority figure, provides such a reward.

To utilize inductive process, the instructor must structure the units of knowledge and skill so that each question is within the student's frame of reference and problem-solving skills. Students must be able to answer the instructor's questions and, at the same time, be challenged. Failure to recognize this critical concept in the design of a program will result in the student being frustrated when the questions are beyond their ability, or bored when they are too easy. In either case, the most immediate result will be decreased participation.

Inductive questioning, when effectively structured, also increases the likelihood that the student will continue to actively participate. Skinner said that "human beings are reinforced by success" and that "behavior is a result of its consequences." The desired student behavior, in this instance, is active participation. If the consequence of participation for the student is failure, then participation will diminish. People have a strong basic need for acceptance and the maintenance of their self esteem. Reproof by the instructor is contrary to these needs. On the other hand, when the program is structured so that students can answer the questions with a moderate degree of success, their motivation to participate is increased. Reinforcement by the instructor of those parts of their answers that are correct or complete relate to the satisfaction of these critical acceptance and esteem needs.

Finally, inductive questioning requires active student participation. To facilitate this, the instructor must establish a non-threatening climate and build a trust relationship with the group. The program introduction outlined in Chap. 13 (pages 220-223) sets the stage for a such a climate. Couple this with instructor willingness to listen and explore answers that are incomplete, incorrect or dissonant to his own and the likelihood of participation is further increased. These techniques are discussed in depth in Chap. 15, Guiding a Discussion to a Conclusion.

E. The Principle of Inductive Process

Questions must be <u>preplanned</u> and <u>relevant to the Conclusions</u> you wish your students to reach and a part of the Instructor Guide.

The preceding principle answers the two most frequently asked questions about the interactive inductive (*Guided Discovery*) style: How do you know the right questions to ask and how do you maintain control of the discussion? It demonstrates that the structure of the lesson and the use of questions are the keys to active student participation and the learning motivation produced by inductive questioning.

An analysis of the principle reveals that:

1. Conclusions must be preplanned.

2. Questions must be preplanned and relevant to the Conclusion.

3. Questions and Conclusions must be part of the Instructor Guide.

The operant concepts in the principle are Conclusions, preplanned questions and the Instructor Guide. We will examine each in depth.

F. Conclusions—Structuring Content

Questions must be preplanned and relevant to **the Conclusions you wish your students to reach** and a part of the Instructor Guide.

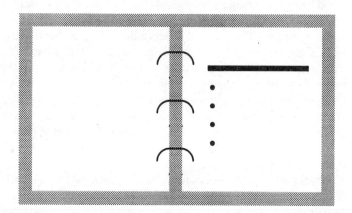

The dictionary defines conclusion, the noun, as a reasoned judgment. The verb "to conclude" means to reach a logically necessary end by reasoning. Therefore, in simplest terms, a conclusion is an idea that the developer of the training wants to communicate to the students. However, rather than tell the students the answer, the developer wishes them to arrive at the answer through a process of logical reasoning.

In effect the developer of the training (we will assume that she is also the subject expert) has acquired a body of knowledge through experience, research, reasoning or prior training. Stated another way, she has discovered, or believes she has discovered, a solution to a particular problem. In effect, her conclusion also represents the answer to a question that she believes to be correct. By posing one or more questions to the students, she hopes that she can have them reach agreement that her solution is correct.

If they agree that the solution is correct and proceed to act on the ideas, change will occur. For example, in Chap. 1 of Part 1 you completed a Technical Knowledge Self Test that asked you to write a definition of a learning objective. This represented the question, **What is the definition of a learning objective?** My answer to this question is Mager's Learning Objective Principle: **"a description of a performance you want the learner to be able to exhibit before you consider them competent."**

Throughout Chap. 2 of Part 1 we acted on Mager's Principle and derived from it the structural components of an objective and the criteria for measuring the usefulness of each. This enabled us to measure the usefulness of any objective or set of objectives. It also enabled us to agree on a system for measuring the student's competence with any desired behavior and, since training is itself a behavior, the effectiveness of the training.

If you, as the reader, did not agree with that definition, you may have stopped reading at that point. If we had been together in a group situation and you disagreed with my answer, we would have had the opportunity to discuss it and explore your ideas. The end product of that discussion could have three possible outcomes: The most desirable, from my viewpoint, would have been agreement that Mager's Principle is a useful definition of a learning objective. This would have enabled us to move forward.

A second possible outcome would have been the modification of my conclusion. In this instance you would have provided me with new information that caused me to recognize that part of my idea was flawed. In this case, we might have made a modification to the definition (principle) or agreed to consider it as presented on the basis that the subsequent ideas would support it. In either case, this would have allowed us to move forward into the content of Chap. 2.

The third possible outcome would be the total rejection of my idea. In this case, you may have argued that my definition was incorrect. You could also have taken the position that learning objectives are irrelevant. Either of these outcomes would, in all probability, result in an inability to move forward. Stated another way, the outcome of my question, and the subsequent discussion would have materialized in an instructor's worst fear—a loss of control.

The Structure of a Conclusion

Human beings learn by organizing and classifying units of knowledge into a hierarchical structure. The process is known as concept formation. Concepts are ideas based on the common properties of a group of objects, events or qualities, usually represented by a word or other symbol. The word "concept" is defined as an abstract or generic idea generalized from a particular instance.

"Concepts are developed through observation and experience. Before a child can associate the label 'apple' with the fruit of that name, he must notice that all apples are approximately round, have stems, can be eaten and so on. This application of a word label to the common properties of different objects is the essence of most concept formation. The process of acquiring these concepts, however, is a long, slow trial and error affair. The child's first concept of apple will probably be so general that it includes most fruits, since plums, peaches, oranges, etc., have many properties in common with apples. With more training and the opportunity to observe the differences between these fruits, the concept will gradually be applied in the more correct, delimited way. Thus concept formation involves learning both similarities and differences." (Goldenson, 1970, p. 245)

You can view this process in the child's development of knowledge. One game I would play with my daughter as she was growing up involved classification. I would ask her, for example, to name five types of animals. To this she would answer, dog, cat, pig, cow and bear. If I asked her to name five types of farm animals she would reply chicken, cow, pig, horse and sheep. Essentially, "Types of Animals" represents an idea or abstraction and the types (dog, cat, pig, cow and bear) the points or ends that she attached to that idea. "Types of Farm Animals" simply represents a more precise classification.

They also represent units of knowledge that she had acquired. Figure 14.4 shows the unit of knowledge "Types of Animals" organized in a manner similar to that found in the sample Instructor Guides (Apps. E and F).

Figure 14.4. A Unit of Knowledge

Types of Animals

- Dog
- Cat
- Pig
- Cow
- Bear

Cash and Crissy provide a particularly concise discussion of how perceiving and thinking interact to form concepts.

> "To gain further understanding about the nature of thoughts and ideas, consider the way in which the mind accumulates information. Even before birth, the surrounding environment impinges on the senses. (There is some research evidence of prenatal learning.) At birth and thereafter, the infinitely more complex and varied environment imposes thousands of stimuli which are sensed by each person each moment of their life. Relatively few of these reach conscious awareness and have meaning attached. When this meaning does take place, *perception* has been added to *sensation*. As similar stimuli are perceived, a generalization occurs. When this generalization is realized, a concept is formed.
>
> The memory then can be thought of as a kind of IBM card sorter—the concept being visualized as the pockets, the perceptions (past and present) as the cards. However the memory is not fixed or static. Through a combination of inductive and deductive processes, the concepts are continually being refined and changed, and new concepts are being formed.
>
> The more varied a person's experiences, the broader his perception is likely to be. The more recurrent his experiences, the more refined and accurate his concepts are likely to be." (Grikscheit, Cash and Crissy, 1981, pp. 77-78)

When a person has formed a concept, she can explain it by citing any number of relevant characteristics. For example, consider the concept (unit of knowledge) "types of sentences." In a recent discussion with my daughter (age 9) she informed me that there are four types of sentences (declarative, exclamatory, interrogative and imperative). She then preceded to define and give me an example of each. These new units of knowledge essentially have a Hierarchical Structure as shown in Fig. 14.5.

Figure 14.5. Units of Knowledge

Types of Sentences

- Declarative
- Interrogative
- Exclamatory
- Imperative

Declarative Sentence

- Makes a statement
- Punctuated with a period
- Example: This is a declarative sentence.

The Need for Structure

In order to bring about an interactive discussion of an idea the instructor must be able to:

1. Decide what units of knowledge and skill are relevant to the Unit Objective.
2. Organize information (units of knowledge) in a manner that leads to their logical discussion.
3. Measure the degree to which the student's answer is correct and complete.

In practical terms this requires a structure that enables the instructor to quickly review the answer. In this case, a series of bullet points rather than text organized as paragraphs is desirable. This type of structure allows the instructor to compare the student's answer to the desired or expected answer.

Appendices E and F contain Instructor Guides that are structured for an interactive inductive discussion of their subject matter. Throughout these guides each unit of knowledge and skill is structured as a Conclusion. Figure 14.6 is a symbolic representation of the Conclusion Structure. Each unit consists of a title (the abstraction or abstract idea) and below the title one or more related points or Ends.

The following is the definition of the Structure of a Conclusion structured as a Conclusion:

Structure of a Conclusion

A unit of desired behavior, skill or knowledge consisting of an abstraction and one or more related Ends at the next lower level of abstraction.

Figure 14.6. A Symbolic Representation of a Conclusion

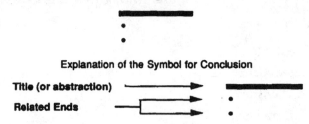

Mager's Principle is an example of a unit of knowledge structured as a Conclusion. It consists of the abstract idea, the **"Definition of a Learning Objective"** and the definition itself: **"A description of a performance you want the learners to be able to exhibit before you consider them competent."** It also can be depicted as shown in Fig. 14.7.

Figure 14.7. A Unit of Knowledge Structured as a Conclusion

Abstraction: <u>Definition of a Learning Objective</u>

Related End: A description of a performance you want the learners to be able to exhibit before you consider them competent.

In both cases, these units of knowledge (Structure of a Conclusion and the Definition of a Learning Objective) are precise definitions that contain only one point or End.

Most units of knowledge have multiple Ends. For example consider a unit of knowledge on the "Benefits of Questions." The question that the developer would ask in preparing this part of the lesson would be "<u>What are the benefits of effective questions in conducting training?</u>" The answer listed in Fig. 14.8 is structured as a Conclusion and represents the answers that I believe to be correct. In this Conclusion I have included a brief justification (italics) for each End.

A Word About the Word "Ends"

The use of the word "End" is significant. End means to conclude or finish. Hence, the Ends, or points, listed in each Conclusion represent an objective to be reached during the discussion of a particular unit of knowledge or skill. In order to maintain control and work within time allocations, there has to be a boundary for each unit of the discussion. If there is a desire to go into additional detail on a given End, it becomes the abstraction (idea or concept) for the next

Conclusion. As such, we must then have one or more new Ends (points) at the next lower level of abstraction which make the idea or concept more concrete and understandable.

This can be demonstrated by the first End **"makes each student think"** in the Conclusion "Benefits of Questions" (see Fig. 14.8). In order to go to the next level of abstraction, we would have to explore the concept of thinking. This would result in a psychological discussion on the functioning of the human mind. (See Fig. 14.9.)

As the developer of a training program you have to decide just how deep into any subject you need to go. The question you must ask yourself is whether or not

---

Figure 14.8. Another Unit of Knowledge Structured as a Conclusion

Abstraction	<u>BENEFITS OF QUESTIONS</u>
Related Ends	**Makes each student think.** *Each must consider their answer to the question.*
	Creates learning motivation. *This is particularly true when the question is asked before the answer is given. When questions are asked in this manner, the student is challenged to use his or her existing knowledge and problem solving skills. A sense of unease is created when the student perceives that their answer is incomplete. There is also a need by the student for reinforcement of their answer.*
	Guides the discussion toward objectives. *One or more units of knowledge and skill may be required to achieve a Unit Objective. Hence the discussion of each unit leads to the achievement of the objectives.*
	Gathers information. *This enables the instructor to gauge the amount of information (knowledge) that the students posses and their viewpoint.*
	Tests effectiveness of communication. *Feedback from students indicate the degree to which they understand and accept the ideas under discussion.*
	Measures learning. *Student responses indicate the degree to which they can use the knowledge and skills under discussion. Questions on a test or the task io be performed in a Competence Performance cause the student to exhibit the desired behavior which enables the instructor to observe and measure their degree of competence.*
	Involves the group. *Questions stimulate the discussion. They provide the license and structure for the student's response.*

Figure 14.9. Going Deeper

Thinking

Cognitive behavior in which we recall or manipulate images or ideas that stand for objects and events: Symbolic behavior.

---

the time and energy invested is necessary for understanding and accepting the idea under discussion. I believe that most people would be comfortable stopping the discussion with the idea that a question makes each student think and the elaboration (justification) that each must consider their answer to the question (before responding).

The Next Lower Level of Abstraction

As discussed earlier, concepts are ideas based on the common properties of a group of objects, events or qualities, which are usually represented by a word or other symbol. For example consider the abstract symbol, "car." Most adults by the time they are in their twenties have acquired a significant amount of knowledge about cars. This would include such things as types of cars, makes of cars, models of cars, financing of cars, purchasing a car, selling a car, parts of a car, assembly of cars, motor vehicle laws, performance of cars and prices of cars.

If you ask a person a question about "types of cars" you are likely to get responses such as sedan, convertible, station wagon, coupe, minivan or hatchback. By contrast, if you ask about "makes of cars" you will get answers like Ford, Chevrolet, Plymouth, Toyota, Audi, Jaguar. Notice that each response is at the next lower level of abstraction. In other words, if people have knowledge, that knowledge is classified in a logical format and can be elicited by a question.

In addition to knowledge of cars people have knowledge about other products they have or will need to purchase. Some of this knowledge is the direct result of experience and some has been acquired through education, television, reading books or talking with people.

The key is that people can draw upon the knowledge they have, manipulate it and through the process come up with new ideas that help them solve problems. For example consider the concept of a buying cycle as it relates to the purchase of a car. Before you proceed further try to answer this question: <u>What are the key events in the process of buying a new car</u>? (See Fig. 14.10.)

Notice that my answer, is organized as a Conclusion. It contains an abstraction, "The Buying Cycle for a Car" and five Ends at the next lower level of abstraction.

If we wish to explore any of these Ends as Units of Knowledge, unto themselves, we can do so by asking another question. For example, take the End "negotiating" and assume that we are conducting a training program for people who will be selling cars to retail customers. We have decided that the salespeople should understand the negotiation process from the customer's view point. Therefore, we ask the question: <u>What does the customer expect during the negotiation process</u>? The likely answers are shown in Fig. 14.11.

Figure 14.10. The Buying Cycle for a Car

1. Deciding: An event triggers the need for a new car.

2. Looking: People consider the type of vehicle they want in relation to their needs.

3. Comparing: Having decided on a type of vehicle, people compare the offerings of several manufacturers to determine the best value for their money.

4. Shopping: People look for the make, model, equipment and color they desire and begin to test the market by getting prices.

5. Negotiating: Having located one or more acceptable vehicles, people bargain with the dealer for an acceptable price.

Again, the answer is organized as a Conclusion with, in this case, seven Ends at the next lower level of abstraction. Any one of these ends could be the subject for another Conclusion.

An important point. Because people organize knowledge as Conclusions, you are not likely to get the End 6 in Fig. 14.11 (The dealer will not generally sell the car at a loss) as a response to the question "What are the key events in the process of buying a new car?"

Figure 14.11. Customer Expectations During Negotiation

1. The dealer's initial price represents a high profit to the dealer.

2. The dealer will claim that the customer's trade-in is worth less than they believe or researched.

3. If the customer makes an initial offer or a counter offer they will be asked for earnest money.

4. The dealer will not generally sell the car at a loss.

5. Knowledge of the dealer's costs increases the likelihood that they get a good deal.

6. The dealer will use one or more negotiation ploys to gain advantage and profit (i.e., offer leasing or payments or an alternative vehicle).

7. The salesperson has limited authority to contract.

Levels of Abstraction

When a term (idea or concept) is abstract or outside a person's frame of reference, the instructor must be prepared to lower the level of abstraction. This can be accomplished by giving specific examples of what we are talking about. The idea that "one picture is worth a thousand words," cannot be over emphasized. In writing this book I have made a conscious effort to illustrate every key point. To that end I built Part 1, Learning Objectives, The Foundation, as a training program so that you would have a concrete example of what I meant when I used the abstract term "effective training program."

S.I. Hayakawa has an excellent discussion of the problems created by the abstract nature of language.

> "An extremely widespread instance of unrealistic (an ultimately superstitious) attitude toward definitions is found in the common academic prescription, 'Let's define our terms so that we shall all know what we are talking about.' As we have already seen..., the fact that a golfer, for example, cannot define golfing terms is no indication that he cannot understand them and use them. Conversely the fact that a man can define a large number of words is no guarantee that he knows what objects or operations they stand for in concrete situations. Having defined a word, people often believe that some kind of understanding has been established, ignoring the fact that the words in the definition often conceal even more serious confusions and ambiguities than the word defined. If we happen to discover this fact and try to remedy matters by defining the defining words, and then, finding ourselves still confused, we go on to define the words in the definitions of the defining words, and so on, we quickly find ourselves in a hopeless snarl. The only way to avoid this snarl is to keep definitions to a minimum and point to extensional levels wherever necessary; in writing and speaking, **this means giving specific examples of what we are talking about**." (Hayakawa, 1978, p. 159)

For a fuller explanation of abstractions, see S.I. Hayakawa's Language in Thought and Action. Specifically Chap. 10, "How We Know What We Know" and Chap. 2, "Symbols."

G. Preplanned Questions

Questions must be **preplanned** and relevant to the Conclusions you wish your students to reach **and a part of the Instructor Guide.**

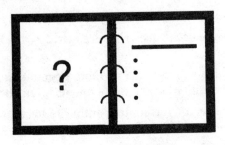

Preplanning questions involves:

- Considering the Conclusion you wish the students to reach
- Defining the questions you will ask
- Deciding how you will pose the questions to the group
- Deciding the point or sequence in the lesson that you will address the issue
- Planning the media you will use in the discussion (flip chart, overhead projector, whiteboard, handout, etc.)

Two critical questions the instructor must ask him or herself are:

1. What knowledge or experience does the student bring to the table?
2. What foundation, if any, has to be laid to enable the student to respond to the question and reach the desired Conclusion?

For example, let's consider the Conclusion, "Benefits of Questions" illustrated on page 267. This is an example of a unit of knowledge that can be easily discussed in a group situation. The instructor can reasonably assume that the students have sufficient knowledge from previous experience to reason their way to each of the Ends listed in Fig. 14.8. Therefore, little or no foundation needs to be established. (Note: Discussions on subjects where the student has limited knowledge and experience are addressed at the end of this chapter.)

Let's further assume that Benefits of Questions is one of several units of knowledge that will be used to achieve the Unit Objective **"Differentiate a Task Question from a Voluntary, Directed and Involuntary Question."** Other relevant units of knowledge are listed in Fig. 14.12.

The discussion of the Benefits of Questions is an excellent lead-in to this unit which deals with the various techniques for posing questions. In fact, the discussion can be started with a simple prefacing statement "Let's talk about the questioning process" followed by the question, "What are the benefits of effective questions in conducting training?"

Figure 14.12. Units of Knowledge to Achieve a Unit Objective

1. Benefits of Questions.
2. Types of Questions.
3. Task Questions.
4. Benefits of a Task Question.
5. Voluntary Questions.
6. Directed Questions and Involuntary Questions.
7. Problems with Directed Questions and Involuntary Questions.
8. Steps for asking a question.

Criteria for Questions

Preplanning of questions also involves the structure of the question. Effective questions:

1. Are relevant to the Conclusion
2. Are indirect (they start with Why, What, How, When, Where or Who)
3. Contain less than 18 words
4. Do not contain any of the "Ends" in the Conclusion (i.e., not give the answer)

The question, "What are the benefits of effective questions in conducting training?," meets each of the preceding criteria. We can see that it is relevant to the Conclusion by the fact that it contains the abstraction, "Benefits of Questions." It is also an indirect question as it begins with the word "what." Finally, it contains less than 18 words and does not contain any of the Ends in the Conclusion.

Questions can exceed 18 words. The limit of 18 words is merely a guideline that reminds you to check your question for clarity. Lengthy questions tend to cause confusion and should be avoided. Also avoid planning questions with two parts. For example, "What are the benefits of asking questions and the steps for asking a question?" Such questions cause confusion and increase the difficulty of conducting a logical discussion.

A question which contains an End or is related to one of the Ends also creates an obstacle to the desired interaction. For example, the question, "How do questions involve the group?," is not likely to stimulate a discussion of the benefits of questions. In order to conduct the discussion, the instructor has to plan one question for each End. This results in a discussion which is too tightly controlled. Highly controlled discussions tend to inhibit future participation.

Core, Secondary and Spontaneous
Secondary Questions

As a general rule, one preplanned question should bring about the discussion of any Conclusion. This is referred to as a Core Question. The question, "What are the benefits of effective questions in conducting training?," is an excellent example of a Core Question.

A second question can also be preplanned. This is referred to as a Secondary Question. A Secondary Question is relevant to one or more Ends in a Conclusion that the developer of the training wants to emphasize. The developer may also be concerned that the Conclusion, as structured, cannot be discussed with only the Core Question. In other cases, the developer may be concerned that the group will have difficulty reaching one of the Ends.

Let's look at an example. "Creates Learning Motivation" is an End in the Conclusion "Benefits of Questions" (see Fig. 14.8) that the developer feels the group may have difficulty in reaching. If the developer feels that the End is important to discuss but, because of time or other constraints, does not warrant a separate unit of knowledge, a Secondary Question is appropriate. To bring about the discussion of this particular End, the following questions could be used: <u>What is the benefit of asking a question before the answer has been given?</u> or <u>How do questions create learning motivation?</u>

A review of the Instructor Guides in Apps. E and F will reveal that 80 percent of the time, only one question has been preplanned. This review will also show that a maximum of two questions, a Core and Secondary, are used to bring about the discussion of any Conclusion. Why?

Back in 1979 when I first developed this system, I wrote numerous questions for each Conclusion; sometimes a Core and a question for each End. This proved impractical. When the Core Question was effective, the discussion of the Conclusion occurred spontaneously. In other words, all the preplanned questions were not needed. Additionally, when the discussion failed to address one or two of the preplanned Ends, it proved to be difficult to locate the appropriate preplanned question from the list of questions. This "Guide clutter" tended to waste time and reduced my focus on the group.

The solution to the problem occurred quite naturally. While I was unable to quickly locate the preplanned question, I was able to clearly identify the Ends which had not been reached. If I wished to bring about a discussion of one particular End, I would spontaneously ask a question related to the missing point (End). This question is referred to as a Spontaneous Secondary Question (SSQ).

Another approach is to explain the remaining points to the group and ask for their reaction. Take the End "creates Learning Motivation" for example. The instructor could say: "Questions create learning motivation; especially those asked before the answer is given." To test the group's reaction to this idea the instructor could then ask: "Why would this technique create learning motivation?" In either case, the question brings about a discussion of the idea.

Selection of Media

Preplanning, as stated earlier, involves decisions with regard to the media to be used. In the discussion of the "Benefits of Questions," the instructor chooses to use a blank flip chart and list the group's responses as each one is discussed. This is particularly useful when the Conclusion has a number of Ends. By listing each, the instructor keeps the discussion on track and can easily measure when the Conclusion is reached. In this case, when all seven of the expected Ends are listed.

Figure 14.13 shows that the framed conclusion was ultimately discussed in a different order than planned, but that all the points (Ends) were identified.

The flip chart also helps the students participate in the discussion. Since the Conclusion has seven Ends, the students do not have to remember which ones have been discussed. They would merely have to look at the flip chart. By knowing which Ends were reached, they would be less likely to repeat those that had been discussed. The use of the flip chart, in this case, would also increase the likelihood of note taking.

Figure 14.13. The Framed Conclusion

<u>Benefits of Questions</u>

- Involves the group.
- Makes each student think.
- Measures learning.
- Gathers information.
- Guides the discussion toward objectives.
- Tests the effectiveness of communication.
- Creates learning motivation.

H. The Instructor Guide Panel

Questions must be preplanned and relevant to the Conclusions you wish your students to reach **and a part of the Instructor Guide.**

The principle states that the Conclusion and question should be part of your Instructor Guide. Figure 14.14 shows a Panel of the Instructor Guide for the Unit of Knowledge "Benefits of Questions." The Panel is the basic building block of the Instructor Guide. It consists of one result or outcome, in this case a unit of knowledge structured as a Conclusion and the techniques that the instructor plans to use to bring about the discussion.

Figure 14.14. A Panel of the Guide

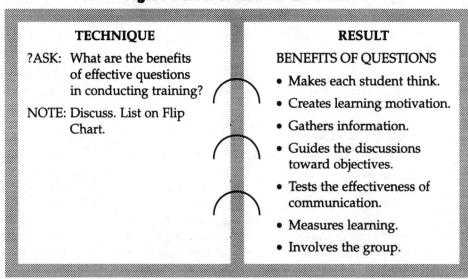

TECHNIQUE	RESULT
?ASK: What are the benefits of effective questions in conducting training?	BENEFITS OF QUESTIONS
NOTE: Discuss. List on Flip Chart.	• Makes each student think.
	• Creates learning motivation.
	• Gathers information.
	• Guides the discussions toward objectives.
	• Tests the effectiveness of communication.
	• Measures learning.
	• Involves the group.

Figure 14.15. Terms with Special Meanings

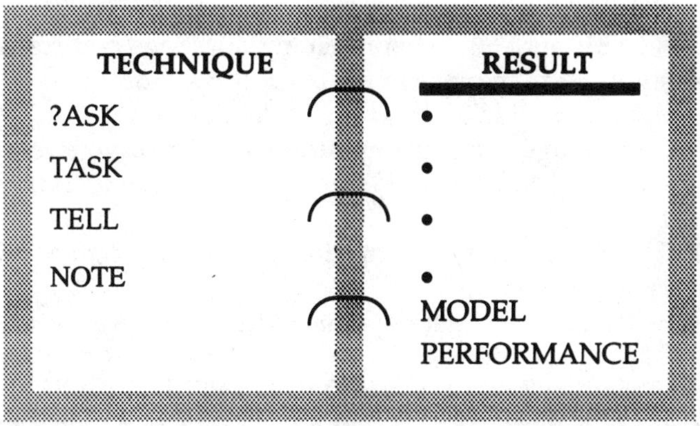

The Panel is the foundation unit of the Instructor Guide. A Panel consists of a left side which represents the specific techniques that will bring about the desired result on the right hand side. In Fig. 14.14, the desired result is a discussion of the benefits of questions. The desired result, as shown in Fig. 14.15, could also be a Performance (Baseline or Competence) or a Model by the instructor.

Listed below the words TECHNIQUE and RESULT are terms and symbols with special meanings. Each will be discussed in detail on the following pages.

Format of an Instructor Guide Panel

The Panel's format evolves from the principle that **"questions must be pre-planned and relevant to the Conclusion you wish the student to reach and a part of the Instructor Guide."** It is divided into two parts. The right-hand side is entitled RESULT and the left-hand side is entitled TECHNIQUE.

1. **TECHNIQUE:** Outlines the questions, tasks, statements and procedures the instructor uses to bring about the specific unit of knowledge or skill or activity defined under RESULT. It consists of:
   a. **?ASK:** Questions to be asked to the group. A question may be followed by a NOTE. For example, the Conclusion is to be listed on the flip chart as the responses occur.
   b. **TASK:** An activity that the group or specific members of the group will engage in. All tasks have a NOTE which lists the instructor action required to maximize the activity's learning value.
   c. **TELL:** A statement which is read to the group. Statements are used to provide information which cannot be efficiently accomplished through a discussion. They are also used as a transition from one Conclusion to another or to frame (provide boundaries for) a question.

    d. **NOTE:** Instructions to the instructor relevant to the subject matter under discussion.

    The symbols **?ASK** and **TELL** (representing questions and statements) are used to permit uniform margins in the Instructor Guide.

2. **RESULT:** The right-hand side of the guide contains:

    a. The units of knowledge and skill organized into Conclusions, each of which represent an objective to be reached during the discussion. Each Conclusion is structured as follows:

        (1) **TITLE:** This represents the abstraction; the idea, concept or procedure to be discussed.

        (2) **END(S):** One or more related points at the next lower level of abstraction.

    b. The desired behavior: The words MODEL and PERFORMANCE appear on the right-hand side. Instructions framing the transaction (defining its beginning and end) are found on the TECHNIQUE page.

        (1) **MODEL:** A demonstration by the instructor which represents the desired behavior the student is to learn.

        (2) **PERFORMANCE:** Student performance of the desired behavior.

Hand-written Versus Computer-written Guides

The guide structure in the illustrations in this chapter appear different from the those in Apps. E and F. Figures 14.16 and 14.17 contrast two formats, one for Panels written by hand and one for those written on a computer.

The hand-written guide Panel consists of two 8 1/2" by 11" pages in a three ring notebook. All instructions (?ASK, TASK, TELL and NOTE) dealing with the techniques to be employed appear on the page labeled TECHNIQUE. The Conclusion, Model or Performance appear on the page labeled RESULT. The reverse side of either page is left blank.

Figure 14.16. Manual (Hand-written) Panel

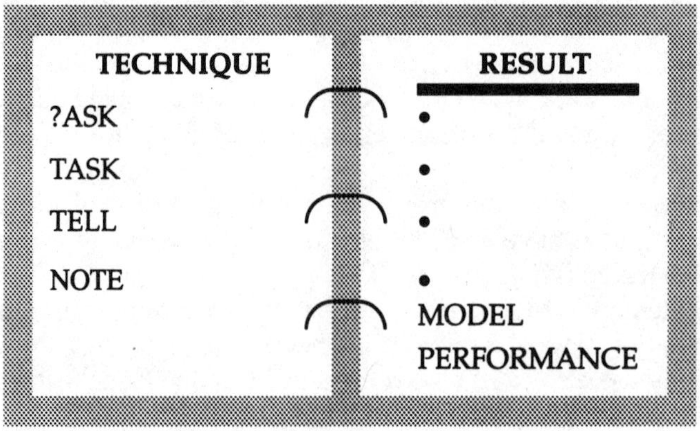

Figure 14.17. Computer (Word Processor) Panel

TECHNIQUE	RESULT
?ASK	
TASK	
TELL	
NOTE	▬▬▬▬▬
	•
	•
	•
	•
	MODEL
	PERFORMANCE

The Computer-written Guide consists of one 8 1/2" by 11" page. All instructions dealing with the TECHNIQUE appear on the left hand side of the page. The Conclusion, Model or Performance appear under RESULT on the right. **One or more Panels can be listed on the same page.** However, a panel may not start on one page and continue to the next.

TECHNIQUE and RESULT

The Panel, whether written by hand or on computer, is divided into two sections. The logic of this structure is particularly important. It recognizes that the instructor (developer) can make errors in the planning process. As such, the techniques to reach any Conclusion may change as could any Conclusion. For example, the question could be correct but the instructor's answer could be incorrect, partially correct or incomplete. The discussion of a particular unit of knowledge or skill could be out of sequence. In other cases, the students may not have sufficient prior knowledge or experience to answer the question thus creating a chasm in the guide (e.g., you can't get from here to there as planned). In other cases, the pre-planned question could be flawed. In any of these situations, some degree of rewriting will be necessary.

The single page structure of the hand-written guide enables this to occur with the least amount of rewriting. In 1980, I worked on a program development project with a team of eight mid-level managers of a finance company in the United Kingdom. My objective was to develop a training program that would enable these managers to train 350 District Managers who called on 2,000 automobile dealerships. These District Managers were trained to conduct sales meetings with 10,000 automobile salespeople on the sale of financing (through the client finance company) and related insurance products. The goal was to reach approximately one million customers annually with a message that they (the customer) should finance their vehicles with our client's finance company and purchase insurance to protect their ability to repay the loan.

The program was developed in Chicago, Illinois, at my company's home office. Subsequently, I rolled the program out in the United Kingdom with the team of eight mid-level managers. The initial sessions had the dual purpose of testing the program (with actual students) and simultaneously certifying the eight managers as instructors.

During the first session we discovered numerous flaws in the structure of our program (sequence of the Unit Objectives) and in the content of our Conclusions. Because of the guide structure we were able to correct the problems with a minimal degree of rewriting. The program was 80 percent correct, it was just in the wrong order. On one particularly long evening we laid the Instructor Guide Panels end to end on the floor and physically changed the order in which the Unit Objectives were covered. We then created the missing Panels to bridge the gaps.

Correcting flaws in a guide written on a computer is simply a matter of inserting new data or cutting and pasting the Panels to change the order of the units of knowledge or skill.

I. Types of Preplanned Questions

Preplanning for an interactive inductive discussion requires specific decisions about the types of questions to be asked during the program. In this section I will differentiate three types of preplanned Core Questions. These are called Voluntary Questions, Task Questions and Tasks. For our purposes any task is the equivalent of a question. Implicit in the task is the question "can you perform?" The students' performance of the given task reveals their knowledge and skills.

Voluntary Question

Any question posed to the group as a whole is referred to as a Voluntary Question. This technique causes each student to think about his or her answer and, as a result, produces a good discussion. The instructor can allow one or more volunteers to respond with answers until the Conclusion is reached. Figure 14.18 contains a Voluntary Question.

Figure 14.18. A Panel Containing a Voluntary Question

TECHNIQUE   **RESULT**

?ASK: How many different ways could an instructor
        pose a question to the group?

NOTE: Use flip chart. Label and illustrate each technique.

WAYS TO POSE A QUESTION (10)

- Task Question: Have each person write down his or her answer before beginning the discussion.

- Voluntary Question: To the group as a whole. Then wait for a volunteer to respond.

- Involuntary Question: To a specific individual. "Bob, How many different ways could an instructor pose a question to the group?"

- Directed Question: First to the group as whole and then to a specific individual. "How many different ways could an instructor pose a question to the group?" (pause and then call on) "Bob?"

Task Questions

In a Task Question the instructor asks each student to write down his or her answer before beginning the discussion. This causes each student to independently consider his or her answer. As a result, the quality of the student's response is significantly enhanced and participation tends to increase.

The Task Question involves every student. This is particularly important. Time does not always allow the instructor to involve every student in the discussion. However, by using a Task Question even those who do not verbally participate, participate vicariously. Their correct answers are reinforced by virtue of the fact that they had written them down.

Voluntary participation is also enhanced. Students compare the answers they have written to those already given. When one or more of the answers that they have written down have not been given, they are more likely to volunteer their answers. Stated another way, the students are more invested in their answer(s) due to their independent thought. As a result, they get involved to see if their ideas are accepted (test the validity of their ideas).

A Task Question can also be used to involve the student who is hesitant or reluctant to participate. In this case, the instructor calls on the student he or she wants to involve in the discussion. The likelihood of a correct and complete or partially correct answer is increased. As a result, the student is reinforced by the instructor's and group's acceptance of his or her answer. This often leads to his or her increased participation.

Figure 14.19 shows that while there are only three Ends in the Instructor Guide, the group has listed anywhere from zero to five responses. As a result the depth of discussion is enhanced. So, too, is note taking as students add or correct the responses they have written down.

The symbol "TASK" is used before a Task Question as shown in Figure 14.20. A Task Question requires a NOTE. As a general rule, the NOTE will include the time allotted to allow students to write down their answer, instructions with regard to media and, where appropriate, procedures for conducting the discussion. In Fig. 14.20, the developer has allowed three minutes for the students to list their answers. The developer has also indicated that only the underlined portion of each End be listed on the flip chart. This eliminates writing extensive answers; a time consuming practice.

Figure 14.19. Task Question Versus a Voluntary Question

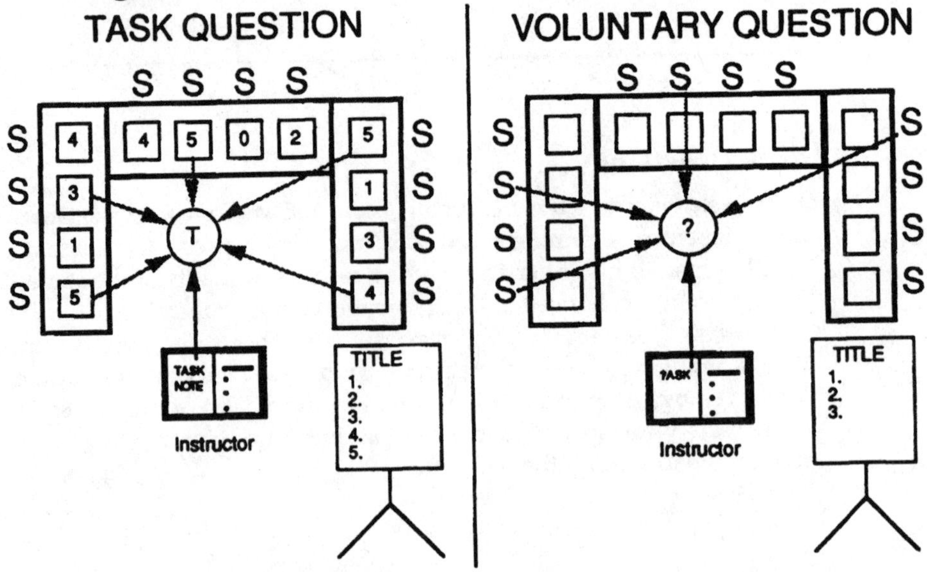

Figure 14.20. A Panel Containing a Task Question

TECHNIQUE   **RESULT**

TELL: During the last 25 minutes, I have been using a group of skills that facilitate a discussion toward a predetermined Conclusion.

TASK: Write down the techniques that you have observed during the last 25 minutes.

NOTE: Allow 3 minutes. Discuss. Record <u>underlined portion</u> of answers on flip chart.

TECHNIQUES THAT FACILITATE DISCUSSION (15)

- <u>Questioning techniques</u>. Posed to the group rather than an individual. They are asked to write down their answers prior to discussion.

- <u>Paraphrase</u>. Used to reinforce the individual and the knowledge or skill under discussion.

- <u>Recording answers on a flip chart</u>. Enables the group to utilize information previously given. Encourages note taking.

- <u>Probing questions</u>. Used to elicit more data or clarify an answer that is perceived to be incorrect.

- <u>Preplanned questions</u>. Questions are listed in the Instructor Guide.

- <u>Preplanned Conclusions</u>. The instructor has committed him or herself to an answer that he or she believes is correct and is willing to test through interaction with a group.

- <u>Spontaneous Secondary Questions</u>. Related to a particular End in the Conclusion.

Tasks

A Task represents a piece of work which one or more member of the group will perform. The practice exercise on page 453 of App. F is an example of a relatively complex task. The group is asked to write a Learning Objective for a training module on the tennis serve. At this juncture of the lesson, the developer is looking for the student to write an objective which contains a clearly identifiable Performer, Performance, Performance Time, Condition and Criteria Component.

The degree of preplanning for the Task in Fig. 14.21 is evident in the instructor note (NOTE). The developer has decided to have all students write an objective. Then, three of the students' objectives will be discussed. The NOTE also reveals that the developer plans to use an overhead projector during the discussion of each student's objective. This will allow the students to participate in the evaluation of the objectives discussed.

Instructor Notes (NOTE)

A NOTE is an instruction to the instructor detailing how the discussion of any unit of knowledge or skill should be brought about. As a general rule, instructor notes should be brief and written as action oriented statements. For example:

1. Allow ___ minutes. This represents the time allocated for student preparation prior to beginning the discussion.
2. Use flip chart (or whiteboard, blackboard, overhead projector, VCR, audio tape recorder, etc.). The developer can designate the matrix (see discussion on page 284) which is appropriate to the unit of knowledge or skill under discussion.
3. Conduct the exercise as follows. The developer provides a detailed outline of the procedures to be followed.
4. Poll group, discuss, use round robin, break into teams, etc. This represents a description of the type of group involvement that is anticipated. For example in the model Guides (Apps. E and F):
   - **Discuss** means to interact with one or more group member until the Conclusion is reached.
   - **Poll group** means to get a response from each group member.
   - **Round Robin** means to move around the room in sequence.
   - **Break into teams** enables group members to formulate a consensus answer and report back to the group.
5. Handout _____, refer to page ___, etc. These instructions remind the instructor to provide the group with the references it needs to participate in the discussion.

Instructor notes permit the developer or the manager responsible for the training to monitor the performance of instructors who have been certified to conduct the program. It enables them to determine whether or not the program is being conducted as it was intended to be.

Figure 14.21. A Panel Containing a Task

TECHNIQUE   RESULT

TASK: You are to teach the serve to a group of 6 students. Your students are beginners who have been taught the forehand and backhand strokes. Write a learning objective for your training module on the tennis serve.

NOTE: Conduct the exercise as follows:

1. Hand out blank acetates and vis-à-vis pens.

2. Instruct group to transfer their objective to a blank acetate.

3. Allow 5 minutes for them to write their answers.

4. Review 3 student answers with the questions below. Place each student's answer on the overhead projector to facilitate discussion.

   ■ What is the performance we want to observe before we consider the student competent?

   ■ How will you know they have accomplished it?

5. Use whiteboard or flip chart to illustrate accuracy and speed.

   ■ Illustrate an overview of the tennis court to establish "accuracy."

   ■ Illustrate a side view of a tennis court and draw a serve with a high trajectory and one with a correct trajectory to illustrate "speed." Ask: Which would be easier to return?

6. Reveal preframed model objective. Have group identify each component.

MODEL OBJECTIVE (25)

Given 10 balls on an indoor court, the player will be able to **serve the ball into the opponent's service court** *7 out of 10 times* at a speed of 50 MPH *while exhibiting prescribed form.*

Notes <u>may</u> appear before or after any Question, Task or Statement. The absence of a Note following a question represents the developer's decision that the unit of knowledge can be discussed without the use of a matrix (Fig. 14.22). This does not mean that the instructor could not use a flip chart or whiteboard to conduct the discussion. However, the developer of the training, by omitting the Note, is suggesting that the point can be made adequately through a discussion. This fact is often reflected in the time allocation for the discussion that is generally lower than those where a flip chart or other matrix is used.

All Tasks must be followed by a Note. This is necessitated by the fact that a Task represents a piece of work which one or more member of the group will perform, and for the most part, a greater allocation of time for student preparation. Stated another way, the students have invested considerable time and energy in formulating an answer. Failure to review their answers negates the effort they invested in class, before class or as homework.

Matrix

Perhaps you're wondering about the use of the term matrix with regard to audio visual resources such as flip charts, overhead projectors, whiteboards, etc. The dic-

---

Figure 14.22. A Panel Without a Note (Open Discussion)

TECHNIQUE   **RESULT**

?ASK: What are the potential problems of conducting a
        role play exercise without a case?

ROLE PLAY WITHOUT A CASE (3)
If the student acting as the customer:

- is too easy, then the performer loses the opportunity to demonstrate his or her skills.

- is too difficult, then the:

  —Performer becomes frustrated.

  —Group's desire to participate in future exercises is reduced.

- portrays an unrealistic situation, then the value of the exercise is lost. The instructor in unable to measure learner competence.

---

tionary defines a matrix as "something within which something else originates or develops." The "something" in interactive inductive training is the students' performance of a desired behavior or their active participation in the discussion of the program's units of knowledge or skill. The flip chart is an excellent example of a matrix. It holds ideas and allows the discussion to develop. The following are the most commonly used matrixes in interactive training.

- Flip chart: Especially useful for recording Conclusions where there is a desire to make future reference to the points listed. Flip chart "frames" can be hung on the walls of the classroom.

- Whiteboard or blackboard: Used for illustrations which support the Conclusion under discussion or for discussing units of skill or knowledge that are unlikely to be referenced later in the program.

- Overhead projector: Especially useful for discussing and evaluating written performance such as learning objectives, questions or other written skills such as business letters, job descriptions, proposals, etc. Allows the performance to be studied and evaluated.

- VCR: Useful for recording interactive sales, management or customer service type transactions where verbal and non-verbal skills are evaluated, as well as individual performance (such as a golf swing or tennis serve) or team performance.

- Audio Tape Recorder: Used for recording vignettes of behavior or verbal behaviors where non-verbal skills are not applicable (telephone transactions).

J. Structure of the Instructor Guide

Relevance to the Conclusion

Questions must be preplanned and relevant to the Conclusions you wish your students to reach and a part of the Instructor Guide.

The structure of a Conclusion relates directly to each level of the **Hierarchical Structure** of a Training Program. The **Hierarchical Structure** enables all of the material in a Training Program to be relevant to the achievement of one or more Result Objectives in a Business Plan. Figure 4.3 from Chap. 4 of Part 1 shows that a related End in a unit of knowledge and skill is directly related to each Objective within the structure.

Each level of the **Hierarchical Structure** is itself a Conclusion; an end or objective to be reached. At the Business Plan level the Result Objective represents an End, which, in this case, is measured by a specified quantifiable result which is to be achieved within a set period of time (i.e., number of sales, gross revenue, gross profit, net profits, etc.). The Core Objective(s) is also an End. In effect, we are saying that the result will be brought about by one or more desired behaviors specified in the Core Objectives.

Figure 4.3. Hierarchical Structure of a Training Program

Business Plan
- Result Objective
- Core Objective(s)

Training Program
- Core Objective
- Module Objective(s)

Training Module
- Module Objective
- Unit Objective(s)

Training Unit
- Unit Objective
- Related unit(s) of knowledge and skill

Unit of Knowledge and Skill
- An idea, concept or procedure
- Related point(s) or End(s)

For example, let's say that we decide to market a line of insurance products through a sales force which we will employ. The Result Objective is to sell $25 million worth of insurance this year, $50 million next year and achieve 20 percent premium growth thereafter with a persistency rate of 75 percent. (In other words, 75 percent of the policies are kept in force for at least 13 months by the policyholders through their continued payment of premiums.)

To achieve this objective we estimate that we will need to recruit and train 80 agents the first year and 40 thereafter to accommodate turnover and sales force growth. These agents will be managed by 10 managers who will also need to be recruited. The Core Objectives that will enable us to achieve the Result Objective involve training agents to sell and managers to select, train, develop and manage the agents. In effect, the Core Objectives represent the desired behaviors to be brought about in two training programs, one for agents and one for managers (see Fig. 14.23—abbreviated Performance Components).

Figure 14.23. Training Programs Evolving from the Core Objectives

Training Program for Agents

- Core Objective: Conduct a sales interview with a prospect.
- Module Objectives:
  A. Make appointments.
  B. Organize time and territory.
  C. Conduct the sales interview.
  D. Select product in relation to client need.
  E. Describe the features and benefits of the products.
  F. Forecast personal performance.

Training Program for Managers

- Core Objective: Conduct an employee performance interview.
- Module Objectives:
  A. Conduct a sales interview. (The agent training program becomes a module of the managers' training program.)
  B. Make a selection decision.
  C. Reinforce sales skills.
  D. Evaluate agent sales performance.
  E. Conduct one on one training.
  F. Conduct sales meetings.
  G. Forecast sales and manpower needs.
  H. Develop an action plan to achieve the forecast.
  I. Conduct an annual performance appraisal.

Structure of the Training Module

A Training Module consists of a Module Objective and one or more Unit Objective. Each Unit Objective represents one or more units of the knowledge and skills that is needed to perform the desired behavior contained within the Module Objective. Each unit of knowledge or skill, as we have seen, forms the basis for a Guide Panel. This is shown in Fig. 14.24.

Figure 14.24. Structure of an Instructor Guide in
Relation to Learning Objectives

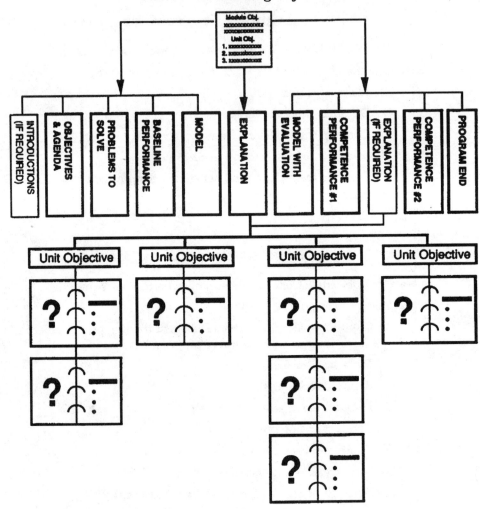

Structure of a Training Unit

Figure 14.25 shows the actual structure of a Training Unit. In this case, we see a
Unit Objective and <u>two Panels</u> (Structure of a Training Unit and Structure of a
Panel) that relate to the objective.

This Training Unit actually consists of several units of knowledge and skill. The
time allocation of 60 minutes (bracketed at the end of the Unit Objective) in relation to the 18 minutes allocated to the Panels indicates that there are more units
of knowledge that need to be reached in order to satisfy the Unit Objective.

Figure 14.25. Two Panels of a Training Unit

TECHNIQUE   RESULT

OBJECTIVE: Describe an Instructor Guide structure that produces discussions that reach agreement on predetermined Conclusions in relation to learning objectives. [60 minutes]

?ASK: What is the structure of a Training Unit?

STRUCTURE OF A TRAINING UNIT (3)

- Contains the **OBJECTIVE** for the unit.
- Contains one or more **units of knowledge** organized as Instrutor Guide Panels.
- States the time frame for each unit (after the objective).

?ASK: What is the structure of a Panel?

NOTE: Discuss. List on flip chart.

STRUCTURE OF A PANEL (15)

- Contains one **unit of knowledge or skill** organized as Conclusion.
- Contains at least one preplanned question (**?ASK**) for each Conclusion.
- States the time frame for each Panel (after the title of the Conclusion).
- Contains instructor **NOTE**s which list procedures and/or media.
- Is divided into **TECHNIQUE** and **RESULT.**

1/3/93   Module #   16

Training Process Objectives and the Training Design

The Training Design also represents a set of Training Process Objectives. Training Process Objectives (Chap. 7) essentially describe the behaviors the instructor will use to enable the learner to understand, accept and perform the desired behavior. Therefore, each of the components of the design represents a Training Process Objective.

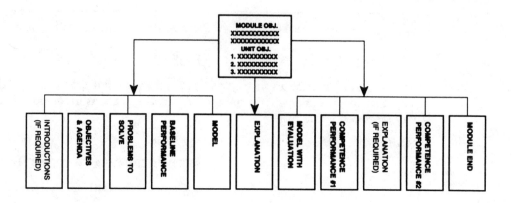

- **Introductions:** Make a personal introduction relevant to the module's learning objectives.

- **Objectives and Agenda:** Reach agreement upon the Module's learning objectives and agenda.

- **Problems to Solve:** Describe the problems experienced when _____
_____.

- **Baseline Performance:** Determine behavioral needs in relationship to the Module Objective.

- **Model (before explanation):** Given a model, describe the structure of the behavior in terms of criteria (as listed in the Performance Evaluation Form).

- **Explanation of the Knowledge and Skills:** Refer to the Unit Objectives.

- **Model with Performance Evaluation (after explanation):** Given a model, evaluate the behavior using the criteria, rating scale and scoring system listed in the PEF.

- **Competence Performance 1 and 2:** Perform and evaluate performance using the criteria, rating scale and scoring system listed in the Performance Evaluation Form.

- **Module End:** State the learning objectives achieved (or not) and value the program's success in meeting their identified needs.

Within the concept of the Hierarchical Structure, Training Process Objectives are treated as Unit Objectives. This concept was demonstrated on pages 99–100 of Part 1. If you refer to Fig. 7.4 you can view Part 1's learning objectives integrated with the Training Process Objectives I used to increase your ability to write useful learning objectives. The integration of Unit Objectives and Training Process Objectives into Training Units is also demonstrated in the model Instructor Guide in App. F (see pages 436–437).

Figure 14.26 (3 pages of a guide) shows a Training Unit for a Baseline Performance. Notice that the unit is based on a Training Process Objective. The Training Process Objective refers to the Module Objective listed below for a class on conducting interactive meetings (refer to pp. 167–169 for a detailed explanation of this program).

Interactive Installation Meetings

Given information about the dealership obtained from the sales interview and a group of 5 students acting as the management team, the consultant will be able to **conduct an interactive installation meeting** *that reaches agreement on the benefits and process of installing the Marcom Technologies System in relation to the goals and challenges facing the client's organization* within 90 minutes.

K. The Role of the Instructor Guide

The Instructor Guide plays an especially important role in the planning, conducting and modifying phases of the development process for a Program or Module that uses interactive inductive process to bring about group participation.

In the planning phase the guide allows the developer to preplan the questions and Conclusions that will bring about the discussion of each unit of knowledge or skill. The guide also permits the instructor to organize the sequence of the units of knowledge within each Training Unit and the order of the Training Units within the Module. Most important, the guide permits the developer to allocate time to the various components and, where necessary, secure additional time to ensure that program objectives are reached. Controlling time is discussed in detail in the next section.

During the conducting phase the guide helps keep the discussion focused toward the objective to be achieved. Essentially the guide answers four questions for the instructor:

A. **Where are we now?** What is the objective (target) to be achieved at this moment? How much time do I have?

B. **Where have we been?** What material has been covered? How much time has been used?

C. **Where are we going?** What material still needs to be be covered? How much time remains?

D. **How are we going to get there?** What activities will bring about the desired discussion or participation and the resultant learning?

The guide increases the instructor's ability to listen. Active listening requires concentrating on the student's responses. However, if the instructor is thinking about how he or she will respond to the student while the student is talking, listening

Figure 14.26. Training Unit for a Baseline Performance

TECHNIQUE

RESULT

OBJECTIVE: Baseline Performance: Determine behavioral needs in relationship to the Module Objective. [195 minutes]

TASK: Write down an outline of the meeting that you currently use. Then transfer your outline to a flip chart and hang it on the wall.

NOTE: Allow 15 minutes.

OUTLINE FOR TRADITIONAL MEETING (50) (Hypothesis)

- Introduce self and give history of Marcom.
- Explain the Marcom System and performance goals.
- List and discuss problems.
- Explain power of words and phrases.
- Show behavioral format.
- Show log sheet.
- Show month end report.
- Define roles (facilitator, tape changer).
- Explain training for managers and salespeople.

TELL: At this point we need to prepare for our exercise.

NOTE: Procedure for setting up the exercise (10 min.):

1. Select a volunteer to act as the Consultant.
2. Designate students to play the roles (General Manager, General Sales Manager, New Car Manager, Used Car Manager). Instructor plays the Dealer.
3. Instruct remaining students to act as observers.
4. Provide players with their roles.
5. Ask student acting as Consultant to leave the room.
6. Hand out and have players read their roles.
7. Allow 2 minutes. Then brief players and observers.

Figure 14.26. *(Continued)* Training Unit for a Baseline Performance

TECHNIQUE	RESULT

?ASK: How do you see your role in this exercise?

?ASK: What is the objective of the exercise?

> **MANAGEMENT TEAM'S ROLE (5)**
>
> - Play your role based on your experience.
> - Our objective is to set up a situation that is challenging while at the same time one that can reach a positive outcome provided that the Consultant:
>
>   —Handles the meeting effectively.
>
>   —Adequately explains Marcom.
>
>   —Addresses your concerns.
>
> - We want to observe performance in a realistic situation.

TELL: Hold your questions and objections until the end. We want to see the degree to which the Rep is able to bring about participation.

TASK: Make a list of problems or issues with the Consultant's handling of the meeting for later discussion. This applies to those playing the roles of the management team and those acting as observers. We will discuss the transaction itself after it is completed.

NOTE: Conduct Exercise. (80 minutes includes briefing)

1. Have Consultant brief dealer (instructor) outside of the room.

2. Dealer and Consultant return to room.

> **PERFORMANCE (80)**

Figure 14.26. *(Continued)* Training Unit for a Baseline Performance

TECHNIQUE   ## RESULT

?ASK: What problems did we observe and
discover during this exercise?

NOTE: List issues on flip chart.

—How would you rate your overall
performance? Why?

—How would you rate your participation?

—How close to your plan was your
actual conduct of the meeting?

—How realistic was the situation we
created?

PROBLEMS (hypothesis)   (40)

- Difficulty getting participation or participation for the sake of itself.

- Unable to access managers' attitudes or understanding of the program.

- Unable to determine if managers accepted the
  ideas.

- One way communication.

- No demonstrations of effective or ineffective
  telephone transactions.

- Limited use of visual aids.

- Problem not clearly established.

- Difficulty responding to objections.

- Lack of an agenda—managers did not know
  where you were going.

- Dealer introduction is too long. Steals thunder.

- Disorganized explanation of the Marcom
  Program.

- Meeting did not have a clear ending.

effectiveness is reduced. The problem is exacerbated when the instructor is thinking about future material and/or the techniques he or she might employ to bring about those discussions. Listening is difficult enough without adding the burden of trying to plan the lesson simultaneously. One consequence of the instructor's failure to listen is the reduction or elimination of the group's active involvement in discussions.

There are a number of other pitfalls that can impact listening. These include:

A. Distractions or irrelevancies. Focusing on the way a person is speaking rather than what they are saying.

B. Getting mentally sidetracked. A comment by the student causes you to think about something else.

C. Not listening when the student presents ideas or beliefs which are dissonant (out of harmony) with your own.

Once the training is completed, the instructor (developer) has the benefit of students' responses during the discussions and his or her evaluation of their performance. This data can be used to make needed modifications to the program. To accomplish this, the instructor (developer) can modify any questions or Conclusions deemed to be flawed, add units of knowledge and skill to fill chasms (gaps in the sequence of the lesson) and, if necessary, reorganize the sequence of the units of knowledge within each Training Unit and the order of the Training Units within the Module.

Other modifications might also need to be made to the Program's or Module's learning objectives, Performance Evaluation Forms, cases or problems.

L. Controlling Time

Time is the critical resource in the design and delivery of training. It, more than any other resource, determines whether or not the training is effective. For example. If time is not allocated for the evaluation of student performance, then training effectiveness is reduced by a factor of 25 percent (in relation to *Standards 1 through 4*). Inadequate time allocations affect whether objectives are achieved and, as a result, the student's acquisition of the desired behavior.

Control of time is especially critical when group participation methods are used. Failure to control time in the explanation phase can result in a program's failure even when the time allocation was adequate. The classic problem is running out of time for student performance due to the "additional time needed for discussion."

Effective time control is also critical when the training program is to be conducted by someone other than the developer. Certified Instructors must be able to conduct the training within the same time frame as the developer. If they are unable to replicate the program within the allotted time, then the resources invested in developing the program and certifying instructors are wasted to the degree that the instructors deviate from the prescribed program.

This section addresses the control of time in relation to the development process. These time management procedures will enable you to determine and obtain the time needed to conduct effective training.

Terms with Special Meanings

Four terms are particularly important. These are Estimated Time, Actual Time, Replicated Time and Representative Group.

- Estimated Time: An estimate of the time required to conduct any Module, Unit or Panel of a Training Program during the planning and writing phases.

- Actual Time: The time recorded by an instructor while conducting any Module, Unit or Panel of a Training Program with a representative group of students.

- Replicated Time: The Actual Time, plus or minus 15 percent, required to conduct the same Module, Unit or Panel of a training program (assuming no modifications) with two representative groups.

- Representative Group: A group of students whose previous training, experience and needs closely parallels the original assumptions made and whose number is within 10 percent of the projected average class size.

Estimated Time

The Terminal (Core or Module) Objectives and the Instructor Guide's structure are the keys to estimating training time during the development process. For our purposes, Estimated Time applies to the planning of the program and the writing of the Instructor Guide. Actual Time and Replicated Time apply to the conducting and modifying phases.

The Performance Time Component of the Terminal Objective provides the foundation for estimating time in the planning phase (Fig. 14.27). Performance Time enables the developer to accurately predict the time required for Baseline Performance, Models (with and without performance evaluation) and Competence Performance. The calculation formulas are listed in Fig. 14.28.

The Guide Panel provides the foundation for estimating time required for the Explanation Component of the training. These estimates are established in the process of writing the Instructor Guide. The Guide Panel is also used to estimate time for the Program Introduction and Conclusion Components as shown by the lighter shading in Fig. 14.29.

To estimate the time for any Panel, the developer must consider:

1. The number and complexity of each of the Ends in the Conclusion.

2. The technique to be used to bring about the desired Conclusion including any references (books, articles, videotapes, etc.), behavior models or visual aids to be used (flip chart, whiteboard, etc.) in the discussion.

Figure 14.27. Training Design Components Directly Affected by the Performance Time Component of the Learning Objective

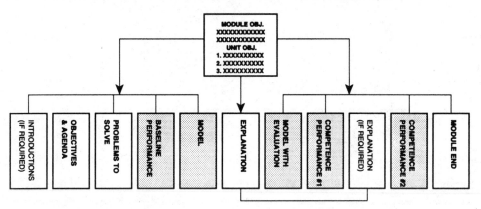

Figure 14.28. Time Allocation for Program Components Involving Performance

BASELINE and COMPETENCE PERFORMANCE

_____ Briefing and set-up before performance.

_____ Preparation: If not completed preclass or as homework.

_____ Taping of performance (if applicable).

_____ Performance or (replay): _____ minutes per student (×) _____ observed.

_____ Discussion/Evaluation: _____ minutes per student (×) _____ observed.

_____ **Total Time Required.**

MODEL and MODEL WITH PERFORMANCE EVALUATION

_____ Briefing and set-up before performance.

_____ Performance Time for the instructor's Model.

_____ Evaluation using the PEF or, if a Model without evaluation, discussion time.

_____ **Total Time Required.**

Figure 14.29. Time Estimates for Design Components that Rely on the Structure of the Instructor Guide Panel

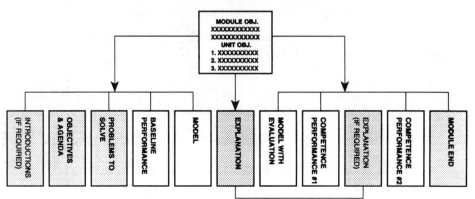

3. The importance of the Conclusion to the achievement of the Unit Objective.

4. The knowledge and experience that the group is likely to possess.

5. The overall time allocated to the training event.

6. The level of participation. The number of students who will participate in the discussion and the degree to which you desire them to discover the answer for themselves.

Time estimates for a Training Unit are determined by adding the estimates for each Panel. The estimated time for a Module is the sum of the estimated times for each Training Unit. A Training Program's estimated time is the sum of the time for the Modules. This principle is demonstrated in App. F. Refer to the section entitled "Training Method" on pages 436 and 437.

Let's consider estimated time for "Benefits of Questions"; a unit of knowledge organized as a Conclusion (Fig. 14.30). In planning this discussion the developer has listed seven ends. Each End also contains a brief justification. As a result, to reach each End, the student or students responding will have to elaborate on their answers. In addition the instructor will want to reinforce each answer by paraphrasing the student's response or by reading the End as written in the Guide. Given these parameters, an estimate of 14 minutes could be justified based on allocating 2 minutes for the discussion of each End.

Additional time must be added if the question is posed as a Task (Task Question). Assuming the instructor allocates 3 minutes for the students to write down their answers, the time estimate for this Panel would then be 17 minutes.

Figure 14.30. Estimating Time for a Panel

?ASK: What are the benefits of effective questions
in conducting training?

NOTE: Discuss. List on flip chart.

<u>BENEFITS OF QUESTIONS (14)</u>

- **Makes each student think.** *Each must consider their answer to the question.*

- **Creates learning motivation.** *This is particularly true when the question is asked before the answer is given. When questions are asked in this manner, the student is challenged to use his or her existing knowledge and problem solving skills. A sense of unease is created when the student perceives that his or her answer is incomplete. There is also a need by the student for reinforcement of his or her answer.*

- **Guides the discussion toward objectives.** *One or more unit of knowledge and skill may be required to achieve a Unit Objective. Hence the discussion of each unit leads to the achievement of the objectives.*

- **Gathers information.** *This enables the instructor to gauge the amount of information (knowledge) that the students possess and their viewpoint.*

- **Tests effectiveness of communication.** *Feedback from students indicate the degree to which they understand and accept the ideas under discussion.*

- **Measures learning.** *Students' responses indicate the degree to which they can use the knowledge and skills under discussion. Questions on a test or the task to be performed in a Competence Performance cause the student to exhibit the desired behavior which enables the instructor to observe and measure the degree of competence.*

- **Involves the group.** *Questions stimulate the discussion. They provide the license and structure for the student's response.*

Actual Time

Actual Time is the time recorded by an instructor while conducting any Module, Unit or Panel of a Training Program with a representative group of students. This is accomplished by keeping a Time Sheet (Fig. 14.31). Recording Actual Time enables you to:

1. Validate your original time estimates and, after two or more programs, establish Replicated Time.

2. Identify Panels that exceeded your time estimates. This could reveal flaws in the question, Conclusion or the Conclusion's sequence within the Training Unit.

Figure 14.31. Time Sheet

Program:				Trainer:		Day #:		Date:
Module		Recorded Time		Actual Time		Planned Time		+/−
#	Page	Begin	End	Min	Cum.	Min	Cum.		Comments

3. Determine progress in relationship to the total time allocation for the module during training. This enables you to make adjustments and, as a consequence, increases the likelihood that you will achieve all of your objectives.

4. Negotiate program changes with management that increase or maintain program effectiveness. Program length, group size, program content or the methodology employed may need adjustment.

5. Bring about and measure the desired behavior specified in the learning objectives.

The last point is particularly critical. As stated repeatedly throughout this book, the only way you can determine the effectiveness of training is to observe and measure the desired behavior contained within the Terminal Learning Objective. When time estimates are significantly flawed, the instructor has to make adjustments to the program. These could include changing methodology or cutting out certain units of knowledge.

One of the benefits of the Instructor Guide's Panel format is that it can be easily changed to a lecture. This is accomplished by making the question rhetorical. The instructor states the question and then proceeds to lecture through the unit of knowledge or skill.

Obviously, the one adjustment that should not be made is to sacrifice Competence Performance. By retaining the Competence Performances, you gain the ability to determine the effect of the adjustment made during the program on student learning. This is analogous to a basketball player who changes his shooting style during the game. The only way he knows if he is successful is by measuring the number of times the basketball goes in the hoop. Making adjustments to a training program in progress and not measuring performance is like shooting baskets without a hoop.

Time Management

In order to conduct the discussion of the units of knowledge and skill and measure student performance within the allocated time, the instructor must be able to determine the group's progress in relation to time. If the group is progressing well, few adjustments will be needed. On the other hand, if discussions are allowed to stretch beyond planned time frames, the instructor must take action. The Time Sheet (Fig. 14.31) provides the vehicle to manage time. It enables the instructor to:

■ Record the beginning and ending times for each page of the guide.

■ Calculate the cumulative Actual Time for each Training Unit or Module.

■ Compare the cumulative Actual Time to the Planned Time allocation for any page of the guide or Training Unit.

The guides in Apps. E and F and Chap. 15 were written on a computer. This allows multiple Panels on each page. When Actual Time is desired for each Panel, the instructor records the Beginning Time next to each question and the Ending Time below the Conclusion.

Keeping track of time while conducting a program requires a considerable amount of discipline. One has to remember to record beginning and ending times each time a page is turned. A digital watch helps increase the accuracy of the times recorded.

Optimizing Classroom Time

When tasks are complex, such as writing a series of questions for a sales interview, writing a proposal to a client or researching the answers to problems using references, the task can be assigned as homework with discussion occurring on the following day (next session). In this way, class time for discussion is maximized.

Another example is practicing for a videotaped sales, management or customer relations type interview. By assigning this as homework, the student can practice until she feels competent. This may involve several attempts.

A third example demonstrates that a combination of in-class and homework preparation is desirable. In a life insurance sales training program an objective required the agent to: "<u>select product and coverage</u> in relationship to the prospect's pre-agreed upon needs and financial capacity to pay premiums <u>and</u> complete a proposal form</u> within a 30-minute time frame."

This objective requires a combination of time, judgment and accuracy of calculation. To accomplish it, students were assigned selection problems as homework. In theory, they could have completed these in 20 minutes. However, in the development of the desired behavior, judgment of product suitability in relationship to the prospect's "situation" was more important than time. The student could spend whatever amount of time they required on the homework problems. These were discussed in class the next day.

The problems given during the class concentrated on reaching the time goal for both the <u>product selection</u> and <u>proposal form completion</u>. Hence, 20 minutes were allowed for selection in class. The student's decisions on product and coverage were discussed and a "best" solution was agreed upon. Then, the student was given the school solution and 10 minutes to complete a proposal form. In this way, selection process and proposal completion could be simulated and measured for speed, judgment and accuracy. The complete performance (product selection and completion of a proposal form) was also later evaluated in videotaped role play exercises.

Why Validate Time Assumptions?

The ability to accurately predict time increases the precision of your planning and the likelihood that the program will bring about the desired behavior in the student. Large time errors can result in your being unable to complete a program within the time negotiated. As a result, students leave without the requisite knowledge or skills.

Replicated Time

Replicated Time is the Actual Time, plus or minus 15 percent, required to conduct the same Module, Unit or Panel of a training program (assuming no modifications) with two representative groups. Once established, Replicated Time is substituted for the time listed in the Instructor Guide.

Certification of instructors is dependent on accurate time estimates. Therefore, certification should not commence until the developer has established Replicated Time for most (80 percent) of the Panels. This effectively requires the developer to test the program with at least two representative groups. In the process accurate time frames are established along with program effectiveness.

Without accurate time allocations you cannot determine if the Instructor Trainee is conducting the program effectively. For example, the Instructor Trainee spends 25 minutes on a Conclusion that has a time allocation of 15 minutes. The program has been tested only one time. Is the amount of time on this particular Conclusion adequate? Is the 10 minute overage a result of the instructor's incompetent leadership of the discussion or is there a flaw in the Conclusion or its sequence within the program? Without adequate testing and the establishment of Replicated Time, the developer may have difficulty determining the cause of the problem.

M. Inductive Process: In Cases Where the Student Has Limited Knowledge

Up to this point we have examined the discussion of subject matter where the instructor can reasonably assume that the students have sufficient knowledge to reason their way to a Conclusion. In this section we will look at situations where the student's knowledge is limited.

An example. Consider the unit of knowledge, "Types of Sentences," (Fig. 14.5). If a person has learned the names of the four types of sentences they can answer the question: <u>What are the four types of sentences?</u> But, what if they have never heard those terms before? Is it possible to teach this subject using inductive process (the question is asked before the answer is given)?

Preplanning involves the answer to two key questions.

1. What relevant knowledge or experience does the student already have the ability to demonstrate?

2. What foundation, if any, has to be laid to enable the student to respond to the question and reach the desired Conclusion?

Let's assume that we are going to teach the concept "Types of Sentences" to a group of 4th graders. We can reasonably assume that they will not know the names of the types of sentences. We can also assume, however, that they have experienced each type of sentence in conversations they have had and in books that they have read. In many ways, we have the situation referred to by

---

Figure 14.5. Units of Knowledge

Types of Sentences

- Declarative
- Interrogative
- Exclamatory
- Imperative

Declarative Sentence

- Makes a statement
- Punctuated with a period
- Example: This is a cat.

Hayakawa: "the fact that a golfer, for example, cannot define golfing terms is no indication that he cannot understand them and use them."

Based on these assumptions, we can structure an inductive discussion of the types of sentences. To accomplish this, we must create a situation that enables the student to figure out the answer (Types of Sentences) for themselves. This creates the foundation that enables the student to reach the desired Conclusion and is demonstrated by Fig. 14.32.

Figures 14.32 and 14.5 demonstrate the subtle difference between inductive and deductive process. Inductive moves from the concrete (the example) to the abstract (the technical name) where deductive moves from the abstract to the concrete.

Prediscussion Assignments

Another technique that can be used to bring about active participation in discussions where the student has limited knowledge is through the use of a prediscussion assignment (i.e., reading a book, an article or completing an exercise). To use this technique effectively the developer must structure the exercise so that the student can learn the material on his or her own.

The following demonstrates how a prediscussion exercise can be used to create discussion on a subject where the student has no prior knowledge. In this instance the students were new agents learning to sell an accident insurance policy. An important aspect of the training involved product knowledge. In order to sell effectively, agents had to understand the policy. This would enable them to better explain the coverage to prospective insureds and to do so without any misrepresentations.

Figure 14.32. A Guide Unit for an Inductive Discussion

TECHNIQUE	**RESULT**

OBJECTIVE: Differentiate four types of sentences. [20 minutes]

TELL: Today we will examine four different types of sentences.

NOTE: Reveal preframed flip chart containing the statements below:

    1. This is a cat.

    2. What is a cat?

    3. Feed the cat.

    4. Look out for the cat!

?ASK: What is different about these four sentence?

NOTE: Label each type of sentence once the group establishes the intent and punctuation differences.

                TYPES OF SENTENCES (20)

                1. <u>This is a cat</u>.

                    —Punctuation: Period.

                    —Intent: Makes a statement.

                    —Technical Name: Declarative.

                2. <u>What is a cat</u>?

                    —Punctuation: Question mark.

                    —Intent: Asks a question.

                    —Technical Name: Interrogative.

                3. <u>Feed the cat</u>.

                    —Punctuation: Period.

                    —Intent: States a task to be performed. A command given.

                    —Technical Name: Imperative.

                4. <u>Look out for the cat</u>!

                    —Punctuation: Exclamation point.

                    —Intent: Contains a warning or sudden emotion (That hurts!)

                    —Technical Name: Exclamatory

In structuring this unit we had to assume that the agents had no understanding of the policy. The key to the training design is the learning objective in Fig. 14.33 and the assumptions made with regard to the students' problem-solving skills.

Our key assumption involved problem-solving skills. We reasoned that any customer who bought one of these policies could, if they had an accident, read the policy and determine if the policy would pay them benefits. Based on this assumption, we created a number of hypothetical claim situations. The student was given these situations (the prediscussion assignment) along with a specimen insurance policy.

The task was to determine if a benefit was payable and if it was, to calculate the amount of the benefit. To accomplish this task the student had to read the policy and decide how it would respond to each situation. The accuracy of the claim decision reflected his or her understanding of the policy. The following lists the training design for this particular Training Unit.

1. Give students a policy and a preclass assignment containing claim examples.

2. Require the students to answer each question by referencing the policy language that supports their answer.

3. Provide an answer sheet that will be turned in prior to the discussion for accountability.

4. Collect the answer sheets prior to discussion to establish accountability and baseline knowledge.

5. Conduct a discussion of the preclass assignment where students describe their rationale for their answers by citing policy provisions.

6. Allow students to correct their answers during the discussion.

7. Administer a short (10 question, 10 minute) post-test (in class), to measure learning.

Figure 14.33. Unit Objective for Product Knowledge

Conditions:	<u>Given an accident policy and a series of hypothetical claim situations,</u>
Performer:	the agent will be able to
Performance:	**verbally explain the coverage, conditions and exclusions**
Criteria:	*by citing the appropriate contract provision, without misrepresentation,*
Performance Time:	within 2 minutes
Performance Std.:	and obtain a score of 90 percent correct responses on a test.

When the students came to class we collected their answer sheets. This allowed us to measure the amount of (baseline) knowledge they had acquired prior to the discussion. Students averaged 65 percent correct responses prior to the discussion.

We then conducted the discussion. Each student, in turn, was given an opportunity to participate. They were instructed to read a problem, state whether the claim was payable and, if payable, the amount of the benefit. They also had to justify their action by citing the policy provisions.

The group was given the task of determining if the student's answer was correct. If incorrect, they had the opportunity to explain why the respondent's answer was incorrect and to offer their solution. The key role for the instructor was to keep a "poker face" even if a student's answer was correct. This prompted students with incorrect answers to challenge the correct answer. As a result, the student or students who defended their correct answer experienced additional reinforcement.

Following the class discussion, we administered the 10-question quiz. The scores obtained validated the effectiveness of the training design. Students scored 95 percent correct after the discussion.

This exercise proved to be extremely effective. Students enjoyed getting the answers correct since the questions were challenging. In addition they had fun during the discussion as they competed with each other to demonstrate their knowledge and ability to explain the contract. In effect, they did 70 percent of the talking.

Prior to the program development effort, the instructor would read the policy to the group, clause by clause. Then he or she would explain each clause in his or her own words. The instructor would also cite examples of claim situations to clarify points when someone raised a question. As a result, the instructor did 70 percent of the talking. He concluded the session by asking if there were any questions.

Incidentally, the "learning objective" for the session read "the student will understand the policy." As we now know, that objective is somewhat flawed. It receives an Effectiveness Rating of zero as it exhibits none of the components found in a useful learning objective.

N. The Module Planner

The ability to conduct training that uses the interactive inductive (*Guided Discovery*) training style to bring about and measure a desired behavior as described in a learning objective is directly related to the developer's ability to effectively plan and organize the Module.

The Module Planner is a job aid designed for this purpose. (See App. H.) It consists of six major sections: **Desired Performance, Training Design, Performance Time Requirements, Resources Required, Notes and The Format for the Instructor Guide.** It should be set up as a template on a word processor and duplicated each time a new module is created.

The first page (Fig. 14.34) contains information about the module and documents the **Desired Performance** (behavior).

Figure 14.34. Module Title and Desired Performance

Module Title

PROGRAM: List program name when the Module is part of a Training Program

PROGRAM DEVELOPER: (Name)

SUBJECT EXPERT(S): (Names)

SCHEDULE: ___ Days from 9:00 a.m. to 5:00 p.m.

NET TEACHING TIME

Gross time per day	480 minutes
Lunch	−60
Breaks (2 × 15)	−30
Available each day	390
Available During the Module	

Desired Performance

STUDENT JOB TITLE:

OBSERVED OR ASSUMED PERFORMANCE DISCREPANCIES:

■

■

ASSUMPTIONS OR DATA RELATED TO PREVIOUS TRAINING OR EXPERIENCE:

■

■

MODULE OBJECTIVE: Insert Core or Module Objective.

■

■

UNIT OBJECTIVES: To accomplish the Module Objective the (job title of the performer) will be able to:

■

■

Expert Criteria TO MEASURE THE PERFORMANCE AS DESCRIBED IN THE MODULE OBJECTIVE(S):

■

■

Listed below the words Module Title are a series of prompts that deal with the Module's origin and time allocation. Since time impacts virtually every decision in the development process it is calculated as the first step. The illustration shows 390 minutes of Net Teaching Time for a day that begins at 9:00 a.m. and ends at 5:00 p.m.

The section entitled **Desired Performance** effectively takes the developer through the first three steps of Program Development Process. The developer lists the:

1. Observed or assumed performance discrepancies

2. Assumptions about the students' previous training or experience

3. Module and Unit Objectives and

4. *Expert Criteria* to measure the performance as described in the Module Objective.

With the *Expert Criteria* identified, the developer has 90 percent of the Performance Evaluation Form completed. All that is left are decisions on the Scoring System, Rating Scale and formula for calculating the rating. The decision to use the 0-4 or 10-5-0 (Criterion Scoring) systems will be dictated by the type of behavior and the precision of the criteria.

Page 2 is entitled **Training Design** and is shown in Fig. 14.35. This provides the developer with a format which integrates the learning objectives and Training Process Objectives into a Training Design that meets the *Total Quality Training Standards.*

The model Training Design contains a subset of Training Process Objectives which are related to the Module Introduction and Conclusion. These are identified by the (>) karat symbol and are deleted when the Module is part of a Training Program.

The parentheses preceding each unit of the design represent each Unit's allocated time. These are totaled at the end of the page and identified as Estimated, Actual or Replicated Total Time.

When the module is in the planning stage, the time estimates for the Explanation Component are "educated guesses." Once the Guide Panels are written, the time allocation can be more accurately established for each Training Unit. As the development process moves from planning to writing and then to the conducting stages, the times shown increase in accuracy. The time estimates for the performance components (Baseline, Model and Competence) can be accurately estimated on the page entitled **Performance Time Requirements** (Fig. 14.36).

Page 3 contains space to identify key issues that are directly related to the Training Design. These include: **Prerequisite Module(s), Preclass Assignment, Homework Assignment and Review and Reinforcement.** Each of these issues should be addressed in the planning stages and are subject to change as the development process continues. (See Fig. 14.37.)

While the first three items are self explanatory, the fourth, **Review and Reinforcement,** enables the developer to identify other Modules of the Training

Figure 14.35. The Model Training Design

Training Design

Delete [>] when the module is part of a training program.

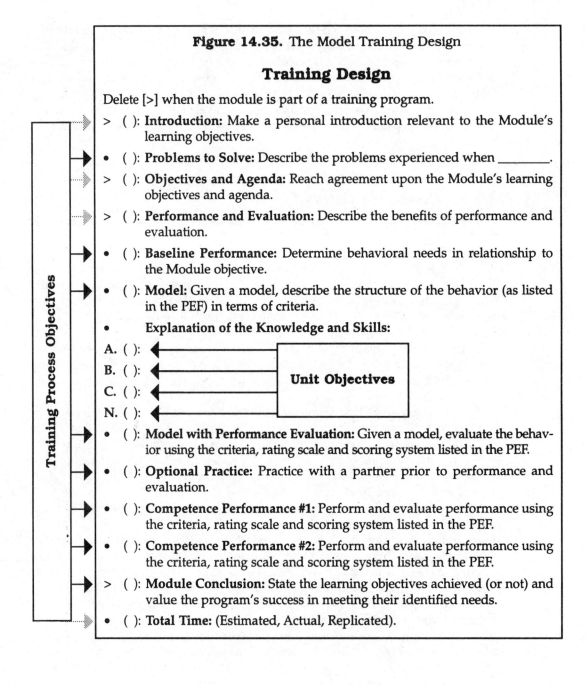

> ( ): **Introduction:** Make a personal introduction relevant to the Module's learning objectives.

• ( ): **Problems to Solve:** Describe the problems experienced when _____.

> ( ): **Objectives and Agenda:** Reach agreement upon the Module's learning objectives and agenda.

> ( ): **Performance and Evaluation:** Describe the benefits of performance and evaluation.

• ( ): **Baseline Performance:** Determine behavioral needs in relationship to the Module objective.

• ( ): **Model:** Given a model, describe the structure of the behavior (as listed in the PEF) in terms of criteria.

• **Explanation of the Knowledge and Skills:**

A. ( ):
B. ( ):   **Unit Objectives**
C. ( ):
N. ( ):

• ( ): **Model with Performance Evaluation:** Given a model, evaluate the behavior using the criteria, rating scale and scoring system listed in the PEF.

• ( ): **Optional Practice:** Practice with a partner prior to performance and evaluation.

• ( ): **Competence Performance #1:** Perform and evaluate performance using the criteria, rating scale and scoring system listed in the PEF.

• ( ): **Competence Performance #2:** Perform and evaluate performance using the criteria, rating scale and scoring system listed in the PEF.

> ( ): **Module Conclusion:** State the learning objectives achieved (or not) and value the program's success in meeting their identified needs.

• ( ): **Total Time:** (Estimated, Actual, Replicated).

Training Process Objectives

Figure 14.36. Performance Time Planning Aid (Page 4)

Performance Time Requirements

AVERAGE GROUP SIZE: ___ Students.

BASELINE PERFORMANCE—TIME REQUIRED: ___ minutes.

A. (__): Briefing and set-up before performance.

B. (__): Preparation: If not completed preclass or as homework.

C. (__): Taping of performance (if applicable).

D. (__): Performance or (replay): ___ minutes per student (×) # ___ observed.

E. (__): Evaluation: ___ minutes per student (×) # ___ observed.

MODEL—TIME REQUIRED: ___ minutes.

A. (__): Briefing and set-up before performance.

B. (__): Performance time for the instructor's model.

C. (__): Discussion time.

MODEL WITH PERFORMANCE EVALUATION—TIME REQUIRED: ___ minutes.

A. (__): Briefing and set-up before performance.

B. (__): Performance time for the instructor's model.

C. (__): Evaluation using the *Expert Criteria* in the PEF.

COMPETENCE PERFORMANCE #1—TIME REQUIRED: ___ minutes.

A. (__): Briefing before performance. (Include any time required for preparation.)

B. (__): Taping of performance (if applicable).

C. (__): Performance or (replay): ___ minutes per student (×) # ___ observed.

D. (__): Evaluation: ___ minutes per student (×) # ___ observed.

COMPETENCE PERFORMANCE #2—TIME REQUIRED: ___ minutes.

A. (__): Briefing before performance. (Include any time required for preparation.)

B. (__): Taping of performance (if applicable).

C. (__): Performance or (replay): ___ minutes per student (×) # ___ observed.

D. (__): Evaluation: ___ minutes per student (×) # ___ observed.

Figure 14.37. Additional Training Design Issues (Page 3)

PREREQUISITE MODULE(S):

■

PRECLASS ASSIGNMENT:

■

HOMEWORK ASSIGNMENT:

■

REVIEW AND REINFORCEMENT:

■

Program which continue the learning process on the subject. This permits Certified Instructors or the manager in charge of the training to quickly ascertain the Module's relationship to the overall Training Design. This section can also detail how the training is to be followed up on the job.

Page 5 provides the developer with a place to list **Resources Required. These include: Equipment, Cases, Materials** (such as handouts or instructor references), **Preframes** (any information that must be written on a flip chart prior to the discussion) and a place for **Notes.** (See Fig. 14.38.)

Figure 14-38. Resources and Notes (Page 5)

Resources Required

EQUIPMENT REQUIRED:

■

CASES REQUIRED:

■

MATERIALS REQUIRED:

■

ACETATES:

■

PREFRAMES:

■

Notes

■

■

The **Notes** section allows the developer to document any issue which is not covered by one of the prompts in the Module Planner. For example, consider the Notes from the model guide <u>Interaction by Design</u> (App. 5). In Fig. 14.39, Notes 1 and 2 are generic instructions that are relevant to Conclusions which will be listed on a flip chart. This saves the developer from repeating these instructions in each note within the Instructor Guide. Notes 3 and 4 deal with the handout and the timing of its use. In this instance the information is related to the Training Design.

Figure 14.39. A Note Found in a Module Planner

Notes

1. Only relevant student answers are recorded on the flip chart.
2. All flip charts will be taped to the wall.
3. The session handout is a modified version of the Instructor Guide. It duplicates the actual guide used by the instructor except for page 428 which represents the discussion of guide structure. This page contains space for students to record their answers. The handout provides the student with a permanent reference.
4. The handout will be given to the group toward the end of the session.

Figure 14.40 provides the structural format for the Instructor Guide Units. Detailed rules for the construction of the Guide Unit follow.

Figure 14.40. The Format for the Instructor Guide

Technique   Result

OBJECTIVE: Title: Performance and, if applicable, Conditions, Criteria and Performance Time [xx minutes]

XXXX: (Replace XXXX with ?ASK,
TASK, TELL or NOTE and
insert the actual question,
task, statement or note.)

CONCLUSION TITLE (__) time
■ (Insert a relevant End)

Rules for Construction of the
Instructor Guide Unit

The following rules will assist you in constructing a guide that helps you facilitate the active participation that you desire:

1. All questions must have a Conclusion. Two exceptions:
   - A Core Question may be followed by one Secondary Question.
   - Questions may appear in a NOTE when the purpose for the questions is to prompt discussions about a student's performance. For example:
     —How would you rate your performance?
     —What would you do differently if you had it to do over again?
     —How closely did the simulation come to the situations you face on the job?

2. All Conclusions must have a title and at least one related End at the next lower level of abstraction.

3. All TASKs <u>must</u> have a NOTE. (Refer to page 284.)

4. A question or statement <u>may</u> have a NOTE, e.g., the developer desires the instructor to use a flip chart.

5. A Panel should contain <u>one</u> RESULT (a Conclusion or the words PERFOR-MANCE or MODEL) and the TECHNIQUE (Questions, Tasks, Statements and Notes) to bring about that RESULT.

6 A Training Unit should contain one Unit Objective and <u>one or more</u> related units of knowledge and skill that enable the student to perform the Unit Objective.

7. The time for any Panel should be listed in parentheses in the title of the Conclusion or immediately after the words Performance or Model.

8. The time for any Training Unit should be listed in brackets immediately following the Unit Objective.

9. Handwritten Guides: The Panel is written on two 8½ by 11 sheets of paper and inserted into a 3 ring binder. One page for RESULT, one page for TECH-NIQUE. Nothing is written on the back of either page.

10. Computer-written Guides: TECHNIQUE and RESULT are written on one page. One or more Panels can appear on a page. Avoid having a Panel start on one page and end on the next.

11. The word "Hypothesis" is added to the title of a Panel to indicate that all of the Ends in the Conclusion do not have to be reached during the discussion. This allows the developer to list the range of problems that the group may be experiencing and is frequently used in Panels which refer to perceived or observed performance problems (i.e., following a Baseline Performance).

Only those performance problems which are relevant are discussed with the group. See examples in Fig. 14.26.

O. Practice Exercise

Here is an opportunity for you to practice writing a Training Unit and apply the Rules for the Construction of the Guide. In this case you will be asked to write a unit on the benefits of interactive communication during a sales meeting.

You may assume that your group consists of 12 sales managers that work for an automobile dealership. These managers hold frequent sales meetings to inform, motivate, problem solve and train. Your client (the dealer) observes that they are not effective in conducting meetings to solve problems or to improve the skills of their salespeople. Specifically, they have difficulty getting people involved in meaningful discussions. They would rather talk than listen.

You have written the following Unit Objective and have allocated 20 minutes for its discussion.

Unit Objective

Describe the advantages of an interactive sales meeting and contrast the interactive style with the conventional presentation (lecture or limited participation).

Your task is to structure the Training Unit for the preceding objective. To accomplish this you will need to:

1. Identify the units of knowledge that will enable you to reach each component of the objective.
2. Structure each as Conclusions and create the Guide Panel or Panels that will bring about the discussion.

You can then compare your Instructor Guide to my answer that follows.

Solution to the Practice Exercise

OBJECTIVE: Describe the advantages of an interactive sales meeting and contrast the interactive style with the conventional presentation (lecture or limited participation). [20 minutes]

?ASK: What are the <u>benefits</u> of an interactive sales meeting?

NOTE: List on flip chart. Hang on wall.

> BENEFITS OF INTERACTIVE (8)
>
> - Tends to be more interesting.
> - Concerns are more likely to be expressed. (Assuming a non-threatening environment.)
> - Feedback through participation indicates understanding and acceptance.
> - Ability to evaluate meeting effectiveness (during the meeting) through reaching agreement on the resolution of the issue.
> - Builds relationship with dealership personnel, especially sales people, by giving them credit for bringing "something to the table."
> - People have to pay attention.
> - Feeling of working together to reach agreements.

?ASK: What are the <u>disadvantages</u> of an interactive sales meeting?

?ASK: Why are people reluctant to use interactive process?

NOTE: List on flip chart. Hang on wall.

> DISADVANTAGES OF INTERACTIVE (4)
> - Takes longer.
> - Potential for losing control.
> - Easier said than done.

?ASK: What are the benefits of lecture or limited participation?

NOTE: List on flip chart. Hang on wall.

> ONE WAY COMMUNICATION
> BENEFIT (3)
> - Faster.
> - Total control.
> - Does not invite objections.
> - Message and delivery can be very professional.

?ASK: What are the disadvantages of lecture or limited participation?

NOTE: List on flip chart. Hang on wall.

> DISADVANTAGE: ONE WAY
> COMMUNICATION (4)
> - Difficult to measure understanding or acceptance until after the meeting (which may be too late).
> - Not as interesting.
> - Needs or concerns or resistance may not be discovered.
> - One way communication does not build relationships.
> - More of the same from the salesperson's viewpoint. Dealer and sales manager are more likely to talk <u>at them</u> or (down) <u>to them</u> rather than with them.

?ASK: What do you learn from this discussion of the advantages and disadvantages of one and two way communication?

> COMMUNICATION LESSON (1)
>
> The advantages of one are the disadvantages of the other.

P. The Optional Sixth Standard

Instructor Guides structured to produce discussions that reach predetermined Conclusions in relation to learning objectives.

This standard can be met as follows:

1. Before Training:
   a. Determine the units of skill or knowledge required to reach each Unit Objective.
   b. Structure each unit of skill or knowledge as a Conclusion:
      (1) Give each unit a title. The title represents the idea under discussion.
      (2) List one or more relevant Ends: Ends are points that directly relate to and support the idea under discussion.
   c. Pre-plan at least one question or construct a task that is likely to bring about a discussion of the Conclusion.
   d. (If applicable) Describe any illustrations, examples, analogies or, where applicable, behavioral models that will graphically or dramatically illustrate the idea under discussion. (Refer to Fig. 15.2 for an example that relates directly to the *Optional Sixth Standard.*)
   e. Structure the Instructor Guide so that each unit of skill or knowledge is a unit unto itself. (Refer to Fig. 14.14, A Panel of the Guide.)
2. During Training: The instructor can (refer to Fig. 15.2):
   a. Ask the preplanned question or give the group the task to perform.
   b. Listen to one or more student responses.
   c. Determine the degree to which the response is correct and complete in relation to the preplanned Conclusion and discuss the response using:
      (1) Paraphrasing to support the answer or demonstrate active listening.
      (2) Probing to cause students to expand their explanation or determine the rationale behind their response.
   d. List relevant responses on a flip chart (if applicable).
   e. Explain and illustrate the Conclusion (as required).

Rationale: Understanding, acceptance and competence increase when people have the opportunity to use their existing knowledge and skills to think through the problem under discussion.

The following lists the *Total Quality Training Standards* including the *Optional Sixth Standard.*

Total Quality Training Standards

To achieve training effectiveness, the initiative should contain:

1. Learning objectives which describe the **desired behavior(s)** to be exhibited during the training program. (Learning Objectives)

2. Evidence of a performance discrepancy in relation to the **desired behavior** resulting from a lack of skill or knowledge. (Needs Analysis)

3. Examples or models of the **desired behavior** during the training program. (Modeling)

4. Evaluation of student performance of the **desired behavior** to determine competence during training. (Performance Evaluation)

5. Evidence that the **desired behavior** has persisted after training and is linked to results. (Post Training Evaluation).

6. Instructor Guides structured to produce discussions that reach predetermined Conclusions in relation to learning objectives. (Optional)

These standards apply to any event which is designed to improve organizational results through the enhancement of knowledge or skills.

An organization that adopts the *Optional Sixth Standard* has made a cultural statement with regard to the communication style that they desire their instructors to use. As a by-product, they have empowered developers, instructors and the employees being trained to examine and challenge the knowledge and skills being taught.

They have also made a statement with regard to program continuity and the development of people. As stated in Chap. 13, an effective Instructor Guide enables the program to survive the promotion, transfer or termination of the employee who created the program or a subsequent instructor who conducts the program. Hence, organizational resources can be committed to the solution of new problems rather than the constant reinvention of the training.

15
Guiding a Discussion to a Conclusion

The process of using preplanned questions to guide a group to a preplanned Conclusion can be broken down into three distinct segments. These involve the techniques for posing the question, the nature of the student's response and the techniques the instructor employs to guide the discussion to the preplanned Conclusion. The process is depicted in Fig. 15.2.

In this final chapter, I have chosen to use the Instructor Guide structure itself to present the ideas. This will enable you to better appreciate and understand the logic of preparing training using the *Guided Discovery* format.

Participating Using the Instructor Guide Format

To interact with me, merely cover the RESULT (found on the right hand side of each page) and answer the questions or complete the task required under the TECHNIQUE (found on the left hand side of the page).

For example, cover the Conclusion "COST FACTORS" and "OTHER COST CONSIDERATIONS" on the right-hand side of the following page and begin reading under the TECHNIQUE section. Then reveal the Conclusion, "COST FACTORS," to compare your answer to mine. You may have identified more or less factors. In any case, the answer provided represents my point of view and the knowledge I had available when I wrote this book.

Remember, the Guide format only contains four words under TECHNIQUE. When you see the word "TELL" I am making a statement. The word "TASK" contains an exercise I would like you to complete. A "NOTE" contains instructions for completing the exercise. In the example, you are asked to: "list your responses on paper. Then compare your answers to those shown." And finally, "?ASK," is the symbol for a question that I would like you to answer.

Technique   ## Result

OBJECTIVE: Describe direct and indirect expense factors that should be considered in determining the cost of a training program.

TELL: Whether effective or ineffective, training represents a considerable expense to an organization.

TASK: Write down the direct and indirect expense factors that should be considered in determining the cost of a training program.

NOTE: List your responses on paper. Then compare your answers to those shown.

COST FACTORS

- Wages paid to employees attending.
- Travel and expenses.
- Fees paid to vendors for materials and/or use of their programs.
- Wages paid to trainers and supervisory personnel.
- Cost of facilities, materials, audio visual support, postage, copies, etc.

?ASK: While not direct expenses, what other tangible and intangible costs occur when the training is ineffective?

OTHER COST CONSIDERATIONS

- Lost opportunity.
- Lost productivity.
- Lowered morale.
- Lowered expectations regarding future training.
- Lost profits or efficiencies which could have been gained from the training if it were effective.

Training Module

TITLE: *Guiding a Discussion to a Conclusion*

PROGRAM: Program Development under the principles of *Guided Discovery.*

PROGRAM DEVELOPER/SUBJECT EXPERT: Les Shapiro

TIME ALLOTTED: 190 minutes

MODULE OBJECTIVE:

Given an Instructor Guide Panel, the Instructor Trainee will be able to conduct a discussion using the prescribed technique in the Instructor Guide and guide the group to the prescribed Conclusion within 15 percent (plus or minus) of the planned time.

UNIT OBJECTIVES: The student will be able to:

A. (18): **Types of Questions:** Differentiate a "Task Question" from a "Voluntary, Directed and Involuntary Question."

B. (13): **Asking Questions:** Describe a 5-step procedure for asking a "Task or Voluntary Question" and seven instructor options for responding and guiding the discussion to a Conclusion.

C. (12): **Types of Responses:** List the possible student responses that can occur from asking a question to a group.

D. (17): **Dealing with Correct and Complete Responses:** Describe the procedure and options available for responding to a student's correct and complete response.

E. (20): **Paraphrase:** Describe the purpose, structure and value of paraphrasing student responses.

F. (5): **Dealing with No Response:** Describe the procedure for bringing about a discussion when there is no response to the question posed by the instructor.

G. (20): **Incorrect or Incomplete Responses:** Describe the procedure and options available for responding to partially correct, incomplete or incorrect answer.

H. (40): **Using Spontaneous Secondary Questions:** Given an Instructor Guide Panel, be able to formulate Spontaneous Secondary Questions and conduct a 1-minute discussion to reach a designated End.

I. (15): **Guide Usage Problems:** Describe instructor practices while using an Instructor Guide that inhibit participation.

J. (30): **Dealing with a Flawed Conclusion:** Describe the process of interacting with the group to correct a flawed Conclusion.

NOTE:

1. The techniques in this module are depicted in Fig. 15.2, Guiding a Discussion to a Conclusion.

2. The objectives within this module are reached through discussion which is based on the students' observation of the instructor's use of the *Guided Discovery* style throughout the training program. Essentially, the students use the instructor's behavior in previous discussions to identify the techniques for conducting a discussion to a Conclusion.

Technique	**Result**

OBJECTIVE: **A. Types of Questions:** Differentiate a "Task Question" from a "Voluntary, Directed and Involuntary Question." [18 minutes]

TELL: Let's explore the process of interacting with a group toward a prescribed Conclusion. We will begin with the process of asking questions and then look at the options the instructor has for responding to student answers.

?ASK: What are the four techniques that we previously identified for asking questions?

NOTE: List on flip chart. Refer to Fig. 15.1, Questioning Techniques on the following page.

TECHNIQUES FOR ASKING QUESTIONS (6)

- **Task Question:** All students write down their answers. "Write down the ...."

- **Voluntary Question:** Question is posed to entire group and instructor selects a volunteer to respond. "What is the ...? Who would like to respond?"

- **Directed Question:** Question is posed to group and then an individual is selected to respond. "What is the ...? Bill?"

- **Involuntary Question:** An individual is selected prior to the question being posed. "Bill, What is the ...?"

?ASK: Which are the optimal techniques for asking a question to a group? Why?

OPTIMAL QUESTIONING TECHNIQUE (3)

- **Voluntary Questions:** All students must think.

- **Task Questions:** All students are given time to individually consider their answers before the discussion begins.

Figure 15.1. Questioning Techniques

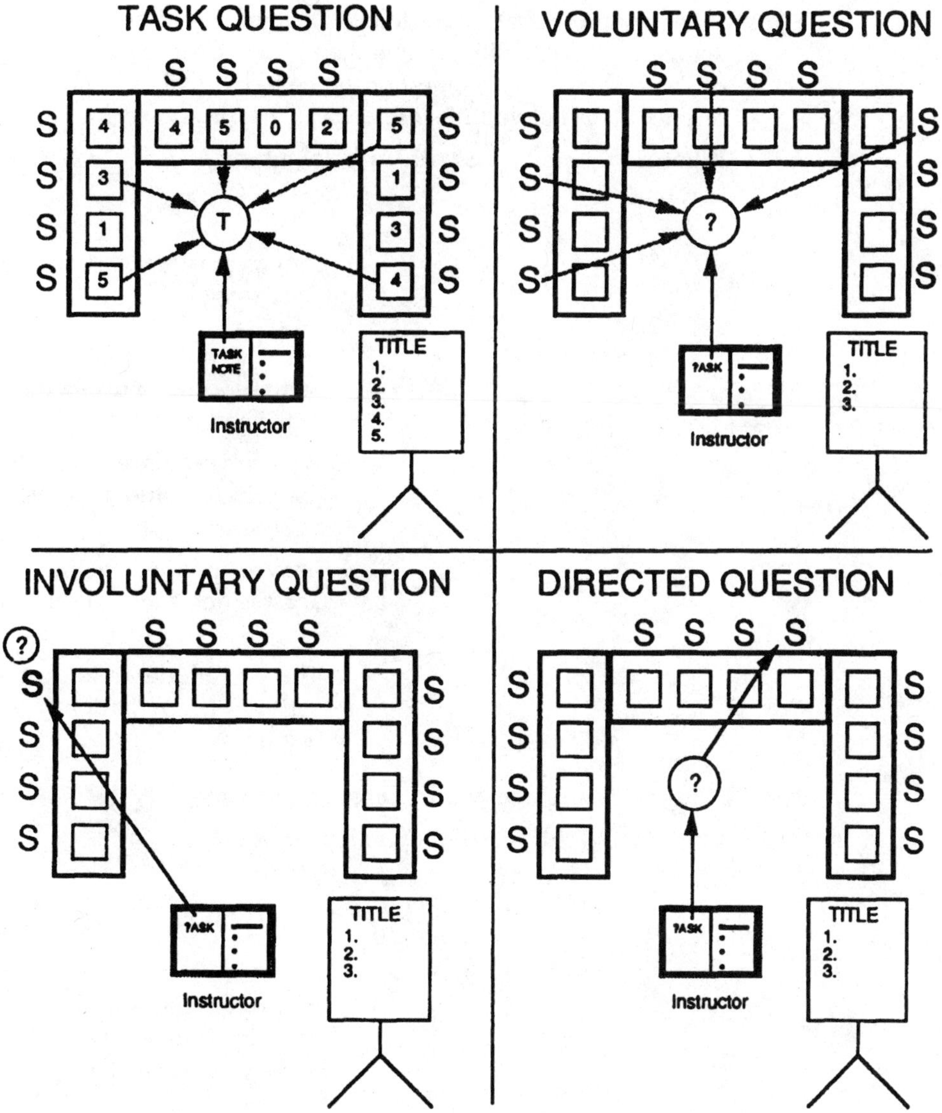

Technique	**Result**

TELL: When an individual is selected prior to the question being posed (i.e., "Bill, What is the …") we refer to this as an Involuntary Question as the individual selected does not volunteer to answer the question.

?ASK: What are the problems with an <u>Involuntary Question</u>?

PROBLEMS WITH INVOLUNTARY QUESTIONS (6)

- The selected student is effectively put on the spot. As a result, his or her level of tension increases.
- As a consequence of fear of exposure, the selected student's response tends to be short.
- Leaves people feeling vulnerable. Trust is not built or builds more slowly.
- The technique does not encourage active participation or quality responses.

?ASK: What is the problem with a <u>Directed Question</u>?

?ASK: How should the Directed Question be used?

DIRECTED QUESTIONS (3)

- Problem: The student you select may not have the best answer. Generally, people volunteer when they feel they have a good answer.
- Use: To bring a student into the discussion.

TELL: As a general rule, a Directed Question is most effective when it is used in conjunction with a Task Question. In this way, the student who you wish to bring into the discussion is more likely to have a correct and complete answer.

Technique

Result

OBJECTIVE: **B. Asking Questions:** Describe a 5-step procedure for asking a "Task or Voluntary Question" and seven instructor options for responding and guiding the discussion to a Conclusion. [13 minutes]

TELL: Let's talk about the mechanics of asking a question.

?ASK: What is the procedure for asking a preplanned Task or Voluntary Question to the group?

NOTE: Discuss. List on flip chart. Refer to the appropriate section of Fig. 15.2.

PROCEDURE FOR ASKING A QUESTION (6)

1. **Ask the preplanned question** from the guide as it was written.
2. **To the group** (as opposed to an individual).
3. **Wait:** Give the students time to think.
4. **Select a volunteer.**
5. **Listen** to the response.

?ASK: What options do you have for responding to student feedback and reaching a Conclusion?

NOTE: List on flip chart.

RESPONSE OPTIONS (7)

- Probe.
- Paraphrase.
- Rephrase the question.
- Explain the answer.
- Ask a Spontaneous Secondary Question related to the next End.
- Matrix the response.

Figure 15.2. Guiding a Discussion to a Conclusion

ASK A QUESTION	FROM GUIDE	TO GROUP	WAIT	VOLUNTEER	LISTEN

THE RESPONSE IS

CORRECT AND COMPLETE	PARTIALLY CORRECT INCOMPLETE INCORRECT (from your viewpoint)	NO RESPONSE

INSTRUCTOR'S CHOICE

PARAPHRASE	PROBE	PARAPHRASE	PROBE
To reinforce the correct response and the individual	To bring out more information: "Please explain?"	To demonstrate active listening	To clarify: "How do you understand the question?"

MATRIX	LISTEN		LISTEN
List response (if applicable)	Is the response correct & complete?		Is the question understood?
	YES / NO		NO / YES

		Is this the first response to the question?	
		NO / YES	

CONCLUSION REACHED	EXPLAIN	LOWER THE ABSTRACTION	REPHRASE
NO / YES	Reveal an END or explain the CONCLUSION	• ILLUSTRATE • GIVE EXAMPLE • USE AN ANALOGY • TELL A STORY • DEMONSTRATE	Frame a question to test understanding
Frame a SSQ for next END / Go to the Next PANEL			

Technique   **Result**

OBJECTIVE: **C. Types of Responses:** List the possible student responses that can occur from asking a question to a group. [12 minutes]

TASK: List all the possible student responses that can occur from asking a question to a group. Assume that you are using either a Task or Voluntary Question and that there is adequate time for the discussion. Also assume that a trust relationship has been established.

NOTE: Allow 2 minutes. Discuss. List on Flip Chart.

RESPONSES TO A QUESTION (12)

- Correct and complete.
- Correct but highly abstract and therefore incomplete.
- Partially correct or complete.
- Incorrect (from your point of view).
- Confusion. Students do not seem to understand the question.
- No response: Students refuse to answer the question.
- Disagreement. Students do not agree with the (developer's) question.
- The student could ask the instructor a question.

Technique	Result

OBJECTIVE: **D. Dealing with Correct and Complete Responses:** Describe the procedure and options available for responding to a student's correct and complete response. [17 minutes]

TELL: Let's consider the optimal situation, a student's correct and complete response.

?ASK: What should be the instructor's response to a student's complete and correct answer?

NOTE: Show <u>appropriate section</u> of Fig. 15.2, Guiding a Discussion to a Conclusion.

COMPLETE AND CORRECT (6)

- Paraphrase the student's response.
- List response on flip chart, whiteboard or overhead (if applicable).
- Probe to have the responding student elaborate further. Additional verification that the student understands.
- Ask other students to respond to determine if they hold the same view before reinforcing the answer.
- Determine if all Ends within the Conclusion have been reached.

?ASK: Why list correct and complete student responses on a matrix (flip chart, whiteboard or overhead)?

LISTING RESPONSES ON A MATRIX (5)

- Reinforces the correct answer.
- Encourages the students to take notes.
- Enables the students to see what ideas have been discussed. This eliminates restating the same ideas over again and aids in drawing out new ideas.
- Helps the instructor measure that all Ends in a Conclusion have been reached. (By comparing the matrixed responses to the Ends in the Guide.)

Technique	**Result**

TELL: While a student's response may be both correct and complete it may not address the entire Conclusion. Often there are Ends that have not been brought out.

?ASK: What technique should the instructor use to bring out unreached Ends?

SPONTANEOUS SECONDARY QUESTIONS (2)

■ Frame a question relevant to the desired End.

■ Follow the procedure for asking a Voluntary Question (To the group, wait, select a volunteer and listen)

?ASK: What is the difference between a Spontaneous Secondary Question and a probing question?

SSQ VERSUS PROBE (4)

■ SSQ: A question formulated by the instructor during the discussion which is relevant to a desired End.

■ Probe: A question (or gesture) to clarify or bring out more information.

A. Please explain?

B. Why do you say that?

C. Could you elaborate?

Technique   **Result**

OBJECTIVE: **E. Paraphrase:** Describe the purpose, structure and value of paraphrasing student responses. [20 minutes]

?ASK: What is a paraphrase?

PARAPHRASE (1)

The restatement of text or an idea
expressed verbally in another form,
such as the words of the receiver.

?ASK: What is the structure of a paraphrase?

NOTE: List on flip chart.

STRUCTURE OF A PARAPHRASE (2)

1. Transition: What I hear you saying is
   (or if I hear you correctly).

2. Restatement: The student's thoughts
   are stated in your own words.

3. Acknowledgment: Is that correct?

?ASK: What does a paraphrase accomplish?

NOTE: List on flip chart.

BENEFITS OF PARAPHRASE (4)

- Reinforces the correct (desired)
  answer.

- Reinforces the individual.

- Demonstrates active listening.

- Helps the instructor understand the
  student's point of view. Instructor's
  response will be more relevant and
  the potential to guide the student to
  the prescribed Conclusion is increased.

Technique   ## Result

?ASK   How does paraphrase reinforce the correct (or
            desired) answer?

REINFORCEMENT OF THE ANSWER (3)

- The correct answer is repeated.

- The instructor is perceived as an authority figure. Therefore, the instructor's answer has more weight, credibility, etc.

- The use of the instructor's words or the words in the Instructor Guide will often be different than those of the student. The difference in phrasing may promote understanding.

?ASK: How does paraphrase reinforce the individual?

REINFORCEMENT OF THE PARTICIPANT (3)

- The behavior, that of participation, is reinforced by the instructor's demonstration of active listening. The student is more likely to participate in future discussions.

- Active listening is an exchange of value between the sender and receiver. It says; "I value you enough to listen to what you have to say (even though I may disagree with you)."

?ASK: Why is paraphrase a demonstration of active listening?

PARAPHRASE AND ACTIVE LISTENING (4)

- It is difficult, if not impossible, to restate another person's thoughts if you have not been listening.

- This is particularly true when the answer you receive is different or dissonant from the view you hold.

Technique	**Result**

OBJECTIVE: **F. Dealing with No Response:** Describe the procedure for bringing about a discussion when there is no response to the question posed by the instructor. [5 minutes]

TELL: Let's look at a situation where a question has been posed, but the group does not respond.

?ASK: What should the instructor do when the group fails to respond to a preplanned question?

NOTE: Show <u>appropriate section</u> of Fig. 15.2, Guiding a Discussion to a Conclusion.

NO RESPONSE TO YOUR QUESTION (5)

- Probe: To clarify the students' understanding of the question: How do you understand the question?

- Listen: Is the question understood?

  A. If NO: Rephrase the question.

  B. If YES: Allow a student to answer?

Technique   **Result**

OBJECTIVE: **G. Incorrect or Incomplete Responses:** Describe the procedure
            and options available for responding to partially correct, incom-
            plete or incorrect answers. [20 minutes]

TELL: Let's look at the more difficult and more common
        transactions, the partially correct, incomplete or
        incorrect answer.

?ASK: What procedure should the instructor follow when
        an answer appears to be incorrect or partially cor-
        rect?

NOTE: Show <u>appropriate section</u> of Fig. 15.2, Guiding a
        Discussion to a Conclusion.

RESPONDING TO AN INCORRECT
ANSWER (5)

- Avoid telling the student that their
  answer is wrong.

- Remember, the answer may be incorrect from your point of view.

- Paraphrase: To demonstrate active listening.

- Probe to bring out more information
  and to understand the student's view
  point.

- Listen: Is the probed response complete and correct?

Technique	**Result**

?ASK: Should you paraphrase an incorrect answer?

PARAPHRASING INCORRECT
ANSWERS (2)

- Demonstrates that you listened.
- Allows the student to hear your interpretation of his answer. The student may reconsider and change it.

?ASK: What is the value of adopting a position that "There are no wrong answers?"

NO WRONG ANSWERS (3)

- To be told you are "wrong" in public is embarrassing. The student's self-esteem is damaged and he may be less likely to participate in further discussions.
- Other students vicariously participate in each transaction and thus may be less likely to participate if their peers are "confronted" over "wrong" answers.

Technique   ## Result

TELL: After listening to the student's explanation, we may determine that the response is still incorrect or incomplete.

?ASK: What options does the instructor have available to lead the discussion to the prescribed Conclusion?

NOTE: List on flip chart. Show <u>appropriate section</u> of Fig. 15.2, Guiding a Discussion to a Conclusion.

OPTIONS FOR A PROBED
INCORRECT ANSWER (6)

- **Paraphrase the part of the answer that is correct.**

- **Ask other students** to respond to determine if they hold the same view.

- **Rephrase the question.** Ask the rephrased question to the:

  A. Group.

  B. Original respondent.

- **Explain the answer.** Reveal an End or explain the Conclusion.

- **Lower the level of abstraction** to help the student(s) understand. An example, illustration, analogy, story or demonstration could be used.

Technique	**Result**

?ASK: What would dictate the appropriate course of action?

NOTE: Show <u>appropriate section</u> of the Algorithm (Fig. 15.2)—Guiding a Discussion to a Conclusion.

FACTORS TO CONSIDER IN CHOOSING OPTIONS (4)

- Time.

- Importance of the content under discussion.

- Number of incorrect responses to the question.

- Availability of students within the group who might know the answer.

Technique	**Result**

OBJECTIVE: **H. Using Spontaneous Secondary Questions:** Given an Instructor Guide Panel, be able to formulate Spontaneous Secondary Questions and conduct a 1-minute discussion to reach a designated End. [40 minutes]

TELL: Let's apply the process of formulating Spontaneous Secondary Questions to reach designated Ends within a Conclusion.

TASK: One of you will act as the trainer and conduct a 1-minute discussion to reach an End which I will designate. I will act as the student and respond to your questions. The remainder of the group will act as observers. We will use the Conclusion entitled "Client Benefits of a Reinsurance Company" and assume that you have given the group the task to write down the benefits to a client of a reinsurance company. We will further assume that our original assumptions about the group's knowledge have proven to be flawed. As we listen to their responses, we realize that they know very little about insurance and reinsurance companies. You are to bring about a discussion of the End "Underwriting Profit" to the extent that the student can explain what it is. Your transaction begins based on my response (as your student) that one of the benefits of the reinsurance company is "additional income."

NOTE: Reveal Conclusion:

CLIENT BENEFITS OF A REINSURANCE CO.

1. **Underwriting profit.** The difference between actual and expected losses.

2. **Investment income.** Interest earned on reserves for losses held by the insurance company.

3. **Leverage with the dealer's bank.** Cash flow (premiums deposited) and reserves held by the dealer's bank translate into the ability to borrow money at favorable terms.

4. **Favorable tax rate** as a life insurance company.

5. **Long term capital gain** treatment upon dissolution or sale.

Technique   ## Result

NOTE: Select a volunteer to act as the trainer. Allow 1 or 2
       students to perform. Instructor acts as the student.
       Record the transaction on audio or videotape.
       Instruct the observers to identify:

   1. Spontaneous Secondary Questions.

   2. Use of paraphrase.

   3. Use of probing questions.

PERFORMANCE (15 w/set up)

NOTE: Discuss performance by replaying the tape. Then demonstrate. Instruct
       the observers to identify:

   1. Spontaneous Secondary Questions.

   2. Use of paraphrase.

   3. Use of probing questions.

MODEL (5)

?ASK: What Spontaneous Secondary Questions did you
       identify (SSQs)?

EXAMPLE SSQs (5)

- How does an insurance company
  make money? (Underwriting profit
  and investment income.)

- What is an underwriting profit? (The
  difference between actual and expected losses.)

- What is the structure of a life insurance
  premium? (Consists of 4 parts: mortality, commission, expenses and profits.)

- What does the word underwriting
  mean? (The process of accepting risk.)

- What happens if the mortality
  assumptions prove to be more favorable than the company originally
  anticipated? (The company realizes an
  underwriting profit.)

Technique	**Result**

?ASK: How would you describe the transaction to reach the End "Underwriting Profit" that you observed?

NOTE: List on flip chart.

REACHING A DESIRED END (5)

- The instructor brought about understanding in the student(s) through a series of questions. SSQ and probes.

- The student was able to define underwriting profit in his or her own words as a result of the issues discussed.

- The instructor did not have to give the answer.

- The instructor paraphrased the student's answers to demonstrate understanding.

- The instructor paraphrased the desired End at the conclusion of the transaction.

Technique   Result

TASK: You are to bring about discussion of the End
       Investment Income to the extent that the student
       can explain what it is. Assume that I have identified
       Underwriting Profit as one of the benefits of the
       reinsurance company.

NOTE: Select a volunteer to act as the trainer. Instructor
       acts as the student. Record the transaction. Instruct
       the observers to identify:

       1. Spontaneous Secondary Questions.

       2. Use of paraphrase.

       3. Use of probing questions.

PERFORMANCE (5)

NOTE: Discuss performance by replaying the tape. Then
       demonstrate. Instruct the observers to identify:

       1. Spontaneous Secondary Questions.

       2. Use of paraphrase.

       3. Use of probing questions.

MODEL (3)

?ASK: What questions were used to bring about the End
       "Investment Income"?

RELEVANT SSQs (2)

- What does an insurance company do
  with the premium it sets aside for
  anticipated claims? (The company
  invests the money.)

- What is an insurance company
  allowed to invest in? (Bonds, real
  estate, stocks, money market instruments, etc.)

Technique   **Result**

OBJECTIVE: **I. Guide Usage Problems:** Describe instructor practices while
            using an Instructor Guide that inhibit participation. [15 minutes]

TELL: The purpose of the *Guided Discovery* style is to bring about active
        group participation and through it, understanding, acceptance and the
        ability to use the ideas under discussion. This is accomplished by asking
        questions that challenge each student to think, listening to their respons-
        es and, through the use of probing, paraphrase and illustration (lower-
        ing the level of abstraction), guiding them to a pre-determined
        Conclusion.

        The Instructor Guide format discussed in Chap. 14 and used throughout
        this chapter is the tool that enables the instructor to bring about and
        control active participation. Like any tool it can be misused. Listed in the
        following are the common problems experienced by people using an
        Instructor Guide prepared according to the *Guided Discovery* format.

        - **Manipulative paraphrase.** The instructor takes a student's incorrect
          response and restates it as the correct response in the guide without
          first probing to determine the student's rationale and paraphrasing to
          demonstrate active listening. This technique will quickly extinguish
          participation as students perceive that the instructor is not genuinely
          interested in their responses.

        - **Reading the Conclusion in the guide while the student is respond-
          ing to the question.** The instructor attempts to measure the com-
          pleteness and correctness of the student's response by comparing it to
          one or more Ends in the guide. Unfortunately, students do not always
          use the exact words in the guide. This practice interferes with listen-
          ing. As a consequence, the instructor is unable to use paraphrase to
          reinforce the student and, if appropriate, the student's response. The
          practice also conveys a message to the students that their ideas are
          not important.

        - **Accepting abstract or incomplete answers.** The instructor accepts stu-
          dent answers without probing and then goes on to elaborate. Students
          perceive that the instructor is not really interested in their ideas and
          participation diminishes. Students should be encouraged to expand on
          their answers. In this way, the instructor can measure the degree to
          which they understand and accept the unit of knowledge under dis-
          cussion.

        - **Trying to get the group to say the exact words in the guide.** The
          instructor frustrates the students by taking acceptable answers and, in
          effect, stating they are incorrect. Student's perceive interactive induc-
          tive process as a guessing game and participation declines.

Technique   **Result**

- **Not using the Core Question as written in the guide.** The inappropriate restatement of the question results in student responses that are not relevant to the Conclusion. As a consequence, time is lost as the instructor attempts to redirect the discussion toward the desired objective. The practice is linked to the instructor's perception that his or her credibility as a subject expert is reduced by making reference to notes (the guide).

- **Phantom Conclusions.** This occurs when the instructor decides to go deeper into the subject than originally intended. He or she begins asking questions which are not in the guide. This practice uses up time that is allocated to other activities such as modeling, performance, evaluation and other key training units.

- **Responding to student questions that are relevant to future material.** The instructor jumps ahead and covers material that was planned for discussion later in the program. Often these units of knowledge and skill require that some foundation be established before they are discussed. The instructor's failure to contract with the group to discuss the issue at a later time results in lengthy explanations. In many cases, the instructor's answers lead to even more student questions. This practice eats up time and often results in incomplete discussion of the units of knowledge and skill. When the instructor gets to the actual Training Unit he or she is likely to say "we already covered that."

  This problem is easily solved with an "Issues List." When the student asks a question which is relevant to future material the instructor acknowledges the fact, contracts with the student to delay the discussion and writes the student's question on the "Issues List." This technique can also be used to defer the discussion of controversial issues that arise from time to time.

- **Asking a question and then turning to write the title of the Conclusion on the flip chart.** This results in a slight but noticeable loss of control as one or more students simultaneously respond to the question. A better approach is to write the title of the Conclusion on the flip chart before asking the question. In this way, the instructor is facing the group when he or she asks the question.

Technique   **Result**

OBJECTIVE: **J. Dealing with a Flawed Conclusion:** Describe the process of interacting with the group to correct a flawed Conclusion. [30 minutes]

TELL: Up to this point we have made the assumption that
the Conclusion is relevant to the group and that
they agree with your Conclusion.

?ASK: What are the other possibilities beyond complete
agreement with your Conclusion (answer)?

VALIDATION OF CONCLUSIONS (4)

- Relevant ideas or techniques are added.

- Disagreement with all or part of your
Conclusion.

- Inability to reach the desired Conclusion due to missing background
knowledge. Example: Attempting to
<u>discuss</u> the presentation of a product
without first establishing some technical knowledge about the product.

?ASK: What are the possible outcomes when the group
disagrees with your Conclusion?

DISAGREEMENT WITH
CONCLUSIONS (3)

- Discussion resulting in a new
Conclusion being reached.

- Dissonance: The dissent restricts the
instructor's ability to proceed resulting in lost time.

- Delay: The instructor has to consult
with a subject matter expert to resolve
the disputed point(s).

TELL: In some cases, the unit of knowledge or skill
(Conclusion) under discussion can be added to an
"Issues List" and resolved later in the program. In
other cases, the issue must be resolved before the
program can successfully continue.

Technique   **Result**

?ASK: What would cause a group or an individual to disagree with your Conclusion?

REASONS FOR DISAGREEMENT
WITH CONCLUSIONS (3)

- The Conclusion or part of it is incorrect.

- The group has a different perspective
or different needs as it regards the
issue.

- The question was inappropriate to the
Conclusion you wrote.

TELL: You attended a training program with Bright and
Associates, a nationally recognized training company on writing learning objectives. Your purpose in
attending their program was to conduct training in
your company on writing objectives for experienced
instructors. They presented the following as a model
learning objective. You incorporated their model
into your program. In your class are several instructors who have read the **Training Effectiveness
Handbook.**

NOTE: Show acetate of Bright's model objective.
"Within three weeks, Sales Representatives should
be able to use the total needs presentation visual to
make presentations that will result in at least 5 fact-
finding interviews and 2 sales per week."

?ASK: What are the chances of your reaching agreement
with the group that Bright's model is a valid example of a correctly stated learning objective? Why?

FLAWED CONCLUSION (3)

The instructors who read the **Training
Effectiveness Handbook** will not accept
Bright's objective as a model as it is
flawed in relation to the (6) Criteria for
Measuring the Usefulness of a Learning
Objective (Part 1).

Technique   ## Result

TASK: Write down the specific problems with Bright's model objective?

NOTE: Allow 2 minutes. Discuss. List errors on flip chart. Refer to page 42 of Part 1.

?ASK: Conceptually, what is the problem with Bright's model objective?

PROBLEMS WITH THE OBJECTIVE (8)

General Problem: Bright's model suggests that training produces results as opposed to behavior. Under *Guided Discovery* theory, "Training produces desired behavior. Desired behavior produces results." The following are the specific flaws:

- **Criteria are "results" as opposed to behaviors.** They cannot be observed or measured during the training.

- **The criteria are beyond the control of training.** The "objective" of getting 5 interviews is a matter of prospecting activity. The performance deals with the interview.

- Desired behavior at program's end is unclear. Is the total needs presentation a discrete behavior? If so, it should be capitalized.

- No time is stated for the performance.

- Within 3 weeks is not a condition. It does not impose a limitation or state a non-implicit resource.

- What about responding to sales resistance from the prospect? Is that part of the training the sales representatives will receive?

Technique   ## Result

TELL: Let's assume that the instructors who read the
       Training Effectiveness Handbook and several other
       group members will not accept Bright's objective as
       a model of a correctly stated learning objective.

?ASK: What action should the instructor take with regard to
       the dissonance caused by the flawed model objective?

NOTE: List on flip chart.

RESPONSE TO GROUP DISSONANCE (5)

- Probe. Have the group identify the
  specific errors and list on flip chart.

- Ask the group to describe their criteria for an effective (useful) objective.

- Ask the group to write an objective
  that they feel meets their criteria.

- Compare their objective to their criteria and determine if their knowledge
  is more or less correct than that held
  by the instructor.

?ASK: How does the process of resolving the dissonance
       with a Conclusion you present relate to the Theory
       Y assumptions postulated by Thomas Kramlinger?

THEORY Y ASSUMPTION 3 (4)

Truth is discovered by participation in
formulating the problem, in drawing on
personal experience, in searching for
resources, by suggesting alternatives
and contrasting them and in testing
options and accepting the consequences.

TELL: Kramlinger's Theory Y Assumption 3 is about learn-
       ing. The students (instructors in this instance) bring
       to the table better knowledge and skills than the
       instructor conducting the training. If the instructor
       recognizes that any Conclusion he has is merely the
       best answer he has at that moment (in other words,
       "truth is transient"), then he can listen to his stu-
       dents and objectively determine if their answer
       ought to replace his.

K. Guided Discovery

Guided Discovery is a teaching method or style which uses objectives and interactive inductive learning to bring about one or more desired behaviors in the student.

The *Guided Discovery* system is based on a modified version of a key assumption that Harold Cash and W. J. E. Crissy used as the basis for their book, *The Psychology of Selling*. It was through their words that I was able to discover the resources that enabled me to formulate the ideas that led to *Guided Discovery* and the principles contained in this book.

Guided Discovery Teaching

The most fruitful way to view teaching is to see it as a learning process which the instructor brings about in the student(s). Thus the process begins with the discovery of needs to be met by the learning objectives to be achieved. (Cash and Crissy, 1966, Vol. 1, Preface)

These words may look innocent or perhaps even trivial at first appearance. However, if you take each part and consider its meaning, you arrive at a teaching method that is highly interactive and productive for both student and instructor. Consider:

- **The most <u>fruitful</u> way.** Not the <u>only</u> way or even the <u>best</u> way but rather the most productive way.

- **To view teaching is to see it as a <u>learning process</u>.** We are told to look at it from the student's point of view. The words learning process also suggest that we look at the change in behavior to determine if the process is working.

- **Which the <u>instructor brings about</u> in the student.** Responsibility for learning is placed upon the instructor, yet, as evidenced by the next line, the focus is on the student. I consider *Guided Discovery* to be an instructor controlled, student-centered teaching method.

- **Thus the process begins with the discovery of needs.** Students must discover a need or deficiency in skill or knowledge to become motivated to learn. When the student is, in fact, a competent performer, he or she is reinforced by the training conducted.

- **To be met by the learning objectives to be achieved.** The process ends with the acquisition of the desired behavior (skills or knowledge) which are contained within the learning objective.

Figure 15.3 shows the principle of *Guided Discovery Teaching* in relationship to the **Total Quality Training Standards.** *Figure 15.3 demonstrates that <u>each key phrase</u> bears a direct relationship to a* **Training Standard** *and the methodology used to meet the* **Standard.**

Figure 15.3. *TQT Standards* in Relation to
the *Guide Discovery* Principle.

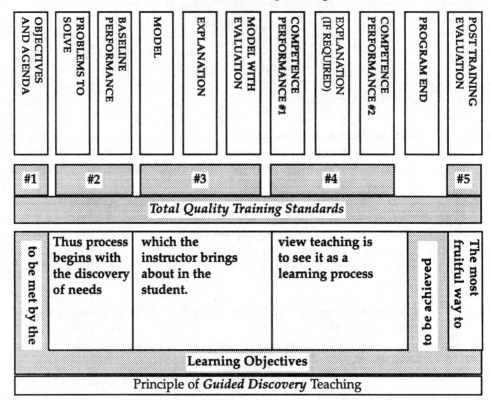

- **The most fruitful way:** As stated in the introduction to the *Training Effectiveness Handbook,* "training is effective to the degree that it produces the desired effect in the population being trained. In concise terms, this means the ability of each participant to use the knowledge and skills contained within the program to bring about a desired result on the job." Hence, the logical relationship to Post Training Evaluation.

- **To view teaching is to see it as a <u>learning process</u>.** Student performance enables us to measure the degree to which change has occurred.

- Which the <u>instructor brings about</u> in the student. The instructor's modeling of the desired behavior and explanation help the student to understand, accept and use the knowledge and skills under discussion.

- **Thus the process begins with the discovery of needs.** Problems to Solve and Baseline Performance enable the students and instructor to identify the performance discrepancies that are inhibiting productivity.

- **To be met by the learning objectives to be achieved.** As indicated by the shading, learning objectives are the foundation for the process.

Notice also that the principle appears in direct opposition to the linear flow of the Training Design. This suggests the importance of the planning and organizing phases of the Program Development Process.

The Mechanism for Change

The word "fruitful" means abundantly productive. I have found the *Guided Discovery* style to be both productive in terms of what my students learned and growth producing in terms of what I learned.

From the early days of January, 1979, I have used the *Guided Discovery* style in every training program I developed. I have also conducted training for program developers. My course, Program Development under the Principles of *Guided Discovery*, is taught with the *Guided Discovery* style. As a result, I have had the opportunity to interact with my groups toward Conclusions that I believed were correct and complete. However, my students, who I empowered to accept or reject the ideas under discussion, did not always agree with me. Their input along with the measurement of their performance helped me correct many of the flawed units of knowledge and skill that I held.

As a result, the system you have learned in this book stands the ultimate test. It can be used to explain itself.

L. The *Guided Discovery* Symbol

The following is a symbolic representation of the *Guided Discovery* process (a registered service mark of the Ryan Insurance Group, Inc.) and my way of ending our journey together.

The Bar represents the objective. The "Y" represents McGregor's Theory Y Assumptions, questions, the question "why" (the motive behind all actions and behavior) and two ideas coming together. The Chairs represent two-way communication, a sender and a receiver, point of view, the Hierarchical Structure and something I call the Concept of Dimensions. Finally, the circle represents the matrix. That within which and from which something grows and develops. The symbol taken as a unit represents:

> *Two people working together*
> *to reach agreement*
> *on a course of action*
> *to achieve their goals.*

The "Concept of Dimensions" represents the idea that an effective transaction between two people can have consequences that extend far beyond the event in which the agreement represented by the symbol took place.

The techniques in the *Training Effectiveness Handbook* will enable you to work with people to help them gain the knowledge and skills that will help them and the people they interact with to achieve their goals and, as a direct result, help you to achieve your goals.

I wish you many fruitful transactions.

Appendix **A**

Total Quality Training Standards

What They Are and How They Can Be Met

Contents

Total Quality Training Standards

To achieve training effectiveness, the initiative should contain:

1. Learning objectives which describe the **desired behavior(s)** to be exhibited during the training program.

2. Evidence of a performance discrepancy in relation to the **desired behavior** resulting from a lack of skill or knowledge. (Needs Analysis)

3. Examples or models of the **desired behavior** during the training program.

4. Evaluation of student performance of the **desired behavior** to determine competence during training.

5. Evidence that the **desired behavior** has persisted after training and is linked to results. (Post Training Evaluation)

The preceding *Standards* apply to any event which is designed to improve organizational results through the enhancement of knowledge or skills.

Questions and Answers

- **What are *Total Quality Training Standards*?**

  Training Standards provide criteria to evaluate the effectiveness of a training program. They enable managers, developers and trainers to approach training projects with a common language and establish guidelines that assist all parties in achieving the greatest return from the investment made in training.

- **What is effective training?**

  Training that transfers knowledge and skills that enable employees to bring about desired results on the job and which justifies the expense incurred.

- **Why should managers, developers and trainers work toward meeting the *TQT Standards*?**

  Training Standards enable the team involved with training to:
  A. Increase employee effectiveness and development.
  B. Increase their business unit profits.
  C. Ensure that their unit's investment in training (time and money) produce the greatest possible return.
  D. Solve business problems.

- **Where are these *TQT Standards* applicable?**

  They apply to any event which is designed to improve organizational results through the enhancement of knowledge or skills. In other words, to all training conducted by our organization. This includes existing programs and those under consideration for development or purchase.

■ **When will the *Standards* be implemented?**

The goal is to have all training programs conducted by our organization meet the *Standards* over a ___ year period. The process begins (insert date). The ___ year period recognizes that change is a gradual and evolutionary process.

■ **How does a manager employ *TQT Standards*?**

By requiring developers and instructors to justify how their programs meet the *Standards*. Instructions for evaluating a program begin on 361.

■ **What is the difference between the terms developer and instructor?**

The term developer refers to the individual responsible for planning, organizing, evaluating and monitoring the training. The term instructor refers to the person who conducts the training. In many cases, the developer and the instructor are the same person.

■ **How does a manager, developer or instructor determine if their program meets the *Standards*?**

There are several alternatives:
A. This booklet (starting on page 356) provides a set of guidelines that allow any person to quickly assess the effectiveness of a training program. Included is the rationale and suggested methods for meeting each *Standard*. Compare your current training practices to those described in this booklet. Evaluation instructions appear on page 361.
B. The *Training Effectiveness Evaluation System* (App. D of the <u>Training Effectiveness Handbook</u>) provides specific criteria that measure the *Standards* in relation to 28 components of a training program design. This method provides:
  * A rating which suggests the:
    — Effectiveness of any program component and the
    — Likelihood of producing the desired behavior as a result of the training program.
  * Guidelines for making corrections to identified discrepancies.

■ **Several *Standards* employ the word "desired behavior." What is the difference between training and desired behavior?**

It is important to differentiate between these two terms.
A. Training is the process and methodology employed to bring about the desired behavior in the person being trained.
B. Desired behavior is the knowledge or skills that the trained person uses to bring about a desired result with the end user (such as a customer or worker).

■ **Who established the *TQT Standards* and what was their goal?**

A team of senior training officers representing all subsidiaries of our organization developed the *Standards*. This team was charged with the responsibility to create a set of guidelines that would assist managers, developers and trainers in making training decisions that would increase the effectiveness of our personnel.

Standard 1—Learning Objectives

Learning objectives which describe the <u>desired behavior(s)</u> to be exhibited during the training program.

1. Before Training: The developer:
   a. **Writes the Module Objective: Given** (insert the conditions), **the** (state the job title of the of the performer) **will be able to** (describe the performance) **that** (describe the principle criteria) **within** (state the time limit for the performance).
   b. **Writes the Unit Objectives.**
      (1) To accomplish the Module Objective **the** (state the learner's job title) **will be able to**
      (2) Describe the performance.
      (3) Add Conditions, Criteria and Performance Time as required.
   c. **Organizes the Learning Objectives into a plan or agenda** that includes the sequence of events and training time allocated to each objective. (Refer to example on page 365.)
2. During Training: The instructor at:
   a. Program Introduction: Displays the objectives and reaches agreement with the students on the relevance of the objectives to their needs.
   b. Program Conclusion: Reviews the objectives with the students to determine if they have been achieved.

Rationale: Objectives provide the basis for:

1. *Before Training: Conducting a needs analysis, determining program content, selecting instructional techniques, allocating time and resources.*

2. *During Training: Focusing student effort toward the acquisition of the desired behavior and assessing the program's success in meeting its objectives and, as a direct result, the student's needs.*

3. *After Training: Evaluating the program's success in terms of its impact on productivity. Refer to Standard 5.*

Standard 2—Needs Analysis

Evidence of a performance discrepancy in relation to the <u>desired behavior</u> resulting from a lack of skill or knowledge.

This *Standard* can be met in one of two ways or disregarded:

1. Before Training: The developer collects behavioral data on the performance of the population targeted for training. In general, the developer collects this data by getting as close to the performance in question as is practically and economically feasible. *A report should contain the data collected, its analysis and the conclusions drawn.* The following are examples of data collection methods listed in order of effectiveness:

    a. Observing performers on the job.

    b. Have performers respond to simulated situations.

    c. Surveying employees or customers of the performer using a reliable survey instrument.

    d. Interviews or surveys with the immediate manager(s) of the performers to identify the problems the performer's are experiencing.

    e. Interviews or surveys where performers describe the problems they are experiencing.

2. During Training: The developer or instructor can (in order of effectiveness):

    a. <u>Give the students problems to solve</u> (before giving the answer) that reveal their present competence with the knowledge or skills to be taught. This produces a baseline performance.

    NOTE: Requires the creation of preclass assignments, cases or practice exercises, etc. prior to conducting training.

    b. Ask the students to <u>describe their perceived</u> knowledge or skill discrepancies or the problems they are experiencing in a given area.

    c. Discuss performance discrepancies identified in a Need Analysis (if one was conducted).

3. Disregarding this *Standard:* It may not be feasible to conduct a Needs Analysis in a situation where a new product or procedure is introduced. In such cases, Post Training Evaluation, once completed, will indicate the desired behavior's impact on results and will identify any discrepancies in performance. In this instance, Post Training Evaluation serves as a Needs Analysis and basis for modification of the training. Refer to *Standard 5.*

Rationale:

1. *Needs Analysis focuses the training on the knowledge and skills needed to perform by identifying the actual discrepancies in current performance.*

2. *Learning occurs, most effectively, when the student perceives a problem and wants to clear up her own uneasiness about the problem.*

Standard 3—Modeling

Examples or models of the <u>desired behavior</u> during the training program.

    This *Standard* can be met as follows:

1. Before Training: Depends on the type of behavior to be exhibited:

    a. Knowledge based: The developer can <u>prepare</u> sample problems and solutions.

    b. Interactive: The developer can either:

        (1) <u>Prepare</u> for a live demonstration:

            (*a*) <u>Create</u> cases and materials for a behavioral simulation (role play).

            (*b*) <u>Ensure</u> that the instructor can competently demonstrate the desired behavior in a role play.

        (2) <u>Produce</u> a video of the desired behavior.

(*a*) Optimal: The complete behavior is shown along with, if applicable, responses to typical questions and objections.

(*b*) Questionable: The behaviors modeled are incomplete, frequently interrupted or do not show responses to resistance.

2. During Training: The instructor can:
    a. Depends on the type of behavior to be exhibited:
        (1) Knowledge based: Show example problems and solutions; e.g., the preparation of a tax return in relation to a case.
        (2) Interactive: <u>Conduct</u> a demonstration of the desired behavior in a role play simulation.
    b. Discuss the relevance, importance and structure of each of the units of knowledge and skill that enables the student to perform the desired behavior.

Rationale:

1. *People commit their energies to that which they perceive as relevant.*

2. *Examples and models provide graphic illustrations which permit the student to structure and compare the desired behavior to her own experience.*

Standard 4—Performance Evaluation

Evaluation of student performance of the <u>desired behavior</u> to determine competence during training.

This *Standard* can be met as follows:

1. Before training the developer can:
    a. Provide adequate time during the program for each student to perform the desired behavior. Two or more performances are optimal.
    b. Establish *Expert Criteria* to measure the desired behavior.
    c. Establish a rating scale to measure levels of competence.
    d. Create an Evaluation Form to record ratings and comments.
    e. Establish a performance standard. A minimum level of competence by which the success of both the student and course can be evaluated.
    f. Create cases (if applicable) to simulate situations likely to be encountered on the job.
2. During training the instructor can:
    a. Employ methods to permit the students to evaluate their own performance.
        (1) Have students identify both strengths and improvement opportunities.
        (2) Use criteria, evaluation forms and the rating scale to measure competence.
        (3) (Interactive Behaviors): Videotape the performance. This allows the student to see the performance rather than to recall it from memory.
    b. Observe, evaluate and comment on student performance.
    c. Ensure that multiple performance and evaluation takes place. (If time is allocated).

Rationale: Evaluation of performance allows both the student and instructor to determine if learning has taken place. Stated another way, we discover that the student has acquired the desired behavior if he is able to perform at a reasonable level of competence. <u>Evaluation also increases the student's learning motivation</u> by creating accountability for the acquisition of the desired behavior.

Note: The criteria, rating scale and Evaluation Form can be used to measure the desired behavior on the job. Refer to *Standard 5,* Post Training Evaluation.

Procedure to Calculate Criterion Score for *Standard 4*:

1. Select the SCORE based on the TRAINING METHOD EMPLOYED.

SCORE	EVALUATION METHOD EMPLOYED
10.0	The student performs the desired behavior more than one time* with formal evaluation using pre-agreed upon criteria. Ratings obtained are compared to a performance standard. Performance is observed and evaluated by the instructor.
	*The first performance provides a baseline to measure from. The second shows improvement and competence. The third is a clear measure of competence.
8.0	Same as above except the student's performance is formally evaluated one time using preagreed upon criteria in relationship to a performance standard.
6.0	Performance is observed and evaluated by the instructor. During the evaluation the student, group and instructor identify strengths and weaknesses.
5.0	Students perform the desired behavior. This is followed by an evaluation of their performance based on criteria. <u>However, the instructor **does not** observe or evaluate their performance</u>.
4.0	Students perform and receive unstructured feedback <u>by the instructor</u> and group. There is no evaluation against criteria to measure competence.
3.0	Students perform the desired behavior in <u>unsupervised</u> teams with <u>unstructured</u> feedback or criteria for measuring competence.
0.0	Students <u>do not perform</u> the desired behavior.

2. Multiply the SCORE by the percentage of the group that performs.

Example: Training Method Employed equals 8.0. Percentage of students performing equals 90 percent. **Final Criterion Score: 7.2** $(8.0 \times .9)$

Standard 5—Post Training Evaluation

Evidence that the <u>desired behavior</u> has persisted after training and is linked to results.

This *Standard* requires evaluation of on-the-job performance. To meet this *Standard* the developer must collect behavioral data on the population trained that demonstrates the program's impact on results in relation to *Standard 1* (Objectives), *Standard 3* (Modeling) and *Standard 4* (Performance and Evaluation). In other words, we observe the worker using the knowledge and skills contained in the training.

<u>The process uses the same techniques as those employed in a needs analysis</u>. The developer collects data by getting as close to the performance in question as is practically and economically feasible. A written report is prepared based on the data. *The report should contain the data collected, its analysis, the conclusions drawn and action plan for correcting, if applicable, performance discrepancies identified.* The following are examples of data collection methods in order of effectiveness:

A. Observing performers on the job.

B. Having performers respond to simulated situations.

C. Surveying employees or customers of the performer using a reliable survey instrument.

D. Interviews or surveys with the immediate manager(s) of the performers to identify the problems the performers are experiencing.

E. Interviews or surveys where performers describe the problems they are experiencing.

Rationale: Post Training Evaluation proves that:

1. *The discrepancies the training sought to correct have, in fact, been corrected or*

2. *The desired behavior that the training was designed to bring about is being used by the performers to produce results or*

3. *The problem persists. In this case, the process acts as a needs analysis and provides data for modification of the training or the desired behavior.*

Without such a study, any increase in productivity may be the result of other factors such as management's institution of accountability, minimum performance standards or pay incentives to motivate performance. It could also be the result of altered attitudes rather than from specific employment of the techniques taught. Post Training Evaluation proves that the organization is getting the most from its training investment.

Evaluation Instructions

1. Compare your current training practices to those described in this booklet. Examples of practices which meet the *Standards* begin on page 356.

2. Score each *Training Standard* as follows:

   10   Meets

   5   Questionable

   0   Does Not Meet or Not Evident

   N   Not Applicable (Only applies to *Standard 2*, paragraph 3. See page 357.)

3. Record each score on the Evaluation Form (example on pages 362 and 363).

4. Describe how the program meets each *Standard* by explaining the methodology employed (on the reverse side of the Evaluation Form) **and** attach a copy of the learning objectives.

5. Calculate the **Effectiveness Rating.** Add the scores for each *Standard* and divide by 5.

6. Determine the program's status in relationship to our organizational goal of training effectiveness based on the Effectiveness Rating.

   > 8.0 Effective: Suggests that your training is enabling employees to bring about the desired results.

   > 5.0 Marginal*:   Suggests an improvement opportunity. Modifications to training methodology or investigations (Needs Analysis—Post Training Evaluation) to link the training to what people do on the job may increase productivity.

   < 4.9 Ineffective*: Suggests that the program is unlikely to produce a desired behavior that can be observed on the job or that can be linked to results. The manager should question resources (time and money) invested in this program.

   *NOTE: Disregard the Effectiveness Rating when <u>Post Training Evaluation</u> proves that the desired behavior is linked to productivity and/or results.

7. Take action with regard to the *Standards* that are not met. This booklet provides suggested training methods that meet the **Standards**. Additionally, you can contact the *Professional Development Division* for assistance.

Total Quality Training Standards Evaluation

Program Name _____

Program Length _____ Days, Vendor Fee $_____ Student Materials Cost $_____

Training Vendor Name _____

Decision Maker _____

Developer _____ Development Date _____

Instructor(s) _____

Students' Job Title _____ Average Class Size ____ Students

Evaluated by _____ Evaluation Date _____

Instructions

1. Score and describe how the program meets each *Standard* (on the reverse side)

    10   Meets

    5   Questionable

    0   Does Not Meet or Not Evident

    N   Not Applicable (Only applies to *Standard 2*—Item 3 on page 357)

2. Attach a copy of the learning objectives.

	Total Quality Training Standards	SCORE or RATING
1	Learning objectives which describe the <u>desired behavior(s)</u> to be exhibited during the training program.	
2	Evidence of a performance discrepancy in relation to the <u>desired behavior</u> resulting from a lack of skill or knowledge. (Needs Analysis)	
3	Examples or models of the <u>desired behavior</u> during the training program.	
4	Evaluation of student performance of the <u>desired behavior</u> to determine competence during training.	
5	Evidence that the <u>desired behavior</u> has persisted after training and is linked to results. (Post Training Evaluation)	
TOTAL (Divide by 5)		
EFFECTIVENESS RATING		

For further explanation of each *Standard* refer to the booklet, *Training Standards,* **What They Are and How They Can Be Met.**

Justification of Ratings

Describe briefly how the training program meets each *Standard*.

1. Learning objectives which describe the <u>desired behavior(s)</u> to be exhibited during the training program. Attach a copy.

2. Evidence of a performance discrepancy in relation to the <u>desired behavior</u> resulting from a lack of skill or knowledge. (Needs Analysis)

3. Examples or models of the <u>desired behavior</u> during the training program.

4. Evaluation of student performance of the <u>desired behavior</u> to determine competence during training.

5. Evidence that the <u>desired behavior</u> has persisted after training and is linked to results. (Post Training Evaluation)

Example Learning Objectives

Module Objective (Describes desired behavior.)

- Write Learning Objectives: Given a performance discrepancy that is caused by a lack of skill or knowledge on a subject that the instructional developer has mastered, the developer (reader) will be able to write a learning objective that contains performance, criteria, conditions and time components within 12 minutes which achieves an Effectiveness Rating of 10 (on a 10 scale) against prescribed criteria.

- Selection Interview: Given notes from a pre-screening interview, the results of the Career Profile, a student acting as the candidate and 15 minutes for preparation, the manager will be able to **conduct a fact-finding interview** and probe for facts or attitudes that would be relevant to candidate suitability within 30 minutes.

- Cold Call (Need Selling): Given the name, position and data available in the financial directory and a student acting as the prospect, the Account Representative will be able to **conduct a preliminary sales interview** and, based on the needs identified, reach agreement on the benefits, time, content and participants for a formal sales interview and, where appropriate, respond to up to three instances of sales resistance within 15 minutes.

- Life Insurance Sales Interview (Need Selling): Given a student acting as a customer, the agent will be able to **conduct a sales interview for life insurance** and, based on the needs agreed upon, select and present a proposal for a suitable insurance product within 60 minutes.

- Sales Presentation (Stimulus Response Selling): Given a student acting as a receptive prospect who does not object, **give a sales talk,** word for word, within 6 minutes with no more than 5 word errors.

Unit Objective (Describes a unit of knowledge or skill.)

- Description of a Procedure: **Describe the structure of precontract training** in context with the selection process with a candidate who is employed and **differentiate the procedures to be followed when the manager wishes to accelerate the process** (such as when a candidate is unemployed).

- Definition of an Objective: Define instructional objectives, explain their purpose and relate the definition of objectives to the definition of learning.

- Verb Selection: Choose an active verb for behaviors in the cognitive domain (think) which represents the level of complexity (difficulty) of a desired behavior.

- Classify Types of Questions: Discriminate a behavioral question from a theoretical, leading or not behavioral question.

Objectives Organized into a Training Plan

PROGRAM NAME: Developing Learning Objectives.

MODULE OBJECTIVE:

Given a performance discrepancy that is caused by a lack of skill or knowledge on a subject that the instructional developer has mastered, the developer (reader) will be able to write a learning objective that contains performance, criteria, conditions and time components within 12 minutes which achieves an Effectiveness Rating of 10 (on a 10 scale) against prescribed criteria.

TOTAL TIME: 360 minutes.

TIME		UNIT OBJECTIVES: To accomplish the above objective, the students will be able to:
(10)	A.	Perform an exercise that provides a baseline measurement of their ability to identify the structure of learning objectives.
(13)	B.	Define learning objectives, explain their purpose and relate the definition of objectives to the definition of learning.
(15)	C.	State the 5 components of a learning objective.
(60)	D.	Write (with instructor assistance) two learning objectives containing a Performer, Performance, Performance Time, Criteria and Conditions Component (for serving a tennis ball with beginning and advanced players).
(15)	E.	Evaluate a series of statements to identify those which contain a description of performance and achieve 80% correct.
(15)	F.	Choose an active verb for behaviors in the cognitive domain (think) which represents the level of complexity (difficulty) of a desired behavior.
(15)	G.	Given a series of objectives, identify (by checking) those which contain a correctly stated performance, criteria and conditions and achieve a score of 70 percent correct.
(10)	H.	Given their pre-test and post-test group scores on the Mager Self Test, be able to measure the change in their ability to identify correctly stated performance, criteria and conditions.
(43)	I.	Evaluate and correct an incorrectly stated objective.
(44)	J.	Write a learning objective for presenting, opening and serving a bottle of wine and analyze the desired behavior (in preparation for writing an Instructor Guide).
(00)	K.	(As homework) Write a set of learning objectives for a 1-hour training program.
(120)	L.	Evaluate each objective against six criteria of a useful objective. (Components 04 and 05 of the Training Effectiveness Evaluation System)

Appendix B

Training Effectiveness Survey

A Key Step in the Goal Toward Training Effectiveness

Contents

Questions and Answers

- **What is the purpose of the *Training Effectiveness Survey*?**

  Our organization has set a goal to have all training programs meet *The Total Quality Training Standards* by (Insert Target Date). The survey will allow us to determine the status of our programs in relation to the *Standards* and yield a number of important benefits. These include:
  A. Promoting a dialogue between managers, developers and trainers.
  B. Raising questions about current practices.
  C. Revealing opportunities to make immediate changes that could increase effectiveness.
  D. Providing a "baseline" measurement that will permit us to assess our progress toward the goal.
  E. Determining if your business unit is maximizing the return from its training investment.

- **What programs are to be evaluated in the survey?**

  Programs which have been developed internally or purchased from vendors should be evaluated and included in the survey. You will receive a list of programs from the *Professional Development Team.*

- **Who conducts the evaluation of the programs?**

  The task of evaluating each program should be assigned to the developer or trainer responsible for the program.

- **What does the survey process consist of?**

  The person who is evaluating the program completes the Evaluation Form (sample found on pages 370 and 371). The booklet, *Training Standards,* **What They Are and How They Can Be Met,** contains the *Standards* and sample methodology that meets the *Standards.* The evaluator:
  A. Rates the program against each of the 5 *Training Standards.*
  B. Describes how the program meets each *Standard.*
  C. Attaches a copy of the learning objectives to the Evaluation Form.
  D. Forwards a copy of the Evaluation Form with attached objectives to the *Professional Development Team.*
  E. Meets with the business unit manager to report her findings.

- **What is the purpose of having a copy of the program's learning objectives attached to the survey?**

  The *Professional Development Team* will be conducting a Needs Analysis on the quality of objectives contained within our Training Programs. Objectives can be precisely measured and provide a reliable predictor of training effectiveness. The measurement of objectives acts as a cross-check to measure the accuracy of the ratings produced by the Survey.

■ **What if the program does not have learning objectives?**

Assign *Standard 1* a numerical rating of 0 (does not meet) and indicate "Program does not contain learning objectives" on the reverse side of the Evaluation Form.

■ **When must the evaluation of the program(s) be completed?**

Insert Target Date.

■ **Where do I send the completed Evaluation Forms?**

The completed evaluation forms should be forwarded to (Team Leader's Name) by (insert target date).

■ **Where can the person assigned the evaluation task get assistance?**

If you have questions or need assistance with the survey, contact (Team Leader's Name) at (insert phone number).

■ **What are *Training Standards*?**

A complete explanation is found in the booklet, *Training Standards*, **What They Are and How They Can Be Met**. A copy can be obtained from (Team Leader's Name and phone number).

■ **What information is contained in the booklet, *Training Standards*, What They Are and How They Can Be Met?**

The booklet contains answers to the following questions:

A. What is effective training?

B. Why should managers, developers and trainers work toward meeting the *Total Quality Training Standards*?

C. How does a manager employ the *Total Quality Training Standards*?

D. What is the difference between the terms developer and instructor?

E. How does a manager, developer or instructor determine if his or her program meets the *Standards*?

F. How does a manager get technical expertise and assistance when he discovers that a program falls short on one or more *Standards*?

G. What is the difference between training and desired behavior?

H. Who established the *Total Quality Training Standards* and what was their goal?

Evaluation Instructions

1. Compare your current training practices to those described in the booklet, *Training Standards,* **What They Are and How They Can Be Met.**

2. Score each *Training Standard* as follows:

   - 10   Meets
   - 5   Questionable
   - 0   Does Not Meet or Not Evident
   - N   Not Applicable (Only applies to *Standard 2,* paragraph 3. See page 357.)

3. Record each score on the Evaluation Form (example on pages 370 and 371).

4. Calculate the **Effectiveness Rating.** Add the scores for each *Standard* and divide by 5.

5. Describe how the program meets each *Standard* by explaining the methodology employed (on the reverse side of the form).

6. Attach a copy of the learning objectives to the Evaluation Form.

7. Forward the completed evaluation forms to (insert Team Leader's Name).

8. Determine the program's status in relationship to our organizational goal of training effectiveness based on the Effectiveness Rating.

   > 8.0 Effective: Suggests that your training is enabling employees to bring about the desired results.

   > 5.0 Marginal*:   Suggests an improvement opportunity. Modifications to training methodology or investigations (Needs Analysis—Post Training Evaluation) to link the training to what people do on the job may increase productivity.

   < 4.9 Ineffective*:   Suggests that the program is unlikely to produce a desired behavior that can be observed on the job or that can be linked to results. The manager should question resources (time and money) invested in this program.

   *NOTE: Disregard the Effectiveness Rating when Post Training Evaluation proves that the desired behavior is linked to productivity and/or results.

9. Take action with regard to the *Standards* that are not fully met.

Total Quality Training Standards Evaluation

Program Name _____

Program Length _____ Days, Vendor Fee $_____ Student Materials Cost $_____

Training Vendor Name _____

Decision Maker _____

Developer _____ Development Date _____

Instructor(s) _____

Students' Job Title _____ Average Class Size ____ Students

Evaluated by _____ Evaluation Date _____

Instructions

1. Score and describe how the program meets each *Standard* (on the reverse side)

> 10   Meets
>
> 5   Questionable
>
> 0   Does Not Meet or Not Evident
>
> N   Not Applicable (Only applies to *Standard* 2—Item 3 on page 357)

2. Attach a copy of the learning objectives.

	Total Quality Training Standards	SCORE or RATING
1	Learning objectives which describe the <u>desired behavior(s)</u> to be exhibited during the training program.	
2	Evidence of a performance discrepancy in relation to the <u>desired behavior</u> resulting from a lack of skill or knowledge. (Needs Analysis)	
3	Examples or models of the <u>desired behavior</u> during the training program.	
4	Evaluation of student performance of the <u>desired behavior</u> to determine competence during training.	
5	Evidence that the <u>desired behavior</u> has persisted after training and is linked to results. (Post Training Evaluation)	
	TOTAL (Divide by 5)	
	EFFECTIVENESS RATING	

For further explanation of each *Standard* refer to the booklet, *Training Standards,* **What They Are and How They Can Be Met.**

Justification of Ratings

Describe briefly how the training program meets each *Standard*.

1. Learning objectives which describe the <u>desired behavior(s)</u> to be exhibited during the training program. Attach a copy.

2. Evidence of a performance discrepancy in relation to the <u>desired behavior</u> resulting from a lack of skill or knowledge. (Needs Analysis)

3. Examples or models of the <u>desired behavior</u> during the training program.

4. Evaluation of student performance of the <u>desired behavior</u> to determine competence during training.

5. Evidence that the <u>desired behavior</u> has persisted after training and is linked to results. (Post Training Evaluation)

Example 1: Program Marginally Meets the Standards
Describe briefly how your training program meets each *Standard*.

1. Learning objectives which describe the **<u>desired behavior(s)</u>** to be exhibited during the training program. **Score: 10**

   Training is based on a Module objective that describes a sales performance. All content and activity is directly linked to Unit Objectives. Students receive the objectives prior to training. The final module of the program is an evaluation exercise of the defined sales performance.

2. Evidence of a performance discrepancy in relation to the **<u>desired behavior</u>** resulting from a lack of skill or knowledge. (Needs Analysis). **Score: 10**

   <u>At the beginning of the training</u>, students are asked to describe specifically the problems they wish to solve. <u>During the program</u>, several perform in role play simulations that reveal their present knowledge or skills. A discussion of the problems experienced is conducted. However, no data is collected. The course is conducted by asking the students questions on each subject discussed. Students reveal their understanding prior to the "school solutions" being given. A formal needs analysis was not conducted.

3. Examples or models of the **<u>desired behavior</u>** during the training program. **Score: 10**

   Students view demonstrations of all sales techniques, responses to 4 common objections and a technique for determining the nature of the objection. Students describe the content and structure of each sales behavior.

4. Evaluation of student performance of the **<u>desired behavior</u>** to determine competence during training. **Score: 8**

   Students perform two 5-minute sales transactions which include resistance and rate their performance against criteria. A performance standard is established. All perform at least one time.

5. Evidence that the **<u>desired behavior</u>** has persisted after training and is linked to results. (Post Training Evaluation) **Score: 0**

   A Post Training Evaluation has not been conducted.

EFFECTIVENESS RATING: 7.6 Marginal (38 divided by 5)

*Example 2: Program Does Not Meet the **Standards***
Describe briefly how your training program meets each *Standard*.

1. Learning objectives which describe the <u>desired behavior(s)</u> to be exhibited during the training program. **Score: 0**

   No learning objectives are found in the instructor or student materials.

2. Evidence of a performance discrepancy in relation to the **<u>desired behavior</u>** resulting from a lack of skill or knowledge. (Needs Analysis) **Score: 0**

   There is no documentation which indicates specific discrepancies in the seller's knowledge or skills. Students are not asked to describe the problems they wish to solve at the beginning of the program. They are not asked to discuss their feeling about the product. They are not given the opportunity to discuss or demonstrate how they would sell the product prior to the explanation of the techniques.

3. Examples or models of the <u>desired behavior</u> during the training program. **Score: 5**

   The instructor does not model any sales behavior during the program. A video contains a model of a safety deposit box inquiry with a cross sell of overdraft protection. Students are not shown a complete sales transaction with or without response to resistance.

4. Evaluation of student performance of the <u>desired behavior</u> to determine competence during training. **Score: 3**

   Students role play in groups of three. The instructor does not observe or evaluate their performance. There are no criteria for measuring competence.

5. Evidence that the <u>desired behavior</u> has persisted after training and is linked to results. (Post Training Evaluation) **Score: 0**

   A Post Training Evaluation has not been conducted.

EFFECTIVENESS RATING: 1.6 Ineffective (8 divided by 5)

Appendix C
Student Evaluation of Training
The Key to Monitoring and Maintaining Training Effectiveness

Monitoring and Maintaining Training Effectiveness

The *Student Evaluation of Training* is a survey that measures the student's <u>perception</u> of the value and effectiveness of training. The survey is completed by the student at the end of a program. It is designed to:

- Measure the program in relation to the *Training Standards.*
- Provide meaningful feedback to instructors, developers and management.
- Encourage the use of effective training methodology.
- Monitor the training effectiveness effort.
- Provide an indication of customer (student) satisfaction with the training.

Figure C.1 contains an example survey for **Learning Objectives, The Foundation,** the training program in which you participated in Part 1.

The *Student Evaluation of Training Analysis* provides management with the tabulated survey data. Illustration C.3 shows the tabulated data for the training program on Conducting Interactive Management Meetings referred to in Chap. 11. Notice that the ratings for Practice and Feedback indicate that the program fell short in this critical area. The reader will recall (on page 188) that only 50 percent of the students were given the opportunity to perform. Also notice that the lowered rating is consistent with the Criterion Score of 4 for *Standard 4* (refer to Fig. 11.19).

The *Student Evaluation of Training* can be used to measure **any** training program. This is accomplished by inserting the program's learning objectives in the appropriate sections. All other sections and questions are generic and apply to **all** training programs. (See Fig. C.2.)

The *Student Evaluation of Training* is introduced to the organization after training is conducted on Developing Learning Objectives and Measuring Performance.

Figure C.1. *Student Evaluation of Training*
Learning Objectives, the Foundation

Student: _____

Instructor: _____ Date: _____

Instructions

You can communicate your feelings with regard to the value of the skills and the effectiveness of the training you just completed by answering the questions below. Answer each by inserting the appropriate number from this rating scale:

4	**Yes significantly**
3	**Yes moderately**
2	**Yes slightly**
1	**Questionable**
0	**No**

Skills: How effectively did the training program enable you to?

___ Write a definition of a learning objective.

___ Describe six components of a useful objective.

___ Describe six criteria (standards) that would measure the usefulness of a Core, Terminal, Program or Module Objective.

___ Calculate the Effectiveness Rating of a learning objective with an accuracy of +/− 1.0 against the author's solution.

___ Differentiate between Core, Module and Unit Objectives.

___ Calculate an Effectiveness Rating for a set of learning objectives.

___ Write a learning objective that contains performance, criteria, conditions and time components within 12 minutes.

Comments:

Figure C.1. *(Continued)* ***Student Evaluation of Training***

Value of the Skills Contained Within the Program

___ **Perceived Need:** <u>Were you aware</u> of deficiencies (gaps) in these skills **before** the training program? (In other words, did you feel that you needed training **before** you attended the program?)

___ **Relevance:** Do you feel that these skills are relevant to the problems you must solve or the task(s) you perform?

___ **Practicality:** Do you believe that these skills are practical and usable by you? (The issue is not how often you will use the skills but rather if they can be used in the situations where they are applicable.)

___ **Applicability:** Will you use these skills often enough to justify the time you spent in the training program?

Comments:

Effectiveness of the Training Program

___ **Discovered Need:** <u>Did you become aware</u> of deficiencies (gaps) in these skills **during** the training program?

___ **Explanation:** Do you feel that the explanation of these skills was sufficiently detailed to help you understand where they are applicable and how to use them?

___ **Modeling:** Do you feel that the examples provided or demonstrations **by the instructor** were sufficient to understand the new skills?

___ **Practice Sessions:** Did you feel that you were provided enough opportunity to practice these skills and receive feedback?

___ **Feedback:** Did the feedback that you received from the instructor and students on your performance(s) enable you to identify competencies and discrepancies?

___ **Challenge:** Were you challenged by the program's activities?

___ **Enjoyment:** Did you enjoy the training program?

___ **Competence:** Do you feel you are confident and able to write a learning objective that contains performance, criteria, conditions and time components within 12 minutes which achieves an Effectiveness Rating of 10 (on a 10 scale) against prescribed criteria?

Comments:

Figure C.1. *(Continued)* ***Student Evaluation of Training***

Effectiveness of the Instructor

___ **Expertise:** Do you feel that the instructor knew the subject matter well?

___ **Facilitation Skill:** Did the instructor facilitate the program competently?

Comments:

SUGGESTIONS

How can we increase the relevance, practicality and effectiveness of the:

1. Training Program? Are there deficiencies in **how we trained you?** How can we fix them?

2. Knowledge and Skills Taught by the Program? Are there deficiencies in **what you were trained to do?** How can we fix them?

GENERAL COMMENTS

Figure C.2. Generic Format: *Student Evaluation of Training*

Program Name

Student: _____

Instructor: _____ Date: _____

You can communicate your feelings with regard to the value of the skills and the effectiveness of the training you just completed by answering the following questions. Answer each by inserting the appropriate number from this rating scale:

4	**Yes significantly**
3	**Yes moderately**
2	**Yes slightly**
1	**Questionable**
0	**No**

Skills: How effectively did the training program enable you to?

___ Insert Module or Unit Objective.

___ Insert Module or Unit Objective.

Comments:

Figure C.2. *(Continued)* Generic Format: ***Student Evaluation of Training***

Value of the Skills Contained Within the Program

____ **Perceived Need:** <u>Were you aware</u> of deficiencies (gaps) in these skills **before** the training program? (In other words, did you feel that you needed training **before** you attended the program?)

____ **Relevance:** Do you feel that these skills are relevant to the problems you must solve or the task(s) you perform?

____ **Practicality:** Do you believe that these skills are practical and usable by you? (The issue is not how often you will use the skills but rather if they can be used in the situations where they are applicable.)

____ **Applicability:** Will you use these skills often enough to justify the time you spent in the training program?

Comments:

Effectiveness of the Training Program

____ **Discovered Need:** <u>Did you become aware</u> of deficiencies (gaps) in these skills **during** the training program?

____ **Explanation:** Do you feel that the explanation of these skills was sufficiently detailed to help you understand where they are applicable and how to use them?

____ **Modeling:** Do you feel that the examples provided or demonstrations **by the instructor** were sufficient to understand the new skills?

____ **Practice Sessions:** Did you feel that you were provided enough opportunity to practice these skills and receive feedback?

____ **Feedback:** Did the feedback that you received from the instructor and students on your performance(s) enable you to identify competencies and discrepancies?

____ **Challenge:** Were you challenged by the program's activities?

____ **Enjoyment:** Did you enjoy the training program?

____ **Competence:** Do you feel you are confident and able to *Insert Core or Module Objective*?

Comments:

Figure C.2. *(Continued)* Generic Format: ***Student Evaluation of Training***

Effectiveness of the Instructor

___ **Expertise:** Do you feel that the instructor knew the subject matter well?

___ **Facilitation Skill:** Did the instructor facilitate the program competently?

Comments:

SUGGESTIONS

How can we increase the relevance, practicality and effectiveness of the:

1. Training Program? Are there deficiencies in **how we trained you?** How can we fix them?

2. Knowledge and Skills Taught by the Program? Are there deficiencies in **what you were trained to do?** How can we fix them?

GENERAL COMMENTS

Figure C.3. Student Evaluation of Training Summary

CLASS TITLE: CONDUCTING INITIAL MGMT TEAM MTG   INSTRUCTOR: LES SHAPIRO

EVALUATION CRITERIA	1	2	3	4	5	6	7	8	9	CLASS AVG	SUMMARY
EVALUATION DATE: 07/31/92											
CONFIDENCE IN SKILLS											Group Avg 3.73
Use of Agenda	4	4	4	4	4	4	4	4	4	4.00	
Establishing Need Awareness	3	4	4	4	4	4	4	4	3	3.75	
Explaining Marcom Solution	4	4	4	4	3	4	4	4	3	4.00	
Obtaining Commitments	3	4	4	4	4	4	4	4	3	3.75	
Respond to Resistance	3	3	3	4	4	4	4	4	3	3.25	
Use of the Meeting Guide	3	4	4	4	4	4	4	4	3	3.75	
CONFIDENCE IN SKILLS	3.33	3.83	3.83	4.00	3.83	4.00	4.00	4.00	3.17	3.75	
PERCEIVED NEED**	2	3	4	2	3	2	2	3	4	2.75	
VALUE OF SKILLS											
Relevance	4	4	4	4	4	4	4	4	4	4.00	
Practicality	4	4	4	4	4	4	4	4	4	4.00	
Applicability	4	4	4	4	3	4	4	4	4	4.00	
VALUE OF SKILLS	4.00	4.00	4.00	4.00	3.67	4.00	4.00	4.00	4.00	4.00	
DISCOVERED NEED**	0	4	4	4	4	4	4	4	4	3.00	
PROGRAM EFFECTIVENESS											
Explanation	4	4	4	4	4	4	4	4	4	4.00	
Modeling	4	3	4	4	4	4	4	4	4	3.75	
Practice Sessions	0	3	1	4	4	2	4	NA	0	2.00	
Feedback	0	2	1	4	4	4	4	4	0	1.75	
Challenge	4	3	4	4	4	3	4	4	4	3.75	
Enjoyment	4	3	4	4	4	4	4	4	4	3.75	
Competence	3	4	3	3	3	4	4	4	0	3.11	
PROGRAM EFFECTIVENESS	2.67	3.00	3.00	4.00	4.00	3.50	4.00	3.33	2.67	3.17	
INSTRUCTOR EFFECTIVENESS											
Expertise	4	4	4	4	4	4	4	4	4	4.00	
Facilitation Skill	4	4	4	4	4	4	4	4	4	4.00	
INSTRUCTOR EFFECTIVENESS	4.00	4.00	4.00	4.00	4.00	4.00	4.00	4.00	4.00	4.00	
OVERALL RATING	3.50	3.71	3.71	4.00	3.88	3.88	4.00	3.83	3.46	3.73	

SCORING SYSTEM

4	Yes significantly
3	Yes moderately
2	Yes slightly
1	Questionable
0	No

SATISFACTION SCALE

3.6–4.0	Extremely
2.7–3.5	Moderately
1.8–2.6	Slightly
0.9–1.7	Questionably
0.0–0.8	Not Satisfied

**Ratings are NOT included in overall rating computation.

Appendix D

Expert Criteria to Measure the Total Quality Training Standards

The Training Effectiveness Evaluation System

Contents

A. Introduction

The *Training Effectiveness Evaluation System* (TEES) measures the effectiveness of a training program. **The system predicts the likelihood of producing a desired behavior that impacts results and justifies the training expense.** The system yields:

- An Effectiveness Rating that suggests the likelihood of producing the desired behavior as a result of the training program.
- Guidelines for making corrections to identified discrepancies.
- Guidelines for validation of both the training program and the behavior being trained. This permits the ability to directly link the behavior to results, productivity or sales.

The system consists of *Expert Criteria* for evaluating 28 training program components (i.e., needs analysis, objectives, performance evaluation forms, instructor guide format, etc.), a Scoring System, a Rating Scale and an Evaluation Form. Each component is evaluated by rating its documentation (i.e., administration manual, facilitator's guide, training manual, instructor guide, student notebook or other materials). There are two methods of evaluation:

1. **Estimated Rating:** A rating is determined by physical evidence of the component listed on the appropriate evaluation form. This can be accomplished in approximately 20 minutes.
2. **Precise Rating:** This is determined by rating each component of the program against the *Expert Criteria*. This is accomplished by examination of each component's documentation. It can be accomplished in 2 to 3 hours depending on the scope of the evaluation.

Scope of Evaluation

TEES also permits the evaluator to choose the scope of the evaluation. When all 28 components are evaluated, the training produced:

- Holds the students accountable for the acquisition of a desired behavior. This means that prior to completing the program, they have exhibited the desired behavior at an acceptable level of competence.
- Can be conducted by subject experts who are certified as instructors using materials that have been prepared, tested and validated. The materials contain sufficient detail to hold instructors accountable for conducting the program as it was designed.
- Uses an instructional style that would be categorized as performance oriented with group participation focused toward reaching agreement on the validity and practicality of the knowledge and skills contained within the program.

Eight of the 28 components are <u>essential</u> to any training program and are referred to as <u>mandatory</u>. These eight are applicable to all training programs regardless of methodology or organizational culture. They measure the existence of a problem to be solved, learning objectives and performance evaluation to ensure that the training produces the desired behavior and program validation to prove that the problem was, in fact, solved by the training created. The rating obtained is non-judgmental with regard to instructional style, method or format.

Instructor use of the training materials and effectiveness of certification methods is evaluated by observing instructors teach the course. The evaluator must observe the training with a copy of the training manual.

B. Evaluation Instructions

1. Determine the scope of evaluation:
   A. **All Components.**
   B. *Total Quality Training Standards 1 through 5* only.

2. Select a rating method:
   A. **Estimated:** Rating is determined by physical evidence of the component listed on the appropriate evaluation form.
   B. **Precise:** Each component of the program is rated (by examination of its documentation) against the criteria in this booklet. Rating instructions are provided for each component.

3. Identify the various components of the program. To accomplish this, the evaluator has the program developer or a certified instructor locate the components in the training manual.

4. Score each component or each criterion (if a Precise Rating is desired). Each can receive a score of:

Estimated Rating		*Precise Rating*	
10	Evident	10	Meets Criteria
0	Not Evident	5	Questionable
N	Not Applicable	0	Not Evident
		N	Not applicable

5. Record each rating obtained on the Evaluation Form.

6. Calculate the **Effectiveness Rating** as follows:
   A. **Estimated:** Divide the "Total Evident Components" by the number of "Components Rated."
   B. **Precise:** Divide the "Total Ratings" by the number of "Components Rated."

7. Locate the **Effectiveness Rating** on the **Rating Scale** (page 386).

C. Rating Scale

Effectiveness Rating*		Description
8.0–10.0	<u>Effective</u>	Program produces or is likely to produce the desired behavior.
5.0–7.9	<u>Marginal</u>	Program appears to be missing components that would ensure the student's acquisition of the desired behavior.
1.0–4.9	<u>Ineffective</u>	Unlikely to produce a desired behavior <u>that can be observed on the job</u> or <u>that can be linked to results</u>.
0.0–0.9	<u>Not Evident</u>	No structured training program exists. The likelihood of producing a desired behavior that can be observed on the job falls between uncertain and nil.

* **Disregard the rating when Post Training Evaluation links the desired behavior to productivity and/or results.**

Stage of Development

A. **Development Stage:** Likely to produce the desired behavior. Post Training Evaluation should be undertaken.

B. **Test or Delivery Stage (no Post Training Evaluation):** Produces desired behavior in the classroom and if <u>desired behavior</u> was:

1. **Validated** prior to training program development: Desired behavior is likely to persist. Post Training Evaluation will confirm.
2. <u>**Not**</u> **validated** prior to training program development: Unknown if desired behavior will persist until Post Training Evaluation is undertaken and completed.

D. Training Program Evaluation Form

PROGRAM _____PROGRAM DATE ___/___/___

DEVELOPER _____ EVALUATOR_____ RATING DATE ___/___/___

PROGRAM USER _____RATING METHOD: ESTIMATED ___ PRECISE ___

Total Quality Training Standard	PROGRAM COMPONENT	COMPONENT RATING
Evidence of a performance discrepancy in relation to the <u>desired behavior</u> resulting from a lack of skill or knowledge. (Needs Analysis)	01. Performance Analysis	
	02. Needs Analysis	
	03. Major Assumptions	
Learning objectives which describe the <u>desired behavior(s)</u> to be exhibited during the training program.	04. Program Objectives—Core and Module	
	05. Module Objectives—Module and Unit	
Evaluation of student performance of the <u>desired behavior</u> to determine competence during training.	06. Performance Standard	
	07. Performance Evaluation Form	
	08. Performance Time Allocation	
	09. Role Play Cases	
	10. Performance Evaluation Method	
Examples or models of the <u>desired behavior</u> during the training program.	11. Interactive Behavior Documentation	
	12. Instruct'l Method: Behavior Modeling	
Evidence that the <u>desired behavior</u> has persisted after training and is linked to results. (Post Training Evaluation)	15. Validation of the Desired Behavior	
	16. Post Training Evaluation	
	17. Student Evaluation of Training	
(Optional) Program documentation.	18. Instructional Design—Program	
	19. Instructional Design—Module	
	20. Training Manual	
	21. Program Specifications	
	22. Module Specifications	
	23. Program Description Booklet	
	24. Instructor Certification Plan	
(Optional) Instructor guides structured to produce discussions that reach predetermined conclusions in relation to learning objectives. *Guided Discovery*	13. Instruct'l Methodology (within program)	
	14. Instruct'l Methodology (within modules)	
	25. Inductive Process	
	26. Conclusions	
	27. Preplanned Questions	
	28. Instructor Guide Format	
RATING **SCALE** Effective 8.0–10.0 Marginal 5.0–7.9 Ineffective 1.0–4.9 Not Evident 0.0–0.9 Not Applicable	TOTAL RATINGS OBTAINED	
	EFFECTIVENESS RATING (Divide Total above by the number of Standards Rated)	

Expert Criteria for Measuring Training Programs and Desired Behavior

01—Performance Analysis

A Performance Analysis identifies the disparity between what subjects are doing (results) and what is desired and <u>hypothesizes the cause(s)</u> with regard to behavior, motivation or other obstacles. The Performance Analysis:

A. Identifies the group to be trained.

B Identifies the difference between what the group is <u>expected to be</u> doing and what they are doing.

C. Identifies the skills or knowledge that the group is lacking.

D. Describes factors relevant to motivation:
   1. Possible punishment for correct performance.
   2. Possible reward for incorrect performance or lack of performance.
   3. Possible lack of accountability. (It doesn't matter whether or not they perform correctly.) [Relationship to performance evaluation.]

E. Describes other obstacles to performing productively.

F. Contains conclusions that state the cost and benefit of solving the problem and identifies, if applicable, relevant systemic or policy changes that must occur for the training to be effective.

Determine rating by adding the score for each criterion and dividing by 6.

02—Needs Analysis

A Needs Analysis provides <u>reasonable evidence that confirms or denies the hypothesized cause of a performance problem</u> by getting as close to the transaction in question as possible.

Select the category which best describes the method used to arrive at conclusions. The methods are ranked in descending order of effectiveness.

Rating: The "ranking" is also the maximum "rating" that can be assigned to the category. If more than one method is used, add 50 percent of the rating obtained for the lower ranked method to the score obtained for the higher ranked method.

Ranked Methods of Needs Analysis

10. <u>Unobtrusive observation</u> of the performer with rating against criteria.

9. Observation of the performer with rating against criteria by a trained, <u>non-participating, observer</u>.

8. Observation of performer by a <u>participant in the transaction</u> (such as a shopper) with rating against criteria.

The following describes **effective methodology** for the above categories (deduct for missing components):

A. Data was collected <u>in the field</u> or <u>on the job</u> by observing subjects perform.

B. Deficiencies in performance are identified by critical incident or narrative describing <u>behaviors observed</u>.

C. The performance evaluation system (criteria) is reliable. (Observers can obtain a rating within +/− 1.0 of one another.)

D. Conclusions identify baseline performance (activity related to productivity and results).

E. Population sampled is appropriate to the training investment.

---

8. Observation of the performer in a <u>simulated situation</u> with rating against criteria by a trained observer. Also known as an Assessment Program.

The following describes **effective methodology** (deduct for missing components):

A. Data consists of observed behaviors in a training situation where student performance was measured using criteria.

B. The performance evaluation system is reliable. (Observers can obtain a rating within +/− 1.0 of one another.)

C. Deficiencies in performance are identified by critical incident or narrative describing <u>behaviors observed</u>.

---

7. Study of the target population using a reliable evaluation instrument.

The following describes **effective methodology** (reduce rating for missing components):

A. The evaluation instrument is reliable for measuring the desired behavior and validation data supports this fact.

B. The instrument is completed by subordinates or customers of the performer.

C. The instrument is completed by the performer on him/herself.

D. The instrument is completed by the immediate supervisor(s) on the performer(s).

---

6. Interviews or focus groups which <u>describe specific incidents</u> in addition to perceived needs (deficiencies).

   The following describes **effective methodology** (reduce rating for missing components):
   A. The interviewer(s) used a consistent set of questions for each level of management interviewed.
   B. Interviews with subordinates or customers of the performer regarding needs which describe specific incidents.
   C. Interviews or focus groups conducted with the performer(s) regarding his/her/their own needs which describe specific incidents.
   D. Interviews or focus groups conducted with the immediate supervisor(s) of the performer(s) regarding needs which describe specific incidents.

   ----

5. Evaluations made from observing performance on the job. Maximum effectiveness occurs when there are written descriptions of deficiencies observed.

   ----

4. Survey of, or interviews with the <u>immediate supervisor</u> of the performer where they describe <u>their perception</u> of their subordinate's needs.

   ----

3. Interviews with <u>middle managers</u> where they <u>describe their perception</u> of subordinates' needs (deficiencies) one layer of management removed.

   ----

2. Survey with the <u>immediate supervisor</u> of the performer regarding <u>desire for</u> training for their subordinates in specific areas, such as by ranking importance of job skills or selecting from a menu of subjects for training.

   ----

1. Survey with <u>middle managers</u> regarding <u>desire for</u> training in specific areas for subordinates one layer of management removed.

   ----

0. <u>Assumptions</u> made by <u>Senior Managers</u> based on results data alone <u>unsubstantiated</u> by data collected in the field or interviews with the subjects. In effect, no needs analysis was conducted.

03—Major Assumptions

A. Lists or references conclusions from a **Performance Analysis and/or Need Analysis** relevant to the training to be conducted. Refer to Components 01 and 02. A complete analysis will document:
   1. <u>One or more performance problems</u> that can be solved with the development of training.
   2. <u>Reasonable evidence</u> that confirms or denies the hypothesized cause of a performance problem.
   3. The value of solving the problem.
   4. Any relevant systemic or policy changes that must occur for the training to be effective (if applicable).

   The **Performance Analysis and/or Need Analysis** <u>is</u> attached as an appendix to the program development document.

B. States specific business reasons for program <u>including desired results</u> (that will be or have been validated).

C. Describes the population to be trained including assumptions about experience or prior training that the participant may or may not have.

D. References the desired behavior which is attached as an appendix to the program development document (if applicable).

E. Contains changes to company policy needed to implement the desired behavior.

F. Describes how the <u>training program</u> and <u>desired behavior</u> will be validated (if not previously done).

G. States a limit on the number of students that can participate. (Explains limitations imposed by instructional methodology or performance evaluation considerations.)

H. States the need for assistant instructors including the reason for assistance and the procedure for scheduling the assistants (if applicable).

I. References or contains an Instructor Certification Plan. (Applicable when the program will be facilitated by anyone other than the developer.)

Determine rating by adding the applicable components and dividing by number applicable.

04—Learning Objectives—
Training Program

Core Objective

A. Contains the **job title of the performer** and the words **"be able to"** immediately before the active verb.

B. Contains **the performance** to be exhibited. (Active verb[s] and the object of the verb describe <u>the desired behavior</u>.)

C. Contains a fixed limit of **time** for the performance.

D. Contains **criteria** to measure the desired behavior <u>at program's end</u>.

E. Contains **conditions** which describe the situation in which the performance occurs, limitations imposed or non-implicit resources.

F. Contains **concrete image provoking language** in both the performance (desired behavior) and criteria. Any abstractions are referenced to criteria.

Determine rating by adding the score for each criterion and dividing by 6.

Module Objectives

A. Contains the **job title of the performer** and the words **"be able to"** immediately before the active verb.

B. Contains **the performance** to be exhibited. (Active verb[s] and the object of the verb describe <u>a desired behavior</u>.)

C. Contains a fixed limit of **time** for the performance.

D. Contains **criteria** to measure the desired behavior <u>during the module</u>.

E. Contains **conditions** which describe the situation in which the performance occurs, limitations imposed or non-implicit resources.

F. Contains **concrete image provoking language** in both the performance (desired behavior) and criteria. Any abstractions are referenced to criteria.

Determine a rating for each Module Objective by adding the score for each criterion and dividing by 6. Then total the ratings and divide by the number of Module Objectives rated.
Add the rating for the Core Objective to the Average Rating of the Module Objectives and divide by 2.

05—Learning Objectives—
Training Module

Module Objective

A. Contains the **job title of the performer** and the words **"be able to"** immediately before the active verb.

B. Contains **the performance** to be exhibited. (Active verb[s] and the object of the verb describe <u>a desired behavior</u>.)

C. Contains a fixed limit of **time** for the performance.

D. Contains **criteria** to measure the desired behavior <u>during the module</u>.

E. Contains **conditions** which describe the situation in which the performance occurs, limitations imposed or non-implicit resources.

F. Contains **concrete image provoking language** in both the performance (desired behavior) and criteria. Any abstractions are referenced to criteria.

Determine rating by adding the score for each criterion and dividing by 6.

Unit Objectives

A. Contains the **job title of the performer** and the words **"be able to"** immediately before the active verb. For convenience, a set of Unit Objectives can be prefaced with a statement such as "To accomplish the Module Objective the (performer job title) will be able to:".

B. Contains a **performance** which describes <u>a unit of skill or knowledge</u> to be exhibited.

C. Contains a fixed limit of **time** for the performance. **(If applicable)**

D. Contains **criteria** to measure <u>the unit of skill or knowledge during the module</u>. **(If applicable)**

E. Contains **conditions** which describe the situation in which the performance occurs, limitations imposed or non-implicit resources. **(If applicable)**

F. Contains **concrete image provoking language** in both the performance (desired behavior) and criteria. Any abstractions are referenced to criteria.

Determine a rating for each Unit Objective by adding the score for each criterion and dividing by 6. Then total the ratings and divide by the number of Unit Objectives rated.

Add the rating for the Module Objective to the average rating of the Unit Objectives and divide by 2.

06—Performance Evaluation
and Standard

A. References a Performance Evaluation Form for each performance to be observed. (Refer to Component 07.)

B. States the Performance Standard as a numeric rating.

C. Lists the number of performances to be observed.

D. Identifies performances where all students are evaluated by the instructor.

E. Identifies performances where only a portion of the group is observed or where performance takes place in unsupervised diads or triads.

F. Contains a Performance Evaluation Summary form which allows the sponsor (manager) to evaluate the overall performance of the employee. (Refer to 06A—Performance Evaluation Summary.)

Determine rating by adding the score for each criterion and dividing by 3.

06A—Performance Evaluation Summary

Used to summarize the student's performance during the training program. Important: The summary is only valid if there is a Performance Evaluation Form linked to criteria for each observed performance. (Refer to Performance Evaluation and Standards.)

A. Contains the Overall Ratings for <u>each observed performance</u> which is counted toward the total rating.

B. Contains the ratings for <u>the component modules</u> of the behavior observed. (See example on page 395.)

C. Defines the formula for determination of "Total Rating" (if there is more than 1 performance).

D. Contains Total Rating <u>for the program</u>.

E. Contains a section for narrative comments by the instructor.

Determine rating by adding the score for each criterion and dividing by 5.

Performance Evaluation Summary
PERFORMANCE EVALUATION SUMMARY

Agent _____ Instructor _____ Date ___/___/___

APPR-OACH	FACT FIND	POOL	CASH NEEDS	PROD SEL'T	PROP/ CLOSE	PIVOT DEC'N	RATING	WEIGHT	SCORED RATING	PERFORMANCE DESCRIPTION
☐	■	■	■	■	■	■	☐			Standard Approach without Resistance
☐	☐	☐	■	■	■	■	☐			Approach, Fact Finder and Pool
■	■	☐	☐	■	■	■	☐			Pool and Cash Needs
■	■	■	■	☐	☐	■	☐			Proposal and Close
☐	■	■	■	■	■	■	☐	X2	☐	Approach with Resistance
☐	☐	☐	☐	☐	☐	■	☐	X2	☐	Complete Sales Int. w/Resist.
■	■	■	■	■	■	☐	☐			Pivot Decisions
☐	■	☐	☐	☐	☐	☐	☐	X2	☐	Need Awareness w/Resist.
☐	■	☐	☐	☐	☐	☐	☐	X4	☐	Partial Sales Int. w/Resist.

8-10 Excellent: Knows material (Product and Sales Interview) - conducts interview smoothly and with confidence.

6-7 Good: Basically knows material - interview is occasionally hesitant or lacking smoothness - needs fine tuning

4-5 Fair: Unsure of material - can present it with coaching or prompting - interview is hesitant and lacking smoothness - needs considerable more practice.

1-3 Poor: Knowledge is inadequate - cannot conduct interview - unable to keep the process moving - gives up

☐ **TOTAL SCORE**

☐ **TOTAL RATING** (Divide Total Score by 10)

_____

_____

_____

_____

_____

_____

_____

_____

_____

_____

Instructor

07—Performance Evaluation Form

A. Contains the component structure of the desired behavior to be observed including, if applicable, any repeating behaviors (paraphrase, probing, illustrating, etc.).

B. Contains *Expert Criteria*. A <u>precise description</u> of the desired behavior which can be observed and measured (i.e., detailed, containing several relevant points) for each component or repeating behavior. **(Weight by 5)**

C. Contains a Scoring System: A numeric rating which links to a one or two word description of the performance (i.e., Effective, Marginal or Ineffective or Meets Criteria, Questionable or Not Evident) and, if applicable, <u>criteria</u> to judge achievement on a scale which starts at "0."

D. Contains a Rating Scale: A numeric rating which links to a one or two word descriptive label (i.e., Expert, Effective, Marginal, Ineffective or Not Evident) and an overall description of the performance on a scale which starts at "0."

E. Contains a matrix for recording scores, any interim ratings and the Overall Effectiveness Rating.

F. Contains a formula and instructions for calculating the Overall Rating.

G. Identifies the performer and the person doing the evaluation.

H. Provides space to record specific observations and/or critical incidents.

Determine rating by adding the score for each criterion and dividing by 12.

08—Performance Time Allocation

A. A limit is set for the number of students who can participate in the training program.

B. Time is allocated for **observation (replay) of performance.** Formula: Number of students evaluated times the length of the performance.

C. Time is allocated for **evaluation of performance.** Formula: Number of students evaluated times the length of the evaluation.

D. Time is allocated for **briefing for the exercise.** Formula: Number of briefings times expected length.

E. Time is allocated for **videotaping the performance** (applicable to simultaneous student performances). Formula:
   1. Performance Time: Number of students performing divided by the number of taping facilities times the length of the performance.
   2. Start-up time: 5 minutes (or longer depending on physical layout of taping rooms).
   3. Movement to and from the classroom: 10 minutes (or longer depending on physical layout of taping rooms).

F. Time is allocated for **more than one performance** of the <u>desired behavior</u> described by the Program or Module Objective (a partial performance can count toward meeting this criterion). **(Weight by 5)**

Determine rating by adding the score for each criterion and dividing by 10.

09—Role Play Cases

A. Contains a synopsis which provides the student playing the receiver (prospect, customer, worker, manager) with an overview of the receiver's role.

B. Contains relevant data to be provided to the sender (seller, supervisor, manager) by the receiver in the normal course of the interview and, if applicable, data to be provided if the sender probes.

C. Contains one or more objections, questions or issues to be raised by the receiver to produce the behavior to be observed and, if applicable, non-verbal cues.

D. Contains instructions to the receiver which indicate when the objection(s), question(s), issue(s) or nonverbal cue(s) is/are to be inserted into the transaction.

E. Provides guidelines for the acceptance or rejection of the proposition (if applicable) by the receiver.

F. Contains a narrative that provides the sender (seller, supervisor, manager) with the situation and relevant background information.

Determine rating by adding the score for each criterion and dividing by 5 or 6.

10—Performance Evaluation Method

A. Documentation of methodology can be found in the program development document or within each performance evaluation module.

B. Students have the performance evaluation form, *Expert Criteria* and (applicable) standards in advance of the performance.

C. Students have the Interactive Behavior Documentation for reference during evaluation. (Applicable to sales, leadership and management behaviors.)

D. Case method and/or a script is used to simulate (to the extent possible) situations which occur with prospects, customers or subordinates. See Case Criteria for details.

E. Students playing the salesperson, manager or leader <u>do not see</u> the case and/or script before the performance.

F. Video (or audio) tape is used to matrix all performances which are to be evaluated. (**Weight by 5**)

G. Discussion of performance encourages self-evaluation augmented with peer and instructor feedback. See Performance Methodology—Interactive Behaviors for details.

Determine rating by adding the score for each criterion and dividing by 11.

11—Interactive Behavior Documentation

A. A document (booklet, sales manual, outline, etc.) contains:
   1. The actual or suggested text or outline of the desired behavior including responses to resistance and/or
   2. The desired behavior structured according to objectives and/or
   3. The structure of the desired behavior in the form of an algorithm or flow chart. For example, if the desired behavior is a communication style that can be applied to a specific transaction, such as the technique for "Guiding a Discussion to a Conclusion," the behaviors such as asking questions of the group, waiting for an answer, allowing a volunteer to respond, probing, para-phrase and secondary questions must be listed. (See Fig. 15.2 in Chap. 15).

B. (If actual text) The document is organized to permit reference to each para-graph of text with a number or letter.

C. Related units of the desired behavior are organized into identifiable modules.

D. A matrix (i.e., sales interview kit) controls the flow of the transaction and/or allows data to captured (if applicable).

E. An algorithm or flow chart identifies the decision points within the transaction including those related to likely resistance encountered.

F. The desired behavior with and without resistance can be modeled by an instructor or is on videotape (if applicable).

   Determine rating by adding the score for each criterion and dividing by 3, 4, 5 or 6.

12—Methodology—Behavior Modeling

Documentation within the Instructor Guide indicates that:

A. The behavior is modeled by the instructor or by video.

B. Students identify (by outlining) the structure of the behavior from the model.

C. The behavior is modeled a second time by the instructor.

D. Students rate the instructor's performance using Performance Evaluation Forms containing *Expert Criteria*.

   Determine rating by adding the score for each criterion and dividing by 4.

13—Instructional Methodology (Program)

A. Creation of a non-threatening environment (see 13A).

B. Process begins with the discovery of needs. (Applicable within the first 3 hours from the beginning of the program.)
   1. Problems to be Solved.
   2. Baseline performance.
   3. Observation of the desired behavior.

C. Agreement is reached by instructor and student on the relevance of the objectives.

D. Students are given a problem(s) to be solved before the solution(s) is/are presented throughout the program.

E Instructional sequence within the overall program allows for reinforcement of skills learned.

F. Tasks increase in complexity.

G. Program ends with specific agreement on whether or not the stated objectives were reached <u>in addition to</u> (if applicable) a review of "Problems to be Solved."

H. Critical behaviors (relevant to those stated in the Core or Module Objectives) are evaluated at least 2 times during the program. (**Weight by 3**)

Determine rating by adding the score for each criterion and dividing by 10.

13A—Nonthreatening Environment

A. Initial statement by the instructor contains language that conveys a "fellow traveler" message to the student(s). Example: "We all bring something to the table" and/or "we will all learn something from each other."

B. The initial statement by the instructor is less than 3 minutes.

C. Students introduce themselves and describe their relevant background before the instructor's self introduction. (Relevant to the learning objectives.)

D. Students are asked for their expectations and reservations as part of the introduction.

Determine rating by adding the scores for each criterion and dividing by 4.

14—Instructional Methodology—
Training Module

A. Case method is used to simulate (to the extent possible) real life situations.

B. A student or all students can test their skills to determine deficiencies and areas of competence. This "baseline performance" occurs before the desired behavior is modeled, illustrated and explained.

C. Discussion of "baseline performance" identifies problems experienced.

D. The behavior is modeled by the instructor or by video or by observation of an expert performer on the job.

E. Students identify (by outlining) the structure of the behavior from the model.

F. The behavior is modeled a second time by the instructor or video.

G. Students rate the instructor's performance using performance evaluation forms and *Expert Criteria.*

H. Students perform the desired behavior <u>as described by the Module Objective</u> and receive evaluation of their performance according to the *Expert Criteria.*

Determine rating by adding the score for each criterion and dividing by 8.

15—Validation of the Desired Behavior

A. Desired behavior, as structured, was observed in actual transactions (i.e., interviews with prospects, customers or employees).

B. The desired behavior was measured with a performance evaluation form linked to criteria.

C. Data lists activity, observations and results achieved.

D. Population sampled is appropriate to the business investment.

Determine rating by adding the score for each criterion and divide by 4.

16—Post Training Evaluation

A. Program was conducted as prescribed. (**Weight by 2**) Documentation:
   1. Development Phase: Narrative and Analysis (see 16A).
   2. Certification Phase: Instructor Performance Evaluation Forms.

B. Time spent on each module is documented by time sheets containing:
   1. Module number or name.
   2. Instructor Guide page number.
   3. Beginning time.
   4. Ending time.
   5. Minutes (for each page).
   6. Cumulative time (for each module).
   7. Comments section.

C. Students' performances were evaluated at or above the defined Performance Standard <u>at the program's end</u>. Documentation: Completed Student Performance Evaluation Forms. (**Weight by 2**)

D. Desired behavior was evaluated <u>on the job</u> (or in the field) at or above the defined Performance Standard. Documentation: Completed Student Performance Evaluation Forms and narrative containing critical incidents. (**Weight by 5**)

Determine rating by adding the score for each criterion and dividing by 10.

16A—Narrative and Analysis

A. Lists each module in the training program.

B. Lists Estimated Time in relationship to Actual Time to conduct each module.

C. Documents all student performance observed in each evaluated exercise.

D. Identifies problems experienced (if any) in any module with:
   1. Sequence of the content.
   2. Performance which is below standard.
   3. Time estimates.
   4. The desired behavior or supporting documents (matrixes, sales aids).
   5. Relevance of the content.

E. Lists solutions in the form of objectives or in such detail as to make corrections possible.

Determine rating by adding the score for each criterion and dividing by 5.

17—Student Evaluation of Training

An evaluation completed by the student at the conclusion of the training to measure the student's perception of the effectiveness of the program. The instrument:

A. Contains a rating system.

B. Enables students to rate their confidence and competence with the skills contained by direct reference to the stated objectives (which are listed on the evaluation instrument).

C. Measures (by rating) the student's perception of <u>the value of the skills</u> in relation to the program's stated objectives:
- **Relevance:** Are the skills applicable to the problems you must solve or tasks you perform?
- **Practicality:** Are the skills usable in situations where they are applicable?
- **Applicability:** Can you use these skills often enough to justify the time you spent in the training program?

D. Measures (by rating) the student's perception of <u>training effectiveness</u> in relation to:
- **Explanation:** Do you feel that the explanation of these skills was sufficiently detailed to help you understand where they are applicable and how to use them?
- **Modeling:** Do you feel that the examples provided or demonstrations **by the instructor** were sufficient to understand the new skills?
- **Practice Sessions:** Did you feel that you were provided enough opportunity to practice these skills and receive feedback?
- **Feedback:** Did the feedback that you received from the instructor and students on your performance(s) enable you to identify competencies and discrepancies?

E. Measures (by rating) the student's perception of <u>instructor effectiveness</u> in relation to:
- **Expertise:** Do you feel that the instructor knew the subject matter well?
- **Facilitation Skill:** Did the instructor facilitate the program competently?

F. Solicits written recommendations related to problems with the <u>training's content</u>.

G. Solicits written recommendations related to problems with the <u>training's methodology</u>.

Determine rating by adding the score for each criterion and dividing by 7.

Expert Criteria for Measuring Organization of Materials and Instructor Guides

18—Training Design—Program

A. The <u>program</u> contains Module Objectives and these Module Objectives can be linked to the modules.

B. A document shows all modules in the program and the time allocated to each on a matrix which allows the program to be viewed on a single document. **(Weight by 3)**

C. A narrative or illustration describes the methodology which will be used to bring about the desired behavior. (Training Process Objectives can also be used.)

D. (If applicable) Homework assignments are listed and cross referenced to the module(s) in which they are reviewed.

Determine rating by adding the score for each criterion and dividing by 5 or 6.

19—Training Design—Module

A. The <u>module</u> contains Unit Objectives which can be linked to the Units of Instruction within the module.

B. Shows all Unit Objectives in the program and the time allocated to each.

C. Training Process Objectives, a narrative or illustration describes the methodology which will be used to bring about the desired behavior.

Determine rating by adding the score for each criterion and dividing by 3.

20—Training Manual

A. Questions, tasks or statements in the manual are not subject to interpretation. For example, the manual exhibits the specific question to be asked as opposed to the instruction "Ask Questions."

B. Instructions relevant to media, time, type of group activity are specific and not subject to interpretation.

C. Documents equipment, materials and other resources (i.e., handouts, reference materials) required to conduct the entire program in relation to their use.

D. Specifically contains: Program Specifications including Major Assumptions, Learning Objectives, Master Training Design and Instructor Certification Plan (see page 405), Performance Evaluation Forms, Instructor Guides, Cases, Resources (i.e., handouts, reference materials).

Determine rating by adding the score for each criterion and dividing by 4.

21—Training Program Specifications

A document which contains the principle components of the training program without the modules or content to bring about the learning. It provides management and instructors with information on the purpose of the training, objectives, design and methods of measuring learner competence. Includes:

A. Major Assumptions. (Refer to COMPONENT 03)

B. Learning Objectives—Training Program (Core and Module Objectives). (Refer to COMPONENT 04)

C. Performance Standard. (Refer to COMPONENT 06)

D. Performance Evaluation Form. (Refer to COMPONENT 07)

E. Training Design Documentation. (Refer to COMPONENT 18)

F. Documentation of the Desired Behavior. (Refer to COMPONENT 11)

G. Instructor Certification Plan (if applicable). (Refer to COMPONENT 24)

H. (Optional) Contains an Administrative Overview. (See 21A)

Determine rating by adding the score for each criterion and dividing by 6, 7 or 9.

21A—Administrative Overview

A. Identifies the unit within the organization that is utilizing the training.

B. Identifies the product, service or work procedures affected by the program.

C. Identifies the population to be trained.

D. Identifies the program developer and qualified instructors.

E. Identifies program length in terms of number of days.

F. Identifies total time allotted (hours and minutes [Net Teaching Time]) along with time allocated for lunch and breaks.

G. Identifies group size.

H. Identifies hotel, break or lunch arrangements (if applicable).

I. Identifies dimensions of the training facility.

J. Identifies major items of equipment required (i.e., videotape, flip chart, etc.).

Determine rating by adding the score for each criterion and dividing by 10 or the number applicable.

22—Module Specifications

A. Contains a Module Objective.

B. Contains Unit Objectives that are relevant to the Module Objective.

C. Contains time estimates for each Unit Objective.

D. Contains a block time allocation for the module.

E. Contains a narrative that describes how the instruction will be conducted. (Training Process Objectives can also be used.)

F. Lists prerequisite modules or prior training required.

G. Lists resources required (i.e., Equipment, Materials, Handouts, Acetates, Cases, etc.).

Determine rating by adding the score for each criterion and dividing by 7.

23—Program or Module Description Booklet

The following documentation is made available to the student in a booklet or student notebook which is distributed at the beginning or prior to the training event. The document contains:

A. The learning objectives for the program or module.

B. Performance evaluation criteria or the Performance Evaluation Form(s) containing *Expert Criteria.*

C. An overview of the program which identifies the location of performance appraised exercises (i.e., videotaped role play).

D. (If applicable) Homework assignments for each day.

E. An agenda or schedule.

Determine rating by adding the score for each criterion and dividing by 5.

24—Instructor Certification Plan

Applicable when the program will be facilitated by anyone other than the developer.

A. Selection criteria are defined for the Instructor Trainee and Certifying Instructor.

B. A Superior Objective (Core or Module) is defined. [Obtain rating from Category 04]

C. Subordinate Objectives are defined. [Obtain rating from Category 05]

D. A Performance Standard is stated.

E. Performance Evaluation Criteria are defined. [Obtain rating from Category 08]

F. Instructor Trainee is evaluated using an Instructor Performance Evaluation Form. [Obtain rating from Category 09]

G. Certification process (main activities) is defined.

H. Documentation evidences that the program has been tested and student performance is at or above the defined standard (prior to certification).

I. Documentation evidences that the program has been validated (on the job) and subject's (salesperson's, manager's, leader's) performance is at or above the defined standard.

J. Documentation evidences that each Instructor Trainee can model the desired behavior at or above the defined certification standard.

Determine rating by adding the score for each criterion and dividing by 10.

Criteria numbers 25–28 are applicable to training prepared according to the *Guided Discovery* **Method.**

25—Inductive Process

A. **Tasks** presenting <u>problems to be solved</u> or **Questions** are asked before the **Conclusion** (answer or solution) is given.

B. The **Instructor Guide** contains a model solution or answer to each question with any applicable illustrations or models.

Determine rating by adding the score for each criterion and dividing by 2.

26—Conclusions

A. Are relevant to the Unit Objectives for the panel.

B. Contain a title.

C. Broken into one or more "ends" that are at the <u>next</u> lower level of abstraction.

D. Ends are related.

E. Ends contain more than four words.

F. Relevant illustrations, examples, analogies and, where applicable, behavioral models are contained within the NOTEs (on the left hand-side of the Instructor Guide).

Determine rating by adding the score for each criterion and dividing by 5 or 6.

27—Preplanned Questions and Tasks

A. Are relevant to the Conclusion.

B. Open ended starting with **Why, What, How,** When, Where or Who (at least 90 percent of the questions).

C. Contain less than 18 words (at least 90 percent of the questions).

D. Do not contain any of the "Ends" in the Conclusion.

Determine rating by adding the score for each criterion and dividing by 4.

28—Instructor Guide Format

A. The Unit Objective relevant to the Conclusion or Conclusions to be reached appears before the Conclusions, Questions, Tasks, Statements and Notes that accomplish the objective.

B. The time allocated to the Unit Objective is stated.

C. Structure of Instructor Guide contains the questions on the left-hand side and Conclusions on the right.

D. Student performance and instructor demonstrations are noted on the right-hand side of the guide with the words PERFORMANCE and MODEL (if applicable).

E. Only Objectives, Questions, Tasks, Statements and Notes appear on the left-hand side.

F. Notes contain instructions to the instructor relevant to materials, audio visual resources, demonstrations and/or student time required to complete tasks (if applicable).

G. All Tasks are followed by a Note.

Determine rating by adding the score for each criterion and dividing by 7.

Expert Criteria for Measuring Instructor Performance

Scoring System

Score	Description	Description of Performance
4	Expert	Conducts transaction with *finesse and confidence* displaying appropriate behaviors <u>90 percent</u> of the time.
3	Effective	Conducts transaction with *confidence* displaying appropriate behaviors <u>70 percent</u> of the time.
2	Marginal	Conducts transaction *mechanically* and displays appropriate behaviors <u>at least 50 percent of the time</u>.
1	Ineffective	Unable to conduct the transaction or displays appropriate behaviors <u>less than 50 percent of the time</u>.
0	Not Evident	*Unable to conduct the transaction* and <u>fails to display appropriate behaviors</u>.

Effectiveness Rating

Rating	Description
3.6–4.0	Expert
3.0–3.5	Effective
2.0–3.0	Marginal
1.0–1.9	Ineffective
0.0–0.9	Not Evident

Instructor Performance Evaluation Form
Expert Criteria for Conducting Interactive Training

<u>Techniques used during the transaction</u>: Rate frequency and appropriateness of observed behavior.

_____ **Questioning:** Questions (except probes) are posed to the group rather than an individual. Preplanned questions are used to start the discussion of each Conclusion. *(TEES 32 and 35)*

_____ **Probing:** Short questions, non-threatening and relevant to the student's response. *(TEES 34)*

_____ **Paraphrase:** Spontaneous, in the leader's own words and appropriate to the student's response. Confirmation is obtained. *(TEES 33)*

_____ **Use of Flip Chart:** Conclusions, where required, are recorded interactively. Contains the title as stated in the guide and related Ends (points). Writing is concise and legible. *(TEES 36)*

_____ **Modeling:** One or more demonstration of the desired behavior occurs during the module. A discussion of the structure of the behavior follows the model. The model achieves a rating equal to 90 percent of Expert Performance. *(TEES 30)*

_____ **Baseline Performance:** One or more students participate in a role play where they use their current knowledge and skills to solve the problem. A discussion of their performance follows.

_____ **Competence Performance:** All students perform after the model. Evaluation using a Performance Evaluation Form and discussion of the performance occur. *(TEES 31)*

_____ *Total and divide by number of techniques used*   *RATING* _____

<u>Quality of Discussion</u>: Rate the following *(TEES 29)*:

_____ **Involvement:** All students participate.

_____ **Scope:** Student participation begins within 2 to 3 minutes of the start of the training event and is continuous.

_____ **Quality of Response:** Student responses are sentence-paragraph.

_____ **Leadership:** Involvement is brought about and guided by the instructor.

_____ *Total and divide by 4*   *RATING* _____

<u>After the Transaction</u>: Rate percentage of achievement in relation to the criterion. (Example: Time stated 60 minutes. Actual time 30 minutes. Rating 50 percent)

_____ **Use of the Guide:** Preplanned questions are used. All Ends are reached, Panel(s) are conducted according to the prescribed TECHNIQUE, Spontaneous Secondary Questions are used to reach Ends. *(TEES 37)*

_____ **Content:** Conclusion and Ends are related to the stated objective. Ends are related and at the next lower level of abstraction. *(TEES 37)*

_____ **Time:** Completed within the time stated. *(TEES 37)*

_____ *Total and divide by 3*   RATING _____

                                OVERALL RATING _____

29—Quality of Discussion

A. Active (involving several participants).

B. No single participant dominates the discussion.

C. Discussion was focused to the stated Conclusion.

30—Instructor's Models

Rating is obtained using the **Performance Evaluation Form** used to measure student competence with the desired behavior. The Performance Standard is a rating equal to 90 percent of the highest level of competence.

31—Performance Evaluation Technique

A. Performance is replayed in module segments. **(Weight by 5)**

B. Performance is evaluated by the performing student, peers and the instructor using the **Performance Evaluation Form and Criteria.**

C. Instructor permits student performing to evaluate herself using the **Performance Evaluation Form.**

D. Encourages the performing student to justify rating by identification of his errors.

E. Obtains ratings and evaluations from peers.

F. Discloses instructor rating and justifies rational.

G. Instructor model(s) the desired behavior or segment of behavior when student performance is 6 or below.

H. The *Expert Criteria* are used to substantiate ratings.

I. (Certification Standard) At least 70 percent of the errors observed by the Certifying Instructor were identified and reviewed by the Instructor Trainee.

J. (Certification Standard) Ratings of the Certifying Instructor and Instructor Trainee are +/− 10 percent of each other.

Components 32–37 are applicable to training conducted according to the *Guided Discovery* Method.

32—Questioning Technique

NOTE: Questions, in this context, also include TASKS

A. Preplanned Questions are <u>asked</u> as written or are relevant to the Conclusion.

B. Questions are posed to the entire group.

C. Instructor waited for answers to the questions.

D. Volunteers were asked for answers.

33—Paraphrase

The following describes Expert and Effective (Score: 3 or 4 points):

- Paraphrase was used to demonstrate active listening.
- Student's response was restated in the instructor's own words and is substantially accurate (in relation to student's response).
- When used to reinforce, the student's response was substantially correct and complete in relationship to the prescribed Conclusion.
- Instructor obtained acknowledgment.

The following describes Marginal (Score: 2 points):

- Paraphrase was used to reinforce a response which is substantially incorrect or incomplete (in relationship to the prescribed Conclusion) without prior probing to determine rationale.
- Paraphrase is used less than 50 percent of the time or when the response is substantially correct and complete in relationship to the prescribed Conclusion.
- Paraphrase is mechanical (contains the exact words of the student).
- Failure to obtain acknowledgment.

The following describes Ineffective (Score: 0 or 1 point):

- No evidence of paraphrase.
- Not listening.
- Waiting for the exact words in the prescribed Conclusion.
- Paraphrase does not relate to the student's response.
- Keeps class guessing for the answer ("right words").
- Fails to reinforce a student's response which was substantially correct and complete in relationship to the prescribed Conclusion.

34—Probing

A. Was used to discover rationale when the student's response was either correct, substantially incorrect or incomplete or when the student did not respond to the question.

B. Evidenced by a short question (Why do you say that? Could you explain how you arrived at that?).

C. Directed to the respondent.

35—Spontaneous Secondary Questions

A. Used when the students' response(s) are/were substantially incorrect or incomplete after probing to determine rationale.

B. Question is relevant to the Conclusion or End to be reached.

C. Directed to the group using the "Questioning Technique." Refer to page 412.

D. Presents the prescribed Conclusion in the Guide after 2 attempts.

36—Matrix

Items "A–E" refer to use of the flip chart.

A. Contains the title as stated in the Guide.

B. Each frame contains one or more related points (Ends) that relate to the title.

C. Entries are concise and legible.

D. Produced prescribed illustration.

E. Flip chart used to promote discussion.

F. (Audio tape recorder) Placement is off to the side and between the instructor and student with the microphone pointed toward the transaction.

37—Overall Use of the Guide

A. Preplanned questions (Tasks) are asked as written.

B. Instructor Notes are complied with.

C. Conclusions, including each End, are reached.

D. Actual time is within +/− 15 percent of the stated time allocation.

Figure D.1. Evaluation Form for a Set of Learning Objectives—Training Program

PROGRAM _____ DEVELOPER _____ DATE _____

Core Objective

A. Contains the performer job title and the words "be able to" before the active verb.

B. Contains a performance which describes the desired behavior to be exhibited.

C. Contains a fixed time limit for the performance.

D. Contains criteria to measure the desired behavior at program's end.

E. Contains conditions which describe situation, limitations or non-implicit resources.

F. Contains concrete language and any abstractions are referenced to criteria.

Total Score

Rating—(Divide Total by 6)

Module Objectives

	1	2	3	4	5	6
A						
B						
C						
D						
E						
F						

Average Group Rating

A. Contains the performer job title and the words "be able to" before the active verb.

B. Contains a performance which describes a desired behavior to be exhibited.

C. Contains a fixed time limit for the performance.

D. Contains criteria to measure the desired behavior during the program.

E. Contains conditions which describe situation, limitations or non-implicit resources.

F. Contains concrete language and any abstractions are referenced to criteria.

Total Score

Rating—(Divide Total by 6) Group Rating—(Divide Total by # of objectives rated)

Total of Ratings (Core plus the Average Group Rating of the Module Objectives)
EFFECTIVENESS RATING (Total divided by 2)

Effectiveness Rating

8.0 to 10	Effective
5.0 to 7.9	Marginal
1.0 to 4.9	Ineffective
0.0 to 0.9	Not Evident

Criterion Scoring

10	Meets Criterion
05	Questionable
00	Does Not Meet or Not Evident

Figure D.2. Evaluation Form for a Set of Learning Objectives—Training Module

PROGRAM _____   DEVELOPER _____   DATE _____

Module Objective

A. Contains the performer job title and the words "be able to" before the active verb.
B. Contains a performance which describes the desired behavior to be exhibited.
C. Contains a fixed time limit for the performance.
D. Contains criteria to measure the desired behavior at program's or module's end.
E. Contains conditions which describe situation, limitations or non-implicit resources.
F. Contains concrete language and any abstractions are referenced to criteria.

Total Score

Rating—(Divide Total by 6)

Unit Objectives

A. Contains the performer job title and the words "be able to" before the active verb.
B. Contains a performance which describes a unit of knowledge or skill to be exhibited.
C. Contains a fixed time limit for the performance.*
D. Contains criteria to measure the unit of knowledge or skill during the module.*
E. Contains conditions which describe situation, limitations or non-implicit resources.*
F. Contains concrete language and any abstractions are referenced to criteria.

Total Score

Rating—(Divide Total by 6) Group Rating—(Divide Total by # of objectives rated)

Total of Ratings (Module plus the Average Group Rating of the Unit Objectives)

EFFECTIVENESS RATING (Total divided by 2)

	1	2	3	4	5	6	Average Group Rating

Effectiveness Rating

8.0 to 10	Effective
5.0 to 7.9	Marginal
1.0 to 4.9	Ineffective
0.0 to 0.9	Not Evident

Criterion Scoring

10 Meets Criterion
05 Questionable
00 Does Not Meet or Not Evident

*If applicable

Appendix **E**

Interaction by Design

**Conducting Interactive Inductive
Training Sessions**

Prepared for the
**National Society for Performance and Instruction
1995 National Conference**

Desired Performance

OBSERVED OR ASSUMED PERFORMANCE DISCREPANCIES:

- Inability to bring about discussion in relation to preplanned conclusions.
- Instructor expresses desire for group participation at the beginning of the class. However, <u>class introduction</u> is not participatory.
- Instructor believes that student participation is brought about through their questions. Hence the instructor lectures and waits for participation.
- Instructor guide format and material is not structured to facilitate discussion.
- Inability to clarify incorrect and incomplete answers. Instructor records student answers that are not correct. Practice diminishes the value of correct and complete answers.
- Accepting one or two word answers at a high level of abstraction.

ASSUMPTIONS OR DATA RELATED TO PREVIOUS TRAINING
OR EXPERIENCE:

- Participants have been exposed to lecture style instruction throughout their educational and business careers.
- Participants have attempted to bring about meaningful discussion and have experienced various degrees of difficulty.

MODULE OBJECTIVE:

Developers of training will be able to plan an interactive inductive discussion that reaches agreement on a predetermined conclusion within 15 percent of the planned time.

UNIT OBJECTIVES: To accomplish the Module Objective the developers will be able to:

1. Describe the problems experienced when trying to conduct a discussion with a large group in a limited time frame (NSPI Concurrent Session) or with any size group.
2. Describe criteria for measuring the quality and quantity of participation.
3. Describe seven observable behaviors that facilitate a discussion toward a predetermined conclusion.
4. Define a conclusion and describe its structure.
5. Given a conclusion, preplan a question that will bring about the discussion of the conclusion and identify criteria for preplanned questions.
6. Describe the structure of a guide that facilitates a discussion.
7. Describe techniques for beginning training programs that lead to participation.

Resources Required

EQUIPMENT REQUIRED:

- Flip Chart
- Overhead Projector

MATERIALS REQUIRED:

- Masking Tape
- Handout (Modified Instructor Guide—see following note) 100 Copies
- Guide page 428—100 copies
- Vis-à-Vis Overhead Projector Pens—50

ACETATES:

- Guide pages 420–428
- Blank Acetates—50

PREFRAMES:

- Module Objective
- Agenda
- Shapiro's Question Principle
- Definition of a Conclusion
- Features of the Platinum Plus
- Benefits of the Platinum Plus
- Beginning an interactive training session
- (Optional) Rating Scale

Notes:

- Only relevant student answers are recorded on the flip chart.
- All flip charts will be taped to the wall.
- The session handout is a modified version of the instructor guide. It duplicates the actual guide used by the instructor except for page 428 which represents the discussion of guide structure. This page contains space for students to record their answers. The handout provides the student with a permanent reference.
- The handout will be given to the group toward the end of the session.

Technique   **Result**

OBJECTIVE: Describe the module's learning objectives and agenda. [2 minutes]

TELL: How many times have you attended a training session where the instructor stated, at the very beginning, that she wanted your participation or wanted you to ask questions? What percentage of the time did the session turn out to be a lecture? What we learn from this is that facilitating group participation is a challenge. Hopefully, you will discover from this session workable solutions to this problem.

NOTE: Reveal preframed flip charts (session objective and Agenda) and describe the session).

INTERACTION BY DESIGN

You will be able to plan an interactive inductive discussion that reaches agreement on a predetermined conclusion within 15 percent of the planned time.

AGENDA

Min	Subject
15	Problems experienced when trying to conduct a discussion.
10	Criteria for measuring the quality and quantity of participation.
25	Behaviors that facilitate a discussion toward a planned conclusion.
10	Definition and structure of a conclusion.
25	Criteria for effective questions.
10	Structure of the Instructor Guide.
10	Techniques for beginning an interactive training session.

TELL: To gain the maximum benefit, I will try to work within these time frames.

Technique   ## Result

OBJECTIVE: Describe the problems experienced when trying to conduct a discussion with a large group in a limited time frame (NSPI Concurrent Session) or with any size group. [13 minutes]

TASK: Write down the problems you have experienced when trying to conduct a discussion with a large group in a limited time frame (such as at an NSPI Concurrent Session) or, for that matter, with any size group.

NOTE: Record responses on flip chart.

?ASK: **Why are people somewhat reluctant to participate?**

PROBLEMS TO SOLVE (Hypothesis) (13)

- Knowing the right questions to ask.
- Responding to answers that are incorrect or incomplete.
- Loss of control.
- Time limitation.
- **Getting people to participate. Inhibiting factors:**
  - **Fear of failure (not knowing the answer).**
  - **Fear of embarrassment (being ridiculed).**
  - **Resistance to change.**
- Lack of time to build a trust relationship.
- Room set up which is not conducive to participation. (Classroom style restricts eye contact within the group. Student ability to observe fellow students in successful transactions encourages participation.)
- Not knowing people's names. (A simple solution: Name tags or tents.)

Technique   Result

OBJECTIVE: Describe criteria for measuring the quality and quantity of participation. [10 minutes]

?ASK: What criteria can we establish to measure the quality and quantity of student participation?

NOTE: Record responses on flip chart.

CRITERIA FOR MEASURING
PARTICIPATION (10)

- Involves several participants.
- No single participant dominates the discussion.
- Discussions relate to the questions posed.
- Students respond in sentences or paragraphs rather than one or two words.
- Participation is voluntary.

TELL: You can use these criteria to judge the effectiveness of my interaction with you.

Technique   ## Result

OBJECTIVE: Describe seven observable behaviors that facilitate a discussion toward a predetermined conclusion. [25 minutes]

TELL: During the last 25 minutes, I have been using a group of skills that facilitate a discussion toward a predetermined conclusion.

TASK: Write down the techniques that you have observed during the last 25 minutes.

NOTE: Allow 1 minute. Discuss. Record answers on flip chart.

TECHNIQUES THAT FACILITATE DISCUSSION (15)

- Questioning techniques. (Posed to the group rather than an individual. Group asked to write down their answers prior to discussion.)

- Paraphrase. (Used to reinforce the individual and the knowledge or skill under discussion.)

- Recording answers on a flip chart. (Enables the group to utilize information previously given. Encourages note taking.)

- Probing questions. (Used to elicit more data or clarify an answer that is perceived to be incorrect.)

- Preplanned questions. (Explain Question Principle—next page.)

- **Preplanned conclusions. (The instructor has committed herself to an answer that she believes is correct and is willing to test through interaction with a group.)**

- Spontaneous Secondary Questions. (Related to a particular End in the conclusion.)

Technique   ## Result

?ASK: How do you know the right question(s) to ask?

NOTE: Reveal preframed Shapiro's Question Principle.

SHAPIRO'S QUESTION PRINCIPLE (2)

Questions must be preplanned and relevant to the conclusion that you wish your students to reach (and part of the instructor guide).

?ASK: What are the operational concepts contained within this principle?

NOTE: List on flip chart.

OPERATIONAL CONCEPTS (4)

There must be:

- Preplanned questions.

- A conclusion. (An answer which you believe to be correct.)

- An instructor guide.

?ASK: What is the value of the instructor guide?

VALUE OF THE GUIDE (4)

- Enables trainer to organize the content into a flow which leads to discussion.

- Allows the trainer to focus on the discussion at hand. The next and subsequent discussions are preplanned.

NOTE: Explain versatility of the Question Principle.

Delete [**and part of the instructor guide**]. Represents Spontaneous Secondary Questions and interactive process without an instructor guide.

Delete [**your students**]. Represents the questioning process used to gain information related to a desired end.

Technique   ## Result

OBJECTIVE: Define a conclusion and describe its structure. [10 minutes]

TELL: We have identified a conclusion as **the answer to a question that the developer believes is correct and which he is willing to test through interaction with a group.** Now, we are going to look at the definition and structure of a conclusion.

?ASK: Look around the room at the flip chart frames that we have prepared thus far. Each of these represents a conclusion that matches a conclusion in my Instructor Guide. Can you identify a common structure?

NOTE: Refer to flip charts on the wall.

STRUCTURE OF A CONCLUSION (4)

■ Contains a title (the abstraction).

■ Contains one or more related ends.

NOTE: Reveal definition.

DEFINITION OF A CONCLUSION (1)

A unit of desired behavior, skill or knowledge consisting of an abstraction and one or more related ends at the next lower level of abstraction.

?ASK: What is the benefit of a preplanned answer to your questions?

NOTE: List on flip chart.

BENEFIT OF A PREPLANNED CONCLUSION (5)

■ Ability to measure the quality of the student's responses.

■ The answer represents an objective. You know when you've arrived.

■ Student's responses will validate your answer.

■ Student may provide information that causes you to modify your answer (or approach).

■ The structure (a series of ends) is manageable.

Technique	**Result**

OBJECTIVE: Given a conclusion, preplan a question that will bring about the discussion of the conclusion and identify criteria for preplanned questions. [25 minutes]

TELL: We are now going to explore the process of preplanning questions. To accomplish this I will give you a conclusion and you will preplan the question to bring about its discussion. We will use this process to establish criteria for an effective question.

NOTE: Reveal preframed conclusion:

FEATURES OF THE PLATINUM PLUS

- *Bumper to bumper protection.*
- *Pays cost of parts and labor.*
- *Low $25 deductible.*
- *Coverage for up to 60 months.*
- *Unlimited mileage.*
- *Useable nationwide.*
- *$25 rental reimbursement and $50 towing.*
- *Transferable.*

TASK: Write down one question that could be used to bring about discussion of this conclusion.

NOTE: Provide acetate and pen. Allow 1 minute. Discuss as follows:

1. Place student questions on overhead projector.

2. Ask: Is this an effective or ineffective question? Why? Why not?

3. Modify or ask for alternative questions.

4. Write an acceptable question (or model) on a separate flip chart.

MODEL QUESTION (15)

- QUESTION: What are the features of the Platinum Plus?

- TASK QUESTION: Write down the features of the Platinum Plus.

Technique   ## Result

NOTE: Reveal second preframed Conclusion:

REASONS FOR BUYING PLATINUM PLUS

- *Eliminates financial loss for unexpected breakdowns. Savings or budget is protected.*
- *Comprehensive coverage means most breakdowns are covered.*
- *Protects against inflation.*
- *Repairs are expensive (engine $2,700, transmission $2,500).*
- *Increases resale value.*

TASK: Write down one question that could be used to bring about discussion of this conclusion.

NOTE: Provide acetate and pen. Allow 1 minute. Discuss as follows:

1. Place student questions on overhead projector.

2. Ask: Is this an effective or ineffective question? Why? Why not?

3. Modify or ask for alternative questions.

4. Write an acceptable question (or model) on a separate flip chart.

MODEL QUESTION (10)

- QUESTION: Why should a customer buy the Platinum Plus?
- TASK QUESTION: Write down 4 reasons why the customer should buy the Platinum Plus.

NOTE: List criteria on flip chart as points are made or ask: What have you learned about preplanned questions?

CRITERIA FOR PREPLANNED QUESTIONS

- Question is relevant to the conclusion.
- Open ended starting with a what, how, why, where, when or who.
- Contains less than 18 words.
- Does not contain any of the "ends" in the conclusion.

Technique   ## Result

OBJECTIVE: Describe the structure of a guide that facilitates a discussion. [10 minutes]

NOTE: Hand out the instructor guide. STUDENT VERSION.

TELL: You will notice that the guide contains the questions and answers for everything we've discussed thus far. However, this page, which represents the discussion we are going to have on the structure of the guide does not contain the answer to the question.

?ASK: Why is the answer to this question omitted?

NOTE: Discuss.

> **HUMAN NATURE (3)**
>
> - Most people will not answer a question when the answer is stated. (People recognize that the question is gratuitous.)
> - Giving answers tends to inhibit thinking.

?ASK: What criteria can you identify with regard to the guide's structure from the pages representing the skills and knowledge we have discussed?

NOTE: Use overhead projector to identify the components of the structure. Record answers on flip chart.

> **STRUCTURE OF A GUIDE UNIT (7)**
>
> - Contains the learning objective for the unit.
> - Contains one or more Conclusions.
> - Contains at least one preplanned question for each conclusion.
> - States the time frame for each unit (after the objective) and for each conclusion (in parentheses after the Title).
> - Contains instructions to the instructor with regard to procedure and/or media.
> - Is divided into TECHNIQUE and the RESULT (discussion or activity) which is expected to be produced by the technique.

NOTE: Hand out <u>this page</u> of the guide after completing the above discussion.

Technique   **Result**

OBJECTIVE: Describe the structure of a guide that facilitates a discussion. [10 minutes]

NOTE: Hand out the instructor guide. STUDENT VERSION.

TELL: You will notice that the guide contains the questions and answers for everything we've discussed thus far. However, this page, which represents the discussion we are going to have on the structure of the guide does not contain the answer to the question.

?ASK: Why is the answer to the question omitted?

NOTE: Discuss.

_____ (   )

■

■

?ASK: What criteria can you identify with regard to the guide's structure from the pages representing the skills and knowledge we have discussed?

NOTE: Use overhead projector to identify the components of the structure. Record answers on flip chart.

STRUCTURE OF A GUIDE UNIT (   )

■

■

■

■

■

■

Technique   ## Result

OBJECTIVE: **Optional—if time permits:** Describe techniques for beginning training programs that lead to participation. [10 minutes]

TELL: Let's talk about techniques for beginning training
programs that lead to participation. We will discuss
short programs, such as this one at NSPI and longer
programs—one or more day's duration.

?ASK: What technique was used to begin this training session and bring about participation?

NOTE: Refer to framed Objective, Agenda and Problems to
Solve.

SHORT TIME FRAME (1)

1. Display Objectives and Agenda.

2. Discuss problems to be solved.

?ASK: What was the benefit of this technique?

?ASK: Why is this a valid method for both beginning a session and getting group participation?

NOTE: Record answers on flip chart.

BENEFIT (4)

- Immediate participation (within one
minute).

- People will talk about problems (especially when they are relevant).

- The objective and agenda let them see
where the discussion is headed.

- The discussion of problems is a form
of (perceptual) need analysis.

Technique	**Result**

NOTE: Reveal preframed flip chart and briefly explain.

TELL: This is a technique for beginning training that is used
            in many of the sales and management programs that
            I have designed. It's used with groups of 10 to 20.

BEGINNING AN INTERACTIVE
SESSION (2)

1. Opening Statement (1-2 minutes).

2. Participant introductions (background,
   experience, prior training, expectations and reservations).

3. Instructor Introduction.

4. Problems to Solve.

5. Learning Objectives and Agenda.

6. Baseline Performance (a behavioral
   simulation).

?ASK: What are the benefits of this technique for beginning
            a session?

NOTE: Record answers on flip chart.

BENEFIT (3)

- **Active, immediate and relevant participation.**

- Group gets to know one another.

- Instructor learns expectations and
  concerns.

- The discussion of problems is a form
  of (perceptual) need analysis.

- The baseline performance enables the
  instructor and students to determine
  behavioral needs (actual performance
  discrepancies).

Technique   ## Result

OBJECTIVE: **Optional—if time permits:** Evaluate instructor performance in relation to criteria for the quality and quantity of participation. [No time allocated]

TASK: To complete this session, I would like you to use the <u>Criteria for Measuring Participation</u> to evaluate my performance. Use the following scale and derive an overall rating.

To accomplish this, rate each criterion with the rating scale. Then add up the scores and divide by the number of criteria rated.

NOTE: Reveal preframed flip chart.

4   Expert Performance
3   Effective
2   Marginal
1   Ineffective
0   Not evident

NOTE: Allow 30 seconds to record several group ratings on the flip chart.

PARTICIPATION RATING (Hypothesis)

4   Expert.

MODULE END

Appendix **F**

Training Module

Developing Learning Objectives

Developing Learning Objectives

PROGRAM DEVELOPER: Lester T. Shapiro, CFP

NET TEACHING TIME: 800 Minutes.

AVERAGE GROUP SIZE: 10 Students.

SCHEDULE: 2 days from 8:30 a.m. to 5:30 p.m.

Gross Time	540	Minutes
Lunch	60	
Breaks	30	(2×15)
Net Teaching Time (NTT)	450	
Total NTT Available	900	

Desired Performance

STUDENT JOB TITLE: Program Developers

OBSERVED OR ASSUMED PERFORMANCE DISCREPANCIES:

- Unable to write a behaviorally stated learning objective.
- Unaware of the impact of abstractions on the usefulness of objectives.
- Unable to measure effectiveness of training they or others conduct.
- Unable to define criteria to measure the usefulness (effectiveness) of an objective.
- Unaware of the hierarchical structure of objectives.
- Marginal utilization of objectives in the design, delivery and evaluation of training.

ASSUMPTIONS OR DATA RELATED TO PREVIOUS TRAINING
OR EXPERIENCE:

- 90 percent of students have developed or conducted a training program.
- 95 percent will acknowledge that a training program should have an objective.
- 20 percent will be familiar with the work of Robert F. Mager.

MODULE OBJECTIVE:

Write a Learning Objective: Given a performance discrepancy that is caused by a lack of skill or knowledge on a subject that the instructional developer has mastered, the developer will be able to write a learning objective that contains performance, criteria, conditions and time components within 12 minutes which achieves an Effectiveness Rating of 10 (on a 10 scale) against prescribed criteria.

UNIT OBJECTIVES: To accomplish the Module Objective the Developer will be able to:

1. Write a definition of a learning objective and define learning.

2. Describe the use of objectives in the design, delivery and evaluation of training.

3. Describe (by listing) six components of a useful objective.

4. Describe (by listing) six criteria (standards) that would measure the usefulness of a Core, Terminal, Program or Module Objective.

5. Given six criteria, a Rating Scale and a learning objective, calculate the Effectiveness Rating of the learning objective with an accuracy of +/− 1.0 against the instructor's solution.

6. Differentiate between Core, Module and Unit Objectives. (List and specifically differentiate 4 types of objectives that are relevant to structuring a training program.)

7. Calculate an Effectiveness Rating for a set of learning objectives.

CRITERIA TO MEASURE THE PERFORMANCE AS DESCRIBED IN THE MODULE OBJECTIVE(S):

Module Objective

A. Contains the **job title of the performer** and the words **"be able to"** immediately before the active verb.

B. Contains **the performance** to be exhibited. (Active verb[s] and the object of the verb describe <u>a desired behavior</u>.)

C. Contains a fixed limit of **time** for the performance.

D. Contains **criteria** to measure the desired behavior <u>during the module</u>.

E. Contains **conditions** which describe the situation in which the performance occurs, limitations imposed or non-implicit resources.

F. Contains **concrete image provoking language** in both the performance (desired behavior) and criteria. Any abstractions are referenced to criteria.

Determine rating by adding the score for each criterion and dividing by 6.

Unit Objectives

A. Contains the **job title of the performer** and the words **"be able to"** immediately before the active verb. For convenience, a set of Unit Objectives can be prefaced with a statement such as "To accomplish the Module Objective the (performer job title) will be able to:".

B. Contains a **performance** which describes <u>a unit of skill or knowledge</u> to be exhibited.

C. Contains a fixed limit of **time** for the performance **(if applicable)**.

D. Contains **criteria** to measure <u>**the unit of skill or knowledge during the module**</u> **(if applicable)**.

E. Contains **conditions** which describe the situation in which the performance occurs, limitations imposed or non-implicit resources **(if applicable)**.

F. Contains **concrete image provoking language** in both the performance (desired behavior) and criteria. Any abstractions are referenced to criteria.

Determine a rating for each Unit Objective by adding the score for each criterion and dividing by 6. Then total the ratings and divide by the number of Unit Objectives rated.

Add the rating for the Module Objective to the average rating of the Unit Objectives and divide by 2.

Training Method

> (40): **Program Introduction:** Make a personal introduction which is relevant to the module's learning objectives.

■ (30): **Problems to Solve:** Describe the problems experienced in the design, delivery or evaluation of training.

> (20): **Objectives and Agenda:** Reach agreement on the learning objectives and the agenda for the program.

■ (45): **Baseline Performance:** Determine behavioral needs in relationship to the module objective.

> (20): Identify problems with objectives written in the Preclass Assignment.

> (10): Technical Knowledge—Self Test.

1. (49): **Definition:** Write a definition of a learning objective and define learning.

2. (22): **Purpose of Objectives:** Describe the use of objectives in the design, delivery and evaluation of training.

3. (20): **Components of an Objective:** Describe (by listing) six components of a useful objective.

■ (20): **Model without Evaluation:** Given a model Module Objective, describe the structure of the behavior (as listed in the PEF) in terms of its components.

■ (50): **Practice:** Write two learning objectives containing a performer, performance, criteria, conditions and performance time components (for serving a tennis ball with beginning and advanced players).

4. (40): **Evaluate a Learning Objective:** Given six criteria, a Rating Scale and a learning objective, calculate the Effectiveness Rating of the learning objective with an accuracy of $+/- 1.0$ against the writer's solution.

■ (20): **Model with Performance Evaluation:** Given a model, evaluate the behavior using the criteria, rating scale and scoring system listed in the PEF.

5. (15): **Practice—Evaluation of an Objective:** Calculate the Effectiveness Rating for an objective and identify flaws.

■ (60): **Practice—Evaluation of Components:** Given a component of an objective which may or may not meet the criteria, score the component using the Criterion Scoring System with an accuracy of 60 percent correct responses.

■ (65): **Competence Performance #1—Writing:** Given a flawed objective containing two performances, write separate Module Objectives for the suggest wine and serve wine performances.

- (44): **Competence Performance #2—Writing:** Write a learning objective for presenting, opening and serving a bottle of wine.

- (45): **Competence Performance #2—Evaluation:** Given an objective rated 7.0 or above, identify content and style problems in the wording used to describe the desired behavior.

6. (60): **The Hierarchical Structure:** Differentiate between Core, Module and Unit Objectives.

7. (60): **Rating a Set of Objectives:** Calculate an Effectiveness Rating for a set of learning objectives (with an accuracy of +/− 1.0 against the instructor's solution).

- (45): **Competence Performance #3—Writing:** Perform and evaluate performance using the criteria, rating scale and scoring system listed in the PEF.

- (30): **Competence Performance #3—Evaluating a Set of Objectives:** Perform and evaluate performance using the criteria, rating scale and scoring system listed in the PEF.

> (20): **Module Conclusion:** State the learning objectives achieved (or not) and value the program's success in meeting their identified needs.

- (800): Total Time

REVIEW AND REINFORCEMENT:

- Throughout the *Guided Discovery* Program.

PRECLASS ASSIGNMENT:

- Students write two sets of learning objectives (refer to Preclass Assignment in the Notes section):
  A. A set of objectives for a program on conducting sales meetings.
  B. A set of objectives for a sales or management training program which they plan to develop.

HOMEWORK ASSIGNMENT:

- Rewrite the set of learning objectives for Task #1, the course on conducting sales meetings.

PREREQUISITE MODULE(S):

- None.

Resources Required

EQUIPMENT REQUIRED:

- Flip Chart
- Overhead Projector

CASES/EXERCISES REQUIRED:

- Participant Workbook

MATERIALS REQUIRED:

- Resource Manual
- Blank Acetates (2 per student)
- Vis-à-Vis Overhead Projector Pens (1 for each student)
- Paper towels
- Cups filled with water (for cleaning acetates)

HANDOUTS:

- Module Objectives and Agenda
- Components of a Useful Objective
- Criteria for Evaluating the Usefulness of an Objective
- Criteria for Measuring the Usefulness of a Set of Objectives

ACETATES:

- How did you do?
- Program Objectives PEF
- Module Objectives PEF

PREFRAMES (see Note #2):

- Module Objective
- Mager's Learning Objective Principle
- Definition of Behavior
- Definition of Learning
- Model Objective—Tennis Serve
- Criterion Scoring System
- Rating Scale
- Model Objective—Sales Talk
- Flawed Objective—The Wine Server
- Model Objective—Suggesting Wine
- Model Objective—Serving Wine
- Model Objective—Phone-up (Salesperson Centered)
- Model Objective—Phone-up (Customer Centered)
- Formula for Calculating the Effectiveness Rating
- Interactive Training Session
- Problem-Solving Meeting

Notes

1. The **Training Effectiveness Handbook,** by Lester T. Shapiro, CFP is the resource for this Instructor Guide.

2. Preframes are used rather than acetates. The item preframed is discussed, altered (if required) and then hung on the wall for further reference.

3. Preclass Assignment.

Preclass Assignment

These tasks help us assess your program development needs by providing a baseline measurement of your knowledge and skills.

Task #1

You have been asked by a dealer with 3 dealerships to conduct a training program for 12 automobile sales managers that enables them to conduct sales meetings with their salespeople. The dealer observes that they are not effective conducting meetings to solve problems or to improve the sales techniques of their salespeople. They also have difficulty getting people involved in meaningful discussions. Task: Write the learning objectives for this program.

Task #2

Write the learning objectives for a sales, management or customer relations training program which you plan to develop or desire to improve.

Preparation for Class

1. Make a copy of Task #1 and #2 and bring it to class. These will be collected at the start of the session.

2. Place the learning objectives for the sales manager class (Task #1) and the learning objectives for your project (Task #2) on separate flip chart pages.

Technique	**Result**

OBJECTIVE: **Introductions:** Make a personal introduction which is relevant to the module's learning objectives. [40 minutes]

TELL: Today's program deals with development of learning objectives. It is designed for subject experts who have a responsibility to design, deliver and evaluate training for their area of expertise. It is also applicable to people who work with subject experts to develop training.

Each of us in this room brings a rich combination of experience to the table: experience as a trainer and experience as a student. In fact, some of us have formed some pretty strong opinions on training from the success we have had as trainers or the things we liked or did not like when we were in the student role.

We will capitalize on your experience during this program, and through our interaction, learn a great deal from each other.

TASK: So that we all get to know each other a little better, please take a moment to introduce yourself. We would like some insight into your background and experience. In particular, we would like you to focus on your teaching experience and any professional training that you received with regard to conducting training or developing programs. Finally, I'd like to know your expectations and any reservations you might have with regard to this program.

NOTE: Write the items below on a whiteboard. Allow 3 minutes per participant. Participants should be seated while introducing themselves. Instructor introduces self briefly (6 minutes) after participants.

- Background and experience.
- Training and program development experience.
- Professional training on conducting or developing programs.
- Your **expectations** and any **reservations** you have about today's training.

PARTICIPANT INTRODUCTIONS (40)

Technique   ## Result

OBJECTIVE: **Problems to solve:** Describe the problems experienced in the design, delivery or evaluation of training. [30 minutes]

TASK: Write down the problems you experience in the design, delivery or evaluation of training.

NOTE: Allow 5 minutes. Discuss.

PROBLEMS TO SOLVE (Hypothesis) (30)

- Bring about greater understanding, acceptance and competence.

- People resist change. They cling to old habits.

- Resistance to training (related to past experience—students have difficulty determining the value at the start of the session).

- Inability to measure student learning.

- Inability to link the knowledge and skills contained within the program to the students' performance on the job.

- Inability to find time for role play and performance activities.

- Resistance to role play and performance evaluation activities.

- Inability to bring about student participation and involvement at the desired level.

- Difficulty planning instruction.

- Inability to use learning objectives in the design, delivery or evaluation of training.

- Inability to produce training guides that can be used effectively by any person other than the developer.

Technique	**Result**

OBJECTIVE: **Objectives and Agenda:** Reach agreement on the program's learning objectives. [8 minutes]

TELL: This is the objective for the program.

NOTE: Reveal and read the preframed Module Objective.

> DEVELOPING LEARNING OBJECTIVES (3)
>
> Given a performance discrepancy that is caused by a lack of skill or knowledge on a subject that the instructional developer has mastered, the developer will be able to write a learning objective that contains performance, criteria, conditions and time components within 12 minutes which achieves an Effectiveness Rating of 10 (on a 10 scale) against prescribed criteria.

TELL: Let's look at the specific skills you need to achieve this objective.

NOTE: Hand out Module Objectives and Agenda.

NOTE: Have a student read the Unit Objectives and the Agenda.

?ASK: What is your reaction to these objectives and our agenda?

NOTE: Discuss and resolve any dissonance.

> REACTION TO OBJECTIVES (5)
>
> ■ Relevance perceived.
>
> ■ Relevance not perceived.

Technique   ## Result

OBJECTIVE: **Baseline Performance:** Determine behavioral needs in relationship to the module objective. [45 minutes]

NOTE: Refer to preclass assignment.

TELL: You were asked to write two sets of objectives as a preclass assignment. Before we examine the objectives you wrote we ought to talk briefly about the purpose and structure of the preclass assignment.

?ASK: What was the purpose of having you write objectives prior to class?

BASELINE PERFORMANCE (5)

- To assess individual as well as group needs.

- To establish a baseline. It will now be possible to measure whether or not the course affects your skill in writing objectives.

?ASK: Why did we ask you to write two sets of objectives?

STRUCTURE OF THE ASSIGNMENT (5)

- To create a common frame of reference. We can compare and contrast the set of objectives that each of you developed for sales meetings.

- To begin the program development process for a training project that is directly relevant to you.

Technique	**Result**

TELL: Let's examine the objectives you wrote.

TASK: Hang your set of objectives for the course on sales meetings and your program development project on the wall. Then take a moment to compare the objectives you wrote to those of the other participants. Write down your observations.

NOTE: Allow 2 minutes. Read each set of objectives. Discuss.

?ASK: What problems did you observe?

OBSERVATIONS (Hypotheses) [20]

- No hierarchical structure.
- Excessive use of abstractions (reduces clarity of Performance Component).
- Unlikely to contain a Conditions Component.
- Unlikely to contain a Criteria Component.
- Unlikely to contain a Performance Time component.
- No uniformity of structure.

TELL: The preclass assignment enabled us to measure your ability to write useful objectives. This next exercise will enable us to establish a baseline with regard to your knowledge about learning objectives. Turn to the Self Test in your Participant Workbook.

There are 4 sections that test your technical knowledge with regard to use, structure and measurement of objectives. Later in the program we will discuss the answers to each section and calculate your Objective Utilization Rating.

TASK: Complete sections #1 through #4.

NOTE: Allow 15 minutes.

PERFORMANCE (15)

Technique   ## Result

OBJECTIVE: **Definition:** Write a definition of a learning objective and define learning. [49 minutes]

?ASK: What is the definition of a learning objective?

NOTE: This was completed as a task on the Self Test. Discuss. Then reveal preframed flip chart.

MAGER'S PRINCIPLE (2)

- A description of a performance you want the learners to be able to exhibit before you consider them competent. (Mager, 1962, p. 5)

- Describes the RESULT rather than the PROCESS of instruction itself.

?ASK: What are the key words in Mager's Principle?

NOTE: Underline key words. Have group score their self test—Value 16 points.

KEY WORDS (3)

A description of a **performance** you want the learners to be able to **exhibit** before you consider them **competent**.

TELL: Mager says that a learning objective describes the RESULT rather than the PROCESS of instruction itself.

?ASK: What is the result of training?

?ASK: What is the result of behavior?

TRAINING VERSUS BEHAVIOR (5)

- Training produces Desired Behavior (performance).

- Desired Behavior produces Desired Results.

Technique   **Result**

TELL: The words perform and behave are synonyms. Let's examine the concept of behavior more closely.

?ASK: What is behavior?

NOTE: Show preframed definition. Hang on wall.

BEHAVIOR (5)

An action or response to a situation.

NOTE: Explain Webster's definitions of behave and perform:

— Behave: To act, function or react in a particular way. Anything that an organism does involving action and response to stimulation.

— Perform: To carry out an action or pattern of behavior.

?ASK: What produces behavior in a human being?

MOTIVATION FOR BEHAVIOR (5)

■ Knowledge.

■ Need (as in Maslow's Hierarchy).

?ASK: What are human needs?

NOTE: Illustrate and explain Maslow's Hierarchy of Needs.

HUMAN NEEDS (4)

■ Knowledge (K)

■ Self Actualization (S.A.)

■ Self Esteem

■ Acceptance

■ Safety and Security

■ Physiological: Air, food, sleep, shelter and sex

Technique   ## Result

?ASK: Should we refer to objectives as learning objectives or
        instructional (training) objectives? Why?

THE CASE FOR **LEARNING**
OBJECTIVES (5)

- The term learning objective looks at
  the process from the learner's point of
  view.

- Mager's principle is learner centered.

- The words "be able to" suggest a
  learner focus.

- We are interested in the student's
  rather than the instructor's performance.

- Success is measured by the student's
  competence rather than the instructor's presentation or techniques.

TELL: We can also gain insight from the definition of learn-
        ing.

?ASK: What is learning?

NOTE: Reveal preframed flip chart <u>after</u> group has read
        Goldenson (see exercise on the following page). Then
        read Gagne's explanation (also on the following
        page).

LEARNING (See next page)

Learning is an observable change in behavior that persists over a period of time.

NOTE: Goldenson, Robert M. Ph. D. (1970) *The Encyclopedia
        of Human Behavior: Psychology, Psychiatry, and Mental
        Health.* New York, Doubleday & Company, Inc.

Technique   **Result**

TASK: In your Student Manual there is a tab marked "Goldenson." Read pages 686–687 up to the section on Learning Plateau. Highlight or underline all key points that relate to the learning process and specifically the answers to the following questions.

NOTE: Allow 10 minutes. Discuss and list the answers to the questions.

1. How does Goldenson define the learning process?
2. What are the criteria of learning?
3. What does Goldenson say with regard to measurement and evaluation of learning?

LEARNING PROCESS (20)

■ Definition: A process in which new information, habits or abilities are acquired; in general any MODIFICATION OF BEHAVIOR due to contact with the environment.

■ Criteria: The contact must:

1. **Bring about change in the way they think, perceive or respond (Modification of Behavior).**

2. **Be the result of observation, practice, study or other activity.**

3. **Be relatively long lasting.** A fact or skill forgotten right after it has been acquired has not really been learned.

■ Measurement/Evaluation: At the present time the only way we can know that anything has been learned is by **observing a change in performance.**

TELL: The following is Gagne's definition of learning. *Learning is a change in the human disposition or capability that persists over a period of time and is not simply ascribable to processes of growth.* The kind of change called learning exhibits itself as a change in behavior, and the inference of learning is made by comparing what behavior was possible before the individual was placed in the *learning situation* and what behavior was exhibited after such treatment. The change may be, and often is, an increased capability for some kind of performance. It may also be an altered disposition of the sort called *attitude or interest or value.* The change must have more than momentary permanence; it must be capable of being retained over some period of time. Finally, it must be distinguishable from the kind of change that is attributable to growth, such as a change in the height or the development of muscles through exercise. (Gagne, 1965, pp. 2–3)

Technique   ## Result

OBJECTIVE: **Purpose of Objectives:** Describe the use of objectives in the design, delivery and evaluation of training. [22 minutes]

?ASK: What is the purpose of learning objectives?

NOTE: List responses on flip chart. Do not expect the group to list all of the uses.

PURPOSE OF OBJECTIVES (10)

- Describe, with precision, the knowledge and skills that the training will bring about.

- Plan the structure of a training program in terms of time and modules.

- Negotiate with management (or a client) the time, money and personnel required to conduct the program.

- Make decisions with regard to content, resources and training methodology for each module of the program.

- Organize the students' efforts and activities toward accomplishing the desired behavior.

- Measure the learner's <u>acquisition</u> of the desired behavior (and, therefore, the program's effectiveness).

- Measure the learner's <u>perception</u> of the value and effectiveness of the training.

- Construct instructor guides (manuals) that enable certified instructors to conduct the training program in a predefined manner.

Technique	**Result**

NOTE: Refer to "Use of Learning Objectives" in the Participant Workbook.

TASK: The handout contains a list of 10 documentable uses of learning objectives in the design, delivery and evaluation of training. It also contains a scale with 3 points: 10, 5 and 0. Rate your present use of learning objectives using the scale:

    10   Can document my use of objectives for this purpose

     5   Questionable or not documented

     0   Never used objectives in this way

NOTE: Allow 2 minutes. List scores on a matrix. Then discuss.

?ASK: What do you learn from your score?

UTILIZATION SCORE (12)

- Maximum is 100 points.

- Average score is less than 40. This indicates that there is a substantial improvement in training effectiveness that can be realized through the use of objectives.

Technique   ## Result

OBJECTIVE: **Components of an Objective:** Describe (by listing) six components of a useful objective. [20 minutes]

TELL: Let's look at the structure of a learning objective. Mager identified three principle components. Les Shapiro in the **Training Effectiveness Handbook** identifies six principle components.

?ASK: What are the components of a learning objective?

NOTE: List on flip chart. Hand out Components of a Useful Objective. [Relate to Mager's Principle.]

COMPONENTS OF A USEFUL OBJECTIVE (15)

A. **Performer:** The job title of the performer and the words "be able to."

B. **Performance:** The desired behavior. What you want the person to be able to do at the end of a set period of time. The action you want to observe.

C. **Criteria:** The standard or standards by which you will measure the desired behavior.

D. **Conditions:** The situation under which the performance will occur including any resources required or restrictions you will impose.

E. **Performance Time:** The time expressed in hours or minutes for the performance (not the length of the training program or module).

F. **Performance Standard:** A benchmark for competent performance stated as a rating which is derived from a set of specific criteria.

Technique	Result

TELL   Let's apply the component structure to a practical problem. In this case we will look at a simple psychomotor skill, tying a shoe lace. We will disregard the Performance Standard in this example.

NOTE: List the content of each component on a flip chart as it is discussed. See following discussion:

TIE A SHOE LACE

A. **Performer:** The 5-year-old child will be able to:

B. **Performance:** Tie a shoe lace.

C. **Criteria:** with a double bow knot.

D. **Conditions:** Given an untied shoe lace.

E. **Performance Time:** within 10 seconds.

?ASK: What is the desired behavior? What do you want the person to be able to do at the end of a set period of time? The action you want to observe?

PERFORMANCE (.5)

Tie a shoe lace.

?ASK   What is the job title of the performer?

PERFORMER (.5)

The 5-year-old child will be able to.

?ASK: What is the standard(s) by which you could measure the desired behavior?

CRITERIA (2)

- With a double bow knot.
- Containing even bows.
- Able to withstand 2 pounds of pull.

Technique	**Result**

?ASK: What is the situation under which the performance will occur?

?ASK: What, if any, resources are required or are there restrictions that you will impose?

CONDITIONS (1)

- Given an untied shoe.
- While blindfolded.

?ASK: How much time will you allow for the performance?

PERFORMANCE TIME (1)

Within 10 seconds.

Technique   Result

OBJECTIVE: **Model without Evaluation:** Given a model, describe the structure of the behavior (as listed in the PEF) in terms of its components. [20 minutes]

TELL: Let's take a moment and identify the component structure of the Module Objective for Developing Learning Objectives. This represents a complex cognitive behavior.

?ASK: What is the _____ Component?

NOTE: Highlight or underline (using different colors) each component.

COMPONENT STRUCTURE OF AN OBJECTIVE (10)

Title:	**Develop learning objectives**
Performer:	The developer will be able to:
Performance:	**Write a learning objective**
Performance Time:	Within 12 minutes.
Criteria:	*that contains performance, criteria, conditions and time components*
Conditions:	<u>Given a description of a performance problem related to a discrepancy in skill or knowledge on a subject that the instructional developer has mastered</u>.
Performance Std.:	which achieves an Effectiveness Rating of 10 (on a 10 scale) against prescribed criteria

Technique   ## Result

NOTE: Write the Components of a Useful Objective and Mager's Principle on a whiteboard as shown below:

COMPONENT	MAGER'S PRINCIPLE
Performer	A description of performance
Performance	you want the learners to be able to
Performance Time	exhibit before you
Criteria	consider them competent
Conditions	
Performance Standard	

TASK: Match the Component of a Useful Objective to the appropriate word or words in Mager's Principle.

NOTE: Allow 2 minutes. Discuss

SOLUTION TO MATCHING EXERCISE (10)

- **Performer:** The learners to be able to.

- **Performance:** Description of performance.

- **Performance Time:** Exhibit.

- **Criteria:** Competent.

- **Conditions:** Exhibit before you

- **Performance Standard:** consider them competent.

Technique   ## Result

OBJECTIVE: **Practice Exercise:** Write 2 learning objectives containing a performer, performance, criteria, conditions and performance time components (for serving a tennis ball with beginning and advanced players). [50 minutes]

NOTE: Establish that the group has at least a general knowledge of tennis. How many of you have played tennis? Observed tennis?

TASK: You are to teach the serve to a group of 6 students. Your students are beginners who have been taught the forehand and backhand strokes. Write a learning objective for your training module on the tennis serve.

NOTE: Conduct the exercise as follows:

1. Hand out blank acetates and Vis-à-Vis pens.

2. Instruct group to transfer their objective to a blank acetate.

3. Allow 4 minutes.

4. Discuss up to 3 student responses with the following questions to arrive at the Conclusion:

   ■ What is the performance we want to observe before we consider the student competent?

   ■ How will you know they have accomplished it?

5. Use whiteboard or flip chart to illustrate tennis court.

   ■ Illustrate an overview of the tennis court to establish "accuracy."

   ■ Illustrate a side view of a tennis court and draw a "serve with a high trajectory" which would be easy to return versus one with a correct trajectory to illustrate "speed."

6. Reveal preframed model objective. Have group identify each component.

MODEL OBJECTIVE (25)

<u>Given 10 balls on an indoor court</u>, the player will be able to **serve the ball into the opponent's service court** *7 out of 10 times* at a speed of 50 MPH *while exhibiting prescribed form.*

Technique   Result

?ASK: How would you measure speed, accuracy and form?

MEASURING PERFORMANCE (2)

- Speed: Radar gun.
- Accuracy: Observe and count.
- Form: Observer with a check sheet listing form criteria.

?ASK: What would be the components of form?

COMPONENTS OF PRESCRIBED FORM (3)

- Grip
- Stance
- Ball Toss
- Swing
- Follow-through

TELL: If we desired to create the check sheet, we would identify criteria for each component.

?ASK: What resources (equipment) would we want to have available to measure the player's form?

RESOURCES (3)

- Performance Evaluation System, i.e., criteria, scoring system, rating scale: Allows both student and instructor (developer) to measure the success of the training.
- Video: Allows student to view and identify his or her own errors. Kramlinger: "Self Evaluation is primary."

Technique	**Result**

TELL: Now, let's examine the Conditions Component.

?ASK: What are you giving the students to work with? What limitations are you imposing?

?ASK: How can you increase the level of difficulty?

> MODEL OBJECTIVE—CONDITIONS (3)
>
> - Easy: <u>Given 10 balls on an indoor court</u>.
>
> - Difficult: <u>Given 10 balls on an outdoor court with the sun in their eyes and a cross wind of 15 MPH.</u>

TASK: Write a learning objective for advanced "A" players preparing for an outdoor competition.

NOTE: Allow 2 minutes. Discuss.

NOTE: Adjust "beginner" objective (page 456) to demonstrate effect of criteria and conditions on the level of difficulty (**items in bold**).

> MODEL: INCREASED LEVEL OF DIFFICULTY (9)
>
> <u>Given 10 balls **on an outdoor court with the sun in their eyes and a cross wind of 15 MPH,**</u> the players will be able to **serve the ball into the opponent's service court** *8 out of 10 times* at a speed of 100 MPH *while exhibiting prescribed form.*

?ASK: What changes were made to the objective to increase its level of difficulty?

> INCREASING THE LEVEL OF DIFFICULTY (5)
>
> A. Changed the Performance Time: A speed of 100 MPH.
>
> B. Changed the Criteria: Increase accuracy to *8 out of 10.*
>
> C. Changed the Conditions: <u>On an outdoor court with the sun in their eyes and a cross wind of 15 MPH</u>

Technique   ## Result

OBJECTIVE: **Evaluate a Learning Objective:** Given six criteria, a Rating Scale and a learning objective, calculate the Effectiveness Rating of the learning objective with an accuracy of +/− 1.0 against the writer's solution. [40 minutes—Objective is met thru the next 2 units]

TELL: Earlier we asked you to list six criteria (standards) that you would use to measure the usefulness of a learning objective. At this point we will review the answers to that portion of the Self Test. Do not change the original answers in your participant manual. In answering the next question you can use the knowledge that you've acquired during the program.

?ASK: What criteria (standards) can we use to measure the usefulness of a learning objective?

NOTE: List on flip chart. Then hand out Criteria for Evaluating an Objective.

CRITERIA TO MEASURE
USEFULNESS (10)

A. Contains the **job title of the performer** and the words **"be able to"** immediately before the active verb.

B. Contains **the performance** to be exhibited. (Active verb[s] and the object of the verb describe <u>a desired behavior</u>.)

C. Contains a fixed limit of **time** for the performance.

D. Contains **criteria** to measure the desired behavior <u>during the module</u>.

E. Contains **conditions** which describe the situation in which the performance occurs, limitations imposed or non-implicit resources.

F. Contains **concrete image provoking language** in both the performance (desired behavior) and criteria. Any abstractions are referenced to criteria.

Technique   **Result**

TELL: In order to measure an objective with multiple crite-
        ria you must have a scoring system, rating scale and
        a formula for determining the rating. The following
        is a system for evaluating criteria that make up an
        objective. You will find that the system is also useful
        for measuring the usefulness of any other component
        of the training process.

NOTE: Preframe Criterion Scoring System.

        10   Meets the Criterion
         5   Questionable
         0   Does Not Meet or Not Evident

?ASK: What do you notice about the Criterion Scoring
        System?

                                    CRITERION SCORING (10)

                                    ■ It forces a decision.

                                    ■ 10 and 0 enable us to say that the cri-
                                      terion is met or not met.

                                    ■ 0 recognizes that the entire compo-
                                      nent can be missing.

                                    ■ 5 allows for skepticism.

                                    ■ Requires precise (binary) criteria.

                                    ■ A scale which recognizes a true "0"
                                      allows for values that can be added
                                      and multiplied.

Technique   ## Result

NOTE   Refer the group to the Criterion Scoring Exercise in their Participant manual.

TASK: Listed below are five statements each containing the performance **"score a criterion."** Each is to be rated against the first Criterion for Measuring the Usefulness of an Objective.

Criterion: Contains the **job title of the performer** and the words **"be able to"** immediately before the active verb.

Decide if the component of the objective meets, is questionable or does not meet the criterion and award the appropriate score: 10, 5 or 0.

NOTE: Allow 2 minutes. Poll group. Discuss.

SOLUTION—CRITERION SCORING EXERCISE (10)

__10__   1. The developer will be able to **score a criterion.**

__5__   2. The student will be able to **score a criterion.**

__5__   3. The developer will **score a criterion.**

__0__   4. The student will understand how to **score a criterion.**

__0__   5. **Score a criterion.**

Technique   ## Result

TELL: Let's look at the Rating Scale.

NOTE: Reveal preframed Description of Ratings.

8.0 to 10	Effective
5.0 to 7.9	Marginal
1.0 to 4.9	Ineffective
0.0 to 0.9	Not Evident

TELL: The **Effectiveness Rating** is derived by dividing the Total Score by the number of criteria. The Total Score is the sum of the Scores for each Criterion. The rating suggests the usefulness of the component, in this case a learning objective, to bring about the desired effect; a change in the behavior of the performer.

The usefulness of a learning objective can also be expressed algebraically: **A useful learning objective equals the sum of the its components divided by 6.** For example:

NOTE: Illustrate on whiteboard.

0	Performer
10	Performance
10	Performance Time
0	Criteria
0	Conditions
10	Concrete Language
30	Total Score
5	Effectiveness Rating (Derived by dividing the Total Score by 6)

?ASK: What do you notice about the system?

VALUE OF RATING (10)

- The rating indicates that there is a problem (or the absence of one).

- The scoring identifies the precise nature of the problem.

Technique   ## Result

OBJECTIVE: **Model with Performance Evaluation (after explanation):** Given a model, evaluate the behavior using the criteria, rating scale and scoring system listed in the PEF. [20 minutes]

TELL: Let's evaluate an objective together.

NOTE: Reveal preframed model objective (Sales Talk).

The agent will be able to give a sales talk word for word in 6 minutes.

TASK: Calculate the Effectiveness Rating for this objective.

NOTE: Allow 3 minutes. Poll group and matrix rating on whiteboard. Expect some disparity in ratings due to failure to isolate the individual components.

RATINGS—MODEL OBJECTIVE (10)

A. 10 Performer

B. 10 Performance

C. 10 Performance Timer

D. 10 Criteria

E.   0   Conditions

F. 10 Concrete Language

Total: 50 divided by 6 = 8.3 Rating

TELL: The ability to evaluate an objective requires the ability to break any statement identified as an objective into its component parts.

?ASK: What is the _____ component of this objective?

NOTE: Label the components of the model objective.

COMPONENTS—MODEL OBJECTIVE (5)

A. Performer: **The agent will be able to**

B. Performance: **give a sales talk**

C. Performance Time: **6 minutes.**

D. Criteria: **word for word**

E. Conditions: Missing

F. Concrete Language: No abstractions

Technique	**Result**

TELL: Earlier we stated that a benefit of the evaluation system, and specifically Criterion Scoring, enables us to identify a missing component or flawed components. In our objective for the sales talk, the Condition Component is missing.

?ASK: Given the fact that this objective is related to a sales training program, what would be an appropriate Condition Component—The situation under which the performance will occur or any limitations you will impose and/or nonimplicit resources.

POSSIBLE CONDITION
COMPONENTS (2)

- "Given a student acting as a customer who does not object."

- "Without reference to notes."

NOTE: Add Condition to the model objective: "Given a student acting as a customer who does not object."

?ASK: What occurred when we added the Conditions to the objective?

?ASK: What is the benefit of the Conditions Component to the developer, manager, instructor or student?

EFFECT OF THE CONDITIONS
COMPONENT (3)

- Raised the Effectiveness Rating to 10.

- Conditions Component enables all parties to see the problem or action in relation to a situation. In this case a role play where the student playing the customer does not object.

Technique   ## Result

OBJECTIVE: **Practice—Evaluation of an Objective:** Calculate the Effectiveness Rating for an objective and identify flaws. [15 minutes]

NOTE: Have group turn to the Test Your Evaluation Skill exercise in the Participant Workbook and refer to Problem #2.

You will learn how to write high level objectives in three domains: cognitive, psychomotor and affective.

TASK: Using the Criteria for Measuring the Usefulness of an Objective and the Criterion Scoring System (10 - 5 - 0), establish a rating for this objective. Be prepared to justify each criterion score.

NOTE: Allow 4 minutes. Discuss.

RATING THE OBJECTIVE ON OBJECTIVES (15)

A. 0 Performer: "You" is not the job title of the performer and the words "be able to" are missing.

B. 5 Performance: This objective contains the words "learn how to" before the *active verb* "write" and the *object of the verb* "objectives in three domains: cognitive, psychomotor and affective." The words "learn how to" cloud the clarity of the objective. What would a person be doing to demonstrate their competence? Write an objective, I suspect. Then why not say so.

C. 0 Performance Time: None.

D. 0 Criteria: **High level** is abstract.

E. 0 Conditions: None.

F. 0 Concrete Language: **High level** is abstract. The concept of **domains** is related to Bloom's Taxonomy of Educational Objectives. Essentially the author of the objective is saying you will learn how to write all kinds of objectives.

Total: 5 divided by 6 = .8.

Technique   ## Result

OBJECTIVE: **Practice—Evaluation of Components:** Given a component of an objective which may or may not meet the criteria, score the component using the Criterion Scoring System with an accuracy of 60 percent correct responses. [60 minutes if exercises are assigned as homework]

NOTE: The Participant Workbook contains a series of Practice Exercises that enable the group to use criteria and the Criterion Scoring System to evaluate the components of an objective. These include:

1. Performance Component—10 problems. (Exercise 1, page 494)

2. Performance Component—13 problems. (Exercise 2, page 495)

3. Conditions Component—10 problems. (Exercise 3, page 496)

4. Criteria Component—14 problems. (Exercise 4, page 497)

5. Concrete Language—23 problems. (Exercise 5, page 499)

6. Classifying Components. (Exercise 6, page 500)

The exercises can be used in any order to assist students in developing their ability to judge the components of objectives according to criteria. The answers are found in the **Training Effectiveness Handbook**—Appendix I, Solution to Tasks and Practice Exercises. Time required: 60 minutes if exercises are completed as homework.

TASK: Complete exercises ___ through ___.

NOTE: Conduct Practice Exercise as follows:

1. Assign at least eight problems for each component as homework.

2. Discuss using a round robin. Have a student read the problem and offer an answer. Have them justify as appropriate. (6 minutes per exercise.)

3. Have group complete an additional five problems during class (to verify accuracy of judgments).

4. Discuss problems completed.

PERFORMANCE (60 minutes)

Technique   **Result**

OBJECTIVE: **Competence Performance #1—Writing:** Given a flawed objective containing two performances, write separate Module Objectives for the suggest wine and serve wine performances. [65 minutes]

NOTE: Refer to Problem #1 in the Evaluating Objectives Exercise in the Participant Workbook. Also Preframe.

<u>"Given that the types of dinners served and the dining room atmosphere of the 94th Aero Squadron Restaurant are conducive to wine consumption,</u> the servers will be able to suggest specific wines to customers and demonstrate knowledge of wine serving etiquette using the server manual as a guide."

TASK: Using the Criteria for Measuring the Usefulness of an Objective and the Criterion Scoring System (10 - 5 - 0), establish a rating for this objective. Be prepared to justify each criterion score.

NOTE: Allow 5 minutes. Discuss.

RATING THE WINE SERVER
OBJECTIVE (15)

A. 10 Performer: Server will be able to.

B. 5 Performance: <u>Demonstrate knowledge</u> is abstract. How will we measure this? <u>Suggest</u> wines is concrete.

C. 0 Performance Time: None.

D. 5 Criteria: Using the Server's Manual as a Guide is vague criteria. What is in the manual? Will the server be able to refer to the manual? Too many unanswered questions.

E. 0 Conditions: The given (<u>underlined</u> above) appears to be a description of the restaurant not the situation in which the performance occurs, limitations imposed or non-implicit resources.

F. 0 Concrete Language: <u>Specific</u> (used as criteria) and <u>demonstrate knowledge</u> (used as performance) are abstract.

Total: 20 divided by 6 = 3.3.

TELL: The word **given** is often used to preface the Conditions Component of the objective. However, it is not a condition unless it meets the stated criteria.

Technique   **Result**

TELL: There also appears to be two different performances contained in the objective, to <u>Serve Wine</u> and to <u>Suggest Wine</u>.

?ASK: What is the difference between the <u>Serve Wine</u> and <u>Suggest Wine</u> performances?

DIFFERENCES (2)

- <u>Serve Wine</u>: Predominantly a psychomotor skill.

- <u>Suggest Wine</u>: An interactive selling skill.

TASK: Rewrite the SUGGEST WINE portion of the objective with an objective that contains a Performer, Performance, Performance Time, Conditions and Criteria Component.

NOTE: Explain procedure. You will:

1. Write an objective individually. (7 minutes)

2. Work as a team and negotiate a solution. (8 minutes)

3. Put their objective on a flip chart. (see #2)

4. Rate another team's objective. (5 minutes)

NOTE: Allow 20 minutes. Discuss their objectives. Then:

1. Reveal MODEL.

2. Have group rate and classify. (10)

MODEL OBJECTIVE (30)

<u>Given a wine list with 9 selections (3 red, 3 white, 3 pink) varying in price and taste and 2 students acting as customers,</u> the server will be able to **suggest 1 or 2 wines to the ordering patron** *which complement the entree he/she has ordered and his or her stated preference* within 3 minutes.

Technique	**Result**

NOTE: Refer to MODEL Objective. <u>Given a wine list with 9 selections (3 red, 3 white, 3 pink) varying in price and taste and 2 students acting as customers,</u> the server will be able to **suggest 1 or 2 wines to the ordering patron** *which complement the entree he/she has ordered and his or her stated preference* within 3 minutes.

?ASK: How would you describe the selling style expressed by this objective? Why?

SELLING STYLE (3)

- **Style:** Customer Centered.
- **Indication of Style:** The words "or her stated preference" suggest that the server will ask a question such as **What kind of wine do you enjoy?** and explain the wines to the customer based on her taste.

NOTE: Show acetate of "flawed" objective Exhibit I:

Given a 50 bottle wine list, the server will be able to suggest a wine which the buyer purchases 8 out of 10 times and which will have an average cost of $15.00.

?ASK: What are the flaws in this objective?

NOTE: Effectiveness Rating is 6.7. (Criteria and Performance Time are scored as zero.)

RESULT VERSUS BEHAVIOR (15)

- The criteria specifies a result which is not measurable in the classroom.
- This is a result objective, not a learning objective.
- No Performance Time.

NOTE: Remind group: *Training produces desired behavior. Desired behavior produces desired results.*

Technique   **Result**

OBJECTIVE: **Competence Performance #2—Writing:** Write a learning objective
for presenting, opening and serving a bottle of wine. [44 minutes]

TASK: Rewrite the SERVE WINE portion of the objective.
Assume that a bottle of wine has been ordered.
Envision the transaction from the point when the
server arrives at the table with a bottle of wine <u>until</u>
he walks away from the table having served wine to
all patrons.

NOTE: Allow 3 minutes. Have students write their objectives on blank acetates. Discuss.

MODEL OBJECTIVE (20)

<u>Given a waiter's corkscrew, an un-
opened bottle of wine and a white towel
and 2 students acting as customers</u>, the
server will be able to **present, open and
serve a bottle of wine** *following the 5-step
procedure (outlined below), without error,
and execute each step with finesse* within 4
minutes.

?ASK: What are the characteristics of the model objective?

CHARACTERISTICS OF MODEL
OBJECTIVE (5)

■ **Performer:** the server will be able to

■ **Performance:** present, open and serve
a bottle of wine.

■ **Performance Time:** within 4 minutes.

■ **Conditions:** <u>Given a waiter's corkscrew, an unopened bottle of wine
and a white towel and 2 students acting as customers.</u>

■ **Criteria:** *following the 5-step procedure
(outlined below), without error, and execute each step with finesse.*

TELL: The Criteria Component should be as precise as possible, yet not be wordy (i.e., contain the linear structure of the desired behavior). Therefore, to clarify the
somewhat abstract term "5-step procedure," list the
steps immediately after the objective.

Technique   ## Result

OBJECTIVE: **Competence Performance #2—Evaluation:** Given an objective rated 7.0 or above, identify content and style problems in the wording used to describe the desired behavior. [45 minutes]

NOTE: Refer to Test Your Evaluation Skill—Advanced Exercise.

Given 12 or less salespeople in a setting that allows for 4 hours of relatively uninterrupted instruction time, the salesperson will participate in three in-class role play phone-ups that will result in a rating of 8.0 or greater on the Evaluation Sheet as scored by fellow salespersons.

TASK: Using the Criteria for Measuring the Usefulness of an Objective and the Criterion Scoring System (10 - 5 - 0), establish a rating for this objective. Be prepared to justify each criterion score.

NOTE: Allow 5 minutes. Discuss.

RATING THE INBOUND PHONE-UP OBJECTIVE (10)

A. 5 Performer: Contains name of performer. Missing "will be able to."

B. 0 Performance: "Participate in three in-class role play phone-ups" is not a description of performance. It is a description of training.

C. 0 Performance Time: None.

D. 0 Criteria: **The statement** "that will result in a rating of 8.0 or greater on the Evaluation Sheet as scored by fellow salespersons" **is not criteria.**

E. 0 Conditions: The given portion of the objective is a description of the training. It does not contain the situation the performer faces, limitation(s) imposed or non-implicit resources.

F. 5 Concrete Language: The word "relatively" is abstract. Although the language is concrete, in the balance of the statement it is not an objective as there is no performance or condition stated.

Total: 10 divided by 6 = 1.7

Technique	**Result**

TELL: A group of people familiar with the transaction in the previous learning objective were asked to rewrite it to correct the apparent flaws.

NOTE: Preframe the following objective on the whiteboard.

Given a student acting as a customer, the salesperson will be able to complete a customer phone inquiry with 2 instances of sales resistance using the prescribed format within 4 to 5 minutes.

TASK: Using the Criteria to Measure the Usefulness of a Learning Objective and the Criterion Scoring System (10 - 5 - 0 rating), establish a rating for this objective.

NOTE: Allow 3 minutes.

RATINGS (10)

A. 10 Performer: Contains the job title of the performer and "will be able to."

B. 10 Performance: "complete a customer phone inquiry."

C. 10 Performance Time: 4 to 5 minutes.

D. 10 Criteria: using the prescribed format.

E. 10 Conditions: Given a student acting as a customer.

F. 10 Concrete Language: No abstractions.

Total Score 60

Effectiveness Rating: 10

Technique   Result

?ASK: What is the problem with the behavior described in this objective (complete a customer phone inquiry using the prescribed format)?

CULTURAL DISCREPANCY (5)

- The behavior, as described, appears to be a linear script that the salesperson is required to complete.

- The objective of the transaction is not described within the learning objective.

- The salesperson is not asked to use him or herself to achieve a goal.

?ASK: What is the problem with a scripted or canned sales behavior?

CANNED PRESENTATIONS (10)

- People tend to abandon them as they are punishing. There is no payoff in the work.

- Does not enable the individual to use his or her own personality.

TELL: The company that trains salespeople to use the scripted responses to customer inquiries:

A. States that the objective of the call is to set up an appointment with the customer. They also want to achieve a percentage of names, telephone numbers and appointments.

B. Experiences that salespeople abandon the script 30 to 60 days after training.

Technique   ## Result

TELL: Here is a model objective for responding to a customer's telephone inquiry.

NOTE: Show preframe or acetate.

MODEL OBJECTIVE (1)

Make an appointment: Given a sales aid and student acting as a prospect or customer who is making an inquiry by phone, the salesperson will be able to *conduct a 5 to 10 minute discussion* and, based on the need identified, reach agreement on the date, time and content of the next transaction and, if applicable, respond to two instances of resistance to an appointment.

TASK: Rate the objective according to the Criteria to Measure the Usefulness of an Objective and identify the components of the objective that represent the desired "customer centered" transaction.

NOTE: Allow 4 minutes. Discuss.

ANALYSIS (9)

- Rating: 10
- Desired Behavior: **Conduct a discussion.**
- Focus of the transaction: **Customer Centered. "Based on the need identified."**
- Objective of the transaction is stated: **Reach agreement on the date, time and content of the next transaction.**

Technique   **Result**

OBJECTIVE: **The Hierarchical Structure:** Differentiate between Core, Module and Unit Objectives. [60 minutes]

TELL: At this point we want to focus on the Hierarchical Structure and the rules for developing a set of objectives. In the Self Test you were asked to differentiate 4 types of objectives that are relevant to structuring a training program. In the handout "Answers to the Self Test" you received the operational definitions for 4 types of objectives: Result, Core, Module and Unit.

?ASK: What are the 4 types of objectives that are relevant to structuring a training program?

NOTE: List on flip chart. Refer to solution.

TYPES OF OBJECTIVES (8)

- Result Objective: The results that the training program will bring about stated in units of sales or production.

- Core Objective: Describes **the desired behavior** to be exhibited **at the program's end** to measure competence that relates to the Result Objective.

- Module Objective: Describes **a desired behavior** to be exhibited **during the program** (within modules of the program, if modules are applicable) that relates to the Core Objective.

- Unit Objective: Describes a **unit of skill or knowledge** to be exhibited **during the module** that relates to the Module's Objective.

Technique   **Result**

?ASK: What is the purpose of the Hierarchical Structure?

NOTE: Refer group to the Module and Unit Objectives. List
       on flip chart.

BENEFIT—HIERARCHICAL
STRUCTURE (7)

- One objective is identified as the
  Superior Objective. This objective will
  contain the desired behavior <u>that will
  be measured</u> to determine learner
  competence.

- All other objectives are considered
  Subordinate. These represent the
  behaviors (or units of knowledge and
  skill) that <u>enable</u> the performer to perform the desired behavior.

- Enables all of the material in a training program to be relevant to the
  achievement of one or more units of a
  business plan.

TELL: The Hierarchical Structure brings order to a poten-
       tially chaotic situation. For example, if all objectives
       were created equal, then each subject covered would
       require some degree of measurement. This is obvi-
       ously unnecessary and if taken literally would
       increase the length of training. Consider, for example,
       the first unit objective: Write a definition of a learning
       objective. What conditions and criteria would be rel-
       evant? We could state "word for word in relation to
       that found in Mager's book." However, what pur-
       pose would having you memorize the definition
       serve? The definition represents a unit of knowledge
       that supports the desired behavior. In other words, a
       means to an end. The Superior Objective represents
       the end. The identification of a Superior Objective
       enables us to say that the objective (the end) was or
       was not achieved.

Technique   **Result**

TELL: Let's look at the idea that the Hierarchical Structure
        enables all of the material in a training program to be
        relevant to the achievement of one or more units of a
        business plan.

NOTE: Explain and illustrate the Hierarchical Structure.

Figure F.1. Hierarchical Structure of a Training Program (10)

Business Plan
- Result Objective
- Core Objective(s)

Training Program
- Core Objective
- Module Objective(s)

Training Module
- Module Objective
- Unit Objective(s)

Training Unit
- Unit Objective
- Related unit(s) of knowledge and skill

Unit of Knowledge and Skill (Panel of the Guide)
- Abstraction, concept or idea (Title)
- Related Ends or points

NOTE: Refer to the framed units of knowledge on the wall.
        Point out the Title (abstraction) and points (Ends).

NOTE: Explain Hayakawa's Ladder of Abstraction.

Technique	**Result**

NOTE: Hand out Criteria to Measure the Usefulness of a Set of Objectives.

TASK: Compare the criteria for Core and Module objectives to that of Unit objectives and identify the differences.

NOTE: Allow 3 minutes. Discuss.

DIFFERENCE: CORE/MODULE vs UNIT (10)

- Performance Time, Criteria and Conditions are optional.

- Desired behavior changes to "unit of knowledge or skill."

- At program's end versus during the module.

?ASK: What is the difference between a Core and a Module Objective?

NOTE: Make reference to the objectives in the Program Description Booklet. Use Play Tennis example if required.

CORE VS. MODULE (10)

- No difference in criteria.

- The Core Objective represents a higher level of skill and a transaction with a broader scope.

NOTE: Example of a Core Objective: **Develop Training:** Plan, organize, conduct, evaluate and modify a training program that uses objectives to bring about a desired behavior. Major Modules would be:

1. Writing an objective.

2. Organizing a guide.

3. Conducting the training.

4. Evaluating student performance.

5. Making modifications.

6. Conducting a needs analysis.

Technique   ## Result

NOTE: Preframe categories on matrix on flip chart. Then list
responses.

?ASK: What are the differences between Core, Module and
Unit objectives as to _____?

HIERARCHICAL DIFFERENCES (15)

	Core	Module	Unit
Scope of performance	Desired behavior	Desired behavior	Unit of Skill or knowledge
Where observed	End of program	End of module	During module
Perspective	Forest	Trees	Branches
Components required	Performer Performance Conditions Criteria Time	Performer Performance Conditions Criteria Time	Performer Performance
Hierarchical relationship	Relevant to the Result Objective	Relevant to the Core Objective	Relevant to the Module Objective
Examples	**Develop a Training Program:** Given 10 hours of preparation and a group of developers acting as students, the developer will be able to plan, organize, conduct, evaluate and modify a training program which uses learning objectives to bring about a desired behavior at a prescribed competence standard within 120 minutes.	**Write a Learning Objective:** Given a performance discrepancy that is caused by a lack of skill or knowledge on a subject that the instructional developer has mastered, the developer (reader) will be able to write a learning objective that contains performance, criteria, conditions and time components within 12 minutes.	Differentiate between Core Module and Unit Objectives.

Technique   ## Result

OBJECTIVE: **Rating a Set of Objectives:** Calculate an Effectiveness Rating for a set of learning objectives (with an accuracy of $+/- 1.0$ against the instructor's solution). [60 minutes]

TELL: Let's talk about measuring a set of learning objectives.

NOTE: Write the formula on a flip chart.

FORMULA FOR CALCULATING THE EFFECTIVENESS RATING

$$\frac{\text{Rating of the Superior Objective} + \text{Average of the Ratings of the Subordinate Objectives}}{2} = \text{Effectiveness Rating}$$

?ASK: What do you learn from this formula?

WEIGHT OF THE SUPERIOR OBJECTIVE (10)

■ The absence of a Superior Objective reduces the Effectiveness Rating to 5.0.

■ The absence of enabling objectives (the plan to accomplish the goal) reduces the Effectiveness Rating by 5.0.

■ The failure to identify a Superior Objective often results in programs that do not attempt to measure learner acquisition of the desired behavior.

Technique   Result

NOTE: Have group locate the evaluation forms for Training Modules and Training Programs.

?ASK: What is the difference between the form to evaluate the objectives for a Training Module from that used to evaluate a Training Program?

EVALUATION FORM DIFFERENCES (5)

- **Program:** Holds the set of objectives to a higher standard. Module Objectives must have Condition, Criteria and Performance Time.

- **Module:** Unit Objectives need only contain a Performer, Performance and Concrete Language.

?ASK: How do you decide which form to use?

CHOOSING THE FORM (5)

- Program length—Several days.

- Nature of behaviors. Focused on one (i.e., <u>Write Objectives</u>) or more (i.e., <u>Write Objectives</u>; <u>Organize Guide</u>; <u>Conduct Training</u>; or <u>Evaluate Performance</u>).

- Developer's description as a program or module.

TELL: Let's use the objectives for this training module as an example.

?ASK: Which form would you use and what is the Effectiveness Rating?

NOTE: Demonstrate rating on an acetate.

RATING—DEVELOPING LEARNING OBJECTIVES (5)

- Form: Training Module.

- Effectiveness Rating: 10

Technique   ## Result

?ASK: What does the Effectiveness Rating mean and what
       does it tell you about the training program?

MEANING OF RATINGS (5)

- Predicts the degree to which behavior
  is likely to change and will be observable on the job.

- Indicates the degree to which the program uses performance and evaluation.

- Suggests focus of program. Programs
  rated below 5.0 usually contain a potpourri of stuff (knowledge). Ratings
  above 8.0 are focused on producing an
  observable and measurable behavior.

NOTE: Have group turn to page 502 of the Participant
       Workbook.

?ASK: Which Evaluation Form would you use for this train-
       ing event? Why?

CHOICE: TRAINING PROGRAM (3)

- 5 days.

- Nature of behaviors. (<u>Conducting a
  Selection Interview</u>; <u>Conducting One
  on One Training</u>; <u>Holding a
  Disciplinary Interview</u>; or <u>Preparing a
  Forecast</u>.)

- Developer states that this is a training
  program.

Technique   ## Result

NOTE: Turn to Page 502 in the Participant Workbook.

TELL: The following are the actual learning objectives from a program conducted with District Managers in the United Kingdom. This set was written by an instructor prior to completing program development training.

TASK: Calculate the Effectiveness Rating for the set of objectives.

NOTE: Conduct exercise as follows:

1. Have all participants calculate the rating for the Core Objective and discuss. (9 minutes)

2. Break group into teams of 2. Assign two Unit Objectives to each team. Have them calculate rating for two objectives. (9 minutes)

3. Poll teams for ratings and resolve differences. (9 minutes)

RATING—DISTRICT MANAGER OBJECTIVES (27)

Core Objective			Module Objectives						
			1	**2**	**3**	**4**	**5**	**6**	
A	5	A	5	5	5	5	5	5	
B	5	B	10	10	5	10	10	10	
C	0	C	0	0	0	0	0	0	
D	0	D	0	0	0	0	5	0	
E	10	E	10	0	0	0	10	0	
F	0	F	0	0	0	10	10	10	
	20		25	15	10	25	40	25	
	3.3	Rating	4.2	2.5	1.7	4.2	6.7	4.2	3.9

Total of Ratings	7.2
EFFECTIVENESS RATING	3.6

Technique	Result

OBJECTIVE: **Competence Performance #3—Writing:** Perform and evaluate performance using the criteria, rating scale and scoring system listed in the PEF. [45 minutes]

TELL: Before we formally measure your ability to write objectives, let's do one more practice problem. Turn to page 504 in your Participant Workbook.

TASK: Complete the Practice Exercise entitled Financial Arrangements.

NOTE: Allow 10 minutes. Have students place their objectives on flip charts. Discuss Effectiveness Rating.

MODEL: Financial Arrangements (15)

<u>Given 10 completed purchase orders, a calculation chart and a pocket calculator,</u> the salesperson will be able to **prepare 10 Retail Installment Contracts** *which achieve 100 percent accuracy in calculations, description of property and contract entries on 9 out of 10 contracts* within 60 minutes.

NOTE: Show preframed model objective.

?ASK: What do you notice about the performance?

THE FINAL EXAM

- The objective describes the exercise that will be used to measure learner competence.

- The completion of 10 contracts, rather than one. A more accurate measurement than the completion of one contract.

- A 60-minute exercise.

Technique   Result

TELL: Let's measure the change in your ability to write objectives.

TASK: Rewrite your set of objectives for the course on sales meetings. You may treat this as a module of training. You must write a Module Objective and at least four (4) Unit Objectives. You may also focus, if you wish, on the training meeting or the problem-solving meeting as separate objectives or you may attempt to combine them.

NOTE: Allow 20 minutes. Evaluate each student privately. Then reveal models and discuss with the group.

MODEL: Interactive Training Session

Given an identified skill or knowledge problem with a sales behavior and a group of students acting as salespeople, the manager will be able to *plan and conduct a 60-minute interactive training session* that brings about a measurable change in performance in relation to the manager's model in at least two salespeople during the meeting.

NOTE: Model of Interactive Problem-Solving Meeting.

MODEL: Problem-Solving Meeting

Given an issue that requires communication with the salesforce and a group of students acting as salespeople, the manager will be able to *plan and conduct a 30-minute interactive meeting* that involves each salesperson and which reaches agreement on an action or plan to address the issue.

Technique   Result

OBJECTIVE: **Competence Performance #3—Evaluating a Set of Objectives:** Perform and evaluate performance using the criteria, rating scale and scoring system listed in the PEF. [30 minutes]

TASK: Evaluate the set of objectives entitled Structuring Training Programs on page 503 as a set of objectives for a Training Program. Rate the Core Objective and the first six Module Objectives.

NOTE: Allow 15 minutes. Evaluate each student privately (as they complete the exercise). Then reveal solution and discuss with the group.

RATING—STRUCTURING TRAINING PROGRAMS (30)

Core Objective			Module Objectives						
			1	2	3	4	5	6	
A	10	A	10	10	10	10	10	10	
B	10	B	10	10	10	10	10	10	
C	0	C	0	0	0	0	0	0	
D	10	D	0	0	10	0	10	10	
E	10	E	10	0	10	0	0	0	
F	50	F	0	10	10	10	10	10	
	20		40	30	50	30	40	40	
	8.3	Rating	6.7	5	8.3	5	6.7	6.7	6.4

Total of Ratings   15

EFFECTIVENESS RATING   7.4

Technique   Result

OBJECTIVE: **Program Conclusion:** State the problems solved (or not) and value the program's success in meeting their identified needs. [20 minutes]

NOTE: Refer to Problems to Solve frame.

TELL: We asked you early in the program to identify the problems you wished to solve with regard to the design, delivery and evaluation of training.

NOTE: Review each item on the Problems to Solve frame.

?ASK: Do you feel that we have begun to address this issue?

NOTE: Discuss.

STUDENTS' NEEDS

- Were fulfilled.

- Were not fulfilled.

TASK: Please complete the **Student Evaluation of Training** form. This allows you to communicate your feelings with regard to the value of the skills and the effectiveness of the training you just completed. You accomplish this by rating the program in four areas:

- Your level of confidence and ability with the **Skills.**

- **Value of the Skills.**

- **Effectiveness of the Training.**

- **My Effectiveness.**

The rating scale is 0 to 4. Zero represents "No," 1 represents "Questionable" and 2 through 4 represent degrees of "Yes"; i.e., "Slightly, Moderately and Significantly." On the last page you can give us suggestions on how the training can be improved. There is also space for general comments.

NOTE: Allow 5 minutes. Collect forms. Verify that the rating scale has been used to rate all questions.

MODULE END

Appendix **G**

Participant Workbook for Developing Learning Objectives

_____

Participant's Name

Technical Knowledge—Self Test

Use the following questions to **test your actual knowledge** with regard to the definition, use, structure and measurement of objectives.

1. *Write a definition of a learning objective.*

2. *List five components of a useful objective.*

   A.

   B.

   C.

   D.

   E.

3. *List and specifically differentiate four types of objectives that are relevant to structuring a training program.*

   A.

   B.

   C.

   D.

4. *List six criteria (standards) that you would use to measure the usefulness of a learning objective.*

   A.

   B.

   C.

   D.

   E.

   F.

Use of Learning Objectives

The following statements describe a particular use of learning objectives. **Rate your ability to use each with this scale.**

> 10   **Can document my use of objectives for this purpose**
> 5   **Questionable or not documented**
> 0   **Never used objectives in this way**

___ Describe, with precision, the knowledge and skills that the training will bring about.

___ Plan the structure of a training program in terms of time and modules.

___ Negotiate with management (or a client) the time, money and personnel required to conduct the program.

___ Measure the learner's need for training.

___ Make decisions with regard to content, resources and training methodology for each module of the program.

___ Organize the students' efforts and activities toward accomplishing the desired behavior.

___ Measure the learner's acquisition of the desired behavior (and, therefore, the program's effectiveness).

___ Measure the learner's perception of the value and effectiveness of the training.

___ Construct instructor guides (manuals) that enable certified instructors to conduct the training program in a predefined manner.

___ Determine the effectiveness and relevance of a vendor's training program.

___ Total. This is your **Utilization Score** (maximum score is 100).

How Did You Do?

Insert your **Utilization Score** and **Knowledge Percentage** in the spaces below. Then calculate your **Objective Utilization Rating**:

> **Utilization Score** _____
>
> **Knowledge Percentage** _____%
>
> **Objective Utilization Rating** _____

Determine your **Objective Utilization Rating** by multiplying your **Utilization Score** by your **Knowledge Percentage**. For example: Your **Utilization Score** was 60 and your **Knowledge Percentage** was 90%. Your **Objective Utilization Rating** is 54. (e.g., $60 \times .90 = 54$)

Here is an interpretation of your **Objective Utilization Rating**:

RATING	EXPLANATION OF RATING
71 to 100	You have specific knowledge of the nature and structure of objectives. *Objectives are the foundation of your training programs* as they are used at every juncture of the program development process. Your programs are totally objective driven.
35 to 70	Your use of objectives in your training is very limited or your technical knowledge of objectives limits their use. Utilization of objectives could result in a substantial improvement in training effectiveness.
Below 34	You have limited technical knowledge of objectives or do not use objectives in your training. *They are not the foundation of your training programs.*

If your **Utilization Score** is high and your **Knowledge Percentage** is low you may want to reread the ten utilization questions. Remember, to score 10 you must be able to <u>document</u> each use.

If your **Knowledge Percentage** is high and your **Utilization Score** is low you are missing the benefits of using objectives. Knowledge without application is of very limited value.

Criterion Scoring Exercise

Listed are five statements each containing the performance **"score a criterion."** Each is to be rated against the first Criterion for Measuring the Usefulness of an Objective:

A. Contains the **job title of the performer** and the words **"be able to"** immediately before the active verb.

Decide if the component of the objective meets, is questionable or does not meet the criterion and award the appropriate score: 10, 5 or 0.

_____ 1. The developer will be able to **score a criterion.**

_____ 2. The student will be able to **score a criterion.**

_____ 3. The developer will **score a criterion.**

_____ 4. The student will understand how to **score a criterion.**

_____ 5. **Score a criterion.**

Test Your Evaluation Skill

Here is an opportunity for you to test your evaluation skill. Calculate the Effectiveness Rating for these objectives. *A suggestion: Identify the various components of the objective (by underlining or circling) before you attempt to score them.*

1. Given that the types of dinners served and the dining room atmosphere of the 94th Aero Squadron Restaurant are conducive to wine consumption, the servers will be able to suggest specific wines to customers and demonstrate knowledge of wine serving etiquette using the server manual as a guide.

2. You will learn how to write high level objectives in three domains: cognitive, psychomotor and affective.

3. As a result of this session, the developer will be able to **classify learning objectives** *according to Bloom's Taxonomy.*

Criterion Scoring System		Effectiveness Rating	
10	Meets the Criterion	8.0 to 10	Effective
5	Questionable	5.0 to 7.9	Marginal
0	Does Not Meet or Not Evident	1.0 to 4.9	Ineffective
		0.0 to 0.9	Not Evident

OBJ #1	OBJ #2	OBJ #3	
____	____	____	Contains the **job title of the performer** and the words **"be able to"** immediately before the active verb.
____	____	____	Contains **the performance** to be exhibited. (Active verb[s] and the object of the verb describe <u>the desired behavior</u>.)
____	____	____	Contains a fixed limit of **time** for the performance.
____	____	____	Contains **criteria** to measure the desired behavior <u>at program's end</u>.
____	____	____	Contains **conditions** which describe the situation in which the performance occurs, limitations imposed or non-implicit resources.
____	____	____	Contains **concrete image provoking language** in both the performance and criteria. Any abstractions are referenced to criteria.
____	____	____	**Total Score**
____	____	____	**Effectiveness Rating (Total Score divided by 6)**

Practice Exercise #1—Performance Component

Let's see if we can help you identify useful Performance Components. Listed below is the criterion for measuring the usefulness of an objective's Performance Component:

> Contains **the performance** to be exhibited. (Active verb[s] and the object of the verb describe <u>the desired behavior</u>.)

To test for a Performance, the statement must contain:

- An active (action) verb and the object of the verb.
- Describe the behavior of the student, not the instructor.
- Be observable during the training event: Can you observe the student performing the desired behavior in the classroom?

The statements below <u>may or may not</u> contain a Performance. Your task is to decide if the statement meets, is questionable or does not meet the above criterion and award the appropriate score: 10, 5 or 0.

A ____ Participants will increase their understanding of organizational change factors.

B ____ Describe the structure of the Performance Component of a learning objective.

C ____ Sell a life insurance policy.

D ____ Appreciate the value of lesson planning with objectives.

E ____ Really understand the components of a learning objective.

F ____ Settle at least 70 percent of all claims in less than 5 days.

G ____ List criteria for measuring evidence of a desired behavior.

H ____ Know how to explain the use of the Criterion Scoring System.

I ____ Use *Guided Discovery* to teach effectively.

J ____ Demonstrate an understanding of the definition of learning.

Practice Exercise #2—Performance Component

Here are some more "objectives" to practice with. Decide if the statement meets the criterion for the Performance Component, is questionable or does not meet the criterion and award the appropriate score: 10, 5 or 0.

Judge each statement on the words shown. Do not assume any prefacing language.

A _____ Analyze a learning objective for words which describe the style of the desired behavior.

B _____ Organize an instructor guide.

C _____ Evaluate the effectiveness of a performance evaluation form.

D _____ Improve interviewing skills.

E _____ Design a performance evaluation form.

F _____ Justify the efficacy of a course of action.

G _____ Increase ability to make selection decisions.

H _____ Provide familiarity with how criterion are obtained.

I _____ Explain the importance of an agenda in a meeting.

J _____ Develop a five-year strategic plan.

K _____ To build skills in detecting errors in written communication quickly.

L _____ Write a business letter.

M _____ Provide participants with a four-hour overview of Arbor Corporation's Quality Assurance Program, policy and procedures.

N _____ To apply principles of management to specific situations.

O _____ To acquaint managers and supervisors with their roles and responsibilities.

P _____ Name the planets in the Milky Way.

Q _____ To ensure that classified documents get appropriate markings.

R _____ Diagnose a malfunction in a copy machine.

S _____ Select a method for analyzing learner needs.

T _____ Conduct a sales meeting.

Practice Exercise #3—Conditions Component

Let's see if we can help you identify a useful Conditions Component. Listed below are five objectives. Each is to be rated against the criterion for measuring the usefulness of an objective's Conditions Component:

> Contains **conditions** which describe the situation in which the performance occurs, limitations imposed or non-implicit resources.

In each case, the objective <u>may or may not</u> contain a useful Condition. All other components will be useful (Performer, Performance, Performance Time and Criteria). Your task is to:

1. <u>Underline</u> the Condition Component or what the author thought was the Condition Component.

2. Decide if the Condition meets, is questionable or does not meet the above criterion and award the appropriate score: 10, 5 or 0.

3. (Optional) Identify (by circling, boxing or highlighting) any evident component of a useful objective.

   A ____   Given a narrative describing an employee's behavior, objectives (Business Plan) and results produced to date, the manager will be able to conduct a performance review.

   B ____   Given that performance of the desired behavior is important to the company and 10 hours of training time, the salesperson will be able to present the features and benefits of the product in relation to the customer's needs.

   C ____   Without references to a price guide, the appraiser will be able to estimate the value of the property plus or minus 15 percent of the expert's valuation within 2 hours.

   D ____   Given five objectives that may or may not contain a useful Condition Component, the reader will be able to identify (by scoring) those that contain a Condition which meets the Condition Criterion.

   E ____   Calculate five lease payments using the Lease Payment Calculation Worksheet and a pocket calculator with 100 percent accuracy in 5 minutes.

Practice Exercise #3 (Continued)—Conditions Component

F ____ Given a case and a student acting as the customer, the service representative will be able to conduct a discussion that reaches agreement on a satisfactory course of action in relation to the problem, the customer's level of frustration and prescribed policy.

G ____ Given five opportunities to practice with feedback prior to the examination, the adjuster will be able to access the computer database that enables him or her to obtain the required information.

H ____ Upon completion of a 50 minute session on affective communication, the workers will be able to recognize in themselves and others the eight different character traits and then modify their behavior or response to the person possessing the trait(s) identified.

I ___ Using handouts and other information provided, the trainer will be able to identify five steps in the design of an evaluation form.

J ____ Given a model of team development, the HRD professional will be able to describe the model's use in facilitating organizational change.

Practice Exercise #4—Criteria Component

Let's see if we can help you identify a useful Criteria Component. Listed below is the criterion for measuring the usefulness of an objective's Criteria Component.

Contains **criteria** to measure the desired behavior <u>at program's end</u>.

To test for a Criterion (one standard) or Criteria (two or more standards), the statement should:

- Contain words that would enable you to judge the competence of the desired behavior. In other words, concrete language. (Abstract words are avoided.)
- Be observable during or at the end of the training event.

In each case, the objective <u>may or may not</u> contain a useful Criterion. All other components shown will be useful (Performer, Performance, Performance Time and Conditions). Your task is to:

1. <u>Circle</u> the Criteria Component or what the author thought was the Criteria Component.

2. Decide if the Criteria Component meets, is questionable or does not meet the above criterion and award the appropriate score: 10, 5 or 0.

3. (Optional) Identify (by circling, boxing or highlighting) any evident component of a useful objective.

A ____ Given 10 documents that require classification, the file clerk will be able to mark each document according to Department of Defense Regulation 60006.

B ____ Design and present effective and interesting training sessions.

C ____ Given a useful learning objective (rated 10), the developer will be able to design a performance evaluation system that contains criteria to measure the structure of the behavior which are not subject to misinterpretation.

D ____ Given a table of acceptable tolerances and unassembled parts of an engine, the mechanic will be able to tighten each with a torque wrench to within +/− 2 lb. within three attempts.

E ____ Conduct an interactive sales meeting that reaches agreement on an action plan to solve an identified problem.

F ____ Select the right training activity to meet your objective.

G ____ Given a letter containing 12 errors, the proofreader will be able to identify correctly each of the errors within 5 minutes.

H ____ Write an acceptable performance plan with measurable criteria.

I ____ Given six learning objectives, the developer will be able to classify the objectives according to Bloom's Taxonomy.

J ____ Given a student acting as a customer, conduct a sales discussion that explains the product in relation to the customer's stated needs.

K ____ Train employees to be better problem solvers and decision makers.

L ____ Use the proper close.

M ____ Select training methods that greatly enhance the effectiveness of training.

N ____ Design a top quality Leader's Guide and Participant Materials.

Practice Exercise #5—Concrete Language Component

Let's see if we can help you identify abstract words. Listed below are words that could be found in the Performance Component of an objective.

In this exercise you will use the Criterion Scoring System to indicate the usefulness of the words (below) as active verbs that would appear in an objective for a sales, management or teaching behavior.

10	Concrete Word(s)
5	Questionable Word(s)
0	Abstract Word(s)

____ Design		____ Understand
____ Know		____ Really understand
____ Demonstrate knowledge		____ Plan
____ Prepare		____ Write
____ Develop		____ Smile
____ Challenge		____ Conduct
____ Respond		____ React
____ Think		____ Become familiar with
____ Grasp		____ Present
____ Comprehend		____ Evaluate
____ Demonstrate		____ Acquire knowledge

Practice Exercise #6—Classifying Components

Here is a learning objective broken into its component parts. <u>Your task is to label</u> <u>correctly each Component.</u>

> **Measure Blood Pressure:** The medical student will be able to measure and record a patient's blood pressure with a stethoscope, sphygomonometer, digital watch and blood pressure chart within 5 minutes. The systolic and diastolic measurements must both fall within +/− 4 points of the attending doctor's readings.

_____	With a stethoscope, sphygomonometer, digital watch and blood pressure chart.
_____	Measure and record a patient's blood pressure.
_____	The systolic and diastolic measurements must both fall within +/− 4 points of the attending doctor's readings.
_____	Within 5 minutes.
_____	The medical student will be able to

The next example is the terminal objective for <u>Developing Instructional</u> <u>Objectives.</u> (Mager, 1964)

> **Classify Objectives:** Given any objective in a subject area which you are familiar, in all instances be able to identify (label) correctly the performance, the condition and the criterion of acceptable performance, when any or all of those characteristics are present. (Mager, 1964, p. 3)

Your task is to write the content which represents the component next to the correct label (below). Each phrase can only be used to represent one component. In other words, you cannot have the same phrase (or part of a phrase) in two places. A suggestion. Put a line through each phrase you've identified.

Performer: _____

Performance: _____

Performance Time: _____

Criteria: _____

Conditions: _____

Test Your Evaluation Skill—Advanced Exercise

Here is another opportunity for you to test your evaluation skill. Calculate the Effectiveness Rating for the following objectives.

4. Given 12 or less salespeople in a setting that allows for 4 hours of relatively uninterrupted instruction time, the salesperson will participate in three in-class role play phone-ups that will result in a rating of 8.0 or greater on the Evaluation Sheet as scored by fellow salespersons.

5. Within three weeks, sales representatives should be able to use the total needs presentation visual to make presentations that will result in at least 5 fact-finding interviews and 2 sales per week.

6. The objective of the workshop is to acquaint people with the concepts, philosophies and methods of accelerated learning as applied primarily to corporate training, seed people's imagination in terms of the infinite possibilities for enhancing human learning and enable people to exercise more of their innate creativity in designing and delivering more effective training.

7. You will learn how to identify important problems worth solving, find the most likely cause of each problem; select practical solutions that will eliminate the causes; effectively implement your solutions; and prevent potential problems.

8. Given a list of tasks to be performed, population to be trained, time and resources available, participants will select an appropriate method of training for each task in relation to task selection criteria.

Criterion Scoring System		**Effectiveness Rating**	
10	Meets the Criterion	8.0 to 10	Effective
5	Questionable	5.0 to 7.9	Marginal
0	Does Not Meet or Not Evident	1.0 to 4.9	Ineffective
		0.0 to 0.9	Not Evident

OBJ #4	OBJ #5	OBJ #6	OBJ #7	OBJ #8	
____	____	____	____	____	Contains the **job title of the performer** <u>and</u> the words **"be able to."**
____	____	____	____	____	Contains **the performance** to be exhibited.
____	____	____	____	____	Contains a fixed limit of **time.**
____	____	____	____	____	Contains **criteria.**
____	____	____	____	____	Contains **conditions.**
____	____	____	____	____	Contains **concrete language.**
____	____	____	____	____	**Total Score.**
____	____	____	____	____	**Effectiveness Rating (Divide Total Score by 6)**

District Manager Training—
One Week Program

Core Objective

Given a dealership scenario, be able to forecast, present recommendations and implement the five key ingredients (right person, proper training, motivational pay plan, systems and controls, management support) fundamental to a successful business manager program.

Enabling Objectives

You will be able to:

1. Given a letter of application and a resumé, telephone screen and conduct two interviews in order to recruit a successful business manager.
2. Present the benefits of the Dealer Development training course to a dealer and respond successfully to resistance.
3. Conduct an effective "Kick-Off" with a newly trained Business Manager.
4. Conduct a "One on One" training session with a Business Manager and record details including goals and follow-up in the dealer's "Development Book."
5. Given a monthly performance analysis, conduct a monthly management meeting with the dealer and Lombard North Central personnel and compile an action plan to address any area of weakness.
6. Plan and conduct a sales meeting to address a referral problem.
7. Given a completed performance projection, design Business Manager, Salesman and Sales Manager pay plans and present their benefits to a dealer principal.

Structuring Training Programs—7 Days

Core Objective

Given information on a client, a product (or specifications) and information on the salesforce that will sell the product to the end-user, the developer will be able to plan a training program and write one instructional and one performance evaluation module. The training program must score 8.0 or greater against the **Training Effectiveness Evaluation System** (TEES) criteria #03 through #12. The training modules must score 8.0 or greater against criteria #18, #23, #24, #25, #26, #27, #28.

Primary Subordinate Objectives

To accomplish the Core Objective the developer will be able to:

1. Write a core or primary subordinate instructional objective which contains a performance, criteria and conditions and which achieves an Effectiveness Rating of 10. (TEES #04 or #05)

2. Differentiate between a core, primary subordinate and subordinate objectives.

3. Given a set of objectives for a training program and TEES criteria #04 and #05, establish an Overall Rating that scores +/– 1.0 against the Guide solution and describe the usefulness of the objectives with regard to changing behavior and structuring a training program.

4. Differentiate between a question, task, task question and spontaneous secondary question and describe the most appropriate use of each.

5. Construct an instructional module which includes specifications and panels which conform to the rules of the guide.

6. Construct a performance evaluation system to measure interactive behaviors related to selling credit insurance or other products which produces a rating variation of no more than +/– 1 point on a 5-point scale by two or more trained observers.

7. Describe the content, purpose and use of Program and Module Specifications in the design of a training program.

8. Given Training Standards with Training Effectiveness Evaluation System criteria, a rating form and assistance, be able to determine an effectiveness rating +/– .5 (against the Guide solution) for any training program and **identify the modifications that are most likely to increase effectiveness (and thereby results).**

Practice Exercise

Financial Arrangements

You are to design a course for a group of salespeople on the preparation of a Retail Installment Contract. These salespeople sell consumer goods with a value between $500 and $1,000. The finance arrangement will enable their consumers to finance their purchases.

The contracts must be 100 percent accurate. Any errors in calculation or description of the property will result in the finance company rejecting the contract. (Salespeople are not paid until the finance company accepts the contract.) The salespeople will use a calculation chart supplied by the finance company to calculate the required contract entries. These include the monthly payment, interest rate, total of payments and deferred payment price. The unpaid balance (cost of the goods purchased) is used to enter the calculation chart. Assuming the salesperson has completed a purchase order and uses a pocket calculator, the required calculations and contract can be filled out in 5 minutes.

Appendix **H**
The Module Planner

Module Title

PROGRAM:

PROGRAM DEVELOPER:

SUBJECT EXPERT(S):

SCHEDULE: ___ Days from 9:00 a.m. to 5:00 p.m.

NET TEACHING TIME:

Gross Time	480 Minutes
Lunch	−60
Breaks (2 × 15)	−30
Net Teaching Time (NTT)	390
Total NTT Available	___

Desired Performance

STUDENT JOB TITLE:

OBSERVED OR ASSUMED PERFORMANCE DISCREPANCIES:

■

■

ASSUMPTIONS OR DATA RELATED TO PREVIOUS TRAINING OR EXPERI-ENCE:

■

■

MODULE OBJECTIVE: Insert Core or Module Objective.

UNIT OBJECTIVES: To accomplish the Module Objective, the student will be able to:

■

■

Expert Criteria TO MEASURE THE PERFORMANCE AS DESCRIBED IN THE MODULE OBJECTIVE(S):

■

■

Training Design

Delete [>] when the module is part of a training program.

> ( ): **Introductions:** Make a personal introduction relevant to the module's learning objectives.

■ ( ): **Problems to Solve:** Describe the problems experienced when _____
_____.

■ ( ): **Objectives and Agenda:** Reach agreement upon the module's learning objectives and agenda.

> ( ): **Performance and Evaluation:** Describe the benefits of performance and evaluation.

■ ( ): **Baseline Performance:** Determine behavioral needs in relationship to the module objective.

■ ( ): **Model (before explanation):** Given a model, describe the structure of the behavior (as listed in the PEF) in terms of criteria.

■   **Explanation of the Knowledge and Skills:**

A. ( ):

B. ( ):

C. ( ):

N. ( ):

■ ( ): **Model with Performance Evaluation (after explanation):** Given a model, evaluate the behavior using the criteria, rating scale and scoring system listed in the PEF.

■ ( ): **Optional Practice:** Practice the behavior with a partner prior to performance and evaluation.

■ ( ): **Competence Performance #1:** Perform and evaluate performance using the criteria, rating scale and scoring system listed in the PEF.

■ ( ): **Competence Performance #2:** Perform and evaluate performance using the criteria, rating scale and scoring system listed in the PEF.

> ( ): **Module Conclusion:** State the learning objectives achieved (or not) and value the program's success in meeting their identified needs.

- ( ): **Total Time:** (Estimated, Actual, Replicated)

PREREQUISITE MODULE(S):

■

PRE-CLASS ASSIGNMENT:

■

HOMEWORK ASSIGNMENT:

■

REVIEW AND REINFORCEMENT:

■

Performance Time Requirements

AVERAGE GROUP SIZE: ____ Students.

BASELINE PERFORMANCE—TIME REQUIRED: ____ minutes.

  A. (___): Briefing and set-up before performance.

  B. (___): Preparation: If not completed preclass or as homework.

  C. (___): Taping of performance (if applicable).

  D. (___): Performance or (replay): ____ minutes per student (×) #____ observed.

  E. (___): Evaluation: ____ minutes per student (×) #____ observed.

MODEL—TIME REQUIRED: ____ minutes.

  A. (___): Briefing and set-up before performance.

  B. (___): Performance time for Instructor's Model.

  C. (___): Discussion time.

MODEL WITH PERFORMANCE EVALUATION—TIME REQUIRED: ____ minutes.

  A. (___): Briefing and set-up before performance.

  B. (___): Performance time for Instructor's Model.

  C. (___): Evaluation using the *Expert Criteria* in the PEF

COMPETENCE PERFORMANCE #1—TIME REQUIRED: ____ minutes.

  A. (___): Briefing before performance. (Include any time required for preparation.)

  B. (___): Taping of performance (if applicable).

  C. (___): Performance or (replay): ____ minutes per student (×) #____ observed.

  D. (___): Evaluation: ____ minutes per student (×) #____ observed.

COMPETENCE PERFORMANCE #2—TIME REQUIRED: ____ minutes.

  A. (___): Briefing before performance. (Include any time required for preparation.)

  B. (___): Taping of performance (if applicable).

  C. (___): Performance or (replay): ____ minutes per student (×) #____ observed.

  D. (___): Evaluation: ____ minutes per student (×) #____ observed.

Resources Required

EQUIPMENT REQUIRED:

-
-
-

CASES REQUIRED:

-
-
-

MATERIALS REQUIRED:

-
-
-

ACETATES:

-
-
-

PREFRAMES:

-
-
-

Notes

-
-

Training Unit Format

Technique   **Result**

OBJECTIVE: **Title:** Performance and, if applicable, Conditions, Criteria and
Performance Time. [xx minutes]

XXXX: (Replace XXXX with ?ASK, TASK, TELL or NOTE
and insert the actual question, task, statement or
note.)

CONCLUSION TITLE (___) Insert time

■ (Insert a relevant End)

Appendix I

Solutions to Tasks and Practice Exercises

A. Solution to Task 3—The Self Test

Compare your answers to mine and award yourself points.

1. Definition of a learning objective: "A description of a performance you want learners to be able to exhibit before you consider them competent." (Robert Mager, 1984, p. 5)

Section 1 Score _____

2. Components of a useful objective. (Each is worth 5 points.)

A. **Performer:** The job title of the performer and the words "be able to."

B. **Performance:** The desired behavior. What you want the person to be able to do at the end of a set period of time. The action you want to observe.

C. **Criteria:** The standard or standards by which you will measure the desired behavior.

D. **Conditions:** The situation under which the performance will occur including any resources required or restrictions you will impose.

E. **Performance Time:** The time expressed in hours or minutes for the performance (not the length of the training program or module).

F. **Performance Standard:** A benchmark for competent performance stated as a rating which is derived from a set of specific criteria.

Section 2 Score _____

3. Types of learning objectives relevant to <u>structuring</u> a training program (each is worth six points):

   A. Result Objective: The results that the training program will bring about stated in units of sales or production.

   B. Core Objective: Describes **the desired behavior** to be exhibited **at the program's end** to measure competence that relates to the Result Objective. (The words Program or Terminal would also be acceptable.)

   C. Module Objective: Describes **a desired behavior** to be exhibited **during the program** (within modules of the program if modules are applicable) that relates to the Core Objective.

   D. Unit Objective: Describes a **unit of skill or knowledge** to be exhibited **during the module** that relates to the Module's Objective. (The words Subordinate or Enabling would also be acceptable.)

   Section 3 Score _____

4. Criteria to Measure the Usefulness of a Core or Module Objective. (Each is worth six points.)

   To be considered a useful learning objective the statement must:

   A. Contain the **job title of the performer** and the words **"be able to"** immediately before the active verb.

   B. Contain **a performance** to be exhibited. (Active verb[s] and the object of the verb describe <u>the desired behavior</u>.)

   C. Contain a fixed **time** limit for the performance.

   D. Contain **criteria** to measure the desired behavior at <u>program's end</u>.

   E. Contain **conditions** which describe the situation in which the performance occurs, limitations imposed or non-implicit resources.

   F. Contain **concrete image provoking language** in both the performance (desired behavior) and criteria. Any abstractions are referenced to criteria.

   Section 4 Score _____

Now total the scores from Sections 1 through 4.

Total Score _____
(Out of 100 points)

Your **Total Score** represents your **Knowledge Percentage** which should be inserted on page 18.

A Word to the Reader: How do we know that the answers to the self test are correct (e.g., Mager's definition or the Criteria to Measure the Usefulness of a Learning Objective)? You have the opportunity to challenge each concept. Within this book are numerous model objectives. Decide for yourself if they are consistent with the concepts.

B. Solution to Task 4—
Test Your Evaluation Skill
and the Key to All Tasks and
Practice Exercises

On the following pages you will find the solutions to the problems you were asked to solve. Each contains:

1. The objective being evaluated identified according to its components:

- **Performances are bolded.**
- <u>Conditions are underlined</u>.
- *Criteria are shown in italics.*
- The job title of the performer, the words, "be able to" and the Performance Time are shown in plain type.
- *Abstract words are shown with this type face.*

2. The author's score for each criterion and, where there is the potential for confusion, an explanation.

3. The objective's **Effectiveness Rating.**

4. A commentary describing any general issues raised.

5. Where appropriate, a model objective.

OBJECTIVE 1

<u>Given that the types of dinners served and the dining room atmosphere of the 94th Aero Squadron Restaurant are conducive to wine consumption</u>, the servers will be able to **suggest *specific* wines to customers and *demonstrate knowledge* of wine serving etiquette** *using the server manual as a guide.*

10   Contains the **job title of the performer** and the words **"be able to"** immediately before the active verb.

5   Contains **the performance** to be exhibited. (Active verb[s] and the object of the verb describe <u>the desired behavior</u>.)

There are actually two performances contained within this objective. The performance, suggesting wine, is fairly concrete although we cannot tell to whom the wines will be suggested. A second performance, that of serving wine is shown with the words *"demonstrate knowledge"* which are abstract. What will the server be doing when he or she is demonstrating knowledge?

0   Contains a fixed **time** limit for the performance.

5   Contains **criteria** to measure the desired behavior <u>at program's end</u>.

Using the Server's Manual as a Guide is vague criteria. What is in the manual? Will it be useful for measuring performance? Will the server be able to refer to the manual? Too many unanswered questions.

0   Contains **conditions** which describe the situation in which the performance occurs, limitations imposed or non-implicit resources.

The given (<u>underlined</u> above) appears to be a description of the restaurant not the situation in which the performance occurs, limitations imposed or non-implicit resources. The word **given** is often used to preface the Condition Component of the objective. However, it is not a condition unless it meets the above criteria.

0   Contains **concrete image-provoking language** in both the performance (desired behavior) and criteria. Any abstractions are referenced to criteria.

The word <u>specific,</u> which we can assume was used as criteria, is abstract, as are the words <u>demonstrate knowledge</u> in the performance.

20   **Total Score**

3.3   Effectiveness Rating (Total Score divided by 6)

Commentary: On an evening in 1988 at 8:00 p.m. I was sitting in my office in Chicago when Mike Maglione, a friend and client called me from St Louis. Mike, who was the Director of Training for a large company, was teaching instructional design at a local college. His purpose in calling was to discuss instructional strategy for his module on objectives. After going around in circles discussing how to teach objectives, I asked Mike to read me his objective for the training he was going to conduct. There was dead silence on the phone for about 20 seconds. When he spoke again he admitted that he did not have an objective for the training. Objective 1, which we rated 3.3 was written by one of Mike's students on the final exam. Mike graciously provided me with all of his students' performances, all of which were ineffective.

Moral: <u>You can't teach what you don't know</u>.

OBJECTIVE 2

You will learn how to **write *high level* objectives in three domains: cognitive, psychomotor and affective.**

0   Contains the **job title of the performer** and the words **"be able to"** immediately before the active verb.

5   Contains **the performance** to be exhibited. (Active verb[s] and the object of the verb describe <u>the desired behavior</u>.)

This objective contains the words "learn how to" before the *active verb* "write" and the *object of the verb* "objectives in three domains: cognitive, psychomotor and affective." The words "learn how to" cloud the clarity of the objective. What would a person be doing to demonstrate their competence? Write an objective, I suspect. Then, why not say so?

0　Contains a fixed **time** limit for the performance.

0　Contains **criteria** to measure the desired behavior <u>at program's end</u>.

0　Contains **conditions** which describe the situation in which the performance occurs, limitations imposed or non-implicit resources.

0　Contains **concrete image-provoking language** in both the performance (desired behavior) and criteria. Any abstractions are referenced to criteria.

　　<u>High level</u> is an abstraction.

5　**Total Score**

.8　**Effectiveness Rating (divide Total Score by 6)**

Commentary: This objective appeared in a list of 16 objectives for a two-day workshop on developing training. Of the 16, it was the only one that addressed learning objectives. My question: What are you likely to learn about developing objectives from the person who wrote this objective?

Model Objective

<u>Given a performance discrepancy that is caused by a lack of skill or knowledge on a subject that the instructional developer has mastered,</u> the developer (reader) will be able to **write a learning objective** *that contains performance, criteria, conditions and time components* within 12 minutes.

Moral: I believe it's worth repeating. <u>You can't teach what you don't know</u>.

OBJECTIVE 3

<u>As a result of this session,</u> the developer will be able to **classify learning objectives** *according to Bloom's Taxonomy*.

10　Contains the **job title of the performer** and the words **"be able to"** immediately before the active verb.

10　Contains **the performance** to be exhibited. (Active verb[s] and the object of the verb describe <u>the desired behavior</u>.)

0　Contains a fixed **time** limit for the performance.

10　Contains **criteria** to measure the desired behavior <u>at program's end</u>.

0　Contains **conditions** which describe the situation in which the performance occurs, limitations imposed or non-implicit resources.

　　The words "<u>As a result of this session</u>," describe training process.

10　Contains **concrete image-provoking language** in both the performance (desired behavior) and criteria. Any abstractions are referenced to criteria.

40　**Total Score**

6.6　**Effectiveness Rating (divide Total Score by 6)**

Commentary: The addition of Performance Time and a correctly stated Condition Component would result in an **Effectiveness Rating** of 10. This particular objective appears to be a unit of knowledge and may not be a candidate for a terminal objective. Therefore, I have not included a model objective.

Now turn to page 53 to continue.

C. Solution to Task 5—Test Your Evaluation Skill

OBJECTIVE 4

<u>Given 12 or less salespeople in a setting that allows for 4 hours of relatively uninterrupted instruction time</u>, the salesperson will **participate in three in-class role play phone-ups** *that will result in a rating of 8.0 or greater on the Evaluation Sheet as scored by fellow salespersons.*

5   Contains the **job title of the performer** and the words **"be able to"** immediately before the active verb.

Does not contain the words "be able to."

0   Contains **the performance** to be exhibited. (Active verb[s] and the object of the verb describe <u>the desired behavior</u>.)

The words "participate in three in-class role play phone-ups" does not describe the desired behavior. Rather, it describes training process.

0   Contains a fixed **time** limit for the performance.

0   Contains **criteria** to measure the desired behavior <u>at program's end</u>.

Again we have a description of training process in the words *"that will result in a rating of 8.0 or greater on the Evaluation Sheet as scored by fellow salespersons."* This is not criteria to measure the desired behavior. While we can infer that there are criteria on the Evaluation Sheet, this inference does not earn any score. The objective itself must contain the criteria (or at least the principal criteria) to measure the desired behavior.

The alleged criterion is actually a Performance Standard *(result in a rating of 8.0 or greater).* As you recall, the Performance Standard is an optional component and <u>is not</u> one of the six criteria for measuring usefulness.

0   Contains **conditions** which describe the situation in which the performance occurs, limitations imposed or non-implicit resources.

Did you get tricked by the alleged condition (<u>underlined</u> above)? Our developer is describing the conditions under which the training will occur, not the situation in which the behavior will occur.

10   Contains **concrete image-provoking language** in both the performance (desired behavior) and criteria. Any abstractions are referenced to criteria.

The concrete language enables us to determine that there is nothing there.

15   **Total Score**

2.5   **Effectiveness Rating (divide Total Score by 6)**

Commentary: An objective is a description of performance you want the learner to exhibit, not a description of the training process. Let's say that you agree that the above objective is not a learning objective. We still have a problem. What should the objective for a telephone sales behavior look like? Listed below are two examples that achieve a rating of 10:

Program A. <u>Given a student acting as a customer,</u> the salesperson will be able to **complete a customer phone inquiry with 2 instances of sales resistance** *using the prescribed format, in sequence, within 4 to 5 minutes.*

Program B. <u>Given a student acting as a prospect or customer who is making an inquiry by phone,</u> the salesperson will be able to **conduct a sales discussion** *and, based on the need identified, reach agreement on the date, time and content of the next transaction* **and, if applicable, respond to two instances of resistance to an appointment** within 5 to 10 minutes.

My question: Which of the preceding training programs would you prefer to attend?

If you chose Program A you would learn a highly structured linear behavior and may be penalized for deviating from the script. The objective clearly states that the transaction must be conducted according to the script (prescribed format) in the prescribed sequence.

In program B, you will be rated on your ability to identify the customer's need and reach agreement on a course of action: *the date, time and content of the next transaction.* The words **conduct a sales discussion** are more customer-centered than the words **complete a customer phone inquiry.**

Objectives, when precisely defined, provide a basis for everyone to decide if the training to be conducted is likely to correct the performance discrepancy, be consistent with the culture of the organization and be a growth producing experience for the participant.

For example, what do the words "use the key elements of accelerated learning" mean? How would we know that a person is using them? What does the performance look like? How is the instructor's performance measured? None of these questions are answerable from the learning objective.

OBJECTIVE 5

<u>Within three weeks</u>, sales representatives should be able to **use the total needs presentation visual to make presentations** *that will result in at least 5 fact-finding interviews and 2 sales per week.*

10 Contains the **job title of the performer** and the words **"be able to"** immediately before the active verb.

The word "should" appears to be a hedge. I prefer the word "will."

10 Contains **the performance** to be exhibited. (Active verb[s] and the object of the verb describe <u>the desired behavior</u>.)

0 Contains a fixed **time** limit for the performance.

0 Contains **criteria** to measure the desired behavior <u>at program's end</u>.

"That will result in at least 5 fact-finding interviews and two sales per week" is describing criteria to measure the results **after the training event** not **at program's end**. Hence, there are no criteria within this objective to measure the learner's competence with the desired behavior during training.

0 Contains **conditions** which describe the situation in which the performance occurs, limitations imposed or non-implicit resources.

"<u>Within three weeks</u>" is a description of process. It refers to a time period for measuring the effectiveness of training **after the training event**.

10 Contains **concrete image-provoking language** in both the performance (desired behavior) and criteria. Any abstractions are referenced to criteria.

30 **Total Score**

5.0 **Effectiveness Rating (divide Total Score by 6)**

Commentary: If this were identified as a Result Objective it would be acceptable as it states a measurable result: *5 fact-finding interviews and 2 sales per week.* It even states a time period.

However, it is not a learning objective. It provides no criteria to judge the sales representative's skill with the "total needs presentation visual." Nor does it describe the situation in which the performance will occur. Will the presentation be made to another student acting as the prospect? Will the agent have some prior knowledge of the customer or is this a cold call? Will there be resistance?

There also appears to be a cultural statement within this objective. The words **make a presentation** suggest another salesperson-centered canned pitch. Where, in this objective, is consideration for the customer's needs?

OBJECTIVE 6

The objective of the workshop is to *acquaint people with the concepts, philosophies and methods of accelerated learning as applied primarily to corporate training, seed people's imagination in terms of the infinite possibilities for enhancing human learning and enable people to exercise more of their innate creativity in designing and delivering more effective training.*

0   Contains the **job title of the performer** and the words **"be able to"** immediately before the active verb.

0   Contains **the performance** to be exhibited. (Active verb[s] and the object of the verb describe <u>the desired behavior</u>.)

0   Contains a fixed **time** limit for the performance.

0   Contains **criteria** to measure the desired behavior <u>at program's end</u>.

0   Contains **conditions** which describe the situation in which the performance occurs, limitations imposed or non-implicit resources.

0   Contains **concrete image-provoking language** in both the performance (desired behavior) and criteria. Any abstractions are referenced to criteria.

0   **Total Score**

0   **Effectiveness Rating (divide Total Score by 6)**

Commentary: I received a brochure announcing a three-day workshop from the vendor at a fee of $695. The brochure contained the usual stuff: benefits, who should attend, speaker credentials, list of clients and a registration form. It also contained a curriculum which listed 53 items. There were no stated learning objectives. So, I called the vendor and asked to see the learning objectives. I promptly received a reply which contained the above objective. The reply misspelled my name and contained three spelling errors.

The curriculum contained statements such as: "<u>Understanding the new learner and the learning environment, using the power of suggestion in the classroom</u> and <u>how to use music as an aid to optimal learning</u>." None of these are learning objectives. The use of the word "curriculum" as a term to describe training also puzzled me. Curriculum refers to courses offered by an educational institution. I suggest that the above statements are topics, not courses.

What are you likely to learn from the person who wrote this objective? Certainly nothing about objectives. What about writing? How about professionalism?

Moral: "<u>Because you say it is, does not necessarily make it so</u>."

OBJECTIVE 7

You will learn how to **identify** *important* **problems** *worth* **solving, find the** *most likely* **cause of each problem; select** *practical* **solutions** *that will eliminate the causes; effectively* **implement your solutions;** and **prevent** *potential* **problems.**

0   Contains the **job title of the performer** and the words **"be able to"** immediately before the active verb.

10   Contains **the performance** to be exhibited. (Active verb[s] and the object of the verb describe **the desired behavior**.)

     In fact, this objective contains multiple performances or the linear structure of the behavior. See following commentary.

0   Contains a fixed **time** limit for the performance.

5   Contains **criteria** to measure the desired behavior <u>at program's end</u>.

     Important, worth, most likely, practical and *effectively,* are abstract words that have been used as criteria. How will we measure the learner's ability to **identify** *important* **problems** *worth* **solving, find the** *most likely* **cause of each problem; select** *practical* **solutions** or *effectively* **implement solutions?**

     It appears that we can measure at least one of the performances by comparing the solution selected to the causes identified. Although, without a situation or case, this will tend to be subjective.

0   Contains **conditions** which describe the situation in which the performance occurs, limitations imposed or non-implicit resources.

0   Contains **concrete image-provoking language** in both the performance (desired behavior) and criteria. Any abstractions are referenced to criteria.

     Important, worth, most likely, practical and *effectively* are abstract words. Since these words are not referenced (linked) to any situational data in a Condition Component, we are unable to determine if the learner's performance is competent. For example, we must know the situation and resources available (money, people and time) in order to measure the practicality of a chosen solution.

15   **Total Score**

2.5   **Effectiveness Rating (divide Total Score by 6)p**

Commentary: The usefulness of this objective has been destroyed by a combination of ineffective techniques or traps. These include the use of abstractions to stand for criteria and multiple performances. When we look closely at the list of performances (identify problems, find causes, select solutions and implement solutions), we actually see a process. What we miss is the measurable product of the process, which is commonly known as performance analysis.

What is the product of a performance analysis? I suggest that it is a written document that enables a decision maker (who could also be the preparer of the analysis) to make a decision. Hopefully, one that would solve the problem and be feasible to implement. Therefore, we would want to measure the formal document for both its analysis process and the practicality of the proposed solution in relation to the problem, causes and resources. Listed in the following is a learning objective that addresses the preparation of a performance analysis and which meets all six criteria.

Model Objective

<u>Given a description of a situation or series of events including relevant background data of the person or group involved and resources available,</u> the manager will be able to **prepare a written performance analysis** *which identifies the most likely causes and proposes a solution which reduces or eliminates each major cause and which can be justified with the data in the analysis and is feasible to implement with the resources given* within 2 hours.

OBJECTIVE 8

<u>Given a list of tasks to be performed, population to be trained, time and resources available,</u> participants will **select** *an appropriate* **method of training for each task** *in relation to task selection criteria.*

5　Contains the **job title of the performer** and the words **"be able to"** immediately before the active verb.

The words "participant will" infers performance. Hence, the instructor will observe the ability to perform the task.

10　Contains **the performance** to be exhibited. (Active verb[s] and the object of the verb describe <u>the desired behavior</u>.)

"Select a method of training for each task" is an observable performance.

0　Contains a fixed **time** limit for the performance.

10　Contains **criteria** to measure the desired behavior <u>at program's end</u>.

The appropriateness of the method selected can be measured against the task selection criteria referred to in the Condition Component.

10　Contains **conditions** which describe the situation in which the performance occurs, limitations imposed or non-implicit resources.

10　Contains **concrete image-provoking language** in both the performance (desired behavior) and criteria. Any abstractions are referenced to criteria.

The word "appropriate" by itself is abstract. However, it is referable to the <u>task selection criteria</u>. This allows it to qualify as concrete language.

45　Total Score

7.5　Effectiveness Rating (divide Total Score by 6)

Commentary: A rating of 7.5 represents the high end of marginal. The addition of a Performance Time, the job title of the performer and the words "be able to" would result in a rating of 10. This objective, because of its structure, contains sufficient information to enable a learner to decide if they need the skill offered.

Corrected Objective

Given a list of 5 tasks to be performed, a population to be trained, time and resources available, the developer will be able to **select** *an appropriate* **method of training for each task** *in relation to task selection criteria* within 10 minutes.

D. Solution to Task 6—
Test Your Writing Skill

You were asked to write a Module Objective that meets an Effectiveness Rating of 10 for the suggesting segment and a separate objective for the serving segment. Listed in the following are two model objectives. Compare yours to mine. Did you achieve a rating of 10 for each?

Note: I have **bolded the performances,** underlined the conditions and *put the criteria into italics.*

Serving Wine

Given a waiter's corkscrew, an unopened bottle of wine, a white towel and 2 students acting as customers, the server will be able to **present, open and serve a bottle of wine** *following the 5-step procedure outlined in the server's manual, without error, and execute each step with finesse* within 4 minutes.

Suggesting Wine

Given a wine list with 9 selections (3 red, 3 white, 3 pink) varying in price and taste and 2 students acting as customers, the server will be able to **suggest 1 or 2 wines to the ordering patron** *which complement the entree he/she has ordered and his or her stated wine preference wine* within 3 minutes.

Were you able to write the objectives without a precise knowledge of the subject? My hypothesis was that your knowledge of wines and experience as a restaurant patron would be sufficient. In fact, you probably could identify the units of the training program. Depending on the degree of sophistication desired, the suggesting wine module could contain one or more of the following Unit Objectives:

1. Describe taste components of wine.

2. Given one or more meals ordered, select an appropriate wine.

3. Describe techniques for ascertaining the patron's stated preference.

4. Explain the procedure for describing a particular wine or comparing two wines.

5. Describe the structure of the sales portion of the wine service.

Assuming you did not have the technical expertise, you could hire a wine expert to assist in writing the program.

E. Solution to Task 7— Evaluating a Set of Objectives

Figure 5.8 on the following page contains my Effectiveness Rating for the set of objectives in Fig. 5.7 based on evaluating them as the objectives for a <u>Training Module</u>. I have **bolded the performances,** <u>underlined the conditions</u> and *put the criteria into italics. Abstract words are shown with this type face.*

Figure 5.7. Objectives from a Training Program

The reader will be able to:

1. **Identify** *two* **characteristics of instructional objectives** and **name the** *three* **functions of an instructional objective.**

2. **Identify the** *three* **components of any given instructional objective.**

3. **Distinguish between** *acceptable and unacceptable* **statements of performance** <u>in a given set of objectives</u>.

4. <u>Determine whether the conditions component of an instructional objective is both concise and complete</u> *according to the criteria* <u>given in this section</u>.

5. Determine whether the standards component in an objective is stated in an *acceptable manner.*

6. <u>Given a task for which training is required,</u> **write a** *clear, complete* **instructional objective.**

(Lutterodt and Grafinger, 1985)

Figure 5.8. Module Evaluation Matrix

Module Objective			Unit Objectives							
			1	2	3	4	5	6		
A	0	A	10	10	10	10	10	10		
B	0	B	10	10	10	10	5	10		
C	0	C	NA	NA	NA	NA	NA	NA		
D	0	D	NA	NA	NA	NA	NA	NA		
E	0	E	NA	NA	NA	NA	NA	NA		
F	0	F	10	10	5	5	0	0		Average Group Rating
	0		30	30	25	20	15	20		
	0		10	10	8	7	5	7	7.8	

Total of Ratings	7.8
EFFECTIVENESS RATING	3.9

Commentary: The absence of a Superior (Module) Objective dramatically decreases the Effectiveness Rating. Our rating of 3.9, <u>Ineffective,</u> suggests that these objectives are not useful. We can also infer from this fact that the program may be flawed. In fact, look at the objectives written by the authors. They are loaded with abstractions.

Rating the Set of Objectives as Those of a Training Program

Now let's look at the ratings for the same set of learning objectives (Fig. 5.9) based on evaluating them as objectives for a training program.

This exercise will also enable us to draw conclusions about the usefulness of these objectives and the flexibility of the evaluation system.

Figure 5.9. Program Evaluation Matrix

Module Objective			Unit Objectives							
			1	2	3	4	5	6		
A	0	A	10	10	10	10	10	10		
B	0	B	10	10	10	10	5	10		
C	0	C	0	0	0	0	0	0		
D	0	D	10	10	0	10	0	0		
E	0	E	0	0	10	10	0	10		
F	0	F	10	10	5	5	0	0		
	0		40	40	35	45	15	30		Average Group Rating
	0		6.7	6.7	6.0	7.5	2.5	5.0	5.7	

Total of Ratings	5.7
EFFECTIVENESS RATING	2.9

Commentary: The rating at 2.9 reflects the absence of a Core Objective and the fact that the six objectives are not Module Objectives. They do not describe a complete behavior. They are merely units of knowledge or skill that enable us to perform a desired behavior that is stated only by the title of the book: How to Write Learning Objectives. A book title does not qualify as a Module Objective.

Another Point of View

For the sake of argument, let's agree that the sixth objective, "Given a task for which training is required, write a *clear, complete* instructional objective," is the Module Objective. This is a logical inference made from the title of the book. Now, we will recalculate the Effectiveness Rating for a Training Module. (See Fig. I.1.)

Figure I.1. Module Evaluation Matrix

Module Objective			Unit Objectives							
			1	2	3	4	5	6		
A	10	A	10	10	10	10	10	NA		
B	10	B	10	10	10	10	5	NA		
C	0	C	NA	NA	NA	NA	NA	NA		
D	0	D	NA	NA	NA	NA	NA	NA		
E	10	E	NA	NA	NA	NA	NA	NA		
F	0	F	10	10	5	5	0	NA		Average Group Rating
	30		30	30	25	20	15	NA		
	5.0		10	10	8	7	5	NA	8.0	

Total of Ratings	13
EFFECTIVENESS RATING	6.5

Commentary: While the rating does come up, all they way to 6.5, it does not ring the bell, a rating of 8.0 or effective. This is due to the fact that the desired behavior is inadequately described in the objective. We are missing the critical components of Criteria, Performance Time and Concrete Language. I suggest that the author's inability to write a Core or Module Objective that achieves an Effectiveness Rating of 10 is related to the author's lack of knowledge with regard to the Hierarchical Structure of Objectives. (See page 56 to review this critical concept.)

A final word: The name of the book is "How to Write Learning Objectives." However, the wording in the objectives refers to instructional rather than learning objectives. Does this suggest that the authors may be slightly confused?

F. Solution to Task 8—
Competence Performance

Compare your answer to mine.

Problem 1—Meetings

You have been asked to conduct a training program for 12 sales managers that enables them to conduct effective meetings with their salespeople. The V.P. of Sales observes that the sales managers are not effective conducting meetings to solve problems and that they have difficulty getting people involved in meaningful discussions. You will have up to 2 full days to conduct the training and access to videotape recording equipment.

MODEL OBJECTIVE—Problem-Solving Meeting

Given an issue (problem or situation) that requires communication with the salesforce and a group of students acting as salespeople, the manager will be able to **plan and conduct an** *interactive* **meeting** *that involves each salesperson and reaches agreement on an action or plan to address the issue* within 30 minutes.

Problem 2—Financial Arrangements

You are to design a course for a group of salespeople on the preparation of a Retail Installment Contract. These salespeople sell consumer goods with a value between $500 and $1,000. The finance arrangement will enable their consumers to finance their purchases.

The contracts must be 100 percent accurate. Any errors in calculation or description of the property will result in the finance company rejecting the contract. (Salespeople are not paid until the finance company accepts the contract.) The salespeople will use a calculation chart supplied by the finance company to calculate the required contract entries. These include the monthly payment, interest rate, total of payments and deferred payment price. The unpaid balance (cost of the goods purchased) is used to enter the calculation chart. Assuming the salesperson has completed a purchase order and uses a pocket calculator, the required calculations and contract can be filled out in 5 minutes.

MODEL OBJECTIVE—Contract Preparation

Given 10 completed purchase orders, a calculation chart and a pocket calculator, the salesperson will be able to **prepare 10 Retail Installment Contracts** *which achieve 100 percent accuracy in calculations, description of property and contract entries on 9 out of 10 contracts* within 60 minutes.

Problem 3—Investment Advice

You are to teach a course to a group of financial advisors. These people must assist clients in selecting investments. The investments must be consistent with the risk tolerance, personal objectives and financial position of the client. The company's products range in risk from commodities, options, stocks, bonds, real estate, mutual funds and real estate investment trusts all the way to money market mutual funds and life insurance. The company that employs these financial advisors desires to maintain a long-term relationship with each client. Sound advice is critical and most advice is put into writing. It takes approximately 30 minutes to write a written justification for a particular recommendation.

MODEL OBJECTIVE—Investment Advice

   Given 4 investment options varying in risk and return, a client's financial statement, risk tolerance and personal objectives, the financial advisor will be able to **select and justify (in writing) one investment** *that is consistent with the client's objectives and risk tolerance* within 30 minutes.

Problem 4—One-on-One Training

You have been asked to conduct training for a group of ten new managers who work with salespeople. These salespeople sell a range of intangible products. The managers must conduct individualized training for each salesperson based on his or her needs. Stated another way, the manager must correct the specific problem with each salesperson's performance. Most of the sales presentations used by the salespeople last about 5 minutes. The company prescribes a method it calls the One-on-One Training Technique that it wants these new managers to use. The One-on-One method consists of contracting with the salesperson on the problem to be solved, having the salesperson conduct a sales discussion with the manager acting as the customer and discussing the salesperson's performance. This is followed by the manager acting as the salesperson and the salesperson acting as the customer. A discussion also follows the manager's "model" (demonstration). Finally, the salesperson is asked to perform again. The manager's objective is to measure the improvement in performance as a result of the session.

MODEL OBJECTIVE—One-on-One Training

   Given an identified discrepancy in a selling skill and a student acting as the salesperson, the manager will be able to **conduct an interactive training session** *that brings about a measurable change in performance in relation to the manager's model using the prescribed "One-on-One" technique* within 40 minutes.

Problem 5—Selection Interview

You have been asked to conduct training for a group of 12 managers who conduct selection interviews. You plan to teach them a behavioral interviewing technique. Behavioral interviewing involves asking preplanned questions to obtain information from the candidate about how they have performed in the past in relation to job relevant selection criteria. The interviewer's objective is to collect two to three complete behavioral examples for each of seven job criteria. A behavioral example is a measurable response that is similar to the components of a learning objective. The candidate describes the situation she faced, the action she took and the result her action (behavior) produced. The interview is structured to cover seven job relevant selection criteria and background information from two previous jobs within 60 minutes. An expert interviewer can achieve 21 behavioral examples. Acceptable performance is 14 behavioral examples. The interview guides that the manager will use were developed by a job analysis process.

MODEL OBJECTIVE—Interview and Collect Behavioral Data

Given a candidate's resumé, an interview guide and 5 minutes to prepare, the manager will be able to **conduct a selection interview** *that collects 14 to 21 behavioral examples and relevant background information* within 60 minutes.

Problem 6—Product/Contract Knowledge

You have been asked to conduct training for a group of 20 life insurance agents on a new life insurance policy. The company wants them to understand the benefits, exclusions and policy conditions. Product knowledge is very important and there is a concern that the agent not misrepresent the product when explaining any policy provision. Expert performance involves the ability to locate data within a policy and describe the policy's features, benefits, limitations and conditions. The agent must also be able to describe the policy's response (to pay or not to pay) in relationship to an event.

Note: The subject of this objective is technical knowledge of contracts. Hence, you may substitute "legal contract" for the words "life insurance policy."

MODEL OBJECTIVE—Explain the Coverage

Given a policy and a series of hypothetical claim and contractual situations, the agent will be able to **explain the contract's response to each situation** *by citing the appropriate contract provision(s), without misrepresentation, and obtain a score of 70 percent correct responses on a preclass assignment.*

G. Practice Exercise 3—
Classifying Components

The Component Format is the basis of the evaluation system. Therefore, to effectively use the system you must be able to take any statement identified as an objective and break it down into its component parts. Listed is the Component Format (from page 51) showing the seven components parts (remember the "title" component is optional).

The Component Format

COMPONENT	INDICATORS
Title:	Describe the transaction
Performer:	**The** (state the job title of the performer) **will be able to.**
Performance:	Describe the performance.
Performance Time:	**Within** (state the time limit for the performance).
Criteria:	**That** (describe the principal criteria). Note: The words **which, in relation to** or **based upon** can be substituted for **that.**
Conditions:	**Given** (insert the conditions).
Concrete Language:	Define or reference, if applicable, any abstract words.

Here is a learning objective broken into its component parts. Your task is to label correctly each Component. You can check your answers on the next page.

Measure Blood Pressure: The medical student will be able to measure and record a patient's blood pressure with a stethoscope, sphygomonometer, digital watch and blood pressure chart within 5 minutes. The systolic and diastolic measurements must both fall within +/− 4 points of the attending doctor's readings. (Lutterodt and Grafinger, 1985, p. 39)

_____	With a stethoscope, sphygomonometer, digital watch and blood pressure chart.
_____	Measure and record a patient's blood pressure.
_____	The systolic and diastolic measurements must both fall within +/− 4 points of the attending doctor's readings.
_____	Within 5 minutes.
_____	The medical student will be able to.

Check your answers on the next page.

Solution and Next Problem

Here is the solution to the problem on the previous page:

Conditions	With a stethoscope, sphygomonometer, digital watch and blood pressure chart.
Performance	Measure and record a patient's blood pressure.
Criteria	The systolic and diastolic measurements must both fall within +/− 4 points of the attending doctor's readings.
Performance Time	Within 5 minutes.
Performer	The medical student will be able to

Here is the same objective rewritten into "Sentence Format"

Measure Blood Pressure: <u>Given a stethoscope, sphygomonometer, digital watch and blood pressure chart,</u> the medical student will be able to **measure and record a patient's blood pressure.** *The systolic and diastolic measurements must both fall within +/− 4 points of the attending doctor's readings,* and the process must be completed within 5 minutes.

Optional Problem

The next example is reprinted with Bob Mager's permission (so you know that it is an acceptable objective). It is the terminal objective for <u>Developing Instructional Objectives</u>. (Mager, 1984)

Classify Objectives: Given any objective in a subject area with which you are familiar, in all instances be able to identify (label) correctly the performance, the condition and the criterion of acceptable performance, when any or all of those characteristics are present. (Mager, 1984, p. 3)

Your task is to write the content which represents the component next to the correct label. Each phrase can only be used to represent one component. In other words, you cannot have the same phrase (or part of a phrase) in two places. A suggestion. Put a line through each phrase you've identified. You can check your answers on the next page.

Performer:	_____ _____
Performance:	_____
Performance Time:	_____
Criteria:	_____
Conditions:	_____

Check your answers on the next page.

Solution

Performer:	Be able to.
Performance:	Identify (label) the performance, the condition and the criterion of acceptable performance.
Performance Time:	Not stated.
Criteria:	In all instances—correctly—when any or all of those characteristics are present.
Conditions:	Given any objective in a subject area which you are familiar.

Notice on the previous page that I identified Bob Mager's objective as acceptable, not perfect. Your next task is to use the Criterion Scoring System to determine its Effectiveness Rating.

Criterion Scoring System		*Effectiveness Rating*	
10	Meets the Criterion	8.0 to 10	Effective
5	Questionable	5.0 to 7.9	Marginal
0	Does Not Meet or Not Evident	1.0 to 4.9	Ineffective
		0.0 to 0.9	Not Evident

____ Contains the **job title of the performer** and the words **"be able to"** immediately before the active verb.

____ Contains **the performance** to be exhibited. (Active verb[s] and the object of the verb describe <u>the desired behavior</u>.)

____ Contains a fixed **time** limit for the performance.

____ Contains **criteria** to measure the desired behavior <u>at program's end</u>.

____ Contains **conditions** which describe the situation in which the performance occurs, limitations imposed or non-implicit resources.

____ Contains **concrete image provoking language** in both the performance (desired behavior) and criteria. Any abstractions are referenced to criteria.

____ **Total Score**

____ **Effectiveness Rating (Total Score divided by 6)**

Check your answers on the next page.

Solution

Classify Objectives: <u>Given any objective in a subject area which you are familiar</u>, *in all instances* be able to **identify (label)** *correctly* **the performance, the condition and the criterion of acceptable performance,** *when any or all of those characteristics are present.* (Mager, 1984, p. 3)

__5__ Contains the **job title of the performer** and the words **"be able to"** immediately before the active verb.

_10_ Contains **the performance** to be exhibited. (Active verb[s] and the object of the verb describe <u>the desired behavior</u>.)

__0__ Contains a fixed **time** limit for the performance.

_10_ Contains **criteria** to measure the desired behavior <u>at program's end</u>.

_10_ Contains **conditions** which describe the situation in which the performance occurs, limitations imposed or non-implicit resources.

_10_ Contains **concrete image provoking language** in both the performance (desired behavior) and criteria. Any abstractions are referenced to criteria.

_45_ **Total Score**

_7.5_ **Effectiveness Rating (Total Score divided by 6)**

Commentary: Bob Mager's objective achieves an Effectiveness Rating of 7.5. The formal addition of the job title of the performer, "the developer," would increase the rating to 8.3. Insertion of a Performance Time would result in a perfect score of 10.

Mager created a 20-question Self Test (Mager, 1984, pp. 124-131) to enable the readers of his book to measure their competence in relation to the above objective. I use Mager's Self Test in my training program both as a pre and post test. Students complete the Self Test in 12 to 15 minutes. The discussion of the Self Test requires an additional 20 minutes.

If you are still having difficulty with classification or wish to compare my views with Bob Mager's or wish to gain additional insight, I would urge you to read Preparing Instructional Objectives. (Mager, 1984)

I recommend you complete Practice Exercises 4 through 7. To do this continue to the next page. Otherwise, return to page 53, "Do You Need Help?"

H. Practice Exercise 4A—
Performance Component

Let's see if we can help you identify useful Performance Components. Listed below is the criterion for measuring the usefulness of an objective's Performance Component:

Contains **the performance** to be exhibited. (Active verb[s] and the object of the verb describe <u>the desired behavior</u>.)

To test for a Performance, the statement must contain:

- An active (action) verb and the object of the verb.
- Describe the behavior of the student, not the instructor.
- Be observable during the training event. Here's a hint: Can you observe the student performing the desired behavior in the classroom?

The statements below <u>may or may not</u> contain a Performance. Your task is to decide if the statement meets, is questionable or does not meet the above criterion and award the appropriate score: 10, 5 or 0.

A _____ Participants will increase their understanding of organizational change factors.

B _____ Describe the structure of the Performance Component of a learning objective.

C _____ Sell a life insurance policy.

D _____ Appreciate the value of lesson planning with objectives.

E _____ Really understand the components of a learning objective.

F _____ Settle at least 70 percent of all claims in less than 5 days.

G _____ List criteria for measuring evidence of a desired behavior.

H _____ Know how to explain the use of the Criterion Scoring System.

I _____ Use *Guided Discovery* to teach effectively.

J _____ Demonstrate an understanding of the definition of learning.

Check your answers on the next page.

Solution to Practice Exercise 4A

The following are solutions to problems A through F.

A __0__ Participants will increase their understanding of organizational change factors.

B __10__ **Describe the structure of the Performance Component of a learning objective.**

C __5__ **Sell a life insurance policy.**

D __0__ Appreciate the value of lesson planning with objectives.

E __0__ Really understand the components of a learning objective.

F __0__ Settle at least 70 percent of all claims in less than 5 days.

Statement A: What will the student be doing when they "increase their understanding?" How will you know? This alleged objective is written from the instructor's viewpoint.

Statement B: This is a Performance. Allow me to perform for you. "The Performance Component contains an active verb and the object of the verb."

Statement C: The only way you can sell life insurance in a training situation is to parade live customers through the training. Somewhat impractical. Hence, the questionable score. If the Condition states "given a student acting as a customer," then sell would be acceptable. However, I would prefer "conduct a sales discussion or presentation" as the performance.

Statement D: What will the student do to demonstrate appreciation? Applaud? Write a testimonial? We have no clue.

Statement E: The word "really" does not increase the effectiveness of the word understand. How will the instructor know if the student understands?

Statement F: Same problem as statement 3. This is a result objective, not a performance to be exhibited during the training event.

The following are solutions to problems G through J.

G __10__ **List criteria for measuring evidence of a desired behavior.**

H __0__ Know how to **explain the use of the Criterion Scoring System.**

I __0__ Use *Guided Discovery* to teach effectively.

J __0__ Demonstrate an understanding of the definition of learning.

Statement G: Turn to page 42. There you will find a list of the criteria for measuring the usefulness of an objective. This also represents an example of the required performance.

Statement H: The passive verb "know" reduces the usefulness. How will we know that the student can explain? By explaining, of course. Then, why not say so? A score of "5" is also justifiable since there is a behavior, "explain the use of the Criterion Scoring System."

Statement I: "Use" is questionable as an active verb for an interactive behavior. *Guided Discovery,* which happens to be my teaching method, is a behavior but the words, *Guided Discovery,* do not give a clue as to the nature of the process.

Statement J: What will the person be doing when they are demonstrating an understanding?

How many were you able to identify correctly? If 80 percent are scored correctly, you are doing fine. If you are still having difficulty continue to Practice Exercise 4B. If not, return to page 53.

Practice Exercise 4B— Performance Component

Here are some more "objectives" to practice with. Decide if the statement meets the criterion for the Performance Component, is questionable or does not meet the criterion and award the appropriate score: 10, 5 or 0.

Judge each statement on the words shown. Do not assume any prefacing language.

A ____ Analyze a learning objective for words which describe the style of the desired behavior.

B ____ Organize an instructor guide.

C ____ Evaluate the effectiveness of a performance evaluation form.

D ____ Improve interviewing skills

E ____ Design a performance evaluation form.

F ____ Justify the efficacy of a course of action.

G ____ Increase ability to make selection decisions.

H ____ Provide familiarity with how criterion are obtained.

I ____ Explain the importance of an agenda in a meeting.

J ____ Develop a five-year strategic plan.

K ____ To build skills in detecting errors in written communication quickly.

L ____ Write a business letter.

M ____ Provide participants with a four-hour overview of Arbor Corporation's Quality Assurance Program, policy and procedures.

N ____ To apply principles of management to specific situations.

O ____ To acquaint managers and supervisors with their roles and responsibilities.

P ____ Name the planets in the Milky Way.

Q ____ To insure that classified documents get appropriate markings.

R ____ Diagnose a malfunction in a copy machine.

S ____ Select a method for analyzing learner needs.

T ____ Conduct a sales meeting.

Check your answers on the next page.

Solution to Practice Exercise 4B

Compare your scores to mine. I have provided commentary for each statement that failed to meet the criterion.

A __5__ Analyze a learning objective for words which describe the style of the desired behavior.

> **The word "analyze" is a covert behavior. You cannot observe a person analyzing. An overt (observable) indication of analysis would be the act of underlining words that describe the style of the behavior. I would rate the Performance Component below as a 10:**

> **Underline the words in a learning objective which describe the style of the desired behavior.**

B __10__ Organize an instructor guide.

C __10__ Evaluate the effectiveness of a performance evaluation form.

D __0__ Improve interviewing skills.

> **This appears to the benefit of participating in the course. It is not a performance.**

E __10__ Design a performance evaluation form.

F __10__ Justify the efficacy of a course of action.

G __0__ Increase ability to make selection decisions.

> **Another benefit of participating in the course. It is not a performance.**

H __0__ Provide familiarity with how criterion are obtained.

> **Written from the instructor's point of view. It describes what the instructor will be doing. What is familiarity? How will we know the student is familiar?**

I __10__ Explain the importance of an agenda in a meeting.

J __5__ Develop a five-year strategic plan.

> **The word "develop" is like the words "use" and "demonstrate." What will the finished strategic plan look like? I would prefer to see: Prepare a written five-year strategic plan.**

K __0__ To build skills in detecting errors in written communication quickly.

> **The word "to" at the beginning of an objective is a red flag. Alleged objectives starting with "to" are usually written from the instructor's viewpoint. The words that are not usually shown are: <u>The purpose of this course is to</u>. The completed statement is shown as follows:**

> **The purpose of this course is to build skills in detecting errors in written communication quickly.**

L __10__ Write a business letter.

M __0__ Provide participants with a four-hour overview of Arbor Corporation's Quality Assurance Program, policy and procedures.

This objective for training on quality lacks quality.

N __0__ To apply principles of management to specific situations.

Again we have the word "to" by itself, a red flag. What are principles of management? What will we observe the student doing when he or she is applying the principles?

O __0__ To acquaint managers and supervisors with their roles and responsibilities.

Another teacher-centered statement. Not a performance and not a learning objective.

P __10__ Name the planets in the Milky Way.

I have observed my 9-year-old daughter doing this. I taught her to remember them with the name "J.V. Spummen." (Jupiter, Venus, Saturn, Pluto, Uranus, Mars, Mercury, Earth and Neptune.)

Q __0__ To ensure that classified documents get appropriate markings.

Another teacher-centered statement. Not a performance and not a learning objective.

R __10__ Diagnose a malfunction in a copy machine.

S __10__ Select a method for analyzing learner needs.

T __10__ Conduct a sales meeting.

How many were you able to identify correctly? If 80 percent are scored correctly you are doing fine. If so, return to page 53. If not, turn to page 21 and review the explanation of the Performance Component.

I. Practice Exercise 5A— Conditions Component

Let's see if we can help you identify a useful Conditions Component. Listed below are five objectives. Each is to be rated against the criterion for measuring the usefulness of an objective's Conditions Component:

Contains **conditions** which describe the situation in which the performance occurs, limitations imposed or non-implicit resources.

In each case, the objective <u>may or may not</u> contain a useful Condition. All other components will be useful (Performer, Performance, Performance Time and Criteria). Your task is to:

1. <u>Underline</u> the Condition Component or what the author thought was the Condition Component.

2. Decide if the Condition meets, is questionable or does not meet the above criterion and award the appropriate score: 10, 5 or 0.

3. (Optional) Identify (by circling, boxing or highlighting) any evident component of a useful objective.

A   ____   Given a narrative describing an employee's behavior, objectives (Business Plan) and results produced to date, the manager will be able to conduct a performance review.

B   ____   Given that performance of the desired behavior is important to the company and 10 hours of training time, the salesperson will be able to present the features and benefits of the product in relation to the customer's needs.

C   ____   Without references to a price guide, the appraiser will be able to estimate the value of the property plus or minus 15 percent of the expert's valuation within 2 hours.

D   ____   Given 5 objectives that may or may not contain a useful Condition Component, the reader will be able to identify (by scoring) those that contain a Condition which meets the Condition Criterion.

E   ____   Calculate 5 lease payments using the Lease Payment Calculation Worksheet and a pocket calculator with 100 percent accuracy in 5 minutes.

Check your answers on the next page.

Solution to Practice Exercise 5A

Listed in the following are my scores for each of the five objectives. Scoring, in this instance, involves searching for: **the situation in which the performance (desired behavior) will occur, a limitation placed on the performer or a description of the resources that the person will work with during the performance.**

Notice that **Performances are bolded,** *Criteria are shown in italics* and the job title of the performer, the words be able to and Performance Time is shown in plain type.

A __10__ Given a narrative describing an employee's behavior, objectives (Business Plan) and results produced to date, the manager will be able to **conduct a performance review.**

B __0__ Given that performance of the desired behavior is important to the company and 10 hours of training time, the salesperson will be able to **present the features and benefits of the product** *in relation to the customer's needs.*

C __10__ Without references to a price guide, the appraiser will be able to **estimate the value of the property** *plus or minus 15 percent* of the expert's valuation within 2 hours.

D __10__ Given 5 objectives that may or may not contain a useful Condition Component, the reader will be able to **identify (by scoring) those that contain a Condition** *which meets the Condition Criterion.*

E __10__ **Calculate 5 lease payments** using the Lease Payment Calculation Worksheet and a pocket calculator *with 100 percent accuracy* in 5 minutes.

Objectives A and D use the word **given** to indicate the presence of a Condition. The Condition in Objective A simulates the type of data that a manager would use to conduct a performance review. Objective D is the objective for this exercise. Its Conditions Component describes the nature of the exercise. Some of the objectives you evaluated contained a useful Conditions Component and some did not.

Objective B: The alleged Condition contains a description of training process and does not meet the Condition Criterion. The remainder of the objective, however, contains a useful Performance and Criterion.

Objectives C and E contain Conditions which are not prefaced by the word given. In Objective C, the absence of a price guide is a limitation. In Objective E the Lease Payment Calculation Worksheet and a pocket calculator are a limitation.

If you are still having difficulty continue to the next page. If not, return to page 53.

Practice Exercise 5B—
Conditions Component

Listed below are objectives F through J. Each <u>may or may not</u> contain a useful Condition. Again, all other components will be useful (Performer, Performance, Performance Time and Criteria). Your task is to decide if the Condition meets, is questionable or does not meet the Criterion and award the appropriate score: 10, 5 or 0:

> E. Contains **conditions** which describe the situation in which the performance occurs, limitations imposed or non-implicit resources.

Additional Tasks:

- <u>Underline</u> the Condition Component or what the author thought was the Condition Component.

- (Optional) Identify (by circling, boxing or highlighting) any evident component of a useful objective.

F ____ Given a case and a student acting as the customer, the service representative will be able to conduct a discussion that reaches agreement on a satisfactory course of action in relation to the problem, the customer's level of frustration and prescribed policy.

G ____ Given 5 opportunities to practice with feedback prior to the examination, the adjuster will be able to access the computer database that enables him or her to obtain the required information.

H ____ Upon completion of a 50-minute session on affective communication, the workers will be able to recognize in themselves and others the eight different character traits and then modify their behavior or response to the person possessing the trait(s) identified.

I ____ Using handouts and other information provided, the trainer will be able to identify 5 steps in the design of an evaluation form.

J ____ Given a model of team development, the HRD professional will be able to describe the model's use in facilitating organizational change.

Check your answers on the next page.

Solution to Practice Exercise 5B

F   10   <u>Given a case and a student acting as the customer</u>, the service representative will be able to **conduct a discussion** *that reaches agreement on a satisfactory course of action in relation to the problem, the customer's level of frustration and prescribed policy.*

G   0   <u>Given 5 opportunities to practice with feedback prior to the examination,</u> the adjuster will be able to **access the computer database** *that enables him or her to obtain the required information.*

H   0   <u>Upon completion of a 50-minute session on affective communication,</u> the workers will be able to **recognize** *in themselves and others the eight different* **character traits and then modify their behavior** *in response to the person possessing the trait(s) identified.*

I   5   <u>Using handouts and other information provided</u>, the trainer will be able to **identify 5 steps in the design of an evaluation form.**

J   10   <u>Given a model of team development</u>, the HRD professional will be able to **describe the model's use in facilitating organizational change.**

Objectives F and J contain useful Conditions. In Objective F we can see a role play exercise by the fact that there will be a student acting as a customer. Objective J states that the instructor will supply a model that will be used in the discussion. It states what the student will work with.

Objectives G and H do not have useful Conditions. <u>Five opportunities to practice with feedback prior to the examination</u> is training process, not the situation in which the performance will occur. The 50-minute time is the length of the training, not the length of the student's performance.

Objective I: This Condition is questionable. It appears to be describing training process. However, you can also argue that the documents referred to contain information that will be useful in identifying the five steps. Hence, the score of 5.

How many were you able to identify correctly? If 4 out of 5 are scored correctly you are doing fine. If so, return to page 53. If not, turn to page 24 and review the explanation of the Conditions Component.

J. Practice Exercise 6A—Criteria Component

Let's see if we can help you identify a useful Criteria Component. Listed in the following is the criterion for measuring the usefulness of an objective's Criteria Component.

Contains **criteria** to measure the desired behavior <u>at program's end</u>.

To test for a Criterion (one standard) or Criteria (two or more standards), the statement should:

- Contain words that would enable you to judge the competence of the desired behavior. In other words, concrete language. (Abstract words are avoided.)
- Be observable during or at the end of the training event.

In each case, the objective <u>may or may not</u> contain a useful Criterion. All other components shown will be useful (Performer, Performance, Performance Time and Conditions). Your task is to:

1. <u>Circle</u> the Criteria Component or what the author thought was the Criteria Component.

2. Decide if the Criteria Component meets, is questionable or does not meet the above criterion and award the appropriate score: 10, 5 or 0.

3. (Optional) Identify (by circling, boxing or highlighting) any evident component of a useful objective.

A ____ Given 10 documents that require classification, the file clerk will be able to mark each document according to Department of Defense Regulation 60006.

B ____ Design and present effective and interesting training sessions.

C ____ Given a useful learning objective (rated 10), the developer will be able to design a performance evaluation system that contains criteria to measure the structure of the behavior which are not subject to misinterpretation.

D ____ Given a table of acceptable tolerances and unassembled parts of an engine, the mechanic will be able to tighten each with a torque wrench to within +/− 2 lbs within 3 attempts.

E ____ Conduct an interactive sales meeting that reaches agreement on an action plan to solve an identified problem.

F ____ Select the right training activity to meet your objective.

Check your answers on the next page.

Solution to Practice Exercise 6A

Listed in the following are my scores for each of the six objectives. Notice that **Performances are bolded,** *Criteria are shown in italics* and the job title of the performer, the words be able to and Performance Time is shown in plain type. *Abstract words are shown in this font.*

A   5   <u>Given 10 documents that require classification,</u> the file clerk will be able to **mark each document** *according to Department of Defense Regulation 60006.*

Criteria such as *"according to Department of Defense Regulation 60006"* are not particularly useful as you must refer to another document to determine the standards upon which the performance will be judged. Hence the score of "5." To solve this problem you can either:

1. State the principle criteria in the "regulation" as the Criteria Component.

2. List the most important criteria immediately after the learning objective.

Notice in objectives "C, D and E" below, the reader can identify the principle criteria upon which the performance will be judged as they are explicitly stated.

B   0   **Design and present** *effective and interesting* **training sessions.**

C 10 <u>Given a useful learning objective (rated 10),</u> the developer will be able to **design a performance evaluation system** *that contains criteria to measure the structure of the behavior which are not subject to misinterpretation.*

D 10 <u>Given a table of acceptable tolerances and unassembled parts of an engine,</u> the mechanic will be able to **tighten** *each* **with a torque wrench** *to within +/– 2 lbs within 3 attempts.*

E 10 **Conduct an** *interactive* **sales meeting** *that reaches agreement on an action plan to solve an identified problem.*

F   0   **Select the** *right* **training activity to meet your objective.**

Practice Exercise 6B—
Criteria Component

Here are eight more problems. In each case, the objective <u>may or may not</u> contain a useful Criterion. Other components shown will be useful or questionable. Your task is to:

1. <u>Circle</u> the Criteria Component or what the author thought was the Criteria Component.

2. Decide if the Criteria Component meets, is questionable or does not meet the criterion and award the appropriate score: 10, 5 or 0.

3. (Optional) Identify (by circling, boxing or highlighting) any evident component of a useful objective.

G ____ Given a letter containing 12 errors, the proofreader will be able to identify correctly each of the errors within 5 minutes.

H ____ Write an acceptable performance plan with measurable criteria.

I ____ Given six learning objectives, the developer will be able to classify the objectives according to Bloom's Taxonomy.

J ____ Given a student acting as a customer, conduct a sales discussion that explains the product in relation to the customer's stated needs.

K ____ Train employees to be better problem solvers and decision makers.

L ____ Use the proper close.

M ____ Select training methods that greatly enhance the effectiveness of training.

N ____ Design a top quality Leader's Guide and Participant Materials.

Check your answers on the next page.

Solution to Practice Exercise 6B

Listed in the following are my scores for each of the eight objectives. Notice that **Performances are bolded,** *Criteria are shown in italics* and the job title of the performer, the words be able to and Performance Time are shown in plain type. *Abstract words are shown in this font.*

G __10__ Given a letter containing 12 errors, the proof reader will be able to **identify** *correctly* **each of the errors** within 5 minutes.

H __5__ **Write an** *acceptable* **performance plan** *with measurable criteria.*

I __10__ Given six learning objectives, the developer will be able to **classify the objectives** *according to Bloom's Taxonomy.*

J __10__ Given a student acting as a customer, **conduct a sales discussion** *that explains the product in relation to the customer's stated needs.*

K __0__ **Train employees to be** *better* **problem solvers and decision makers.**

L __0__ **Use the** *proper* **close.**

M __0__ **Select training methods** *that greatly enhance the effectiveness of training.*

N __0__ **Design a** *top quality* **Leader's Guide and Participant Materials.**

How many were you able to identify correctly? If 6 out of 8 are scored correctly you are doing fine. If so, return to page 53. If not, turn to page 25 and review the explanation of the Criteria Component.

K. Practice Exercise 7—
Concrete Language Component

You indicated that you were having difficulty with abstract words. Let's see if we can clear up your problem. Listed in the following are words that could be found in the Performance Component of an objective.

In this exercise you will use the Criterion Scoring System to indicate the usefulness of the words as active verbs that would appear in an objective for a sales, management or teaching behavior.

10	Concrete Word(s)
5	Questionable Word(s)
0	Abstract Word(s)

____ Design	____ Understand
____ Know	____ Really understand
____ Demonstrate knowledge	____ Plan
____ Prepare	____ Write
____ Develop	____ Smile
____ Challenge	____ Conduct
____ Respond	____ React
____ Think	____ Become familiar with
____ Grasp	____ Present
____ Comprehend	____ Evaluate
____ Demonstrate	____ Acquire knowledge

Check your answers on the next page. How many were you able to identify correctly? If 80 percent are scored correctly, you are doing fine. If so, return to page 53. If not, turn to page 31 and review the explanation of Concrete Language.

Solution to Practice Exercise 7

_10_ Design: An action word and observable behavior.

_0_ Understand: This is an abstract term which is generally followed by the words "how to."

_0_ Know: Same as understand.

_0_ Really understand: The use of really does not make understand more concrete. Really represents useless verbiage.

_0_ Demonstrate knowledge: What will the person be doing when they are demonstrating knowledge? Conducting a meeting? Writing an objective? Preparing an agenda?

_10_ Plan: An action word and observable behavior.

_10_ Prepare: Same.

_10_ Write: Same.

_5_ Develop: Refers to a process. What is the difference between writing learning objectives and developing them? I can observe you write. And once you have written one, I can measure it (and so can you). What are you doing when you're developing one? It is not clear.

_10_ Smile: An action word and observable behavior.

_10_ Challenge: I bet that you have challenged some of the ideas in this book. And, I suspect, that if we were together, people could observe you challenging me on some of my points.

_10_ Conduct: An action word and observable behavior.

_10_ Respond: Same.

_10_ React: Same.

_0_ Think: Abstract.

_0_ Become familiar with: What does familiar mean?

_0_ Grasp: Abstract, a synonym for understand.

_10_ Present: I can watch you do it.

_0_ Comprehend: Abstract, another synonym for understand.

_10_ Evaluate: An action word and observable behavior which we are doing.

_5_ Demonstrate: See Develop above.

_0_ Acquire knowledge: Another abstract term. I can tell when you have acquired a car. However, the only way I know you have learned (acquired knowledge) is to observe your behavior.

Glossary

Abstraction: An idea (word, term, concept or operation) stripped of its concrete attributes.

Actual Time: The time recorded by an instructor while conducting any Module, Unit or Panel of a Training Program with a representative group of students.

?ASK: A term used in an Instructor Guide that denotes a question to be asked of the group.

Behavior: An action or response to a situation.

Behavior modeling: A demonstration of the desired behavior by the instructor. See also Desired Behavior and Model.

Baseline performance: A performance which reveals the learner's present level of competence with a desired behavior.

Business Plan: The reason or justification for a training program. The Business Plan, as it relates to training, is characterized by a set of objectives containing a Result Objective and one or more Core Objectives.

Classification: Arrangement according to some systematic division into classes or groups.

Component Format: A method for expressing a learning objective that identifies the desired behavior in relation to the six components found in the Criteria for Measuring the Usefulness of Objectives (see pages 49 and 50).

Conclusion: A unit of desired behavior, skill or knowledge consisting of an abstraction and one or more related Ends at the next lower level of abstraction.

Concrete Language Component: An optional component of a learning objective containing a definition or reference to any abstract word used in the Performance or Criteria Components.

Condition Component: A component of a learning objective that describes **the situation under which the performance occurs, limitations imposed or non-implicit resources.**

Core Objective: Describes <u>the desired behavior</u> to be exhibited **at the program's end** to measure competence that relates to the Result Objective.

Core Question: A preplanned question that is designed to bring about the discussion of a Conclusion.

Criteria Component: A component of a learning objective that describes **the standard or standards by which you will measure the desired behavior.**

Criterion: A standard upon which a judgment or decision can be based.

Criterion Scoring System: A ratio scale containing three points which each have a numeric value starting from true zero that measures each component of an object or process against a criterion.

Desired Behavior: An action or response to a situation where the performer uses certain knowledge and skills to bring about a desired <u>result</u>.

Effective: Producing or designed to produce the expected effect, impression or response.

Effectiveness Rating: An indicator that suggests the likelihood of producing an expected effect. The rating is derived by measuring the components of an objective or process against criteria that rate each component's competence. The rating is calculated by dividing the sum of the scores for each criteria by the number of criteria evaluated.

End: A point, idea or concept representing an objective to be reached during the discussion of a unit of knowledge or skill.

Estimated Time: An estimate of the time required to conduct any Module, Unit or Panel of a Training Program during the planning and writing phases.

Expert Criteria: The observable behaviors (performance) of a person having knowledge and skill derived from training or experience that can be used to judge the performance of learners or performers.

Explanation Component: The phase of the training process where the instructor explains the knowledge and skills that enable the learner to perform the desired behavior described in a Superior Objective.

Guided Discovery: A training method which uses objectives and interactive inductive learning to bring about one or more desired behaviors.

Hierarchical: A group of persons or things arranged in order of rank, grade or class.

Hierarchical Structure: An organized ranking of a set of learning objectives that identifies the objective containing the desired behavior that will be observed to measure learner competence as the Superior Objective, and which identifies the Subordinate Objectives that enable the learner to perform the desired behavior.

Hypothesis: A word which is added to the title of a Panel to indicate that all of the Ends in the Conclusion do not have to be reached during the discussion. This allows the developer to list the range of problems that the group may be experiencing and is frequently used in Panels which refer to perceived or observed performance problems (i.e., following a Baseline Performance). Only those performance problems which are relevant are discussed with the group.

Instructor Guide: A document that contains the Module Objective, Unit Objectives and units of knowledge and skill and sufficient instructions (directions) that would enable an instructor to conduct the training as it was designed.

Learning: An observable change in behavior that persists over a period of time.

Learning objective: Describes the **desired behavior,** skill or knowledge you want the learner to be able to exhibit before you consider him or her competent.

Master Training Design: A matrix containing the modules of the program and the time allocated to each. It represents the overall plan for developing and later conducting the program.

Model: A demonstration of the desired behavior by the instructor that achieves an Effective Rating of 90 percent of the rating specified for expert performance.

Module Objective: Describes **a desired behavior** to be exhibited **during the program** (within modules of the program if modules are applicable) that relates to the Core Objective.

Module Planner: A job aid that enables a developer to organize a Training Module.

NOTE: A term used in an Instructor Guide that denotes an instruction to the instructor relevant to the subject matter under discussion.

Panel: A section of an Instructor Guide consisting of a unit of knowledge or skill structured as a Conclusion and the techniques (i.e., questions, tasks, notes and statements) that the instructor plans to use to bring about the discussion.

PEF: See **Performance Evaluation Form.**

Performance Component: A component of a learning objective that describes **the desired behavior you want the learner to exhibit.**

Performance Evaluation Form: A **tool** used to measure performance which contains: the criteria to judge each component of the behavior, a scoring system, a rating scale and instructions to calculate the rating.

Performance Evaluation System: A **system** containing criteria to judge each component of the behavior, a scoring system, a rating scale, **a formula for determining the rating,** instructions for calculating the rating and, **for most situations, a role play case which simulates the conditions under which the behavior is used.**

Performance Standard: An **optional** component of a learning objective that describes **a benchmark for competent performance stated as a rating which is derived from a set of specific criteria.**

Performance Time Component: A component of a learning objective that describes **the time for the performance expressed in hours, minutes or seconds.**

Performer Component: A component of a learning objective that contains the job title of the performer and the words "be able to."

Replicated Time: The Actual Time, plus or minus 15 percent, required to conduct the same Module, Unit or Panel of a training program (assuming no modifications) with two representative groups.

Representative Group: A group of students whose previous training, experience and needs closely parallels the original assumptions made and whose number is within 10 percent of the projected average class size.

RESULT: A term used to denote the right hand side of an Instructor Guide. See TECHNIQUE.

Result Objective: The results that the training program will bring about stated in units of sales or production. Describes the _results_ you want the learner to produce as a result of acquiring the **desired behavior** described in the **learning objectives**.

Secondary Question: A preplanned question that is relevant to one or more Ends of a Conclusion that the developer wants to emphasize. A supplement to a Core Question.

Spontaneous Secondary Question: A question formulated by an instructor during a discussion that is relevant to one or more Ends of a Conclusion that the instructor wants to draw out of the group.

Standard: Something established by authority, custom, or general consent as a model or example. Synonym: Criterion.

Standard: See _Training Standard._

Structure: A manner of building, constructing or organizing.

Subordinate Objective: A Module or Unit Objective which, when learned, enables the student to perform the behavior contained within the Superior Objective. (A means to an end.)

Superior Objective: A Core or Module Objective containing the desired behavior that will be observed to measure learner competence. (An end in itself.)

TASK: A term used in an Instructor Guide that denotes an activity that the group or specific members of the group will perform.

Task Question: A question posed to the group where the instructor asks each student to write down his or her answer before beginning the discussion.

Taxonomy: The science of classification, laws and principles covering the classifying of objects.

TECHNIQUE: A term used to denote the left hand side of an Instructor Guide which outlines the questions, tasks, statements and procedures the instructor uses to bring about the specific unit of knowledge or skill or activity defined under RESULT.

TELL: A term used in an Instructor Guide that denotes a statement which is read to the group.

Terminal Objective: An objective which describes the desired behavior to be observed and measured at the end of a training event. A Core Objective is the

Terminal Objective for a Training Program while a Module Objective is the terminal objective for a Training Module.

Total Quality Training Design: A Training Design organized in relation to the *Total Quality Training Standards*.

Total Quality Training Standards: See *Training Standards*.

Training Design: An agenda for conducting a Training Module that integrates the module's Unit Objectives and Training Process Objectives. When used in a Module Planner it also shows the time for each objective.

Training Manual: A document consisting of the Program or Module's: Learning Objectives, Training Design, Instructor Guide(s), Cases, Performance Evaluation Form(s), program resources and the Student Evaluation of Training.

Training Module: A unit of training characterized by a set of objectives containing a Module Objective and one or more Unit Objectives.

Training Process Objective: Describes, from the learner's viewpoint, the behaviors the instructor will use to enable the learner to understand, accept and perform the desired behavior.

Training Program: A unit of training characterized by a set of objectives containing a Core Objective and one or more Module Objectives.

Training Standards: A set of principles that permit a judgment to be made with regard to the effectiveness of a training methodology in relation to the desired behavior described in a learning objective.

Training Unit: A unit of training characterized by a set of objectives containing a Unit Objective and one or more related units of knowledge and skill.

Unit of knowledge or skill: An idea, concept or procedure and related points. (See also Conclusion and Ends.)

Unit Objective: Describes a **unit of skill or knowledge** to be exhibited **during the module** that relates to the Module's Objective.

References

Bloom, Benjamin S., ed. *Taxonomy of Educational Objectives. Book 1: Cognitive Domain.* New York: Longman, 1984.

Bloom, Benjamin S., Krathwohl, David R. and Masia, Bertran B. *Taxonomy of Educational Objectives. Book 2: Affective Domain.* New York: Longman, 1964.

Brandenburg, Dale C. "Training Evaluation: What's the Current Status?" *Training and Development Journal,* August 1982.

Brandenburg, D.C., and Schultz, E. *The status of training evaluation: An update.* Presentation at the National Society of Performance and Instruction Conference, Washington, DC, April, 1988.

Burton, W.H. "Basic Principles in a Good Teaching-Learning Situation." *Readings in Human Learning.* Edited by L.D. and Alice Crow. New York: McKay, p. 7, 1963.

Cash, Harold C., and Crissy, W. J. E. *The Psychology of Selling.* Flushing, New York: Personal Development Associates, 1966.

Cook, Mary F. "What's Ahead in Human Resources?" *Management Review,* pp. 41–44, April, 1988.

Cormier, Stephen M., and Hagman, Joseph D. *Transfer of Learning: Contemporary Research and Applications.* Academic Press, Inc., San Diego, CA, 1987.

Cronbach, L.J. *Educational Psychology.* 2nd ed. New York, Harcourt, Brace and World, p. 71, 1963.

Davies, Ivor K. *Instructional Technique.* New York: McGraw-Hill, 1981.

Deming, W. Edwards. *Out of Crisis.* Cambridge MA, Massachusetts Institute of Technology, 1986.

Gagne, Robert M. *The Conditions of Learning.* New York, Holt, Rinehart and Winston, 1965.

Goldenson, Robert M. Ph.D. *The Encyclopedia of Human Behavior: Psychology, Psychiatry, and Mental Health.* New York, Doubleday & Company, Inc., 1970.

Griksheit, Gary M., Cash, Harold C. and Crissy, W.J.E. *Handbook of Selling.* New York: John Wiley & Sons, 1981.

Haggard, E. A. "Learning A Process of Change." *Readings in Human Learning.* Edited by L.D. and Alice Crow. New York, McKay, p. 20, 1963.

Hayakawa, S.I., Berger, Arthur A. and Chandler, Arthur. *Language in Thought and Action.* Harcourt Brace and Company, New York, 1978.

Kapfer, Miriam B. *Behavioral Objectives in Curriculum Development.* Educational Technology Publications, Englewood Cliffs, New Jersey, 1971.

Kidder, Louise H. and Judd, Charles M. *Research Methods in Social Relations.* Holt, Rinehart and Winston, New York, 1985.

Knowles, Malcom. *The Adult Learner, A Neglected Species.* Gulf Publishing Company, Houston, Texas, pp. 126–130, 1973.

Kramlinger, Thomas. "Teach 'Win-Win' Selling with 'Win-Win' Training." *Successful Meetings,* July 1975.

Lutterodt, Sarah A., and Grafinger, Deborah J. *How to Write Learning Objectives.* GP Courseware, Columbia, MD, 1985.

Lutterodt, Sarah A., and Grafinger, Deborah J. *Classifying Learning Objectives.* GP Courseware, Columbia, MD, 1985.

McGregor, Douglas. *The Human Side of Enterprise.* McGraw-Hill, Inc., New York, pp. 33–34, 47–48, 1960.

Mager, Robert F. *Preparing Instructional Objectives.* Fearon · Pitman Publishers, Inc., California, 1962.

Mager, Robert F., and Peter Pipe. *Analyzing Performance Problems.* Lake Publishing Company, Belmont, California, 1984.

Morrison, John E., ed. *Training for Performance.* John Wiley & Sons Ltd., Sussex, United Kingdom, 1991.

Walton, Mary. *Deming Management at Work.* The Putnam Publishing Group, New York, 1991.

Wedman, John, and Tessmer, Martin. "Instructional Designer's Decisions and Priorities: A Survey of Design Practice." *Performance Improvement Quarterly.* Volume 6, Number 2, pp. 43–57.

Index

About the Author

Lester Shapiro is Vice President Program Development of Aon Corporation, an international diversified financial services company which is headquartered in Chicago, Illinois.

He is an expert in the area of learning objectives, program development, training evaluation and interactive inductive training methodology with over two decades of experience.

Acting as an internal consultant, he has developed over 2,000 hours of training on sales, management, customer relations, training design and technical subjects. Over 100,000 individuals have participated in programs which he developed for the insurance, finance and automotive industries.

His student-centered, performance-based *Guided Discovery* training method has received broad acceptance by developers and instructors in both the United States and United Kingdom.